Civil Society and Activism in Europe

How do voluntary organizations contribute to civic and democratic health? What impact do specific organizational types or discrete organizational characteristics have on the generation of various forms of social capital?

This book examines the role of civil society organizations in several advanced European democracies: Germany, the Netherlands, Spain, Switzerland and the United Kingdom. Building on *Citizenship and Involvement in European Democracies* (2007) and *Social Capital and Associations in European Democracies* (2007), this volume seeks to widen and deepen the analysis by introducing new data on activists and combining these with the organizational data and the population data. Based on an innovative research design (and a unique data set) this volume evaluates the impact of the organizational context on individual activity profiles and attitudes and values of activists, and provides a unique assessment on the contribution that voluntary associations make to civil and democratic society.

This book is essential reading for students and scholars of civil society, democracy, political participation, politics and sociology.

William A. Maloney is Professor of Politics and Head of Politics in the School of Geography, Politics and Sociology, Newcastle University. **Jan W. van Deth** is Professor of Political Science and International Comparative Social Research at the University of Mannheim.

Routledge research in comparative politics

1 **Democracy and Post-communism**
   Political change in the post-communist world
   Graeme Gill

2 **Sub-state Nationalism**
   A comparative analysis of institutional design
   Edited by Helena Catt and Michael Murphy

3 **Reward for High Public Office**
   Asian and Pacific Rim States
   Edited by Christopher Hood and B. Guy Peters

4 **Social Democracy and Labour Market Policy**
   Developments in Britain and Germany
   Knut Roder

5 **Democratic Revolutions**
   Asia and Eastern Europe
   Mark R. Thompson

6 **Democratization**
   A comparative analysis of 170 countries
   Tatu Vanhanen

7 **Determinants of the Death Penalty**
   A comparative study of the world
   Carsten Anckar

8 **How Political Parties Respond to Voters**
   Interest aggregation revisited
   Edited by Kay Lawson and Thomas Poguntke

9 **Women, Quotas and Politics**
   Edited by Drude Dahlerup

10 **Citizenship and Ethnic Conflict**
    Challenging the nation-state
    Haldun Gülalp

11 **The Politics of Women's Interests**
    New comparative and international perspectives
    Edited by Louise Chappell and Lisa Hill

12 **Political Disaffection in Contemporary Democracies**
    Social capital, institutions and politics
    Edited by Mariano Torcal and José Ramón Montero

13 **Representing Women in Parliament**
A comparative study
Edited by Marian Sawer, Manon Tremblay and Linda Trimble

14 **Democracy and Political Culture in Eastern Europe**
Edited by Hans-Dieter Klingemann, Dieter Fuchs and Jan Zielonka

15 **Social Capital and Associations in European Democracies**
A comparative analysis
Edited by William A. Maloney and Sigrid Roßteutscher

16 **Citizenship and Involvement in European Democracies**
A comparative analysis
Edited by Jan van Deth, José Ramón Montero and Anders Westholm

17 **The Politics of Foundations**
A comparative analysis
Edited by Helmut K. Anheier and Siobhan Daly

18 **Party Policy in Modern Democracies**
Kenneth Benoit and Michael Laver

19 **Semi-Presidentialism Outside Europe**
A comparative study
Edited by Robert Elgie and Sophia Moestrup

20 **Comparative Politics**
The principal–agent perspective
Jan-Erik Lane

21 **The Political Power of Business**
Structure and information in public policymaking
Patrick Bernhagen

22 **Women's Movements**
Flourishing or in abeyance?
Edited by Marian Sawer and Sandra Grey

23 **Consociational Theory**
McGarry and O'Leary and the Northern Ireland conflict
Edited by Rupert Taylor

24 **The International Politics of Democratization**
Comparative perspectives
Edited by Nuno Severiano Teixeira

25 **Post-communist Regime Change**
A comparative study
Jørgen Møller

26 **Social Democracy in Power**
The capacity to reform
Wolfgang Merkel, Alexander Petring, Christian Henkes and Christoph Egle

27 **The Rise of Regionalism**
Causes of regional mobilization in Western Europe
Rune Dahl Fitjar

28 **Party Politics in the Western Balkans**
Edited by Věra Stojarová and Peter Emerson

29 **Democratization and Market Reform in Developing and Transitional Countries**
Think tanks as catalysts
James G. McGann

30 **Political Leadership, Parties and Citizens**
The personalisation of leadership
Edited by Jean Blondel and Jean-Louis Thiebault

31 **Civil Society and Activism in Europe**
Contextualizing engagement and political orientations
Edited by William A. Maloney and Jan W. van Deth

Civil Society and Activism in Europe

Contextualizing engagement and political orientations

Edited by William A. Maloney and Jan W. van Deth

LONDON AND NEW YORK

First published 2010
by Routledge
2 Park Square, Milton Park, Abingdon, Oxon OX14 4RN

Simultaneously published in the USA and Canada
by Routledge
270 Madison Avenue, New York, NY 10016

Routledge is an imprint of the Taylor & Francis Group, an informa business

© 2010 William A. Maloney and Jan W. van Deth selection and editorial matter; individual contributors, their contributions

Typeset in Times by Wearset Ltd, Boldon, Tyne and Wear
Printed and bound in Great Britain by TJI Digital, Padstow, Cornwall

All rights reserved. No part of this book may be reprinted or reproduced or utilized in any form or by any electronic, mechanical, or other means, now known or hereafter invented, including photocopying and recording, or in any information storage or retrieval system, without permission in writing from the publishers.

British Library Cataloguing in Publication Data
A catalogue record for this book is available from the British Library

Library of Congress Cataloging in Publication Data
Civil society and activism in Europe: contextualising engagement and political orientation/edited by William A. Maloney and Jan W. van Deth.
p. cm. – (Routledge research in comparative politics)
1. Civil society–Europe. 2. Political participation–Europe. I. Maloney, William A. II. Deth, Jan W. van.
JN40.C578 2010
322.4094–dc22   2009037933

ISBN10: 0-415-56043-8 (hbk)
ISBN10: 0-203-85535-3 (ebk)

ISBN13: 978-0-415-56043-6 (hbk)
ISBN13: 978-0-203-85535-5 (ebk)

Contents

List of figures	ix
List of tables	x
Notes on contributors	xiii
Acknowledgements	xvii

1 **Introduction: contextualizing civil societies in European communities**   1
JAN W. VAN DETH AND WILLIAM A. MALONEY

PART I
General social and political orientations   17

2 **Mobilizing voluntary work: the interplay between organizations and municipalities**   19
TOBIAS SCHULZ

3 **Governing associations: member involvement and efficacy towards associational decision-making**   40
HERMAN LELIEVELDT

4 **Associations and political empowerment**   56
BENGÜ DAYICAN, BAS DENTERS AND HENK VAN DER KOLK

5 **Schools and schoolyards: the associational impact on political engagement**   77
JAN W. VAN DETH

6 **Civil society organizations as 'little democracies'?**   100
PATRICK BERNHAGEN AND WILLIAM A. MALONEY

PART II
European political orientations 127

7 Voluntary associations and support for Europe 129
   MANUELA CAIANI AND MARIONA FERRER-FONS

8 EU legitimacy and social capital: empirical insights into a complex relationship 156
   SONJA ZMERLI

9 The relational basis of attachment to Europe 180
   HAJDEJA IGLIČ

10 Political trust in the EU: active idealists and rational non-actives in Europe? 207
   SILKE I. KEIL

11 Conclusion: activists, active people and citizens in European communities 231
   WILLIAM A. MALONEY AND JAN W. VAN DETH

   Bibliography 242
   Index 257

Figures

1.1	The three main parts of the integrated data set	11
5.1	Political interest among activists, socially actives and non-actives (averages)	80–82
5.2	Typology of engagement in European affairs	85
5.3	Distributions of *Committed Multipliers* in various types of associations (percentages)	88–90
7.1	Interest in European politics, and trust in European institutions among activists, socially actives, and non-actives (means)	133
7.2	A typology of 'support for Europe', combining interest in European politics and trust in European institutions	135
7.3a	Distribution of 'Euro-disaffected' for associational sector (percentages)	140–141
7.3b	Distribution of 'Euro-enthusiasts' among different types of associations (percentages)	142–143
9.1	A typology of attachment: municipality and Europe	187
10.1	Two perspectives on political trust	211
10.2	Means of trust in the EU	215
10.3	Explained variance of two tested models	216
10.4	Typology of voluntary associations, differentiated according to size and degree of professionalization	226

Tables

1.1	Main characteristics of the three data sets used	8
1.2	Main characteristics of activists, socially actives and non-actives in various cities and countries (percentages and means)	14
2.1	Comparison of the 'socially active' population (S) and the activists (A); logistic regression, dependent variable: volunteered (or not)	28
2.2	Estimates of multi-level ordinal logit regression of amount of volunteering for an organization	32–33
2.3	Mean random intercepts for sectors	36–37
3.1	Associational participation of activists and socially actives	46
3.2	Associational participation and efficacy of activists	48
3.3	Predictors of associational participation	50
3.4	Predictors of associational efficacy	52
4.1	Mean levels of subjective political empowerment by different levels of activism (citizens and activists)	63
4.2	Mean levels of subjective political empowerment by breadth of involvement (citizens only)	65
4.3	Mean levels of subjective political empowerment by groups of organizations (citizens only)	66
4.4	Subjective political empowerment of citizens	68
4.5	Subjective political empowerment of activists	70–71
5.1	Distributions of types of people interested in European politics and engaging in political discussions (percentages)	86
5.2a	Antecedents of Committed Multipliers (activists only) (binary logistic regression; Nagelkerke R^2)	93
5.2b	Antecedents of Uncommitted Multipliers (activists only) (binary logistic regression; Nagelkerke R^2)	94
5.2c	Antecedents of Silent Committers (activists only) (binary logistic regression; Nagelkerke R^2)	95
5.2d	Antecedents of Politically Unconcerned (activists only) (binary logistic regression; Nagelkerke R^2)	96
6.1	Civic-spiritedness, voter turnout, and protest participation among non-actives, socially actives and activists	110–111

6.2	Least squares regression estimates of organizational effects on civic spirit: East Germany	116
6.3	Least squares regression estimates of organizational effects on civic spirit: Swiss municipalities	117
6.4	Logit estimates of organizational effects on protest: East Germany	119
6.5	Logit estimates of organizational effects on protest: West Germany	120
6.6	Logit estimates of organizational effects on protest: Spain	121
6.7	Logit estimates of organizational effects on protest: Swiss municipalities	122
6.8	Summary of findings from multivariate analysis	123
7.1	Distribution of types of support for Europe among activists, socially actives and non-actives (percentages)	137
7.2	Prediction of euro-enthusiasts (activists only)	147
7.3	Prediction of Euro-pragmatics (activists only)	148
7.4	Prediction of Euro-disaffected (activists only)	149
7.5	Prediction of critical Europeanists (activists only)	150
8.1	Mean values of confidence in the EU amongst non-actives, socially actives and activists	162
8.2	Mean values of social trust amongst non-actives, socially actives and activists	163
8.3	Principal component analysis of different types of trust amongst activists	164
8.4	Mean values of group-related, social and personalized trust amongst activists	165
8.5	Predictors of confidence in the EU amongst European citizens, OLS regressions, beta coefficients	168
8.6	Predictors of confidence in the EU amongst activists, OLS regressions, beta coefficients	169
8.7	Predictors of confidence in the EU amongst activists, OLS regressions, beta coefficients	170–171
8.8	Predictors of group-related trust amongst activists, OLS regressions, beta coefficients	174
8.9	Predictors of social trust amongst activists, OLS regressions, beta coefficients	175
8.10	Predictors of personalized trust amongst activists, OLS regressions, beta coefficients	176
9.1	Distribution of types of attachment across countries (percentages)	188
9.2	Distribution of types of attachment among activists, socially actives and non-actives (percentages)	189
9.3a	Two dimensions of attachment to territories among citizens (principal component analysis of attachment)	191
9.3b	Two dimensions of attachment to territories among activists (principal component analysis of attachment)	192
9.4	Predictors of strength of attachment among citizens	196

xii *Tables*

9.5	Predictors of direction of attachment among citizens	198
9.6	Predictors of strength of attachment among activists	200–201
9.7	Predictors of direction of attachment among activists	202–203
10.1	Determinants of political trust in EU, East Germany (beta coefficients)	218
10.2	Determinants of political trust in EU, West Germany (beta coefficients)	219
10.3	Determinants of political trust in EU, the Netherlands (beta coefficients)	220
10.4	Determinants of political trust in EU, Spain (beta coefficients)	221
10.5	Determinants of political trust in EU, Switzerland (beta coefficients)	222
10.6	Determinants of political trust in EU, United Kingdom (beta coefficients)	223
10.7	Determinants of political trust, differentiated by professionalization and size of organizations (beta coefficients)	227

Contributors

Patrick Bernhagen is a lecturer in the Department of Politics and International Relations at the University of Aberdeen. His main research interests concern the political participation of citizens and firms, as well as their strategies and success in gaining political influence. Patrick Bernhagen's research has been published in international peer-reviewed journals, including *Democratization*, *Electoral Studies*, *European Union Politics* and *Political Studies*. He is the author of *The Political Power of Business: Structure and Information in Public Policymaking* (London: Routledge, 2007) and co-editor (with Christian W. Haerpfer, Ronald Inglehart and Chris Welzel) of a new textbook on *Democratization* (Oxford: Oxford University Press, 2009).

Manuela Caiani is a research assistant at the European University Institute for the comparative project VETO on 'Processes of Radicalization in Political Activism', focused on right-wing extremism in Europe and USA. She received a PhD in Political Science at the University of Florence. Her main research interests concern social movements and civil society, political participation, political violence and terrorism, Europeanization and the public sphere. Among her publications are *Quale Europa, Europeizzazione, Identità e Conflitti* (Bologna: Il Mulino, 2006; with Donatella della Porta) and *Social Movements and Europeanization* (Oxford: Oxford University Press, 2009; with Donatella della Porta).

Bengü Dayican is a researcher and PhD candidate at the Department of Political Science and Research Methods at the University of Twente (The Netherlands). Her main research interests include democratic theories, political culture and political participation (in particular electoral turnout and political protest) in a comparative perspective.

Bas Denters is full Professor of Public Administration and Extraordinary Professor for Urban Policy and Urban Politics in the School for Management and Governance at the University of Twente (the Netherlands). He is Program Director for the Master and Bachelor programs in Public Administration. He is the Convener of the Standing Group on Local Politics and Government (LOGOPOL) of the European Consortium for Political Research (ECPR),

xiv *Contributors*

Member of the Executive of the European Urban Research Association, and Vice-Chairman of the Netherlands Institute of Governance. He has published on issues of urban governance, social capital, citizen involvement and local democracy. His recent publications include *Local Governance Compared; Trends and Developments* (edited with L.E. Rose; Houndmills: Palgrave, 2005).

Mariona Ferrer-Fons is Associate Lecturer at the Department of Political and Social Sciences of the Universitat Pompeu Fabra (Barcelona, Spain). She received her PhD from the European University Institute, and a Diploma in Social Science Data Analysis from the University of Essex. Her research interests are political behaviour (in particular, political consumerism and protest mobilization), and the effect of public policies fostering citizen political participation. Her most recent publication is 'Explaining the determinants of public support for cuts in unemployment benefits spending across OECD countries', *International Sociology* 20(4): 459–481, 2005 (with M. Fraile).

Hajdeja Iglič is Associate Professor of Sociology at the University of Ljubljana (Slovenia). Her main research areas are social networks analysis, social cohesion, social capital, and political attitudes and engagement. She studied networks of Slovenian elites before and after democratic transition, and networks of general population in their relationship to political mobilization and creation of democratic political culture. She is a coordinator of the Erasmus Mundus joint European Master Program on Comparative Local Development at the University of Ljubljana. Recent publications include 'Trust, governance and performance: the role of institutional and interpersonal trust in SME development' (with Andrej Rus), in *International Sociology* (2005), 'The role of institutions in raising the political engagement in new democracies' (with Helena Kovačič), in *Lokale Politische Eliten und Fragen der Legitimation*, edited by K. Pähle and M. Reiser (Baden-Baden: Nomos, 2007), and 'Social networks' (with Joan Font Fabregas), in *Citizenship and Involvement in European Democracies: A Comparative Analysis*, edited by J.W. van Deth, J.R. Montero and A. Westholm (London: Routledge, 2007).

Silke I. Keil is Assistant Professor of Political Science and Political Sociology at the University of Stuttgart (Germany). Her main research area is political sociology, particularly political attitudes, participation, social capital and electoral behaviour. She is general manager of the German national team for the European Social Survey. Recent publications include *Participation in France and Germany* (edited with Oscar W. Gabriel und Eric Kerrouche, Baden-Baden: Nomos, 2009).

Herman Lelieveldt is Associate Professor of Political Science at Roosevelt Academy, a liberal arts and science college of Utrecht University, Middelburg, The Netherlands. His research focuses on political participation, public policy, and the development of undergraduate research in the classroom. Recent publications include a chapter on 'Neighborhood politics' in the

Handbook of Social Capital (Oxford: Oxford University Press, 2008), as well as an article on the use of exit polls as educational tools in *European Political Science* (with Gregor Rossen, 2009).

William A. Maloney is Professor of Politics and Deputy Head of School (Politics) in the School of Geography, Politics and Sociology, Newcastle University (UK). His main research interests are in the areas of interest group politics (internal and external dynamics), social capital, political involvement and non-participation. He has published extensively in these areas, and his recent publications include *The Politics of Organized Interests in Europe: the state of the art*, a special issue of *West European Politics* (December, 2008) Vol. 31, no. 6, (co-edited with Jan Beyers and Rainer Eising); *Civil Society and Governance in Europe: From National to International Linkages* (co-edited with van Deth, Cheltenham: Edward Elgar, 2008); *Interest Groups and the Democratic Process: Enhancing Participation?* (co-authored with Grant Jordan, Houndmills: Palgrave, 2007); and *Social Capital and Associations in European Democracies: A Comparative Analysis* (co-edited with Sigrid Roßteutscher, London: Routledge, 2007).

Tobias Schulz is a research fellow at the Swiss Federal Research Institute for Forest, Snow and Landscape (WSL), and a lecturer in research methods at the Institute for Political Science, University of Zürich. He is mainly interested in research on political behaviour, political positions, and the impact of institutions on political behaviour or the effects of policies. After graduating in economics, he was visiting researcher at the University of California at Berkeley and San Diego, before he earned his doctorate at the University of St Gallen (Switzerland) for his research on voting anomalies in environmental referenda. Subsequently, he was engaged as a research fellow and lecturer at the Institutes for Political Science at the Universities of St Gallen and Zürich. Results of his contributions to Swiss and European research projects have recently been published in journals such as *European Union Politics*, *Party Politics* and the *Swiss Political Science Review*.

Henk van der Kolk is Assistant Professor of Political Science at the University of Twente (The Netherlands). His main research areas are electoral systems, electoral behaviour and local politics. He was Director of the Dutch National Election Studies in 1998 and 2006. He is co-Director of the Euroloc-Summerschool Series on Local Government. Recent publications appeared in *PS, Representation, Electoral Studies, Acta Politica, Local Government Studies* and various Dutch journals. He has co-edited various books on Dutch elections and the European Constitutional Referendum, and contributed to various volumes edited by others.

Jan W. van Deth is Professor of Political Science and International Comparative Social Research at the University of Mannheim (Germany). His main research areas are political culture (especially social capital, political engagement and citizenship), social change, and comparative research methods. He was Director of the Mannheim Centre for European Social Research (MZES), Convener of the international network Citizenship, Involvement, Democracy (CID) of the European Science Foundation, and Book Series Editor of the Studies in European Political Science of the European Consortium for Political Research (ECPR). He is a Corresponding Member of the Royal Netherlands Academy of Arts and Sciences (KNAW), and National Coordinator of the German team for the European Social Survey. Recent publications include *Civil Society and Governance in Europe. From National to International Linkages* (edited with William Maloney; Cheltenham: Edward Elgar, 2008).

Sonja Zmerli is a researcher at the Institute of Political Science at the University of Technology Darmstadt and at the Department of Social Sciences at the Goethe-University Frankfurt/Main (Germany). Her main research interests include social capital, social and political behavior, political orientations, and social identity theory. Recent publications include 'Social trust and attitudes towards democracy', in *Public Opinion Quarterly* (with Ken Newton, 2008); *Inklusives und exklusives Sozialkapital in Deutschland. Grundlagen, Erscheinungsformen und Erklärungspotential eines alternativen theoretischen Konzepts* (Baden-Baden: Nomos, 2008); 'Trust in people, confidence in political institutions, and satisfaction with democracy' (with Ken Newton and José Ramón Montero, 2007), in J.W. van Deth, J.R. Montero and A. Westholm (eds), *Citizenship and Involvement in European Democracies. A Comparative Analysis* (London: Routledge); and 'Networking among voluntary associations: segmented or integrated?' (with Ken Newton, 2007), in W.A. Maloney and S.Roßteutscher (eds), *Social Capital and Associations in European Democracies. A Comparative Analysis*, London: Routledge.

Acknowledgements

In the last decade, empirical research on social capital, citizenship, and civil society has expanded significantly. The international research network Citizenship, Involvement, Democracy (CID), funded by the European Science Foundation (ESF), was set up in 1999 and was predicated on the idea that close international collaboration could provide much of the evidence required in these areas (co-ordinated by Jan W. van Deth, Mannheim; see www.mzes.uni-mannheim.de/projekte/cid). In the first stage, participants included Jørgen Goul Andersen (Aalborg), Klaus Armingeon (Bern), Paul Dekker (Den Haag), Bas Denters (Enschede), Oscar W. Gabriel (Stuttgart), Peter Geurts (Enschede), Tore Hansen (Oslo), Hanspeter Kriesi (Geneva), William A. Maloney (Aberdeen), José Ramón Montero (Madrid), Ken Newton (Essex), Sigrid Roßteutscher (Mannheim), Per Selle (Bergen), Jan Teorell (Uppsala), Lise Togeby (Aarhus), Mariano Torcal (Madrid), Peter A. Ulram (Vienna), Jan W. van Deth (Mannheim), Anders Westholm (Uppsala) and Paul Whiteley (Sheffield). Some of these colleagues left the project after the initial phase and new members joined the network. The list of participants who remained at the final phase is identical to the list of contributors to the three CID volumes.

The CID research design includes three major components: (i) a survey of representative samples of the population in European countries, (ii) a study of voluntary associations in several European cities/communities, and (iii) a survey of people active in these associations. The three parts address similar questions about citizenship and involvement. For each part, similar research designs have been developed (including common core questionnaires) and implemented in a number of countries. The population project provides analyses of individual citizens' involvement and the antecedents of different modes of social and political behaviour. However, before much participation can take place, groups must exist as vehicles for citizen engagement. Thus, the organizational study focuses on the collective opportunities and routes for social and political involvement. In the third part of the project, the focus is on volunteers and active citizens within specific organizations. The logic behind the surveys of organizations and their members was that organizational features are directly linked to the attitudes and behaviour of volunteers and activists. Furthermore, the characteristics of volunteers and activists are compared with the evidence obtained for the 'average

xviii *Acknowledgements*

citizen' provided by the population surveys. The third part of the project aims to systematically combine the results of the three parts of the CID project.

Although it is clear that the various parts of the CID project are highly complementary, they differ in their research designs and empirical evidence. For that reason, the results published in three volumes have discrete aims. All volumes share the general concern with democratic citizenship and the comparative perspective, and each one is based on collaborative efforts of international groups of scholars. The results of the population surveys are presented in the first volume, devoted to *Citizenship and Involvement in European Democracies: A Comparative Analysis* (edited by Jan W. van Deth, José Ramón Montero, and Anders Westholm; London: Routledge, 2007). The results of the organizational study are presented in the second volume, devoted to *Social Capital and Associations in European Democracies: A Comparative Analysis* (edited by William A. Maloney and Sigrid Roßteutscher; London: Routledge, 2007).

The organization and collection of data in each of the 13 societies and 26 European communities was made possible with a number of generous grants. Data collection and preparing the information for our analyses of the populations surveys and the organizational studies was accomplished with support of a number of national foundations and institutes: Denmark (Democracy and Power Study, conducted on behalf of the Danish Parliament), Germany (German National Science Foundation DFG, grant DE630/7-1, Fritz Thyssen Foundation, and the Anglo-German Foundation for the Study of Industrial Society), Great Britain (Anglo-German Foundation for the Study of Industrial Society), Moldova and Romania (International Research and Exchanges Board IREX under the auspices of the Black and Caspian Sea Collaborative Research Program funded by the Starr Foundation), the Netherlands (Institute for Governance Studies at the University of Twente), Norway (Norwegian Research Council; Power and Democracy Group; Stein Rokkan Center), Portugal (Science and Technology Foundation; Ministry of Science and Technology; Institute for Sociological Research ISCTE), Russia (Bank of Sweden Tercentennary Foundation), Slovenia (Ministry of Higher Education, Science and Technology, grant J5-3039-0582-04), Spain (Ministry of Science and Technology, grant SEC2000-0758-C02, and Autonomous University of Madrid, grant 9/SHD/001), Sweden (Bank of Sweden Tercentenary Foundation, Mechanisms of Democracy program) and Switzerland (Swiss National Science Foundation SNF).

In five of the participating countries it was possible to interview/survey a large number of citizens active in one of the associations we approached for the organizational studies. Interviewing of activists in Aberdeen was organized and carried out by William Maloney and Linda Stevenson (grant of the Anglo-German Foundation for the Study of Industrial Society). In Germany, activists in Mannheim and Chemnitz and some minor communities were interviewed. Sigrid Roßteutscher, Jan W. van Deth and Marina Berton were in charge of data collection in Mannheim (grant of the Anglo-German Foundation for the Study of Industrial Society), and Oscar W. Gabriel and Angelika Vetter, with the help of Kathrin Silber, collected data in Chemnitz and the other communities (grant of the Fritz Thyssen Foundation). In the Netherlands, interviewing of activists and volunteers was supervised and carried out by Peter Geurts, with support from Bengü Dayican, Bas Denters and Henk van der Kolk (grant of the Institute for Governance Studies at the University of Twente). Hanspeter Kriesi organized the interviews in Switzerland, assisted by Simone Baglioni (Swiss National Science Foundation, grant 1214-057261.99). The interviews in Spain were supervised by Joan Font, and data collection was organized and carried out by Josep Sanmartin, Laura Morales, Patxi Juaristi, Javier Astudillo, Gerard Coll, Eloi Moya, Alba Seguranyes and Josep Masferrer (Spanish Ministry of Science and Technology, grant SEC2000-0758-02 and Madrid Autonomous Community, grant 06/0288/2002).

Analysing the interviews of the volunteers and activists as well as combining the results from the various parts of the CID project was mainly carried out within the framework of the Network of Excellence CONNEX ('Connecting Excellence on European Governance') funded by the European Union under the 6th Framework Programme. This network was dedicated to the analysis of efficient and democratic multi-level governance in Europe (see www.connex-network.org) and offered an outstanding opportunity to discuss our findings within the much broader context of Europeanization and the prospects for a European civil society. We are very grateful to Beate Kohler-Koch (Network Coordinator) and Fabrice Larat (Network Manager) for their enthusiastic support during all stages of our work.

The design of the integrated data set combining information from citizens, organizations and activists was initially developed by Jan W. van Deth for Aberdeen and Mannheim. Using this design, Silke Keil constructed the data set for the other German communities, Bengü Dayican did so for Enschede, Tobias Schulz for the Swiss communities, and Mariona Ferrer-Fons for the Spanish communities. Daniel Stegmüller and especially Christian Schnaudt (both University of Mannheim) spent many hours harmonizing the various data sets, correcting errors, and computing scales and indices. The time-consuming task of converting a set of heterogeneously formatted papers into uniformly formatted book chapters was carried out by Benjamin Engst (University of Mannheim) and Caitlin Maloney.

After more than ten years, the CID project is finished, with the publication of this third volume. We gratefully acknowledge the generous grants for distinct parts of the project in such a large number of countries and communities. Besides, the Mannheim Centre for European Social Research (MZES) provided substantial resources at all stages of the CID project to smooth communication, build various extensive integrated data sets, and document the various tasks. Yet the successful completion of an unusually large international project dealing with questions about complex social and political developments depends on the help of very many people over a long period of time. We cannot list all the colleagues, research assistants, secretaries and managers who made this project possible, but we are highly appreciative of the generous support that was provided to us without hesitation over so many years. Most importantly, we are grateful to those scholars who contributed to the generation of such rich data sets. It was that unreserved collaboration and support that made working in the CID project both a privilege and an intellectual challenge over the past ten years.

William A. Maloney, Newcastle
Jan W. van Deth, Mannheim
February 2010

1 Introduction
Contextualizing civil societies in European communities

Jan W. van Deth and William A. Maloney

1.1 Democracy and engagement

Since the early 1990s we have witnessed a reinvigorated academic interest in the role of civil society organizations in democracies. This interest has in large part been stimulated by Putnam's seminal volume, *Making Democracy Work* (Putnam 1993) and his *Journal of Democracy* article 'Bowling Alone: America's Declining Social Capital' (Putnam 1995). A subsequent deluge of academic research and the activities of bodies such as the European Commission have maintained high levels of interest in the role of civil society organizations in democratic politics. The EU Commission has focused on reducing the 'democratic deficit' through the development of a more engaged and vibrant European civil society that will promote an active and participatory citizenship – i.e. 'bring citizens closer to the European Union and its institutions' (CEC 2001a). Civil society (and social capital) are seen as promoting effective and efficient democratic governance through the deeper and more meaningful involvement of a wider range of (civil society) actors in the European policy-making process. It is envisaged that this will increase openness, transparency, accountability and democracy.

The EU Commission and democratic governments have been responding to the argument that advanced democracies are under threat from citizen disengagement, growing apathy and a decline in civicness. Dalton (2004: 1) argued that 'the challenge comes from democracies' own citizens, who have grown more distrustful of politicians, sceptical about democratic institutions, and disillusioned about how the democratic process functions'. Some current (2009) perceptions appear to be that democracy is in mortal danger. Scholars such as Hay (2007) and Stoker (2006a, 2006b) are respectively discussing *Why We Hate Politics* and *Why Politics Matters*. Hay (2007: 1) argues that 'Politics, or so it seems, is not all that it was once cracked up to be'. Citizen disengagement is a symptom

> of a more worrying and deep-seated condition. For each individual pathology might be seen as indicative of a more pervasive – indeed, near universal – disdain for 'politics' … 'politics' has increasingly become a dirty word.
> (Hay 2007: 1)

Stoker (2006a, 2006b) perceives cynicism, political disenchantment and disengagement as rising to levels that put democracies on a potentially dangerous track:

> It is difficult to get away from the idea that a general and widespread disengagement from and disenchantment with formal politics does not sit comfortably with the long-term health of democracy. Indeed a pessimistic reading of the degree of disenchantment from formal politics is that it will in the end undermine support for democracy and democratic decision-making.
>
> (Stoker 2006b: 182–183)

Others, while agreeing that citizens are possibly not as interested, active and engaged as they used to be, do not share such pessimism. Hibbing and Theiss-Morse (2002) see citizens' lack of enthusiasm as less problematic, and highlight that in democracies the key issue is that citizens can participate if they want, and that if they choose not to *get involved*, then so be it. Hibbing and Theiss-Morse (2002: 1–2; 3) argue:

> The last thing people want is to be more involved in political decision-making: They do not want to make political decisions themselves; they do not want to provide much input to those who are assigned to make these decisions; and they would rather not know all the details of the decision-making process ... Evidence of the people's desire to avoid politics is widespread, but most observers still find it difficult to take this evidence at face value ... when people say they do not like politics and do not want to participate in politics, they are simply ignored. Elite observers claim to know what people really want – and that is to be involved, richly and consistently, in the political arena. If people are not involved, these observers automatically deem the system in dire need of repair.

However, Hibbing and Theiss-Morse (2002: 171) also note that several studies have demonstrated that when citizens are involved in voluntary associations, they become *better democrats*. Involved citizens are far more likely than their uninvolved peers to display higher levels of trust, tolerance and generalized reciprocity, and to behave less opportunistically. They are also more likely to act in a community- and politically-orientated way – by voting in elections, signing petitions, contacting elected representatives, boycotting or buying specific products for political reasons, taking part in demonstrations and marches, or donating to charities and exhibiting higher levels of interest and knowledge about political issues. Howard and Gilbert (2008: 13, see also p. 26) conclude that 'our results provide general support for the Tocquevillian argument. On average those persons with greater levels of involvement in voluntary associations also engage in more political acts', while Diamond (1999: 242) argued that associations instil 'participatory habits, interests, skills of democratic citizenship ... [and] deeper values of a democratic political cultures, such as tolerance, moderation, a willingness to compromise, and a respect for opposing viewpoints'.

Some scholars maintain that the notion that associations inculcate pro-democratic and civic values in members is somewhat overstretc.hed. Drawing on the CID population data, Wollbæk and Strømsnes (2008: 250) argue that 'the primary contribution of voluntary organizations ... lies not in socializing individual active members but in institutionalizing social capital'. In addition to this, there is not unanimous agreement that more participation equals better democracy. Schumpeter (1943) and Huntington (1981: 219) did not perceive widespread participation as universally beneficial. Huntington famously cautioned against a 'surge of participatory democracy' as generating too many irreconcilable conflicting demands on government. Even scholars who are more sympathetic to greater involvement levels nevertheless have exhibited elitist tendencies, possibly, as Dalton (2006: 19) argues, driven by 'the realities of political life – or at least the hard evidence of survey research'. For example, Berelson and colleagues (1954: 314–315) asked, '[h]ow could mass democracy work if all the people were deeply involved in politics?... Some people are and should be interested in politics, but not everyone is or needs to be' (cited in Hudson 2006: 13). Almond and Verba (1963: 478–479) maintain that 'the democratic citizen ... must be active, yet passive; involved, yet not too involved; influential, yet deferential' (cited in Dalton 2006: 19).

Finally, it is also widely documented that there is a 'dark side' to social capital (Fiorina 1999; Orr 1999; Warren 2008). Social capital can assist the mobilization of non-civic and anti-democratic entities just as easily as it can contribute to a healthy civil society and democratic system. As Warren (2008: 123) notes, 'the social bads sometimes facilitated by social capital can also be considerable, including terrorism, organized crime, clientelism, economic inefficiencies, rigid communities that stifle innovation and are dysfunctional within broader societies, ethnic rivalries, and unjust distributions of resources'. While forms of social capital can be created in oppositional and conflictual settings and in closed communities, the down-side of social capital does not have to be so civically or democratically pathological. Knoke (1990: 8) reminds us there can be contradictory qualities to collective action organizations – groups promote internal unity and external conflict. However, in most cases this conflict does not have a deleterious democratic effect – resolving conflict is at the heart of politics. As Stoker (2006a: 202) argues, 'politics remains about people expressing conflicting ideas and interests and then finding a way to reconcile those ideas and interests in order to rub along with one another'.

1.2 Voluntary associations and democracy in Europe

The rapid rise of neo-Tocquevillean approaches underlines the increased importance of voluntary associations and social activities for democracy. If politics for many citizens has become 'interesting but irrelevant' (van Deth 2000), activities in voluntary associations provide an almost ideal alternative or substitute for apparently less attractive modes of political engagement. Besides, for many people voluntary associations offer a conducive environment for developing skills, attitudes and social contacts, which can be useful for political mobilization and political activities. People don't become members in bird-watching associations or choral societies to be politically active, but that does not mean that those memberships cannot or will not have benevolent consequences for democracy. With the shifting focus from national towards European politics in the past few decades, this idea seems to be especially relevant in the EU member states.[1]

1.2.1 Civil society in Europe

Voluntary associations are an important part of European societal and political systems at various levels. Strongly relying on a top-down approach, the European Commission ascribes a crucial role to a vast amount of associations such as interest groups, voluntary associations, social movements, social movement organizations, non-governmental organizations (NGOs), clubs, political initiatives, foundations, etc.etera. For this heterogeneous mixture of associations, the term 'civil society' is used. The EU presumes that civil society plays a major role in increasing the density, diversity, breadth and depth of the links between citizens and decision-makers in Europe – i.e. the Commission increasingly relies on these associations in order to promote good governance in terms of democracy, accountability and efficiency. The involvement of many civil society organizations in political decision-making within the EU is further evidence of *Europeanization* in this area. The EU *White Paper on Governance* (CEC 2001a) was essentially a rallying call for a more engaged and vibrant European civil society, not as a luxury, but as a necessity. Ever since, the debates about the (potential) contribution of civil society have been at the foreground of political and academic debates on democratizing decision-making in Europe at various levels.

The empirical record for these claims is modest at best (cf. Maloney and van Deth 2008a). Most citizens do not attach much importance to associational activities as an alternative or substitute for political participation or democratic engagement; nor do they consider those activities to be very important for a more democratic Europe. Irrespective of this reluctance and scepticism among average citizens, the idea that democracy depends on an active and vibrant civil society and a healthy stock of social capital is widely held. In the current era (and from the Commission's perspective), groups are seen as representative vehicles delivering 'good fit' public–policy outcomes, and as generating pro-democratic attitudes and values. Civil society possibly even increases citizens' attachment to, trust and confidence in, and identification with, European institutions – and in that way might be an important factor for the ongoing democratization of European social and political systems.

The revival of the idea that a vibrant democracy depends on a well-developed civil society implies a renewed attention to the democratic impact of activities in voluntary associations. From a macro-societal perspective, the benevolent consequences for democracy seem plausible and important – as a wide range of pluralists and neo-corporatists authors have claimed for a very long time. What is less clear, however, is the way associational activities might be related to democratic attitudes and European orientations at the micro-level. Yet the strong impulse provided by the Commission's *White Paper* and the subsequent debates on strengthening civil society in Europe certainly have renewed the interest in the functioning of these organizations and their impact on members, activists, and volunteers. If voluntary associations are a crucial part of European democracy, how do they reach citizens, and what consequences do associational activities have for citizens? And if voluntary associations increasingly become a more active part of a growing European civil society, how do they influence attitudes towards Europe and European institutions?

1.2.2 The context of civil engagement

This volume seeks to address the role of civil society organizations in several advanced European democracies (Germany, the Netherlands, Spain, Switzerland and the United Kingdom). How do voluntary organizations contribute to civic and democratic health? What impact do specific organizational types or discrete organizational characteristics have on the generation of various democratic attitudes and orientations towards Europe? Is Putnam's (1993) initial argument that bird-watching associations and choral societies (not forgetting bowling clubs) undergird and enhance a vibrant civil society robust? In the analyses contained in this volume the authors address the impact of various features on the civic and democratic well-being of these democracies, including: organizational concerns (e.g. 'Family', 'Sports', 'Culture/Music', 'Politics', 'Welfare' and 'Religion'); the extent to which internal democracy is institutionalized (e.g. the existence of an elected assembly and the opportunities for involvement); the extent to which internal democracy is meaningfully practised (e.g. the intensity of participation within groups); organizational size (membership levels and income); organizational homogeneity or heterogeneity (age, gender, educational attainment levels, ethnic background); and the impact of other individual-level characteristics (political interest, satisfaction with democracy). Much participation and social capital research has argued that voluntary associations contribute to civil society and democracy in specific ways, both (normatively) positive and negative. However, few if any have systematically focused on associational universes in a comparative context, or intra-organizational aspects. Thus, herein we can assess the impact of various organizational characteristics, traits and attributes, AND country-specific differences. In addition to this, the authors draw on population data and compare those sections of the population that are civically and politically active – *activists* (those respondents who have been surveyed as members of specific organizations) and *socially actives* (those in the general population who are supporters or members of organizations) – with those who eschew political and civic involvement – *non-actives* (no involvement with any group) (these categories are defined in greater detail in Section 1.4).

1.3 Research strategy and data

Empirical research on the consequences and meaning of associational engagement usually focuses on individual features of participants or on the perceptions of activists. When the different opportunities provided by various organizations are taken into account, it is usually via case studies or reports about perceived opportunities for engagement. The pitfalls and limitations of these research strategies are obvious. Instead of relying on specific cases or subjective assessments and opinions, contextual information has to be considered systematically. Only by analysing the combined impact of (i) individual features of participants, (ii) features of the type and scope engagement, and (iii) objective features of the specific associations concerned, can the *organizational impact of voluntary activities on political orientations and behaviour* be assessed empirically. Furthermore, country-specific characteristics of associational engagement cannot be neglected. By combining these types of information, the associational impact on political orientations can be *contextualized* – i.e. the usual survey responses can be analysed by taking into account the objective features of the organization concerned as well as the specific 'associational universe' or context. In summary, this project moves beyond the 'regular' single focus on organizations, or (representative) samples of activists and volunteers. The research design provides the opportunity to evaluate the impact of the organizational context on individual activity profiles, and attitudes and values of activists. The existing research that looks at members drawn from population surveys and develops arguments and inferences from these data about what is going on inside groups and what impact groups have on citizens' values, attitudes and behaviour is of limited value. However, our data locate citizens (as members) within groups of all types, and thus enable us to make more robust claims regarding the contribution or otherwise that voluntary associations make to civil and democratic society. The novel and innovative aspect of this research project is the direct link that can be established between the *specific* organizational context and the *actual* activist in the associational universes in several European countries.

1.3.1 Studies and data sets

As noted above, comparative empirical research linking aspects of civil society and organizational features on the one hand to attitudes of people engaged in these associations on the other is very rare. To date (2009), comparative data of this kind have only been collected by the Citizenship, Involvement, Democracy project (CID).[2] This project encompassed three main parts: (i) a study of voluntary associations (the 'CID Organization Study'), (ii) a study of activists in selected voluntary associations (the 'CID Activists Study') and (iii) a study of citizens (the 'CID Population Study'). The main characteristics of these three parts are as follows.

The CID Organization Study

In this component the associational 'landscape' was extensively investigated and mapped in six European cities and communities: Mannheim (West Germany), Chemnitz (East Germany), Enschede (The Netherlands), Sabadell (Spain), Bern (Switzerland) and Aberdeen (UK). (In several of these countries there were also some analyses of associations in smaller communities.[3]) The major aim of the CID Organization Study was to identify as many voluntary associations as possible and to uncover a wide variety of types of organizations in terms of relevant characteristics (size, internal participation, resources, institutionalization, etc.). Once mapping was completed, all organizations received a short questionnaire which sought information on: organizational demographics (organization name, year founded, membership and/or supporter size, staffing levels, income and expenditure); sources of income; main objectives; organizational structure (including management and internal democratic procedures); and external organizational activities (nature, type and frequency of contact with external bodies, organizational outputs).

For each organization the information was included in an integrated data set. Here, the primary unit of analysis – the 'case' – is the organization. The main characteristics of this study are summarized in the first part of Table 1.1. Comparative analyses of associational features based on the Organization Study were published in Maloney and Roßteutscher (2007).

The CID Activists Study

In a second step, active members within specific organizations (drawn from the CID Organization Study) were surveyed. In the Activists Study, selected associations were asked to forward extensive questionnaires to a number of their active members. These active members in turn mailed the questionnaire directly back to the research coordinator. The questionnaire consisted of a number of questions about the type and scope of associational involvement, as well as an extensive section on social and political orientations and behaviour. The questionnaire on orientations and behaviour was broadly similar to that used for the CID Population Study (see below).

To select activists and volunteers in each city/community, a range of organizations was drawn from the 'associational universe' mapped by the Organization Study on the basis of an empirical typology of voluntary associations (see Maloney and Roßteutscher 2007: 62–68). The objective was to collect a subsample that contained all possible associational variations. A maximum of 20 organizations (if possible) were selected per issue area in each city/community on the basis of a casually drawn sample. In this way, the selection procedure focused on representation of variations and not on representation of the population of voluntary associations or activists.[4]

It is important to note (and it is worth emphasizing again) that the research design for the Activists Study does not follow the regular design by selecting

Table 1.1 Main characteristics of the three data sets used

	East Germany	West Germany	The Netherlands	Spain	Switzerland	United Kingdom
Organization study:						
Main city	Chemnitz	Mannheim	Enschede	Sabadell	Bern	Aberdeen
Year of survey	2001	2001	2001	2002	2000	2001
Number of available organizations	687	1,618	832	360	742	497
response rate (%)[a]		36.0	50.2	31.9	55.0	36.5
Activists study:						
Year of survey	2001	2001	2001	2002	2000	2001
Number of available activists	1,266	1,868	439	1,272	968	859
Number of organizations with activists	283	429	56	240	161	156
Average number of activists per organization	4.47	4.35	7.84	5.3	6.01	5.51
Population study:						
Year of survey	2001	2001	2001	2002	2000	2001[b]
Number of available citizens	1,013	1,991	1,649	4,252	2,145	809
Response rate (%)[c]	56.1	55.2	30.0	31.0	44.3	67.0

Notes
a The response rate is the number of responses collected divided by the number of existing organizations at the time of the survey (as a percentage).
b For the British population, data from the so-called 'Citizen Audit of Great Britain' are used.
c The response rate is the number of responses collected divided by the number of potential respondents (as a percentage).

people randomly and asking them about their organizational experiences, but starts by locating individuals within 'their' specific associations. For each respondent we had extensive information about her/his social and political orientations and associational engagement based on the activists' questionnaire. Furthermore, we knew in which organization the activities were carried out. The resulting data set consists of the questionnaire responses from active members; the primary unit of analysis ('case') here is the activist. The main characteristics of this study are summarized in the middle part of Table 1.1. No publication based on these data is available yet.[5]

The CID Population Study

The CID Population Study was developed in parallel with but mainly independently of the Organizational and Activists Studies. The samples for the Population Study were representative of the population[6] of 12 European countries (Denmark, Switzerland, [East and West] Germany, Russia, Portugal, Norway, Spain, The Netherlands, Slovenia, Moldova, Romania, and Sweden).[7] An extensive questionnaire was created where the main topics included political participation at different levels and in several areas; social participation and voluntary associations; engagement in 'small democracy' (workplace, health, education); social trust and confidence; political equality; and networks and social contacts. An integrated data set covering the responses by the respondents in a standard form (the primary unit of analysis – the 'case' – here is the respondent) is available.[8] Comparative analyses of citizens' orientations based on the full set of 13 societies available have been published (van Deth *et al.* 2007).

For our research on the contextual effects of associational engagement, we focus on the six communities for which we have information regarding both the organizations and the activists (Mannheim, Chemnitz, Enschede, Sabadell, Bern and Aberdeen). For these cities, the relevant five countries from the Population Study (Germany, The Netherlands, Spain, Switzerland and the UK) were added.[9] Twenty years after the fall of the Berlin Wall the two parts of Germany are still rather different, and we will therefore treat Germany as two separate entities – East Germany and West Germany – according to the lines into which the country was divided for 45 years. The very differential experiences faced by the populations of the two parts still render them significantly different with respect to the development of civil society and a democratic political culture. As a rule, then, we proceed as though we had a sample of six rather than five countries. This information about six representative samples of the populations allows reliable estimates for the citizenries of these countries.[10] The main characteristics of this selection of country studies are summarized in the bottom part of Table 1.1.

1.3.2 Integrating information from three studies

At the core of our research interests is the question regarding the contextual conditions of associational engagement, and its consequences for political and social orientations and behaviour. Both the information on associational features (the Organization Study) as well as the information on the population characteristics (the Population Study) can be used to explore the orientations and behaviour of active members of voluntary associations (the Activists Study) and to compare these results with the information obtained from average citizens.

The country-specific conditions for associational engagement can be seen as a first contextual layer for our analyses. Cross-national differences have been documented in a number of empirical studies, and this finding is most likely to be corroborated by the six countries selected. The second contextual layer consists of the particular cities and communities which provide the direct environment for the associations selected. The varying historical, institutional and cultural settings of these six localities result in different 'associational universes' (see Maloney and Roßteutscher 2007), but do not necessarily have consequences for the orientations or behaviour of activists. The primary context here, however, is established by the specific association and its impact on individual orientations and activities. How do we assess the impact of organizations on active members? In other words, how do we obtain an empirical assessment of the link between specific organizational characteristics and demographics on the one hand, and the social and political orientations of active members on the other? To answer these questions, the first key is to link the information from the Activists Study with the Organization Study. Second, in order to assess the similarities between active members of associations and average citizens, a link between the Activists Study and the Population Study is required.

Since the first two contextual layers (country and city/community) are only indirectly relevant for the main contextual layer (voluntary associations), the empirical analyses are carried out for each country/city separately. In this way the analyses are replicated six times, and both the interrelationships between various factors and the levels or distributions of specific factors can be studied. For each country or city the three parts of the CID project are merged and extended. The Activists Study contains the most relevant information, and is used as a starting point for the construction of the six integrated data sets by adding information from the Organization Study to each of the activists in the following way:

1 The rectangular data set of activists' information (see Matrix A in Figure 1.1) consists of activists' responses to the questionnaire (one case for each activist). For a particular voluntary association V, the number of activists can be p.
2 For each volunteer or activist, the specific organization (V) in which he or she is socially active is known. This information can be used to establish a direct link to the Organization Study.
3 The rectangular data set of organizations, however, consists of cases of organizations. In order to provide the organizational information for each activist p within organization V, the organizational information has to be replicated for each activist; that is, the information for organization V is provided p times in the expanded organizational data set (Matrix B).

4 After the replication of the organizational information for organization V, each activist p obtains the same organizational information by simply merging the two matrices. In this way, the associational features of organization V are transformed into individual features p of each active member of organization V separately.

5 The merged data set (Matrix A + Matrix B) can be used for the analyses of various features of individual activists (for instance, for a comparison of the average age of activists in small and large associations, or for a comparison of associational resources available for men and women). Since the new

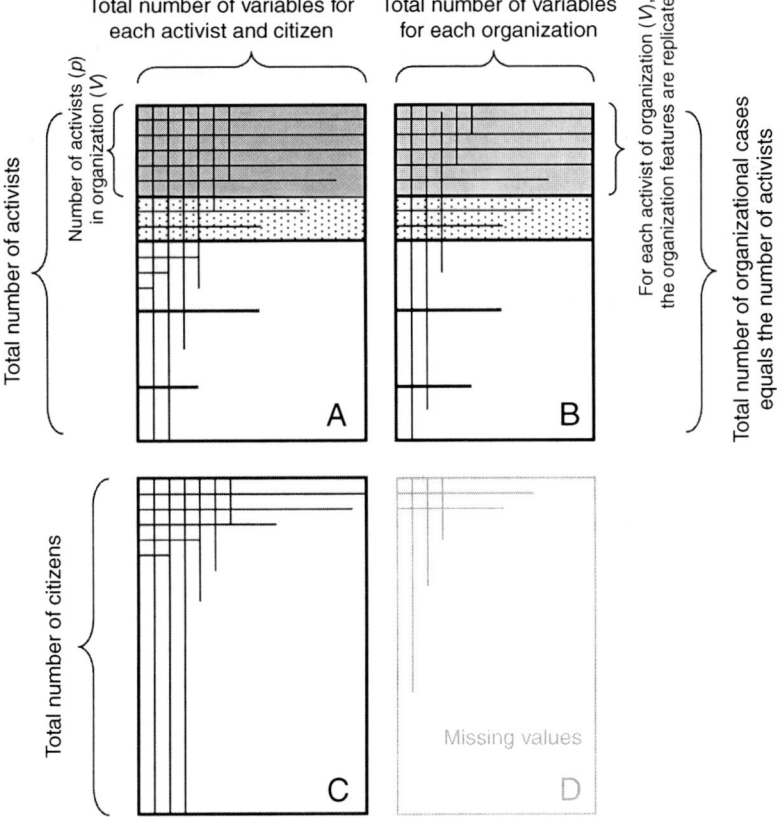

– Matrix A: Activists Study
– Matrix B: Expanded Organizational Study
– Matrix C: Population Study

– Total number of cases in the final data set equals the sum of activists and citizens
– Total number of variables equals the sum of the number of variables in the Activists Study and in the Organizational Study.

Figure 1.1 The three main parts of the integrated data set.

organizational data set (Matrix B) is now weighted by the number of activists interviewed within each organization, the organizational features in the new data set should not be used to estimate organizational properties.[11]

The addition of the population information is carried out in the next step. The questionnaires for the activists and the citizens are highly similar, and so the respective variables can be easily identified and matched. The rectangular data set for the Population Study (Matrix C) can be used to expand the number of cases of the Activists Study (Matrix A). In this way, the features of activists can be directly compared with corresponding features of average citizens (for instance, the differences in the level of education between activists and citizens, or possible over-/under-representation of specific orientations among active members of voluntary associations as compared with other citizens). Although a number of these citizens interviewed indicated that they were engaged in voluntary associations, none of them is active in any of the organizations in the Organization Study.[12] For that reason, the lower right-hand part (Matrix D) of the resulting data set consists of missing values only.

The resulting data set (Matrices A+B+C+D) offers a large number of opportunities to relate features of activists to organizational characteristics, and to compare them with the total population.[13] By constructing similar data sets for each of the six countries/cities separately, a unique data source is obtained which can be used to study the contextual impacts on voluntary engagement systematically.

1.4 Activists, socially actives, and non-actives

By definition, the Activists Study contains information about citizens active in a voluntary association. Yet a substantial proportion of the citizens involved in the Population Study also indicated that they were actively involved in some association. For these respondents, however, the information about their activities is restricted to *reported behaviour and perceptions of organizational opportunities* only. Therefore, the resulting integrated data set enables us to distinguish three types of respondents:

- *Activists*: we have objective information about their activities and the specific organizational context available (from the Activists Study). The fact that they are active in a voluntary association is not based on self-reporting, and their inclusion in our study is not on a self-selection basis.
- *Socially actives*: these are the respondents in the Population Study who explicitly indicate that they 'participate in activities' and/or 'do voluntary work' in at least one of the 27 types of associations presented in the questionnaire. By excluding respondents who are members only or who donate money to their organization, the socially actives selected are, in principle, similar to the activists interviewed in the Activists Study. However, being identified as socially active is based on self-reporting only.

- *Non-Actives*: these are the respondents in the Population Study who neither volunteer nor participate in activities of voluntary associations. They can, however, be engaged in these organizations in less active ways (by being a member and/or donating money). Being identified as non-active depends on self-reporting only. Some may object to the inclusion of passive members and donors in the non-active category; however, we are specifically interested in examining *actual activity*, and not *passivity*.

Some main characteristics of activists, socially actives, and non-actives in the six countries included in our project are summarized in Table 1.2. The differences between the three categories of respondents are clear. This first dip of the toe into the empirical water demonstrates the relevance of associational activities as suggested by neo-Tocquevillean theories. Compared with other groups, activists tend to be relatively highly educated, relatively interested in politics, more supportive of left-wing positions, and relatively satisfied with democracy and their life as a whole. However, even a cursory glance at these findings also shows that the differences between the various countries/cities are considerable.

1.5 Research focus and plan of the book

The six integrated data sets allow for a large number of comparisons of relationships, levels and patterns. The main research focus of the contributions prepared for this volume consists of a comparison of the features of activists, socially actives and non-actives for a number of social and political attitudes, as well as European orientations. The selection of the explanatory concepts (or independent variables) at the individual level is grouped in three blocks: (i) sociodemographic variables orientations; (ii) variables about the type and scope of engagement (subjective measures); and (iii) variables about the associational context and opportunities (objective measures). If possible, and where relevant, comparisons of results obtained from the Activists Study with similar analyses based on the Population Study were conducted. Any deviations from this common procedure are driven by the specific topic under consideration. However, each contribution addresses contextualizing effects on the basis of the information available from the Organization Study.

The volume consists of 11 chapters which focus on the two main topics mentioned. In Part I of the book, empirical analyses are presented dealing with the neo-Tocquevillean claim that associational activities have positive consequences for a number of democratic social and political orientations. Tobias Schulz opens the analyses of contextual effects in this part of the volume with his study on the mobilization of voluntary work, especially the interplay between organizations and municipalities (Chapter 2). The impact of associational activities on members' involvement in associational decision-making processes is studied by Herman Lelieveldt (Chapter 3). While Lelieveldt focuses on the effects on involvement within organizations, Bangü Dayican, Bas Denters and Henk van der Kolk focus on the extent to which associational involvement increases

Table 1.2 Main characteristics of activists, socially actives and non-actives in various cities and countries (percentages and means)

	East Germany			West Germany			The Netherlands			Spain			Switzerland			United Kingdom		
	Activists	Socially actives	Non-actives	Activists	Socially actives	Non-actives	Activists	Socially actives	Non-actives	Activists	Socially actives	Non-actives	Activists	Socially actives	Non-active	Activists	Socially actives	Non-actives
Gender (percentage male)	53.95	51.29	43.88	53.21	47.45	39.30	62.04	45.73	48.23	49.72	52.66	46.17	55.50	47.86	41.40	37.88	37.82	41.82
Age (mean years)	48.18	48.65	49.11	52.54	48.49	51.88	51.19	48.14	46.20	41.67	43.22	45.62	47.67	47.06	49.72	55.08	48.36	51.66
Education (percentage tertiary)	40.22	19.62	11.36	33.24	15.36	8.34	48.02	33.50	22.22	47.80	25.37	11.25	31.97	27.69	18.47	37.95	26.63	23.42
Political interest (mean 1–4)	2.90	2.82	2.21	2.99	2.61	2.18	2.74	2.66	2.42	2.53	2.16	1.71	2.75	2.76	2.48	2.71	n.a.	n.a.
Left–right placement (mean 0–10)	4.06	4.41	4.61	4.82	4.92	5.12	4.93	5.17	4.99	3.57	4.50	4.62	4.44	5.01	5.16	5.05	5.12	5.18
General trust (mean 0–10)	5.97	4.44	3.95	6.10	5.55	4.16	7.01	6.40	6.00	6.01	4.97	4.29	6.62	6.34	5.37	6.22	6.82	6.57
Satisfaction with democracy (mean 1–4)	2.25	2.49	2.31	2.72	2.97	2.85	2.98	3.00	2.91	2.17	2.65	2.66	2.80	2.73	2.68	2.65	2.95	2.99
Satisfaction with life (mean 0–10)	7.63	7.62	6.68	7.75	8.11	7.54	8.04	8.10	7.93	n.a.	7.67	7.40	8.08	8.31	8.10	8.03	3.90	3.84
N (min)	1,196	390	483	1,773	1,043	699	423	938	601	1,191	1,202	2,152	893	895	1,022	789	730	1,571

Notes
– Spanish data weighted.
– Satisfaction with democracy/Satisfaction with life in UK population file scaled 1–5.

feelings of empowerment among activists (Chapter 4). The latter two chapters in Part I examine the effects of associational involvement on political orientations. The impact of this involvement on political interest is analysed by Jan van Deth (Chapter 5), while Patrick Bernhagen and William Maloney turn to behavioural attitudes in their search for the effects of democratic associational opportunities on the political participation of citizens and activists (Chapter 6).

Part II of this volume consists of four contributions expanding the scope of the social and political orientations concerned. The spread of European integration and the success of the EU have confronted many citizens with political issues, questions and institutes that clearly lie beyond the borders of the conventional nation-state. Do activities in voluntary associations – which are locally based – have consequences for attitudes towards Europe? Manuela Caiani and Mariona Ferrer-Fons search for support for European arrangements among citizens and activists (Chapter 7), and Sonja Zmerli examines the associational determinants of the EU legitimacy, especially looking into the relationships with social capital (Chapter 8). Hajdeja Iglič focuses on the relational basis of attachment to Europe (Chapter 9), while Silke Keil presents a comparative analysis of idealism and rational abstention as important explanations of political trust in the EU (Chapter 10).

The two main topics discussed in the two parts of the book – democratic political attitudes and European orientations – are brought together in the conclusion by Jan van Deth and William Maloney, in an attempt to formulate general findings from the various empirical analyses (Chapter 11). The unique combination of CID data sets enables examination of the claims of positive effects of engagement in voluntary associations.

Notes

1 Additional support for this idea is provided by Miller (2009), who presents empirical evidence that members of 'translocal groups' are considerably more politically engaged than members of local or national voluntary associations.
2 The CID-network was funded by the European Science Foundation; see www.mzes.uni-mannheim.de/projekte/cid, or the edited volumes by van Deth *et al.* (2007) and Maloney and Roßteutscher (2007) for further information.
3 See Maloney and Roßteutscher (2007: xv–xvii) for extensive acknowledgements, funding and principal investigators for the Organization Study.
4 See the Acknowledgements in this volume for principal investigators, funding and support for the Activist Study.
5 First analyses of parts of these data sets for Aberdeen and Mannheim are presented by Maloney *et al.* (2008).
6 The sample is of citizens 18 years and older – 18 is the minimum voting age in all the countries included in the population project.
7 See van Deth *et al.* (2007: xxi–xxiv) for extensive acknowledgements, funding and principal investigators for the Population Study.
8 Data from the CID Population Study can be obtained from the Zentral Archiv in Cologne, Study number 4492 (http://info1.za.gesis.org/DBKSearch12/SDesc2.asp?no=4492&search=CID&search2=&db=E).
9 Five of the countries do not provide any problem, and data can be simply selected

from the integrated CID Population Study file. For the UK the situation is a little more complicated, since country representatives from Britain dropped out of the CID project at an early stage. However, they consequently developed the 'Citizen Audit of Great Britain', some of which is compatible with parts of the CID project and can be used as a surrogate data set for the UK population. For the 'Citizen Audit of Great Britain', see www.data-archive.ac.uk/findingData/snDescriptionasp? n=5099 and the analyses presented by Pattie *et al.* (2004).

10 Since the Spanish part of the Population Study is based on regional samples, the population data for Spain are weighted. Weighting procedures for the other five countries would result in very minor differences only, and are not used here (see van Deth *et al.* 2007: 30).

11 The replication of organizational features is likely to result in complications when standard OLS estimation procedures are used. Accordingly, OLS estimations are used for explorative analyses only in the contributions to this volume.

12 Since the citizens are drawn from the national populations of each country, the chances of being involved in a voluntary association in the specific city selected are extremely low.

13 The combined matrix and the accompanying algorithms were designed by Jan van Deth. Daniel Stegmuller and especially Christian Schnaudt constructed the data matrices for Mannheim/West Germany, Chemnitz/East Germany, and Aberdeen/UK. Tobias Schulz constructed the Bern/Switzerland matrix, Bengü Dayican was in charge of the Enschede/Dutch data, whereas Mariona Ferrer-Fons took care of the construction of the Sabadell/Spanish matrix.

Part I
General social and political orientations

2 Mobilizing voluntary work
The interplay between organizations and municipalities

Tobias Schulz

2.1 Introduction

The relationship between welfare policy and volunteering is of great importance in most western welfare states. One constant and controversial policy-relevant question is whether higher levels of welfare spending will 'crowd out' private initiative or whether, on the contrary, volunteering is supported by state expenditure. Quantitative examinations have tried to explore this issue (Menchik and Weisbrod 1987; Day and Devlin 1996) by relating overall government expenditure to measures of (organized) voluntary work. Although 'crowding-out' clearly predicts a negative relationship between these measures, the effects that have been identified are not very consistent across different policy areas (education, social services, health, etc.). However, the prominent Johns Hopkins Comparative Nonprofit Sector Project (Salamon and Sokolowski 2001) started from a different assumption – that is, that state expenditure should be supportive of the voluntary sector. This research finds positive correlations between respective measures, although on a highly aggregated (cross-country) level. Their indicators for both social expenditure and volunteering are somewhat rudimentary, and therefore should be treated as indicative.

Unfortunately, the research in this realm suffers from two insufficiencies. First, incorporating overall government expenditure fails to take account of the fact that government spending can take different forms. Direct social security transfers to individuals certainly have the potential to substitute some of the efforts that are rendered by volunteers. However, some of the money can also be attributed as subsidies that go to voluntary organizations directly, or to the infrastructure support of these organizations (Schulz and Häfliger 2007). In the latter case, government spending can indirectly foster voluntary engagement. Second, the survey data in this realm usually do not include measures that would describe attributes of the voluntary organizations. How the internal rules as well as the external relations of voluntary organizations might influence the engagement of the activists cannot be examined with this data.

The CID data offer the opportunity to largely overcome both these limitations. First, the organizational level can be taken into account explicitly because each activist is linked to an organization and important attributes of these organizations have been measured. Second, the list of organizational attributes contains the amount of subsidies an organization received from the local and regional administration, as well as the number of contacts the organization has with important local (administrative) actors. In this chapter, we examine the relationship between voluntary work in general and subsidies to (voluntary) organizations in the six countries that make up the empirical background of this volume. The two main questions to be addressed are: (i) To what extent is the amount of volunteering dependent upon the organization in some way? (ii) How is this related to funding (from the local government), or is it a result of the strong ties the organization has established with the local elite?

The results are mixed. Although the hierarchical regression model indicates that the organizational level does play some role with respect to the mobilization of voluntary work in all but one of the cases, the actual mechanisms remain unclear. One substantial insight is that money is more predictable in its impact than contacts. The subsidies from the local administration have a more or less consistent positive, and in some cases also significant, impact on the amount of volunteer work. Generally, however, the results do not provide us with a categorical understanding of how organizations relate to the (local) administration and what makes the difference with respect to the mobilization of voluntary work on the organizational level. Further research is required to understand how the work of voluntary organizations could be supported and complemented by government programmes.

In what follows, we briefly discuss the determinants of voluntary engagement at the individual level, and then give a short review of theoretical and empirical contributions that have examined how voluntary engagement is dependent on public policy (i.e. welfare expenditure and subsidies to organizations) or how much it might be dependent on organizational attributes.

2.2 Individual-level determinants of voluntary engagement

Individual-level examinations of voluntary work usually differentiate between the decision to volunteer and the amount of time volunteered. Conceptually, these two are connected. Menchik and Weisbrod (1987) conducted a seminal study for the USA, based on explicit economic models – i.e. a 'consumption model' and an 'investment model' of volunteering. The investment model supposes that volunteering is aimed at increasing potential earnings (in the future), because such an activity provides experiences and contacts that potentially raise one's value in the job market. In addition, voluntary work can also be advantageous for a single employee in a more immediate sense – for example, if that employee receives a wage surplus because his or her voluntary engagement improves the reputation of the employer. The consumption model proceeds from the assumption that people engage in volunteer work simply because they are altruistic. Hence, working on a volunteer basis increases individual utility by the same token as normal consumption.

According to Menchik and Weisbrod (1987), however, the investment model does not allow us to come to unambiguous conclusions regarding the effect of income on volunteering. Alternatively, the consumption model posits a positive relationship between 'full income' (including income from real-estate property and from assets but excluding wages) and volunteering, since this is income that is earned independently from a time-consuming job. The 'net-of-tax wage', however, is the opportunity cost of time, and hence one would expect that the higher this kind of income, the less one could afford to give away one's time for free.

These economic models have been elaborated somewhat further and in some detail by Day and Devlin (1996),[1] Segal and Weisbrod (2002)[2] and Cappellari and Turati (2004).[3] However, applying such sophisticated economic models of volunteer work is beyond the scope of this chapter. We are primarily concerned with establishing the impact of co-variates of volunteer work at the organizational level. Furthermore, a differentiation between wage and non-wage income is not possible with the CID data, which include 'total income' only. The value of income as an explanatory variable is thus questionable, since wage and non-wage income exert opposing effects within a consumption model. It follows that no clear prediction for income can be made.

Alternatively, one could try to measure opportunity costs of time indirectly, by differentiating between the non-, the part-time and the fully employed, as done by Day and Devlin (1996). One has to bear in mind, however, that having a job creates social contacts and hence new opportunities for volunteering. Accordingly, one should expect part-time workers to be most prone to volunteering, because they are less disconnected than the unemployed but have more time available than the fully employed.

Menchik and Weisbrod (1987) employ a number of control variables – for example, the background of the respondent with respect to civic engagement (whether the parents had been active already or whether the parents went to church regularly), education, children, marital status, sex, age, and the size of the city. In a similar study for Canada, Day and Devlin (1996) employed age, sex, marital status, the number of children, education level, strength of religious beliefs and health as explanatory variables. The language spoken at home is used as an indicator of the cultural background of the subject. Segal and Weisbrod (2002) also included an indicator variable that identifies whether the respondent is a community newcomer.

For most of these variables, the expected correlation with the amount volunteered is self-evident. People who feel attached to a place, were raised in a socially active family and have received higher education should have a higher propensity to volunteer. On the contrary, community newcomers should have a lower propensity to do so. For some of these proxies clear theoretical foundations are lacking, and, accordingly, the results are not consistent. Women are assumed to be more likely to take up action for other people, and Menchik and Weisbrod (1987) confirm this with the amount volunteered as the dependent variable. However, Day and Devlin's (1996) results suggest that while men are less likely to take up action, they are more likely to supply more hours of work. Other expected relationships for which the theoretical foundations are not fully discussed but which are employed in the studies mentioned include the assumption that religious people should be more altruistic, and people living in anonymous suburbs should be less inclined to engage for other people.

Similarly, Menchik and Weisbrod (1987) add variables that measure 'demographic life-cycle characteristics', without fleshing out the theoretical expectations in full detail. With respect to age, younger and elderly people are expected to be less motivated for volunteering than the middle-aged – a result that is also confirmed by Day and Devlin (1996). While the general expectation is that married people should engage more often in volunteer action, possibly because they get involved in the activities of their partners, the impact of the number of children is assumed to be ambivalent (Day and Devlin 1996). While caring for small children is time consuming, grown children give their parents the opportunity to become engaged in those clubs their children participate in.

2.3 Voluntary organizations and the state

2.3.1 Substitutive vs supportive relationship

Scholars claiming a negative relationship between state expenditure and volunteering are proceeding from the point of view that volunteering is simply a reaction to 'government failure' (Dollery 2003) – that is, the inability or unwillingness of the public sector to provide a public good. This could be described as a 'substitutive' relationship between governmental programmes (mostly direct monetary transfers to individuals) and volunteering.[4] The other side of the coin, the 'crowding-out hypothesis', has been examined by Weisbrod (1977, 1988): motivations of volunteers could be damaged if the government takes up new activities and starts to provide services in fields where voluntary organizations are active. This hypothesis states that with unchanged demand, an increase in government service provision results in a decrease in volunteer effort (Weisbrod 1977: 103).

Menchik and Weisbrod (1987), in their examination of US data between the late 1970s and the mid-1980s, were unable to confirm this hypothesis for all sectors. While they found a substitutive effect for volunteering in the social welfare and higher education sectors; overall government expenditure was linked slightly positively with volunteer time (Menchik and Weisbrod 1987: 179). Day and Devlin (1996) have also tested the 'crowing-out' hypothesis explicitly at the individual level. However, they do not differentiate between volunteering in different realms; rather, they look at it from the opposite perspective and estimate the impact of government spending in different policy areas on volunteering. They find that government spending has an impact on the decision to volunteer, but not on the amount of time volunteered.

In opposition to the 'crowding-out' approach is the argument that government expenditure supports the voluntary sector. Salamon *et al.* (2000) claim that there must be a positive relationship between the size of the nonprofit sector and the size of the public sector: 'Recruiting volunteers and sustaining their participation over time require organizational resources, and such resources are typically proportional to the size of the nonprofit sector' (Salamon and Sokolowski 2001: 11).[5] This is what they call the 'interdependence-theory', and the 'Comparative Nonprofit Sector Project' has produced an impressive amount of empirical work to support this view (compare, for example, Skocpol *et al.* 2000: 538).

Based on parts of the CID data, Kriesi (2006) conducted an analysis at the aggregated level to shed light on the impact of financial and organizational resources on the mobilization of volunteers and the organizational activity of members. He concluded that financial resources are concentrated in the segment of the larger organizations that have the largest territorial scope and non-traditional modes of financing – i.e. in addition to membership dues they also receive subsidies from government and other sources. Although his analysis leads him to conclude that 'associational life is intertwined with governmental policies and politics' (Kriesi 2006: 130), he is not analysing whether subsidies actually influence the voluntary activity in these organizations. His expectation is, however, that professionals (who are more likely to be found in organizations that receive subsidies) could either substitute volunteer engagement or provide appropriate organizational skills to support mobilization of volunteers. While not directly comparing these two factors, Salamon and Sokolowski (2001) conclude that paid nonprofit employment encourages rather than 'crowds out' private volunteer action.

This discussion reveals that the relationship between public policy and volunteering should be conditional on the differentiation between different forms of government expenditure. It is plausible that direct transfers to individuals (for example, for social welfare or for medical treatment) can substitute for voluntarily provided social or medical services, while subsidies to voluntary organizations should help build up the organizational resources needed for the mobilization of volunteers. The CID data allow us to measure subsidies to voluntary organizations coming from the local and the regional administrative levels. Under the assumption that the local administrative level is better able to target the subsidies, a positive relationship between subsidies and volunteering is expected particularly at this level.

2.3.2 Connections between organizations and local government

One key to the examination of the supportive relationship is obviously voluntary organizations. However, this part of the puzzle is still not very well understood, and therefore the relationship between voluntary organizations and the state has received increased attention in recent research. Oxendine *et al.* (2007) take as a point of departure 'contextual influences' on civic behaviour. They proceed from research that tries to establish an impact of governmental institutions on civic engagement, mainly in the USA. Whether or not people are given a choice to which public school they send their children increases their involvement (Schneider *et al.* 1997). Also, the design of policies might influence whether and how people engage in civic activities (Kumlin and Rothstein 2005). The structure of the voluntary sector is to some degree dependent on the institutional context of the respective country (Kriesi et al. 2006). A recent study that examined determinants of volunteer participation in Japanese municipalities concludes that 'it is the practices of the state and society – how well they legitimise, fund, and organise volunteers – that determine the level of volunteer participation in a community' (Haddad 2004: 26).

However, money is not the only kind of relationship that can be established between the (local) government and organizations. Opportunities for organizations to provide services related to governmental programmes can also be created simply through communication. An additional hypothesisis, therefore, is that the stronger the links between organizations and local authorities, the more voluntary work the activists of organizations will provide. The question therefore is whether it is simply money that makes a difference, or whether the success of voluntary organizations depends on the strength of the ties between the association and the local actors.

Lelieveldt and Caiani (2006) have already examined the CID (organizational, but not members) data with respect to the contacts an organization has with relevant governmental actors. They use a cumulative 'contacts score', which is based on the idea that types of contacts can be structured hierarchically because they usually develop in a common pattern. Contacts with civil servants are most frequent, and contacts with the executive, and then with counsellors, are usually built upon these. Based on this, Lelieveldt and Caiani are able to establish a rather clear but not very strong positive correlation between their local contacts score and the subsidies an organization receives from local authorities.[6] However, the relationship between political contacts and the number of volunteers is not very strong and clear cut. What seems to be more effective with respect to the mobilization of volunteers are the contacts between organizations (Zmerli and Newton 2006).

In the empirical model, in order to make the established relation between an organization and the local administration more reliable, one should also include controls for how likely individuals are to volunteer because they think the organization is important in the local context, or whether it is because they are simply interested in local administrative issues. Without those controls, it would not be clear if a positive correlation between the contacts score of the organization and volunteering is only due to the possibility that people that are at the same time socially engaged and politically interested tend to assemble in better-connected and more influential organizations. Of course, we expect a positive impact of perceived influence of the organization and political interest on the amount volunteered.

2.3.3 Other organizational determinants of volunteering

Similarly important for the current context is the contribution of Torpe and Ferrer-Fons (2006), who have examined whether the organizations' structure of management, their mode of representation and organization as well as their size matters with respect to their capacity to mobilize volunteers. They operationalize this capacity as the ratio between passive members and volunteers, and find rather strong and highly significant correlations between measures of organizational type and volunteering. According to their analysis, the less the management of an organization is differentiated, the less formal its representational rule is and the fewer members the organization counts the better it is able to mobilize volunteers. Kriesi (2006) found a similar effect of size: membership organizations generally have fewer resources available. Whether or not the organization is itself an umbrella organization or part of such a hierarchical structure, or whether it is rather freestanding or part of a more loosely tied network, does not seem to matter much with respect to the mobilization of volunteers. Of the factors mentioned here, size seems to matter most, whereas the representational rule does significantly influence volunteering in some cities only.

Civil society organizations are usually specialized in one or several sectors, such as social policy, sports or religion, and most of them can be attributed to broad task domains. It is obvious that organizations that are active in different thematic fields with different goals might vary with respect to their effect on political participation. However, possible differences with respect to the mobilization of volunteers are less obvious.

Theoretical typologies usually divide the universe of voluntary organizations into two dimensions. Lelieveldt *et al.* (2006) distinguish between 'policy-oriented' (representation, mobilization) and 'service-oriented' (service and activation) organizations. Kriesi and Baglioni (2003: 10) differentiate between services for constituencies and mediation between government and constituencies on the one hand, and between low and high membership involvement on the other. Hence, 'service' organizations provide (professional) services (low membership involvement), whereas organizations for 'activation' comprise sports clubs or clubs for cultural activities (high membership involvement). Organizations that take over the function of 'representation' provide advocacy based on low membership involvement (e.g. parties), whereas citizen groups that engage for broader interests (such as peace or human rights) require high membership involvement and thus are labelled as 'mobilization' organizations.

Maloney and Roßteutscher (2006) have also established a typology of civil society organizations that is based on a factor analysis of the CID data and thus purely empirical. The resulting 11 sectoral types of civil society organizations range from family, sport and culture to the municipality, different forms of politics and welfare, as well as economics and religion.

Whether or not such typologies are useful for the examination at hand is largely an empirical question. Although we would expect, for example, sports organizations to rely more on volunteers in contrast to organizations concerned with representing some minority, it is not clear whether this is also the case when the *amount* of volunteering is examined. However, as we will see in the empirical part of this chapter, the proposed typologies shed some light on the latent influence of the organization, which cannot be well explained otherwise.

2.4 Econometric model and data

One key question regarding the analysis of volunteer work concerns the choice of the dependent variable and the econometric model. One could look exclusively at the decision whether or not to volunteer, which brings into focus how many volunteers could be mobilized. However, this disregards the amount of work that is accomplished. In the econometric model of Menchik and Weisbrod (1987), decision and amount are treated as being naturally interrelated: the dependent variable that measures the time volunteered is interpreted as being left-censored at 0. Consequently, they apply a Tobit regression model. Day and Devlin (1996) take into account the twofold decision process by jointly estimating two interrelated equations, one for the decision to volunteer and one for the time supplied.

Mobilizing volunteer work can be done by either looking for new people that are willing to engage, or by convincing existing volunteers to increase the amount of time supplied – although the time a single volunteer is willing to supply is probably limited, and it therefore always advisable for organizations to seek new volunteers. The differences in the amount volunteered among activists are considerable, and it is reasonable to assume that these differences are somehow related to the type of volunteer work or the realm the organization is active in. It is hence not advisable to dismiss the information about how much time is spent on volunteering and to simply rely on the numbers of volunteers.

The CID data employed in this chapter measure the amount of volunteer work using a four-point ordinal scale.[7] Applying a Tobit model to an ordinally-scaled dependent variable is not advisable, since the conditional distribution of the errors is not likely to be normal. In addition, what is most important for the present analysis is that the nested structure of the data (volunteers nested in organizations which are in turn nested in municipalities) allows us to apply a multi-level random effects modelling approach, which is important for several reasons. First, a hierarchical model accounts for the clustering of observations (individuals from the same organization and the same municipality are more likely to supply similar amounts of time), and thus corrects possible biased standard errors. Of course, this could also be corrected by allowing for clustered standard errors in a conventional regression approach. Second, a hierarchical random effects approach allows for the identification of the variance components of the different levels of analysis (organizational level and municipalities; Rabe-Hesketh and Skrondal 2005). It also allows us to identify how much the intercepts for groups of observations belonging to single units (e.g. organizations) on these various levels deviate from the overall intercept. Again, to some extent this can also be reached by applying a so-called fixed-effects model that includes k−1 dummy variables for the k organizations the volunteers belong to. Most importantly, however, a hierarchical random effects model allows the identification of random intercepts and, at the same time, the inclusion of co-variates that measure attributes of the units on the different hierarchical levels – i.e. the organizations and the municipalities. In addition to identifying the latent effect of the different levels by examining whether or not the random intercepts of the single units (i.e. organizations) deviate significantly from the overall intercept, it is also possible to check whether some attributes (e.g. the size of the organization) might provide the explanation for this latent influence. We will pursue this here, because the nature of the influence of organizations on volunteering is still relatively poorly understood.[8]

2.4.1 Comparing activists with the 'socially active population'

Before we examine volunteering, we first explore whether activists (A) deviate perceivably from the socially active population[9] (S) of these countries. All respondents – activists and population – were asked whether they ever conducted voluntary work for an organization. The first question, therefore, is about the decision to volunteer or not. Based on this binary variable, Table 2.1 presents logistic regression models for each group in each country. We have also applied those models to the whole population, and we refer to those results occasionally although they are not included in Table 2.1.

As independent variables, we employ a number of proxies of individual taste and abilities related to volunteer engagement as they were applied in the studies reported above. These include the respondents' sex and marital status, whether they have lived at their current home for less than two years, whether their parents are or have been active in organizations, whether respondents are regular church attenders, the degree of their attachment to the municipality or the quarter, their political interest, and their age and education. Furthermore, a set of variables is related to the opportunity costs of time, as employment (full- and part-time) and household income. With respect to children, the CID survey only allows an indicator for whether or not there are children living with the respondent. However, since the impact of children depends on their age (compare Menchik and Weisbrod 1987, for example), we will not use this variable.

For each country, there are two columns in Table 2.1; one for the socially active population of the country (S) and one for the activists of the selected town or municipalities (A). For the activists, we included two additional variables that are only available in the Activists Study: an indicator of whether or not the activist perceives his or her own organization as influential, and an indicator of whether or not the parents of the activist are or have been activists. It is obvious from Table 2.1 that there is a serious problem with missing information for the UK and Spain: all of the time-constraint variables as well as the information about the attachment to the town are missing in the Spanish population data, and the latter information is also missing in the activist data.

For the UK all time-constraint variables, as well as the variables for political interest, marital status and attendance at religious services, are missing, which heavily constrains the comparison. There is thus not much to say about this case. The only somewhat significant effect for the activist model reveals that an activist is more likely to volunteer if his or her parents are or have been activists. In addition, part-time working activists are somewhat more likely to volunteer than

Table 2.1 Comparison of the 'socially active' population (S) and the activists (A); logistic regression, dependent variable: volunteered (or not)

Variable	East Germany S	East Germany A	West Germany S	West Germany A	The Netherlands S	The Netherlands A	Spain S	Spain A	Switzerland S	Switzerland A	UK S	UK A
Married	-0.132 (0.251)	0.006 (0.170)	0.323** (0.142)	0.160 (0.137)	-0.152 (0.177)	-0.011 (0.384)	0.004 (0.141)	0.271* (0.165)	0.059 (0.174)	0.217 (0.216)		0.013 (0.314)
Community newcomer	0.140 (0.696)	0.135 (0.447)	-0.355 (0.327)	-1.047** (0.481)	-0.817*** (0.284)	-0.845 (0.967)	-0.075 (0.275)	0.243 (0.589)	-0.216 (0.240)	0.401 (0.351)	-0.012 (0.269)	0.380 (0.807)
Male	-0.149 (0.158)	0.209 (0.158)	-0.031 (0.145)	0.132 (0.133)	0.184 (0.175)	0.417 (0.377)	-0.052 (0.132)	0.015 (0.139)	0.402** (0.200)	-0.302 (0.220)	-0.025 (0.182)	-0.337* (0.173)
Parents active		0.195 (0.146)		0.225** (0.114)		0.318 (0.331)		0.382** (0.170)		0.168 (0.197)		0.450** (0.191)
Organization perceived as influential?		0.047 (0.029)		0.061** (0.025)		-0.146* (0.076)		0.026 (0.033)		0.011 (0.035)		-0.011 (0.038)
Attachment to place	0.127* (0.065)	0.044 (0.030)	0.059* (0.035)	0.040* (0.021)	0.087** (0.034)	0.047 (0.076)		0.024 (0.154)	0.042 (0.032)	0.025 (0.036)	-0.018 (0.034)	0.019 (0.038)
Politically interested	0.872*** (0.259)	0.121 (0.170)	0.230* (0.138)	0.274** (0.128)	0.028 (0.161)	0.430 (0.395)	0.561*** (0.137)		0.082 (0.172)	0.136 (0.201)		0.144 (0.178)
Goes to church regularly	0.123 (0.430)	0.635*** (0.186)	0.736*** (0.157)	0.280** (0.137)	0.769*** (0.177)	1.298*** (0.457)	0.362** (0.148)	0.547*** (0.218)	0.570*** (0.197)	0.242 (0.303)		
Age	-0.008 (0.008)	0.003 (0.005)	-0.008* (0.005)	-0.016*** (0.004)	0.003 (0.006)	0.001 (0.014)	-0.017*** (0.004)	-0.008 (0.006)	-0.001 (0.007)	-0.001 (0.008)	0.003 (0.005)	-0.003 (0.007)
Level of education	-0.222 (0.310)	0.148 (0.167)	0.166 (0.194)	-0.073 (0.119)	0.308** (0.166)	-1.012*** (0.273)		-0.126 (0.169)	0.042 (0.188)	0.052 (0.190)	-0.163 (0.201)	-0.033 (0.202)
Part-time working	0.196 (0.607)	0.392 (0.277)	0.340 (0.257)	-0.050 (0.197)	0.408* (0.215)	-0.295 (0.468)		0.340 (0.252)	0.100 (0.243)	-0.075 (0.268)		0.585* (0.325)
Full-time working	-0.159 (0.285)	-0.055 (0.159)	-0.034 (0.156)	-0.016 (0.139)	0.173 (0.217)	-0.455 (0.323)		0.040 (0.196)	0.030 (0.243)	0.120 (0.241)		0.100 (0.226)
Household income	0.000 (0.000)	0.041 (0.027)	0.210 (0.164)	0.217* (0.131)	-0.121 (0.175)	0.962** (0.403)		-0.342** (0.193)	0.000 (0.000)	0.084** (0.035)		
Constant	-0.430 (0.670)	-1.612*** (0.383)	-0.018 (0.332)	-0.095 (0.302)	-0.866** (0.410)	0.075 (0.955)	0.386** (0.194)	0.291 (0.294)	0.084 (0.429)	-0.662 (0.520)	-0.626* (0.336)	0.053 (0.567)
N	311	896	1,106	1,324	789	304	1,375	858	727	633	581	553
Log-Likelihood	-199	-598	-681	-887	-516	-171	-929	-562	-451	-395	-371	-368
χ^2-Test	18.406*	30.227***	52.682***	42.862***	45.521***	68.812***	33.044***	23.293***	18.801**	18.479	1.149	16.165

Note
Significance levels: *10%; **5%; ***1%.

those who are not working, but this effect is not very reliable. The model does not perform very well with the British data.

It performs somewhat better with the Spanish data, although in this case too some variables have to be dismissed. These results are interesting, since we encounter significant effects for some important variables. The pattern for the population is that the politically interested and those who go to church regularly are more likely to volunteer. For the 'real' activists, the effect remains only for those who are connected to the church more strongly. This result is not very surprising for Spain, because the church is involved in the provision of many social services – for example, childcare. What is more surprising is that household income bears a weakly significant negative effect for the activists; this is surprising because for most of the other cases we actually find a positive coefficient for this variable.

One such case is Switzerland, where we find a significant positive influence of household income. Curiously, the influence of income cannot be detected in the population data, as it is also the case for the other two countries that show a (weak) significant and positive correlation between household income and volunteering: the Netherlands and West Germany.

Otherwise, the performance of the model for the Swiss activists is disappointing. None of the remaining variables becomes truly significant, although some of them actually perform rather well for the data on the whole population (not reported).[10] Even among the socially active population, only the churchgoers are significantly more likely to volunteer.

Similarly, also for the East German case, only a few predictors significantly contribute to our understanding of why the population or the activists volunteer. For the whole population, as in the Spanish case, three variables stand out as having a significant positive effect: attachment to the place, political interest, and connection to the church. For the socially active, however, only interest and attachment remain (weakly) significant. In comparison, among the activists it seems that the churchgoers are those who are most likely to volunteer.

It remains that the results are most comparable between activists and the population for the Netherlands and for West Germany. Those are also the cases for which the models perform best in terms of significant effects to be found. The effects of those variables are mostly consistent across samples, and they turn out as expected. For West Germany, the results remain largely the same if one compares the whole population with the socially active population: all ability and preference measures affect volunteering positively except age. Thus, the West Germans are more likely to volunteer the more they are attached to the places they live in, the more they are politically interested, and the more regularly they go to church. In addition, married people are more likely to volunteer – a result that is also reported by Day and Devlin (1996). These effects are much weaker and less reliable for the sample of the socially active. The differences from the 'real' activists are not very pronounced: obviously, the newly introduced variables (parents and perception of organization) are also affecting volunteering positively. The impact of the remaining variables is more or less the

30 T. Schulz

same, but it also seems that those activists that have not lived at their current homes for more than two years are actually significantly less likely to volunteer.

For the Netherlands, the results are similar. Newcomers are less likely to volunteer – at least in the population – and attachment, interest and connection to the church all significantly and positively affect volunteering. Compared to the population, among the activists, only the churchgoers remain with a significant effect. Education is the only variable in the whole analysis that reverses its sign, although it remains significant. Thus, although education has a positive impact in the population, the effect turns out to be negative for the activists in Enschede. Whether this has to do with local circumstances in Enschede or other factors remains unclear.

To summarize, the 'time-constraint' variables work less well than expected. What seem to be more important as predictors for the decision to volunteer are how strongly individuals are attached to the place where they live, and how strongly they are engaged in the church or politically interested. It appears that the comparison between the socially active population and the 'real' activists is hindered by the different sample sizes and by the restricted availability of variables for different samples. However, in those cases, where a comparison seems to make sense (the Netherlands and West Germany) the differences do not appear to be very pronounced.

2.4.2 A multi-level-model for the activists

Turning to the multi-level analysis of the activist data, we examine the impact of the organizational level with the random intercept of this level in a first step. In a second step, we then employ several organization-level variables such as the number of members, the share of paid staff relative to the number of members, and the proportion of financial resources received from the municipality and the regional government.[11] Furthermore, we employ the sum of the variables that measure whether the organization has occasional or regular contact with important actors in the municipality (the local administration, etc.). While the expectation is that subsidies will generally support the mobilization of volunteers, the impact of paid staff is ambiguous. The number of organizational contacts, on the other hand, is again expected to influence volunteering positively.

The results for the ordered logit random intercepts analysis are listed in Table 2.2. To save space, the 'reduced' models are suppressed – that is, the models with no co-variates but just the random intercepts at the level of the municipalities and the organizations, or with the individual-level co-variates only.

One should keep in mind that the dependent variable now includes the amount of time volunteered in addition to the decision to volunteer. We should thus not expect the results of Table 2.1 to be identically replicated. Nevertheless, as far as the individual-level co-variates are concerned, most of the coefficients show the same sign as in the respective columns of Table 2.1. A lot of unexplainable changes and even some clear reversions of signs can only be found for Enschede. This is probably due to the very low number of observations. The analyses for Aberdeen and Spain also suffer from this shortcoming, although it less obviously influences the results. Hence, the results for these cases should be seen as indicative. For Aberdeen, no effects on the individual level can be found. For Spain, it is now education rather than income that shows a negative coefficient, but since education and household income tend to be correlated, this change is negligible. For the other cases, the results are rather consistent: in East Germany it is still the churchgoers that stand out in their propensity to volunteer, and in Mannheim 'attachment to the place' becomes most significant whereas some of the other predictors lose some reliability. The most pronounced difference appears for the Swiss municipalities: household income loses its significance and gives way to some rather inconclusive predictors such as age and sex.

Looking first at the level of the municipalities (Switzerland, Spain and East Germany), no significant effect can be found for this level. Given the low number of municipalities, it was not really expected to find such an effect. Hence, there is not much sense in including co-variates that measure differences between municipalities, for example, the sum of government expenditures.

What is more surprising is that the random intercepts for the organizations vary significantly for all cases except Enschede (the Netherlands). This result is also remarkable because it persists despite the inclusion of co-variates at the organizational level. The results remain stable even if more organizational characteristics are considered – for example, the formalization of the organization, its regional scope, whether or not it is an umbrella organization, etc.[12] None of these factors prove to be significant. Two such explanatory variables (the size of the organization in terms of members and the share of paid staff) that have been stressed by Kriesi (2006) are listed in Table 2.2 despite their lack of influence.

The co-variate that actually shows (albeit weakly) a significant coefficient in some cases (East Germany, Spain, Switzerland and the UK) is the share of subsidies from the local government. For all cases except Spain, this effect is positive, as expected. My interpretation of this finding is that the more the organization is financially supported by the government, the more it is able to build up an infrastructure that also helps with mobilizing volunteers. Alternatively, subsidies from the local government might be distributed on a project basis, for which additional volunteer time must be found. The prominent exception is Spain, where such subsidies seem to reduce the level of volunteering. However, this result is ambiguous, because for Spain (and Enschede), unfortunately, it is not possible to include the amount of subsidies that are given by the regional government, which means that the effect of subsidies is probably biased in these cases. As the other cases reveal, subsidies from the higher level (the region) are counter-productive (although not significantly).

With respect to the number of political contacts an organization has with local actors – such as the administration, for example – the finding is that such contacts seem to have a positive impact on volunteering in just two cases (Aberdeen and Mannheim), but none of these effects turns out to be significant. In all other cases, having intensive contacts with the administration is a characteristic that

Table 2.2 Estimates of multi-level ordinal logit regression of amount of volunteering for an organization

Variable	East Germany	West Germany	The Netherlands	Spain	Switzerland	United Kingdom
Married	−0.026	0.248	−0.064	−0.345	0.200	−0.242
	(0.212)	(0.213)	(0.430)	(0.318)	(0.234)	(0.514)
Community newcomer	−0.234	−1.099*	−1.941**	−1.008	−0.064	0.611
	(0.555)	(0.646)	(0.806)	(1.786)	(0.396)	(0.957)
Male	0.418**	0.220	−0.709*	0.347	0.463**	−0.293
	(0.185)	(0.194)	(0.430)	(0.288)	(0.236)	(0.283)
Parents active	0.156	0.047	0.706*	−0.193	0.331*	−0.029
	(0.174)	(0.157)	(0.401)	(0.275)	(0.185)	(0.269)
Organization perceived as influential?	−0.002	−0.004	0.187**	0.034	−0.031	−0.016
	(0.039)	(0.037)	(0.080)	(0.050)	(0.035)	(0.065)
Attachment to place	0.010	0.126***	−0.088		0.027	0.067
	(0.038)	(0.032)	(0.083)		(0.036)	(0.055)
Politically interested	−0.042	−0.001	−0.462	0.372	0.149	0.004
	(0.202)	(0.201)	(0.463)	(0.270)	(0.201)	(0.274)
Goes to church regularly	0.478**	−0.067	0.605	0.344	−0.051	
	(0.237)	(0.203)	(0.561)	(0.376)	(0.249)	
Age	0.002	−0.013*	0.041**	0.000	−0.027***	
	(0.007)	(0.007)	(0.017)	(0.011)	(0.008)	
Level of education	−0.090	0.010	0.937**	−0.754***	0.292	0.275
	(0.190)	(0.182)	(0.417)	(0.292)	(0.186)	(0.264)
Part-time working	−0.389	−0.163	0.318	0.690	0.158	0.530
	(0.324)	(0.281)	(0.539)	(0.481)	(0.287)	(0.404)
Full-time working	−0.058	−0.380*	0.485	0.149	−0.308	−0.025
	(0.205)	(0.211)	(0.488)	(0.348)	(0.248)	(0.304)
Household income	0.053	0.339*	−0.939**	−0.144	−0.010	
	(0.035)	(0.190)	(0.425)	(0.355)	(0.034)	
Subsidies from local government	0.010*	0.010	−0.006	−0.012*	0.012*	0.048***
	(0.005)	(0.007)	(0.008)	(0.007)	(0.007)	(0.015)

	(1)	(2)	(3)	(4)	(5)	(6)
Subsidies from regional government	0.009 (0.007)	−0.011 (0.012)			−0.011 (0.009)	−0.051 (0.033)
No. of political contacts	0.049* (0.058)	0.067 (0.049)	−0.039 (0.064)	−0.045 (0.094)	−0.042 (0.049)	−0.002 (0.122)
Total number of members	0.000 (0.000)	0.000 (0.000)	0.196 (0.183)	0.000 (0.000)	0.000** (0.000)	0.000 (0.000)
Share of paid staff	0.054 (0.192)	0.309 (0.405)	0.033 (0.340)		−0.044 (0.091)	0.562 (1.548)
cut1	−0.950* (0.557)	−1.880*** (0.612)	1.183 (1.488)	−2.601*** (0.993)	−2.933*** (0.640)	−1.142 (0.816)
cut2	1.099* (0.563)	0.600 (0.612)	3.427** (1.511)	−1.234 (0.980)	−0.635 (0.631)	1.270 (0.821)
cut3	2.797*** (0.582)	2.432*** (0.621)		0.056 (0.979)	1.094* (0.641)	2.711*** (0.844)
Organization (standard error)	0.617*** (0.156)	1.102*** (0.146)	0.000 (0.255)	0.824*** (0.219)	0.481*** (0.150)	0.878*** (0.217)
Municipality (standard error)	0.000 (0.110)			0.362 (0.282)	−0.315 (0.223)	
No. of municipalities	3			5	8	
No. of organizations	160	201	24	62	115	63
No. of activists	541	715	144	251	505	261
Log-likelihood	−689.095	−877.722	−135.124	−322.462	−623.514	−316.064

Note

Standard errors in parentheses. *$P < 0.1$; **$P < 0.05$; ***$P < 0.01$.

rather seems to prevent – although not significantly – the mobilization of voluntary work by an organization – or, to put it differently, organizations that have close relations with the local elite rely less on volunteer time. Maybe this is because such organizations are active in a certain realms or pursue tasks for which it is not necessary to mobilize voluntary work.

2.4.3 Patterns for groups of organizations

This leads us to the final question: the nature of the latent organizational influence that can be measured by the variance of the random intercepts. The first part of this question concerns the importance of this latent influence. It is considerable, as is revealed by an analysis of the variance components of the multilevel models in Table 2.2. For the 'null models' (i.e. the models without co-variates but only the random effects), the variance of the organizational level covers between 15 and 35 per cent of the total variance in most cases; Enschede is the exception, where it is only 10 per cent. The inclusion of co-variates at this level reduces this unexplained latent influence of the organization to between 6 and 21 per cent of the total variance. Hence, the organization matters with respect to the mobilization of volunteers, although most of this influence remains unexplored and thus is difficult to comprehend.

One way to explore this a little further is to group the organizations – or their intercepts respectively – by the civil society sector-classification offered by Maloney and Roßteutscher (2006).[13] This should reveal, for example, that sports organizations are generally more reliant on volunteers than are economic interest organizations.

In Table 2.3, for each country/town[14] the means of the significant[15] random intercepts are listed by sector, and below this mean we list the number of organizations that belong to these sectors as well as the number of organizations per sector for which a significant random intercept could be predicted. The number of significant predicted intercepts per organizational sector is remarkably and consistently low for Mannheim and Aberdeen (only between 2 and 12 per cent of the organizations showed a significant intercept). For Spain, a relatively high share of significant intercepts could only be found for some sectors ('family' and 'sports'). The other cases have rather high shares of significant intercepts in some sectors. For some sectoral types of organizations, the ability to mobilize volunteers (or their reliance on volunteer time, respectively) differs rather strongly across countries. We find more or less the same number of positive and negative means of significant intercepts for the sectors 'family', 'new politics' and 'religion'. More consistent are the means for sectors 'sports', 'culture', 'community concerns' and 'economic interest': these sectors obviously rely less on volunteer time. If we include all (and not only the significant) intercepts in the calculation of the mean, the 'group-specific welfare' sector also becomes consistently negative across countries. The means are consistently positive for the 'politics' sector – which seems to have existed in East Germany only – as well as the 'general welfare' sector.

2.5 Conclusion

The results can be summarized as follows: for East Germany, Switzerland and Spain we have only a very limited sample of municipalities at hand, and it is not surprising that a substantive effect cannot be found. On the other hand, at the level of the organizations, the data reveals a latent influence of the organizations in all cases but the Netherlands. Unfortunately, we were unable to clearly identify the factors at the organizational level that are responsible for this latent influence.

Among the organizational factors that exhibit a perceptible and somewhat consistent effect across samples is the share of local subsidies an organization receives. It positively (but not very reliably) influences the level of volunteering which is provided by the members of the organization in all cases for which it was possible to unambiguously test this hypothesis. This supports the view that the 'crowding out' hypothesis is overly simplistic, and that it is important for the examination of government expenditure to differentiate between transfers to individuals and subsidies to organizations coming from different levels of government. Curiously, no effect can be found for the subsidies that come from a higher level. There possibly is some qualitative difference between the two forms of subsidies that causes this distinction.

In any case, the impact of these subsidies is actually more important and consistent than the influence of the amount of contacts the organization has with the actors at the local level. This is probably due to the fact that the variables are somewhat related: receiving subsidies generates contacts, and having contacts probably helps in directing subsidies to an organization. Although the coefficients do not turn out to be significant, it is noticeable that the contacts score is negatively correlated with volunteering in four of six cases. This uncovers the ad hoc nature of the corresponding hypothesis – stronger local ties should increase the opportunities for volunteering – and raises the suspicion that deeper theoretical considerations are needed to better understand the interrelatedness between voluntary organizations and the local government.

Further, apart from organizational size having a positive impact on the amount volunteered in Switzerland only, no clear and consistent effects could be found for all other possible explanatory variables that have been discussed above – for example, the regional scope of the organization, its formalization, etc. This is an important result, since it makes it clear that although the organization is something that should be considered important, thus far its role is not clearly understood. Differentiating between different types of organizations according to the sectors they are active in does somewhat improve the interpretation of the latent influence. Organizations concerned with sports, culture and economic interests obviously rely less on the mobilization of volunteers in most of the countries examined. For the remaining sectors, the results differ across countries, and this supports the view that voluntary sectors of different countries should not be lumped together. However, one main conclusion of the current examination is that organizational attributes do not matter much for the mobilization of volunteers. What seems to

Table 2.3 Mean random intercepts for sectors

Variable	East Germany	West Germany	Spain	Switzerland	United Kingdom
Family	−0.52	−2.03	0.57	0.24	–
No. of intercepts	169	123	69	98	15
No. of significant intercepts	49	3	3	39	0
Sports	−0.88	1.32	−1.61	−0.23	−1.48
No. of intercepts	267	146	153	122	76
No. of significant intercepts	82	3	25	66	1
Culture	−0.82	1.08	−1.13	−0.78	–
No. of intercepts	107	123	339	84	35
No. of significant intercepts	34	9	28	30	0
Community concerns	0.75	–	−0.14	−0.73	−2.37
No. of intercepts	41	92	52	–	11
No. of significant intercepts	4	0	6	–	9
Politics	0.92	–	–	–	–
No. of intercepts	1	–	–	–	–
No. of significant intercepts	1	–	–	–	–
New politics	−0.62	0.73	–	–	–
No. of intercepts	11	49	9	11	11
No. of significant intercepts	5	6	0	0	0
General welfare	−0.10	–	.	0.69	0.99
No. of intercepts	17	143	26	21	55
No. of significant intercepts	11	0	0	5	4
Group-specific welfare	−1.02	0.47	1.54	−0.87	−1.44
No. of intercepts	88	66	89	56	101
No. of significant intercepts	28	4	4	9	7
Economic interest	–	–	−1.44	−1.05	–
No. of intercepts	3	50	42	40	11
No. of significant intercepts	0	0	3	21	0
Religious	0.87	−2.79	–	−0.78	0.75

No. of intercepts	102	79	25	13	208
No. of significant intercepts	13	2	0	4	12
Other	−0.30	−0.34	−0.53	0.15	−1.13
No. of intercepts	203	549	243	141	165
No. of significant intercepts	80	24	32	43	20
Missing	−0.53	−1.92	0.86	0.04	−2.09
No. of intercepts	257	448	225	355	171
No. of significant intercepts	39	36	8	129	16

Note

A mean is missing in this table if either the sectoral type was not identified in the respective data set, or all organizations of a sectoral type had to be excluded from the analysis because of the structure of missing data in the data set. In addition, if no significant predicted intercepts could be found for a sector, no mean was computed (compare, for example, sector 'Economic interest' for the UK as well as East and West Germany).

matter more is the type of task the organizations have to fulfil in different sectors of the society, which is probably also related to how government programmes are designed in these sectors. This emphasizes the structure of the voluntary sector as a whole, and advocates sectorally differentiated examinations of the role organizations play in voluntary engagement.

Notes

1 These authors take into account the possibility that volunteering may generate a part of the subject's income by substituting it with the income of the spouse and some proxies for human capital (family size, number of grown-up children, labour market experience).
2 Segal and Weisbrod (2002) apply estimates of opportunity costs derived from responses to questions related to wages and taxes in the questionnaire. Their study is designed to compare volunteering in different sectors (health, education and religion) and, interestingly, they find significant differences not only for the demographic variables but particularly also for their economic variables for different sectors. For example, while the 'tax status' of an individual has no (significant) influence in the health sector, it has a highly significant *negative* influence in the education sector and the opposite effect (also highly significant) for religious services.
3 This study focuses on the decision to volunteer, and is based on a survey among Italian workers. While their set of demographic characteristics is rather limited, they employ a proxy for 'intrinsic motivation' (i.e. whether or not a respondent placed 'solidarity' as their most important value among others) and for 'extrinsic motivation' (i.e. whether or not they indicate that the salary is the most important reason to change a job).
4 Despite the notion 'substitutive', this does not mean, of course, that it is possible (or desirable) to entirely replace services provided by the government by voluntary work in the same quality and amount, and vice versa.
5 There is also a considerable body of research dedicated to the role of 'social capital' that would support this view (see, for example, Ostrom and Ahn 2003).
6 For none of the countries examined did we find an exceptionally high correlation between the contacts score and the subsidies from the local level.
7 Question: Do you provide voluntary services for THIS ORGANIZATION? Answer categories: 1, Some times per week; 2, Some times per month; 3, Some times per year; 4, Never or virtually never. We have reversed the scale to make interpretation more intuitive.
8 Of course, applying this technique does not come without costs. Most importantly, it is widely believed that there should be a minimum number of observations within clusters, to justify the application of such estimation routines. In the CID data set, the number of individual-level observations is rather low relative to the number of organizations (cf. Table 2.2). However, Gelman and Hill (2007) still recommend using a random effects modeling approach, despite the fact that for some organizations there is a low number of observations, or even just one single individual-level observation. The consequence is that the estimation routine will put less weight on clusters with a low number of observations. We have applied the gllamm package in Stata to estimate the hierarchical three-level ordered logit models reported below. We have also estimated the identical models applying multi-level Tobit regression using the xttobit routine in Stata (which, however, allows for only one level of clustering). For most of the countries, the results do not deviate very much from those reported in Table 2.2 and, by and large, the conclusions are the same for both types of analysis. Further, we have also conducted ordered logit regression with a correction for clustered standard

errors. For some countries (namely Switzerland, Aberdeen and Mannheim), the results are more optimistic as far as the organizational-level variables are concerned: local subsidies consistently significantly foster the amount volunteered.

9 The socially active population consists of those subjects from the population study that indicated that they had either 'participated in activities' or 'done voluntary work'. The proportion of volunteers among the 'socially active' lies around 25 and 40 per cent in most cases. Only Spain (14 per cent) and Aberdeen (9 per cent) have a rather low share of volunteers.
10 I have also computed variance inflation factors for all of the logit models presented here, but was not able to detect any serious multi-colinearity problems.
11 I do not employ the budget, since this is already incorporated in the two measures just mentioned. Furthermore, we ran additional models including the the remaining variables on the organizational level discussed above. However, none of these variables exerted a significant influence on the dependent variable and we decided to exclude them from the analysis to render the models more parsimonious.
12 As explained in the previous note, the results for the models that incorporate these additional organizational attributes are not listed in Table 2.2.
13 In the Organization Study, the representatives of the organization were asked to which of about 35 civil society sectors their organization mainly contributed. The sectoral classification of the organization was computed from the answers to this question.
14 Enschede had to be excluded from this table because the variance of the random intercepts at the organizational level was virtually non-existent and failed to be significant. As a result, meaningful random intercepts could not be predicted.
15 The gllamm package of Stata allows computation of so-called 'posterior standard deviations' of the predicted intercepts (Rabe-Hesketh and Skrondal 2005).

3 Governing associations
Member involvement and efficacy towards associational decision-making

Herman Lelieveldt

3.1 Introduction

Voluntary associations have always been strongly associated with notions of democratic governance. One of the earliest and most prominent observations came from Alexis de Tocqueville, who in his *Democracy in America* points out why egalitarian societies are more prone to develop a rich associational landscape compared to their aristocratic counterparts:

> In aristocratic societies men do not need to combine in order to act, because they are strongly held together. Every wealthy and powerful citizen constitutes the head of a permanent and compulsory association, composed of all those who are dependent upon him or whom he makes subservient to the execution of his designs. Among democratic nations, on the contrary, all the citizens are independent and feeble; they can do hardly anything by themselves, and none of them can oblige his fellow men to lend him their assistance. They all, therefore become powerless if they do not learn voluntarily to help one another.
>
> (de Tocqueville 1945 [1835]: 115)

While Tocqueville focuses here on the system-level relationship between democracy and a strongly developed associational life, there is in addition the important micro-level observation that most voluntary associations are in fact democratic associations.

Voluntary associations resemble the formal democratic polities of the public sphere – cities, provinces, states – in at least two important respects. First, they allow each of its members to participate in decision-making – and often on a one person one vote basis. Second, they are being run by members themselves through the principle of self-governance: the government and management of associations are in the hands of the members who most often have been elected to such offices by their co-members.

According to Warren, voluntary associations are so 'intrinsically connected to the strongest meanings of self-governance' (Warren 2001: 46), precisely because they are communities of choice. Given the voluntary nature of associational life, members would leave associations that were perceived as unresponsive. Democratic procedures are therefore an important device to maintain organizational cohesion (Warren 2001: 53), and this explains to a large extent why many voluntary associations are also democratic associations.

Gauging these levels of participation is important because it tells us to what extent associations actually function as schools of democracy, by giving members experience in self-government. Moreover, for advocates of participatory democracy, there is an inherent value in such participatory practices because in their view democracy amounts to 'something very much wider than a set of "institutional arrangements" at the national level' (Pateman 1970: 35). Pateman would be offended by the qualification of associations as mere schools of democracy, because the associational sphere constitutes one of the 'alternative arenas where the individual can participate in decision-making in matters of which he has first hand everyday experience' (Pateman 1970: 35). In this perspective, a healthy associational life in terms of an involved group of members is as important as an extensive involvement of citizens in formal politics. Given the relevance of these factors for associational life itself and their spillover effects into the realm of formal politics, it is somewhat surprising that there is still relatively little knowledge about the 'political infrastructure' of groups (Barakso 2005: 315).

In this chapter, we focus upon the extent to which voluntary associations live up to this picture of democratic self-governance by examining the *participation* of members in decision-making and the management of the organization. The analysis of participation will be accompanied by measuring the extent to which members *feel* they can affect decision-making. The analysis of these two concepts in tandem bears a strong resemblance to studies examining the relationship between political efficacy and political participation. They are similar in the expectation that people who feel they are able to affect decision-making will also show higher levels of actual participation in decision-making.

Obviously, part of the difference in the level of engagement will be caused by the fact that some people are simply more active in an association than others, and as a result will also tend to be more active in decision-making processes. A second group of factors relates differences in participation and efficacy to socio-structural factors such as gender, education and age. Measuring the effect of these variables enables us to find out to what extent levels of participation are biased with regard to a number of characteristics that have been identified as crucial with respect to issues of representation in formal politics (Verba *et al.* 1995: 163–266).

The third, and most important, question that we will try to answer is to what extent the organizational context affects participation in decision-making and associational efficacy. To what extent do factors such as size, professionalization, budget and formal structure affect people's involvement in the management of the organization? The data that will be presented here enable us to perform an analysis similar to the pioneering work of Knoke on the impact of organizational characteristics on detachment and attachment of volunteers (Knoke 1981, 1990).

The empirical results show first that among both socially actives and activists there is a considerable amount of participation in decision-making and management. The analysis of activists furthermore replicates Knoke's finding that efficacy and participation are strongly related, and the strongest predictor in their respective equations. Finally, when it comes to the effect of organizational factors, there is no impact of these on actual participation rates of activists. Size and the presence of paid staff, however, do have a small negative effect on the efficacy of activists. Although the effect is small, it indicates that even the most engaged group of members feels less able to affect decision-making when the organization becomes larger and makes use of professional staff.

3.1.1 Associations as participatory spaces

Ever since Roberto Michels claimed that every nominally democratic association will in the end develop into an oligarchic organization that leaves little influence for ordinary members (Michels (1959 [1911]), sociologists have focused upon organizational-level factors that may account for such developments. While many studies have focused upon processes of oligarchization within organizations over time – most notably increases in size as well as the professionalization of organizations (Zald and Garner 1990) – there have been relatively few large-scale empirical studies which examine the relation between organizational characteristics and involvement in decision-making.

One notable exception is the work of David Knoke on the commitment and detachment of volunteers (Knoke 1981, 1990). Commitment focuses upon the willingness of social actors to give their energy and loyalty to social systems, such as voluntary associations, while detachment 'expresses a sense of personal remoteness from the collectivity and feelings of inability to influence organizational activities and policies'. Knoke characterizes this latter term as the 'organizational analog to powerlessness and inefficacy at the societal level' (Knoke 1981: 142). In terms of its meaning and operationalization, the concept is very similar to what has come to be known as (internal) political efficacy in the political science literature.[1] Campbell and colleagues originally defined that term as 'the feeling that individual political action does have, or can have, an impact upon the political process' (Campbell *et al.* 1954: 187).

Knoke's empirical analysis shows that members feel more efficacious if they are more involved in decision-making, and if they communicate more frequently with fellow members about organizational matters. This positive correlation between participation and efficacy should not surprise us. Given the more or less *voluntary* nature of associational life, it would be odd to find people participating while not feeling efficacious about it. However, it is important to note that the arrow runs in the other direction as well: members who feel more efficacious will be more inclined to take part in decision-making and in organizational management. This latter finding clearly matches what has been found in studies of political involvement, where political efficacy has been repeatedly shown to be an important determinant of levels of political participation (Craig *et al.* 1990; Parry *et al.* 1992; Verba *et al.* 1995: 342). The results of these studies clearly show that actual participation and efficacy need to be analysed in tandem, and should be included as control variables in any wider analysis of the determinants of participation and efficacy respectively.

3.1.2 Organizational characteristics

Now what would be the impact of different organizational settings on people's involvement in associational decision-making? First, one could posit the hypothesis that any polity – be it an association or a city – will experience a negative relationship between its size and the involvement of its members. Oliver reports such a relationship between the number of inhabitants of a city and civic engagement (Oliver 2000), while Knoke finds the same relationship at the level of voluntary associations.

The effect works on both actual levels of participation as well as efficacy. A decline of participation can be expected, because there is not a linear relationship between the size of an association and the amount of people that need to be involved in associational management. As the association grows in size, a relatively smaller number of members are needed to run the organization. Turning to the effect on efficacy, we can also expect that people will feel more distance from the association as it grows in size. They will have to compete with many other participants in making their voice heard, while the associational leadership will have to cope with all these possible conflicting demands. All in all, this makes it likely that associational efficacy decreases as the organization increases in size.

The next organization-level factor that is relevant is professionalization of the organization. I hypothesize that an organization that employs professionals will exhibit lower levels of member efficacy and participation in decision-making. Compared to associations that are fully driven by volunteers, it is likely that the decision-making processes in associations with paid staff will be dominated to a greater extent by these employees. First, looking at participation in associational management, there will be less need for ordinary members to be involved in management issues because some of these tasks will be performed by the paid staff. A similar effect will be expected for levels of efficacy: activists will moderate their expectations regarding their ability to influence decision-making because paid staff will be intent on setting the organization's agenda and having a stake in decision-making. In conclusion, organizations with paid staff should exhibit lower rates of participation and efficacy than those that are fully run by volunteers.

The final organizational level factor that will be examined refers to the impact of the level of formalization on associational participation and efficacy. Putnam has been critical about newer and looser groups in the associational landscape, and claims that they 'certainly do not represent "participatory democracy"' (Putnam 2000: 160). Part of the reason may be the lack of a formal decision-making structure as well as role specification for the management of the association.

First, it could be argued that more formalized and well-organized voluntary associations foster higher levels of involvement in decision-making and efficacy than do more loosely, informally organized organizations. While trust-building may take place in any associational context in which members regularly interact, the experience of being involved in a democratic polity might demand a more formalized structure that provides channels for participation and having a say in the decision-making process of the association. A general meeting, a governing board, by-laws and special committees all constitute participatory venues that give members the opportunities to be involved.

Even if these structures turn out not to be used to a very great extent by the associational members, they can act as a democratic safety net, and in any case boost the sense of efficacy. Many associations do not need to hold formal elections for board positions because they have a hard time finding people to stand. However, in those cases where members are unhappy with the candidates that are being proposed, there is always the opportunity to come up with competing candidates and force an election. The resulting expectation is higher levels of efficacy in more formalized associations.

In Knoke's study, the role of these venues is measured through the concept of 'authority role systems', which he defines as 'roles and formal procedures for the legitimate exercise of power by its participants' (Knoke 1990: 152). It is very similar to what Torpe and Ferrer-Fons call the 'differentiation of management' (Torpe and Ferrer-Fons 2007). Knoke finds a positive relationship between the size of differentiation and detachment.

A second measure of the extent to which members are able to affect decisions is to look at 'formal representative rule', which refers to those procedures that specifically focus upon giving members a say in decision-making. Torpe and Ferrer-Fons (2007) point out that these concepts overlap, but need to be assessed separately. Knoke finds a positive effect of such democratic 'structures' on efficacy.

Thus, we could expect to find positive effects of both types of measures on associational efficacy and participation in decision-making. It will first provide more opportunities for participation, and thus also boost actual involvement in decision-making. A clearer organizational structure will also give members a higher perceived level of control over the association's decisions (differentiation), in particular when this is accompanied by a specific body that organizes member participation (general assembly).

Summarizing the above expectations, four organizational-level factors are expected to affect participation in decision-making and management as well as member efficacy in being able to influence decision-making. Size and professionalization will be negatively related to participation and efficacy, while the level of formalization and the existence of a formal assembly will be expected to be positively correlated. Before turning to the empirical analysis, we briefly discuss the individual-level variables that will be examined in conjunction with the above variables.

3.1.3 Individual-level determinants of associational participation and efficacy

Knoke's analysis points to the importance of incorporating measures of members' level of general activity in the association as a predictor of both efficacy and participation. First, we expect length of membership to be positively related to both concepts. Long-standing members are more knowledgeable of the workings of the association and the key figures, which will increase their likelihood of both being engaged in decision-making as well as feeling competent to affect decisions (Ohmer 2007, 114). Moreover, we can expect a self-selection effect, which leads less active and efficacious members to leave the association at an earlier stage, and results in higher levels of involvement for those cohorts that have been in membership for a longer time. Second, efficacy and participation will be related to higher objective levels of involvement, as measured by the number of hours spent in the association. This supposes that involvement in decision-making, and the feeling of being able to affect this, increases as members devote more time to their association. Third, as a more subjective factor of involvement, feeling committed to the association is expected to be related positively to involvement in decision-making and associational efficacy. By and large, this third factor seeks to measure the intensity of a member's engagement with the association.

These three variables function as control variables to take into account the different levels of associational activity of the associational members. In addition, I will look at four individual-level factors that may be related to different levels of participation and efficacy: age, gender, education and being employed.

3.2 Empirical results

3.2.1 Participatory activities of socially actives and activists

We start the analysis with an overview of participation in decision-making using data from the Population Study, which will enable us to compare socially actives (all respondents who indicated that they were active or volunteered in at least one of the 27 types of associations that were presented to them) with activists.

Participation has been measured on the basis of a question that taps the frequency of being involved in four activities: participation in official meetings of associations, planning or chairing a meeting, preparing for or giving a speech at a meeting, and writing a text other than a private letter. All four of these focus upon the management and decision-making within the organization, and enable us to find out to what extent these associations function as 'participatory spaces'. Volunteering has been excluded from this measure, as this is generally understood to be a type of activity that is not concerned with directly affecting decision-making.

The figures show that participation rates are considerable for both types of respondents. Looking first at the socially actives, Table 3.1 shows that in all

Table 3.1 Associational participation of activists and socially actives

	East Germany		West Germany		The Netherlands		Spain		Switzerland		United Kingdom	
	A	S	A	S	A	S	A	S	A	S	A	S
Participate in an official meeting	81	55	85	49	76	57	84	59	90	64	84	n.a.
Plan or chair a meeting	39	15	43	15	36	27	53	21	51	33	43	n.a.
Prepare or give a speech	47	20	48	20	38	26	44	18	53	31	43	n.a.
Write a text	36	11	45	13	40	30	53	23	54	37	40	n.a.
N	799	422	1,393	1,557	425	961	1,272	1,402	774	773	805	

Note
Percentage of respondents at least active a few times a year. A, activists; S, socially actives.

countries except West Germany, more than half of the respondents participate in official meetings at least a few times a year. Furthermore, around 30 per cent of the socially actives prepare or give a speech at such meetings. Rates are lowest for planning or chairing a meeting and writing a text for the association, but even here it is an activity that is not uncommon among the socially actives. All in all, the figures indicate that socially actives are not merely involved in volunteering, but also take part to a considerable extent in the management of associations as well as in decision-making.

These participation rates are even higher for activists. In all countries, well above 80 per cent of activists attend meetings at least a few times a year. Furthermore, for all countries except the Netherlands more than 40 per cent of the activists are involved in writing or preparing a speech, while planning or chairing a meeting is done by between 27 per cent (the Netherlands) and 53 per cent of the activists (Spain). Finally, writing a text is done by more than 50 per cent of the activists in Switzerland, but only 11 per cent in Spain.

Compared to the socially actives, activists are even more active in decision-making and management, and seem to constitute what one could call a participatory elite. In this context, it is important to recall that the activists were recruited for the survey by associational leaders, and that the mean number of activists surveyed per association was relatively small (between four and eight – see Chapter 1). Although the survey did not ask the activists whether they occupy a formal position within the association, there is no doubt that many of these activists are in fact in such positions – and, in the case of less formalized associations, have a de facto role as organizational leaders. The considerable number of activists involved in planning or chairing a meeting demonstrates this.

3.2.2 Participation and efficacy of activists

The remainder of the analysis will make use of data from the Activists Study. It is for this group only that we possess information on both their involvement as well as associational efficacy. Moreover, only for this group of respondents is it possible to estimate the impact of organizational characteristics.

Table 3.2 first shows the participation rates of the activists on the basis of the Activists Study. It reveals that these figures closely match the numbers they gave in the earlier survey, which were still referring to all associations together. Once again, rates for participation in general meetings are very high, while the rates for other activities are still substantial. The four items regarding participation in the organization's affairs form a highly reliable scale (Cronbach's α ranging between 0.77 and 0.95) and have been used to construct a scale score which will be used in further analyses. This brings us to the overview of their perceived influence on organizational matters.

Associational efficacy was measured on the basis of a four-item question that asked the activists to rate the opportunities they have to influence (i) *decisions* that are made, (ii) the *range and types of activities* the organization undertakes, (iii) the *management structure* of the organization, and (iv) *how* decisions are

Table 3.2 Associational participation and efficacy of activists

Variables	East Germany		West Germany		The Netherlands		Spain		Switzerland		United Kingdom	
	%	Score	%	Score	%	Score	%	Score	%	Score	%	Score
Participation												
Participate in an official meeting	84	2.2	83	2.2	69	2.2	84	2.7	89	2.3	79	2.2
Plan or chair a meeting	34	1.5	36	1.5	29	1.4	53	2.0	44	1.6	34	1.5
Prepare or give a speech	44	1.6	43	1.5	28	1.3	44	1.7	46	1.6	35	1.4
Write a text	33	1.5	39	1.5	30	1.3	53	1.9	49	1.6	31	1.4
Scale score participation		1.7		1.7		1.5		2.1		1.8		1.7
Cronbach's α		0.82		0.94		0.77		0.85		0.82		0.95
Efficacy – opportunity to affect:												
Decisions that are made		6.5		6.2		6.4		n.a.		6.5		5.9
Range and types of activities		6.4		6.3		6.2		n.a.		6.2		5.6
Management structure		5.2		5.1		5.0		n.a.		5.5		4.6
How decisions are made		5.9		5.7		6.0		n.a.		5.9		5.1
Scale score efficacy		6.0		5.8		5.9		5.9*		6.0		5.3
Cronbach's α		0.93		0.82		0.89		n.a.		0.92		0.82
Pearson R participation × efficacy scale		0.54		0.54		0.39		0.55		0.48		0.49
N		1,237		1,868		418		1,272		899		807

Note
%, Percentage of activists at least active a few times a year. Score, mean score on participation scale: 1 (almost) never to 4 (a few times a week); efficacy scale: 0, no opportunity at all, to 10, very great opportunity. * For Spain, there was only a general question on the ability to affect decision-making.

Governing associations 49

made on a ten-point scale, with the lowest score designated for the category 'No opportunity at all' and the highest score for 'a very great opportunity'.

Table 3.2 gives the mean scores for these four items, as well as a summary mean score (in Spain only, a question was asked on the perceived possibility of respondent to influence the decisions the organization takes). On a scale running from zero to ten, scores hover around the value of six, suggesting a fair overall amount of efficacy. On average, activists have a somewhat greater efficacy regarding decisions and activities than regarding their perceived ability to change more fundamental aspects such as structures and procedures (the differences between the means are significant at a 95 per cent level). This, of course, makes intuitive sense, as changing the fundamentals usually involves the need to modify the by-laws of an association, often through lengthy formal procedures. The highest levels of efficacy can be found among activists in East Germany and Switzerland, and the lowest among those in United Kingdom. What is much more remarkable is the fact that the difference is less than a full point, on a ten-point scale, between the different countries. The efficacy items are, like the participation items, strongly correlated, and form a highly reliable scale (Cronbach's α ranges between 0.82 and 0.93).

The final row of Table 3.2 gives correlation coefficients for the participation and efficacy scales that were constructed, and shows that correlations are moderate to strong, ranging between 0.39 for the Netherlands and 0.55 for Spain. All in all, this justifies the conclusion that participation in decision-making and perceiving opportunities to affect decision-making go together. Within the group of activists, those with higher levels of factual participation also express a higher level of confidence in their ability to affect decision-making. Still, the relationship is far from deterministic.

3.2.3 Predicting participation in decision-making

Tables 3.3 and 3.4 list the results of regression analysis of the three groups of variables on participation and efficacy respectively. The three groups have been entered in a blockwise procedure, starting with individual-level variables, followed by associational involvement and, finally, organizational characteristics.

As individual-level variables, age was operationalized as an interval variable, gender was a dummy variable with males scoring zero and females scoring 1, and education was measured as a dummy variable that measures having completed tertiary education. Occupation was a dummy variable indicating whether someone is currently employed (0=no, 1=yes). Associational involvement was measured by taking the number of years active in the association as an indicator for membership length, taking the number of hours active in the association on a monthly basis as a measure for actual involvement, and asking the question 'how committed do you feel to this organization' as a measure for commitment.

At the organizational level, size was operationalized as the number of members of the association. The professional staff variable was operationalized as a simple dummy measuring the presence of at least one person being active as

Table 3.3 Predictors of associational participation

Independent variables	East Germany	West Germany	The Netherlands	Spain	Switzerland	United Kingdom
Age	−0.034	−0.019	0.031	0.028	−0.018	0.010
Gender	−0.048*	−0.064**	−0.026	0.020	−0.027	0.032
Education	0.125****	0.043**	0.090**	0.029	0.062**	0.024
Employment	−0.034	0.055**	−0.027	0.040	0.044	0.067
Years member	−0.007	0.044	−0.014	0.076***	−0.032	0.078
Time membership	0.165****	0.324****	0.100**	0.218****	0.221****	0.261****
Commitment to organization	0.037	0.053**	0.258****	n.a.	0.133****	0.084
Associational efficacy	0.472****	0.407****	0.289****	0.491****	0.377****	0.311****
Size (activists)	0.025	0.015	−0.006	0.044	−0.034	0.051
Employees (dummy)	0.071**	−0.026	0.038	0.003	0.182****	−0.089
Degree of formalization	−0.080**	0.047	−0.025	−0.030	0.024	0.022
Assembly		−0.044	−0.060	−0.005	0.027	−0.098
Adj R indiv	0.053	0.046	0.070	0.015	0.030	0.000
Adj R indiv + assoc involve	0.358	0.415	0.219	0.373	0.320	0.231
Adj R indiv + assoc involve + org vars	0.368	0.414	0.218	0.374	0.358	0.237
N	878	1,156	360	1,093	708	311

Note
Standardized beta coefficients. *$P<0.1$; **$P<0.05$; ***$P<0.01$; ****$P<0.001$.

paid staff. Formalization of the association was measured using a formalization index that measured the fraction of possible institutional devices such as having a constitution, the extent to which the organization has different formal positions, and the existence of general meetings. Finally, the general meeting variable was a dummy indicating the existence of such a body in the association (0=no, 1=yes).

The regression results are reported in a cumulative manner, starting from the individual level, adding individual involvement in the association and, finally, adding associational characteristics. The tables list the standardized beta coefficients of the final equation, which includes all variables. The bottom of the tables gives the adjusted R-squares after each block has been entered. The model estimates for participation and efficacy will be discussed in turn.

Table 3.3 shows that the bulk of the explained variance of levels of participation in decision-making is explained by the associational involvement variables (second block of variables). First, in all countries associational efficacy is the most important determinant of participation in decision-making, reflecting the modest correlation between the two concepts observed already. The second strongest factor affecting participation in decision-making and management is the amount of time devoted to the association. In all countries, there is a significantly positive effect. Finally, in some countries the more subjective measure of commitment to the organization also significantly affects participation.

Despite the overwhelming influence of these involvement variables, there are still some significant effects at the individual and organizational levels, albeit small. First, we consider the individual-level variables. In four of the six countries, education has a positive significant effect on decision-making participation. This means that within the stratum of activists – who already constitute a more highly educated group compared to socially actives and passives – there is still a somewhat more educated subgroup that is more heavily involved in associational decision-making. Furthermore, in East and West Germany women are somewhat less inclined to take part in decision-making than men. Finally, age and employment status exert no significant influence on being involved in decision-making (except for age in the Netherlands, and employment status in West Germany). Within the group of activists, only education has some effect on the extent of involvement in decision-making, but it is relatively small.

This brings us finally to the most important group of variables, measuring the possible impact of organizational properties. First, and contrary to expectations, size does not have a suppressing effect on actually taking part in decision-making. It is not significant in five countries, while in Spain it is significantly positive. A similar result is obtained for the effect of paid staff. Once again contrary to expectations, we do not see a suppressing effect, but notice that in two countries (East Germany and Switzerland) the effect is significantly positive. Having paid staff, then, seems to facilitate instead of hinder the involvement of members in decision-making and management.

Results for the two formal structure variables exhibit the same pattern. The effect of the degree of formalization on participation is absent, except for East

Table 3.4 Predictors of associational efficacy

Independent variables	East Germany	West Germany	The Netherlands	Spain	Switzerland	United Kingdom
Age	−0.001	−0.078***	−0.076	−0.006	0.029	0.043
Gender	−0.039	−0.068***	0.047	−0.078***	−0.007	0.039
Education	0.027	0.059**	0.067	0.059**	0.059*	0.056
Employment	0.101****	0.089****	0.089	0.053**	0.099***	0.055
Years member	0.036	−0.011	0.152***	0.064**	0.012	0.034
Time membership	0.041	0.058***	0.066	0.128****	0.056	0.126**
Commitment to org	0.211****	0.212****	0.125**	n.a.	0.202****	0.206****
Associational participation	0.470****	0.434****	0.287****	0.506****	0.402****	0.316****
Size (activists)	−0.124****	−0.073***	−0.157***	−0.083***	0.026	0.063
Employees (dummy)	−0.045	−0.109****	−0.166****	−0.028	−0.144****	−0.097
Degree of formalization	−0.033	−0.007	0.113*	−0.040	−0.020	−0.072
Assembly	−0.038	0.024	−0.146**	0.009	0.009	−0.052
Adj R indiv	0.044	0.065	0.08	0.032	0.047	0.06
Adj R indiv + assoc involve	0.358	0.364	0.168	0.345	0.3	0.214
Adj R indiv + assoc involve + org vars	0.371	0.381	0.223	0.355	0.316	0.224
N	878	1,156	360	1,093	708	311

Note
Standardized beta coefficients. *$P<0.1$; **$P<0.05$; ***$P<0.01$; ****$P<0.001$.

Germany, where it seems to decrease participation instead of facilitating it. Finally, we do not see any significant effects for the existence of a general assembly.

It is important to note that these effects hold by and large if we examine the contribution of these groups of variables block by block. As Table 3.3 shows, the explained variances of only the individual-level variables are negligible. The same applies for the contribution of the contextual variables. If we drop the most important involvement variable (efficacy), the only change at the organizational level is that in West Germany and the UK paid staff has a negative effect on participation, while in Spain formalization decreases participation somewhat. Although these results are more in line with expectations, they in fact attest to the robustness of the above results, rather than forcing us to reconsider the original findings.

3.2.4 Predicting associational efficacy

Given the fact that there is a modest correlation between participation and efficacy, we should not expect drastically different results when looking at the determinants of efficacy. In terms of the contribution of the different blocks of variables to the explained variance, the results are similar. Activity in the association is most important, while background variables and organizational characteristics also exert a modest influence here. Still, the regression results reveal a number of interesting differences.

First, starting with the group of variables measuring activity in the association, associational participation in decision-making is the most important determinant of efficacy, just as efficacy has turned out to most strongly affect participation.

Time invested in membership also has a positive effect – but not in as many countries as in the case of predicting participation. Instead, commitment to the organization exerts a consistent positive effect on associational efficacy. The explanation for this is probably that the concepts of efficacy and commitment both tap into the same attitudinal predisposition, and thus are somewhat related to each other. Finally, in two countries we witness a positive effect of the length of membership on efficacy, providing *some* support for the expectation that long-standing members are more confident about their ability to affect decision-making.

If we take a look at the individual-level variables and their relation with efficacy, we notice that education has significant positive effects but not in all countries, as was the case when predicting associational participation. Instead, being employed exerts a stronger and more consistent effect on efficacy. Employed people feel more confident about their ability to affect decision-making than those who are not employed. The effects for gender and age are similar when predicting participation – mostly absent.

This, then, brings us to the effect of organizational variables. Contrary to our previous findings, both size and the existence of paid staff are related to lower levels of efficacy in several countries. Size depresses efficacy in all countries except Switzerland and the UK. The existence of employees negatively affects efficacy in West Germany, the Netherlands and Switzerland. The effects for formal structure remain negligible, and are only significant in the Netherlands, where the degree of formalization positively affects efficacy, but the existence of an assembly has a negative effect.

The most notable difference between involvement in associational decision-making and management and the perceived influence on decision-making revolves around the impact of size and paid staff. While there is no influence of these two variables on actual involvement, in several countries these variables affect efficacy in the expected direction: keeping a host of individual level factors equal, larger organizations and organizations with paid staff are characterized by a lower perceived level of efficacy of its activists.

3.3 Discussion

What do these results mean for the participatory spaces that voluntary associations are supposed to offer? First and foremost, the data regarding the activities of the *socially actives* show considerable levels of the involvement of more or less 'ordinary' members of associations. In terms of the functioning of associations as democratic organizations in which there is room for deliberation among members, the high level of members attending meetings more than several times a year attests to the vitality of these organizations as democratic spaces. Their involvement in planning meetings, preparing speeches and writing texts highlights the fact that these associations are to a very large extent being run by the members themselves. It also indicates the substantial role of associations as 'skill producers' (Verba *et al.* 1995: 377–390), a factor that has important spill-over effects to the political domain.

The analysis subsequently focused upon the activities of activists and the relationship between participation in decision-making/organizational management and associational efficacy. First, dominance of associational activity as an explanation of both participation and efficacy replicates the findings of Knoke in his study of associational involvement in the United States. Individual-level background variables and organizational-level factors have relatively modest effects, leading to the somewhat sobering conclusion that the most important factors are also the least surprising. Those who are heavily involved in conducting the associations' business are also the ones having the strongest feelings about the possibility to influence these decisions, and vice versa. In addition to being good news for those scholars who value the role of voluntary associations as participatory spaces in their own right, these results also suggest that associations function as important contexts in which citizens acquire civic skills that are relevant resources for different forms of political participation and levels of political efficacy as well.

To further assess the meaning of these results, it is important to recall that in many instances the surveyed activists consisted of very small groups of respondents for each of the associations surveyed, and in no way constitute a cross-section of the membership population. First of all, this means that it should not come as a surprise to find relatively high levels of both participation in decision-making and efficacy among these respondents. This group of respondents has been selected by the leaders of the association; it is likely that fellow members were picked with considerable levels of activity in running the association as well. The general absence of an effect of organizational characteristics on the propensity to be actually active may be partly explained by this. A comprehensive survey of the engagement of members in associations might have shown more substantial effects on the four factors that were included in the analysis: size, paid staff, formal structure, and the existence of a general assembly.

The picture looks more interesting if we turn to the determinants of associational efficacy. We notice that even for this highly engaged substratum of the association's members, we witness lower efficacy scores if they are active in larger and professionalized associations. In other words, the most efficacious subgroup of members still displays lower levels of efficacy in larger associations, and in associations where paid staff are employed. While the effect for this subgroup is relatively modest, one could argue that ordinary members might be even more susceptible to this effect of size and professionalization.

The results as such are not consoling regarding Michels' (1959 [1911]) worries about the consequences of professionalization for the government of associations. If the essence of associational life lies in making sure members run and control the organization, it is important to make sure that members feel efficacious, as levels of efficacy are important determinants of these activity levels. The analysis helps to understand how prospering associations which grow in size, and as a result decide to professionalize part of their management, indeed run the risk of becoming more bureaucratized and less democratic. Somewhat tragically, the consequence of their success might be that they enter a downward spiral in which lower levels of efficacy and member involvement feed into each other, necessitating a further professionalization of management tasks, which in turn reduces the involvement of ordinary members. Successful associations that experience a substantial growth might thus pay a price in terms of their ability to function as democratic polities. When it comes to preserving the essence of associational democracy, small may indeed be beautiful.

Note

1 Knoke's measure of detachment is somewhat different from political efficacy measures because it also focuses upon the distance members feel toward fellow members.

4 Associations and political empowerment

Bengü Dayican, Bas Denters and
Henk van der Kolk

4.1 Introduction

On the occasion of the opposition to the Maastricht Treaty in 1992, Robert Dahl asked how the vitality of the democratic process in such a large-scale transnational political community could be maintained (Dahl 1997). One of his recommendations pertains to the enhancement of democratic life in smaller communities below the level of the nation-state. He argues that it is essential that the enlargement of scale inherent in the extension of trans-national democracy should not lead to a 'widening sense of powerlessness', by giving citizens opportunities to 'exercise significant control over decisions on a smaller scale of matters important in their daily lives' (Dahl 1997: 440).

The ideas presented by Dahl are, of course, not new. Pateman refers to John Stuart Mill when she identifies the potential benefits of political participation. Mill argued, 'We do not learn to read or write, to ride or swim, by merely being told how to do it, but by doing it, so it is only by practising popular government on a limited scale, that the people will ever learn how to exercise it on a larger scale' (Pateman 1970: 31).

On this basis, Vetter has developed her thesis of local political competence as a resource for the legitimacy of large scale EU democracy (Vetter 2002). She argues that involvement in small-scale communities might provide a training ground for acquiring communicative skills, knowledge and appreciation of democratic procedures, etc. All these authors commonly refer to local government as such a training ground.

Similar to this, scholars from the Political Culture tradition (and later Social Capital theorists) have argued that voluntary associations, the workplace and other forms of social engagement might have similar empowerment effects (Almond and Verba 1989 [1963]); Putnam *et al.* 1993; Putnam 2000). Associational life may enable more democracy in more domains of life, and it can at the same time help to form and develop the capacities and dispositions of democratic citizenship (Warren 2001). In a rather similar vein, Robert Putnam has argued that participation in voluntary associations provides a form of social capital which is essential for 'making democracies work' (Putnam *et al.* 1993, Putnam 2000).

Almond and Verba investigated the effects of participation in voluntary organizations, and found that the sense of political efficacy was higher among members of organizations than among non-members and highest of all among active members, particularly of explicitly political organizations (Almond and Verba 1989 [1963]): 252–265; see also Pateman 1970: 47). This finding has since 'been repeated quite routinely' (Hooghe 2008: 569).

The argument that participation in voluntary organizations fosters empowerment and citizenship was also supported by the EU ministers in 2001 at the Troika meeting of the 7th European Conference on Social Economy:[1]

> People participating in decision-making as members in associations and cooperatives are continuously practicing and experiencing the realities of democracy. Ministers underlined the opportunities, for young, adults and old, women and men with various backgrounds, of such participation as one of the most effective and relevant means for active democratic citizenship.

In this chapter, we focus on the role that engagement in voluntary associations plays in the process of civic empowerment. We focus on subjective political empowerment, or people's sense of political efficacy. This is a relevant concept within the notion of democratic citizenship, since the democratic quality of a political system becomes questionable if large numbers of citizens believe they lack effective channels to influence political decision-making. Therefore, studies of democratic citizenship over the years have devoted a lot of attention to people's sense of political powerlessness.

Our main question is:

How is engagement in civic associations related to the subjective political empowerment of citizens?

In our analysis, we will focus on different types of individual engagement (non-members; different types of membership) as well as on different structures of associations (purpose and size, for example). By carefully focusing on the context in which people may get empowered, we hope to add to the existing body of literature. The data used in this chapter to test our preliminary thoughts allow us to further focus on this context.

In the next section, we discuss the main dependent variable 'political empowerment' and the factors that are supposed to contribute to this feeling of empowerment. These expectations are tested using data from various sources from five different societies. The data sources are discussed in the third section, although we refer to the Notes for a more detailed description of all variables. Subsequently, we describe the levels of empowerment for various types of involvement using data both from random samples of citizens and from a sample of activists. In the fifth section, we test our main hypotheses using data sets which consist of all citizens. We then zoom in on various groups of activists. The final section discusses the results. We conclude that although activism is related to political efficacy, it is not a very strong explanation of this important aspect of democratic citizenship.

4.2 Concepts and expectations

4.2.1 Efficacy

'Political efficacy' has a relatively long conceptual history. In its original formulation, the term referred to 'the feeling that individual political action does have, or can have, an impact upon the political process' (Campbell *et al.* 1971 [1954]: 187). In the original formulation there is some ambiguity, because the definition refers to both actual (*does have*) and potential (*can have*) influence on the policy-making process. In our research, we focus on the possible effects of engagement in voluntary organizations on potential efficacy (*can have*) – i.e. citizens' perceptions of their possibilities and opportunities to have an impact upon the political process.[2]

Lane (1959: 149) pointed out that, with regard to this aspect of political efficacy, two analytically distinct dimensions are relevant. The first dimension pertains to the citizen's self-image: how a person assesses his or her personal knowledge and capacity to act competently in political processes. Subsequently, this dimension has been referred to as *internal political efficacy*. The second dimension refers to the citizen's perceptions of the openness of the system and political officeholders for the needs and demands of citizens. In subsequent work, this dimension has been referred to as *external political efficacy*.

The CID questionnaire contains two items[3] that refer to such personal 'possibilities' for presenting political opinions. Linguistically, the term 'possibilities', which is used in the formulation of both items, refers both to (perceived) personal capacities and competences (internal efficacy) and to the perceived systemic opportunities (the political opportunity structure, external efficacy) in a similar way. It is therefore appropriate to use the general term 'political efficacy' to refer to the composite measure based on these items.

4.2.2 Mechanisms

As we argued in the introduction, participation in voluntary associations is often hypothesized to have a positive effect on citizens' perceptions of their personal possibilities and the systemic opportunities to act politically (see also Bowler *et al.* 2003: 1113; Hooghe 2003: 48).[4] At least two different mechanisms have been mentioned to account for the relationship between joining and empowerment; participation in voluntary groups both improves individual capacities as well as self-confidence, and establishes useful social ties (for this distinction, see Teorell 2003: 50–51).[5]

The first and, according to some, most prominent mechanism is that associations provide citizens with opportunities to learn skills such as talking in public, writing official letters and meeting skills that may also enhance their capacity to act competently. In this first line of argument, it is emphasized that participation in associations increases a person's human capital (see, for example, Becker 1964; Berry *et al.* 1993: 256; Verba *et al.* 1995; Teorell 2003: 50; Green and Brock 2005: 3; Howard and Gilbert 2008: 14).

The second mechanism is that involvement in an association extends the social network of its members by establishing social ties, both directly and indirectly, with others. Such ties may be important for providing actual access to politically relevant resources and information, and may therefore broaden individuals' knowledge and perceptions of opportunities for political influence and thus increase their political empowerment (Granovetter 1973, 1983; Wollebaek and Selle 2002: 34).

4.2.3 Types of involvement

Several of the aforementioned claims regarding the effects of associational involvement tend to be too general. To begin with, the *depth of people's engagement* in associations may vary considerably. Some authors have found that the level of activism is indeed a relevant factor in the explanation of civic virtues and political participation (see, for example, Howard and Gilbert 2008: 26). It indeed seems plausible that an involvement effect on political orientations will be more pronounced for the more active ('deep') forms of associational involvement, although some have argued that the differences between active and passive membership are rather small (Wollebaek and Selle 2002: 54–55; Hooghe 2003: 52; Hooghe 2008: 573–574).

A related characteristic is the *breadth of engagement*. This refers to the multiplicity of a citizen's memberships. In addition to people who are not involved in any association, there are differences between people who have engaged themselves in one type of association and those who are engaged in a variety of associations. This breadth of engagement increases the likelihood that someone is directly and indirectly linked to a variety of others, providing wider access to politically relevant resources and information (Teorell 2003; Iglič and Font Fábregas 2007: 189).[6]

4.2.4 Associations

In some of the older literature on the consequences of voluntary associations, it is implicitly assumed that most associations are alike. More recently, however, authors have started to argue that the *type of association* a person is involved in may be relevant, too (Joye and Laurent 1997: 166; Moyser and Parry 1997: 27; Eastis 2001; Stolle and Rochon 2001; Bowler *et al.* 2003; Hooghe 2008: 574). There is a wide variety of associations that people may join. One important characteristic is the sphere of action or social domain in which associations and their members operate. They range from an association of pigeon-fliers to a branch of the Hell's Angels, and from a sewing circle to a debating club. Obviously, the political socialization effects of group memberships may differ for each of these spheres (see, for example, Stolle and Rochon 2001: 148–149). In this chapter, we distinguish between organizations on the basis of their activities – leisure, politics, economic and religious – although more subtle distinctions are presented too.

Despite the emphasis many authors have placed on distinguishing between various types of organizations, the mechanisms relating the type and various consequences of voluntary participation are not clear yet (Newton 2001a). As Bowler and colleagues write with regard to the creation of democratic values; 'To the extent that [differences between types of organizations; DDvdK] holds up elsewhere this suggests the neo-Tocquevillians may have to develop more nuanced arguments with regard to the kinds of social groups that might instill democratic virtues' (Bowler et al. 2003: 1128).[7]

Part of the mechanism explaining differences between organizational types can be found in their structural characteristics. The *size of the organization* in terms of membership may differ. System size is likely to affect the opportunities for direct, active member involvement (see, for example, Dahl and Tufte 1973); this in turn is likely to increase the chances of people acquiring politically relevant social skills and contacts and, as a consequence, to increase their sense of personal efficacy. Size also affects the number of social relationships that will be enabled by the organization.

A second characteristic of organizations may be their *linking social capital* (Szreter 2002, see also Gitell and Vidal 1988: 15; Woolcock 1998). This refers to the linkages of the organization with other voluntary organizations and with political and state agents such as political and bureaucratic state institutions, political parties and politicians. Our expectation is that members of organizations providing linking social capital will consider themselves more efficacious than members of other organizations.

In our analysis, we will therefore focus on the type, the size and linking aspects of organizations.[8]

4.2.5 Additional individual and other contextual determinants of political efficacy

In explanations of political orientations, some scholars primarily focus on long-term processes of socialization while others focus on political and social contexts (see, for example, Mishler and Rose 2001; see also Denters et al. 2007). When we explore the relevance of the associational involvement factors discussed above, it is important to compare the explanatory contribution of associational involvement with these two alternative explanations (socialization and context).

First, political socialization not only occurs in voluntary associations; it also (and probably predominantly) occurs in the family, informal social networks, schools and the workplace. Accordingly, we have to consider the effect of these alternative forms of association as well. We therefore take marital status, having children at home (and thus, for example, having contacts via schools and children's sports clubs) and employment status into account.

Second, people's political orientations are also shaped by their current personal context. People who are placed in a context where they lack politically relevant resources are in a relatively disadvantaged position, which is likely to be reflected in their sense of political efficacy. There are at least two mechanisms that may be at work here (Denters and Geurts 1993: 451–452). Possession of resources (such as money and education) is associated with one's position in the 'social pecking order'. The higher people are placed in this hierarchy, the more likely they are to develop politically relevant skills. It is also plausible that positions relatively high up in the social pyramid will provide easier access to politically influential circles. To the extent that this is the case, such resources will also have a positive effect on the availability of opportunities to have an impact on political decisions. At the same time, being high in the social stratification means that one is likely to be a winner in social and political interactions (Converse 1972: 326), and such success is likely to boost people's sense of personal (political) efficacy.[9]

4.3 Data and research strategy

In our data analysis, we will apply the following strategy. In the next section, we will first provide a descriptive analysis in which we compare non-actives (citizens within the population who neither participate nor do voluntary work), and socially active citizens with respect to their levels of subjective political empowerment. This analysis will be based on the CID Population Study. Alongside the results of this comparison of socially active and non-active citizens in the mass surveys, we will in some instances also present information about the subjective political empowerment of the activists that we questioned in our survey of organizational activists. We will also describe the relationship between the breadth, depth and type of organizational involvement and empowerment in the various countries.

In a subsequent explanatory section, we shall then specify a causal model which includes individual level explanatory factors (*depth* and *breadth of engagement*) as well as the organizational characteristics (*type of organization*, *size of organization* and *linking capital*).

We will control for the explanatory power of these variables by using socio-economic status indicators such as income, education, social integration (marital status, children, and employment status), age and gender. We will first test our model using the data on citizens, and then extend the analysis to activists, focusing on the effect of organizational characteristics on the empowerment of activists.

Subjective political empowerment, the main dependent variable of our study, has been defined as citizens' perceptions of their possibilities and opportunities to have an impact upon the political process (see above). In this chapter, we measure empowerment on the basis of an additive index constructed from two items: perceived personal potential for presenting opinions to politicians,[10] and perceived personal potential for making politicians take account of own opinions.[11]

4.4 Descriptive analysis

We will first focus on subjective political empowerment among people having different degrees of associational involvement. As discussed above, we expect that the feeling of empowerment will be higher among more 'deeply involved' citizens. Table 4.1 shows the mean levels of political empowerment in different levels of engagement in associations in all countries for both samples from the population and the activists. We describe here four levels of engagement. *Uninvolved* refers to those respondents not involved in any way in any of the 23 associations listed in the survey. The category *Only member* refers to those whose activities do not go beyond being a member of any of the organizations. *Participating and/or Volunteering* are the respondents who, in addition to being a member, either take an active part in activities or do voluntary work in at least one organization. *Management* refers to respondents who do at least one of the following management activities: take part in decision-making at meetings, planning or chairing a meeting, preparing or giving a speech, and writing a text other than a private letter.

The overall picture in Table 4.1 supports our expectation that the feeling of efficacy is lowest among those who are not at all involved in any association, and increases with the level of activeness. This is the case in almost all societies, and applies both to citizens and activists. Even respondents who are just members of an organization have a slightly greater feeling of efficacy, compared to those who are not involved in any organization. Among the most active groups, individuals who take active part in the organization management generally have a higher level of subjective political empowerment than those who just participate in organizational activities and/or do voluntary work. This supports the idea that involvement in decision-making in a smaller context such as the association strengthens the belief of citizens that they can also be efficacious in more general decision-making processes.

There are significant country differences. East German citizens feel substantially less politically empowered than do citizens in other countries. Spanish and Swiss citizens feel more empowered than East German citizens, but Dutch and West German citizens feel most empowered.

The general comparison between the general population and the group of activists shows that the latter group feels more politically empowered. This should not surprise us at all, because in the general population there is a strong relationship between involvement and political empowerment. What is slightly more surprising, however, is that among activists participating in the organization (the row 'Socially active' in Table 4.1) political efficacy is *higher* than among citizens, indicating they are socially active too. Even activists who are only members of at least one organization show a higher level of political efficacy than do people in the general population.

These differences are probably due to two factors. First, we expect that the way we approached potential respondents for the organizational study resulted in self-selection, resulting in over-representation of more socially-active activists.

Table 4.1 Mean levels of subjective political empowerment by different levels of activism (citizens and activists)

Levels of activism	East Germany		West Germany		Netherlands		Spain		Switzerland		UK	
	Population	Activist	Population	Activist	Population	Activist	Population	Activist	Population	Activist	Population	Activist
Not socially active	2.33 (468)	2.73 (111)	4.42 (706)	3.36 (47)	4.89 (372)	4.88 (8)	3.27 (2,083)	–	2.63 (151)	3.58 (13)	–	5.03 (31)
Uninvolved	2.28 (407)	2.31 (51)	4.40 (607)	4.88 (8)	4.54 (120)	8.00 (1)	3.24 (1,872)	–	3.04 (57)	7.75 (2)	–	5.75 (6)
Only member	2.63 (61)	3.08 (60)	4.53 (99)	3.05 (39)	5.06 (252)	4.43 (7)	3.56 (211)	–	2.38 (94)	2.82 (11)	–	4.86 (25)
Socially active	3.26 (401)	3.89 (912)	5.21 (1,078)	5.63 (1,614)	5.38 (910)	5.60 (403)	4.14 (1,208)	–	4.08 (722)	5.14 (847)	–	5.53 (748)
Participating/volunteering	3.25 (164)	3.33 (280)	5.21 (1,078)	5.17 (219)	5.38 (910)	5.63 (97)	3.82 (461)	–	3.42 (273)	4.54 (170)	–	5.41 (159)
Management	3.26 (237)	4.14 (632)		5.71 (1,395)		5.59 (306)	4.34 (747)	–	4.48 (449)	5.29 (677)	–	5.57 (589)
Total	2.75 (958)	3.66 (1,222)	4.87 (1,922)	5.45 (1,810)	5.24 (1,545)	5.54 (427)	3.61 (3,742)	–	3.68 (1,251)	5.01 (924)	–	5.49 (830)

Note
Entries are the mean levels of subjective political empowerment (a variable ranging from 0 to 10, see Appendix). Between brackets is the number of respondents. Unfortunately, the political empowerment questions were not asked of Spanish activists. In the United Kingdom, these questions were asked of the Aberdeen activists but not the whole population.

Secondly, we think that some people in the population may have overestimated their level of involvement (while not overestimating their level of political empowerment). This may have reduced the average level of political efficacy among the members classified as socially active in the population.

Although we should be cautious about these observations, they do confirm the central expectation of this chapter: the degree of engagement in associations has a consistent positive relationship with subjective political empowerment. This relationship is evident across all six societies being studied here.

We continue by taking a closer look at the relationship between subjective political empowerment and the breadth of associational involvement.[12] Here we restrict ourselves to the observation of the general population, since among activists a great majority of respondents are involved in three or more organizations, which makes a comparison between the two groups meaningless. We expected citizens to feel more efficacious the broader their organizational involvement – i.e. the higher the number of associational involvements. Again here we find the expected relationship in all societies (see Table 4.2). The relationship is somewhat less pronounced in the Netherlands and in Switzerland, since we can not observe a linear increase of subjective political empowerment parallel to the number of organizations. However, bivariate correlations between the two variables indicate that there is a significant relationship between breadth of involvement and political empowerment in these two countries.

The final descriptive results we shall discuss here pertain to the types of organizations.[13] We used membership as the distinctive characteristic. People can, of course, be members of various organizations. The results are presented in Table 4.3.

Table 4.3 shows that the sphere of action of the associations and their members does indeed matter for the level of subjective political empowerment. Overall, citizens who are actively engaged in associations show higher levels of political empowerment compared to non-active citizens, yet these levels obviously differ depending on the type of associational involvement. The feeling of personal political efficacy is in all countries markedly higher for those who are active in political parties. With respect to other types of organizations, the evidence is rather mixed. People who are actively involved in societal-economical interest groups (such as general welfare and economic interest associations) display relatively higher levels of subjective political empowerment, whereas other groups (such as organizations involved in community concerns and group-specific welfare) do not seem to foster citizens' sense of political efficacy. Among participants of leisure groups, those who are engaged in family associations feel most politically empowered, especially in Germany and the Netherlands. In sum, the results confirm the idea (see Almond and Verba 1989 [1963]) that political empowerment is most strongly developed among those active in political organizations, especially among those involved in political parties.

Table 4.2 Mean levels of subjective political empowerment by breadth of involvement (citizens only)

Breadth of involvement	East Germany	West Germany	The Netherlands	Spain	Switzerland
Uninvolved	2.28 (407)	4.40 (607)	4.54 (120)	3.24 (1,872)	3.04 (57)
One organization	2.93 (290)	4.92 (497)	5.15 (174)	3.67 (891)	2.68 (111)
Two organizations	3.03 (137)	4.98 (408)	4.97 (229)	3.94 (457)	3.41 (162)
Three or more organizations	3.62 (119)	5.41 (410)	5.40 (1,022)	4.53 (522)	3.89 (921)
Total	2.75 (958)	4.87 (1,922)	5.24 (1,545)	3.61 (3,742)	3.68 (1,251)

Note
Entries are the mean levels of subjective political empowerment (number of respondents in brackets). The figures for the UK are not included in the table, since empowerment items are missing in the UK population data file.

Table 4.3 Mean levels of subjective political empowerment by groups of organizations (citizens only)

Types of organizations	East Germany	West Germany	The Netherlands	Spain	Switzerland
Sports	3.32 (152)	5.31 (571)	5.36 (412)	4.23 (382)	4.15 (350)
Family	4.34 (34)	5.39 (79)	5.41 (121)	4.31 (233)	4.21 (131)
Culture	3.61 (43)	5.41 (251)	5.75 (185)	4.24 (257)	4.29 (156)
Leisure	**3.50 (209)**	**5.30 (748)**	**5.45 (576)**	**4.21 (708)**	**4.13 (498)**
Community concerns	3.80 (15)	5.83 (23)	5.54 (130)	4.29 (100)	4.08 (95)
Politics	5.38 (30)	6.34 (51)	6.72 (53)	6.07 (88)	5.63 (76)
New politics	4.50 (28)	5.67 (65)	5.66 (67)	4.29 (80)	4.12 (98)
Political	**4.50 (66)**	**5.87 (126)**	**5.73 (223)**	**4.77 (242)**	**4.41 (228)**
General welfare	3.79 (34)	5.41 (120)	5.71 (153)	4.25 (237)	4.20 (139)
Group-specific welfare	3.04 (25)	5.16 (47)	5.49 (87)	3.95 (95)	4.42 (89)
Economic interest	4.40 (21)	5.23 (40)	5.92 (87)	5.12 (94)	4.94 (99)
Economical	**3.64 (69)**	**5.40 (187)**	**5.68 (283)**	**4.29 (381)**	**4.31 (266)**
Religious	**3.36 (58)**	**5.33 (181)**	**5.51 (180)**	**4.56 (121)**	**4.31 (111)**
Other	3.02 (202)	4.97 (449)	5.42 (412)	4.17 (440)	4.11 (321)
Uninvolved	2.28 (407)	4.40 (607)	4.54 (120)	3.24 (1,872)	3.04 (57)
Total	2.75 (958)	4.87 (1,922)	5.24 (1,545)	3.61 (3,742)	3.68 (1,251)

Note
Entries are the mean levels of subjective political empowerment of citizens. As people can be member of several organizations, the numbers of respondents indicating membership of one of the constituting organizations do not add up. For the UK, empowerment items are not available.

4.5 Explanatory analysis

Of course, on the basis of the aforementioned analyses, we cannot say that membership and depth and breadth of involvement 'cause' empowerment. There are two potential problems here. First, there may be a problem of '*endogeneity*': while membership may result in political empowerment, it might also be the case that those feeling politically empowered might be more inclined to join a voluntary organization or more prone to becoming actively involved (Hooghe 2008). There are increasing numbers of scholars who argue for the latter possibility. They maintain that the correlation between associational membership and efficacy may be the result of self-selection: more efficacious citizens might be more prone to join an association than are their less efficacious peers (see Stolle 1998; Newton 1999a: 16; Hooghe 2008: 571, 578–579). Such self-selection based on subjective political empowerment may be more likely in some contexts than in others – for example, in joining political organizations. On the other hand, it is by no means obvious that politically efficacious people should be more inclined to join a football club or a choir than are less efficacious persons. Nevertheless, when interpreting the results of our analyses we will have to consider the issue of reciprocal causation.

Second, we must avoid drawing conclusions on the basis of spurious effects. To avoid this second problem, we will test our hypotheses in a multivariate model by controlling for a number of socio-economic status indicators that are supposed to explain both empowerment and membership.

In the next sections, we will first investigate our theoretical expectations on the basis of the citizen surveys. However, because we are also interested in the effects of some as of yet unanalysed characteristics of organizations (such as size and the linking capital of an organization) on the empowerment of activists, analyses of the data collected among activists allows us to draw some inferences about this relationship.

4.5.1 The citizens' model

We start with a basic model based on the data from citizens only. This model includes two dummies indicating the 'depth of involvement': active participation and having management tasks. Unfortunately, we were unable to distinguish between those who are just actively involved in an organization and those who also have management tasks, in Germany and the Netherlands (see Table 4.1). For these two countries we included only one dummy variable. Because the nominal variable 'type of organization' (measured by dummies for membership in organizations for leisure and sports, political organizations, economic organizations and religious organizations) is by definition related to 'breadth of involvement', we chose not to include the latter variable in our model. Finally, we controlled for effects by using a number of additional individual factors, such as socio-economic status and personal context.[14]

The results of our multivariate analysis are presented in Table 4.4. The overall fit, as measured by the adjusted R-square is small in all countries. Only some of

Table 4.4 Subjective political empowerment of citizens

	East Germany		West Germany		The Netherlands		Spain		Switzerland	
	b	Beta	b	Beta	b	Beta	b	Beta	b	Beta
Constant	2.00***		5.05***		5.06***		3.38***		2.80***	
Participating/volunteering (yes)	0.60*	0.11	0.36	0.09	−0.16	−0.05	0.18	0.03	0.06	0.01
Management (yes)	0.24	0.05					0.35*	0.07	0.67**	0.14
Involvement in organizations: leisure	0.52*	0.10	0.28	0.07	0.30*	0.09	0.11	0.02	0.12	0.02
Involvement in organizations: political	0.92**	0.10	0.50*	0.06	0.44**	0.09	0.69***	0.08	0.39*	0.06
Involvement in organizations: economic	0.44	0.05	0.02	0.00	0.25	0.06	0.14	0.02	0.23	0.04
Involvement in organizations: religious	−0.18	−0.02	0.24	0.04	0.13	0.03	0.58*	0.05	0.07	0.01
Marital status (married)	0.44*	0.10	−0.19	−0.04	0.18	0.05	−0.06	−0.01	−0.13	−0.03
Children in household (yes)	0.15	0.03	−0.62***	−0.13	−0.07	−0.02	n.a.	n.a.	−0.07	−0.01
Employment status (works)	0.08	0.02	−0.22	−0.05	0.06	0.02	−0.13	−0.03	0.17	0.03
Gender (male)	0.28	0.07	0.35**	0.09	−0.04	−0.01	0.20*	0.05	0.30*	0.06
Income	0.07	0.04	0.20***	0.13	0.18***	0.14	0.30***	0.18	0.35***	0.20
Age (Ref. cat. = born 1950–60)										
Born before 1940	0.23	0.05	0.09	0.02	−0.12	−0.03	0.32*	0.06	0.03	0.01
Born 1940–50	−0.07	−0.01	0.12	0.02	0.04	0.01	0.01	0.00	−0.12	−0.02
Born 1960–70	−0.20	−0.04	0.05	0.01	−0.32*	−0.08	0.12	0.02	0.32	0.06
Born 1970 and later	0.17	0.03	−0.07	−0.01	−0.25	−0.06	0.08	0.02	−0.08	−0.01
Education	0.32**	0.11	0.38***	0.13	0.27***	0.10	0.35***	0.09	0.79***	0.21
Adjusted R^2	0.08		0.08		0.07		0.08		0.19	
N	680		1107		1172		2661		1006	

Notes
Not involved in any organization is the implicit reference category (the constant); ***P = 0.001; **P ≤ 0.01; *P ≤ 0.05; Ref. cat. = Reference category.
b and Beta refer, respectively, to unstandardized and standardized regression coefficients.

the variables are significantly related to political empowerment. The model confirms the strong impact of income and education, the two most prominent socio-economic status variables. The combined effect of income (having five categories) and education (having three categories) is even quite substantive. Most other variables, however, are only weakly (if at all) related to political empowerment, and their effects are far from identical across countries. In West Germany, for example, having children at home reduces the level of political efficacy, while in the other societies this relationship is not significant.

We are, however, more than anything else interested in the characteristics related to organizational involvement. The impact of the 'depth of involvement' seems to be significant in the expected direction, although perhaps not as consistently as one might have anticipated. In three out of five countries, the contribution of activism beyond mere membership is significantly positive, but in two societies activism does not significantly contribute to higher levels of political efficacy.

Moreover, being a member of and/or being active in a *political* organization is related to a somewhat higher level of empowerment. In two countries, membership of a leisure organization increases political efficacy too, albeit to a smaller extent. Effects of religious organizations are only significant in Spain, whereas the impact of economic organizations is never significant. The overall impact of being involved in all organizations (as compared to being involved in none of the organizations at all), the 'breadth of involvement', is relatively small in Switzerland and largest in East Germany, where, in particular, membership of political organizations is especially strongly related to political empowerment.

4.5.2 *The activists' model*

In the final model, we restrict our analysis to activists. We use largely the same model, but add two variables to our analysis: organizational size and linking capital.[15] We also added length of membership and average monthly time spent on organizational activities to see whether these individual characteristics affect empowerment: longer and stronger involvement may enhance a person's efficacy. The results of the analysis are presented in Table 4.5.

The overall fit of the activists' model is better than for the citizens' model. The constants are somewhat higher in the citizens' model, indicating that activists on average are feeling more empowered than citizens. The activists are, of course, a very specific sub-set of citizens. There are also other reasons why we should be cautious in interpreting the differences between results from this model and those reported in Table 4.4. First, we have no data on activists for Spain. Second, the set of explanatory variables differs slightly. These differences notwithstanding, we find that active engagement in political organizations has a consistent positive association with political empowerment. In addition to this, we find that engagement in economic organizations in Germany and Switzerland increases one's sense of political empowerment. Amongst the activists, we do not find an effect of activism in religious and leisure organizations.

Table 4.5 Subjective political empowerment of activists

	East Germany		West Germany		The Netherlands		Switzerland		UK	
	b	Beta	b	Beta	b	Beta	b	Beta	b	Beta
Constant	2.33***		3.69***		4.61***		2.27***		3.87***	
Participating/ volunteering (yes)	0.05	0.01	0.46**	0.09	0.93*	0.25	0.96**	0.17	0.13	0.02
Management (yes)	0.35	0.08	0.51**	0.07	0.93*	0.26	1.23***	0.24	0.03	0.00
Involvement in organizations: leisure	0.09	0.02	−0.13	−0.03	−0.29	−0.09	−0.31	−0.07	−0.06	−0.01
Involvement in organizations: political	0.62***	0.11	0.90***	0.17	0.86***	0.24	0.84***	0.18	0.58*	0.09
Involvement in organizations: economic	0.52**	0.10	0.29*	0.06	0.10	0.03	0.30	0.07	0.13	0.03
Involvement in organizations: religious	0.50**	0.08	0.20	0.03	−0.38	−0.09	0.07	0.01	0.18	0.04
Marital status (married)	−0.25	−0.05	−0.31	−0.06	−0.30	−0.07	−0.31	−0.06	−0.24	−0.03
Children in household (yes)	0.16	0.04	−0.15	−0.03	0.11	0.03	−0.16	−0.04	−0.24	−0.05
Employment status (works)	0.13	0.03	0.10	0.02	0.14	0.04	0.46*	0.10	0.02	0.00
Gender (male)	0.23	0.05	0.58***	0.12	−0.38*	−0.11	0.28	0.06	0.29	0.06
Income	0.17**	0.11	0.19**	0.10	0.29***	0.25	0.20**	0.12	n.a.	n.a.

	b	Beta	b	Beta	b	Beta	b	Beta	b	Beta
Age (Ref. cat.=born 1950–60)										
Born before 1940	0.46	0.10	−0.38	−0.07	0.63	0.18	−0.17	−0.03	0.57	0.11
Born 1940–50	0.07	0.01	0.24	0.04	0.20	0.05	−0.08	−0.02	0.40	0.07
Born 1960–70	0.52*	0.10	0.25	0.04	0.26	0.06	−0.72***	−0.13	0.15	0.02
Born 1970 and later	0.74**	0.13	0.85***	0.11	−0.38	−0.07	0.05	0.01	0.24	0.03
Education	0.40***	0.15	0.53***	0.17	0.32*	0.14	0.34*	0.09	0.72***	0.24
Length of membership	−0.14*	−0.07	0.02	0.01	0.07	0.05	0.03	0.02	0.01	0.00
Time spent for organization	0.09	0.05	−0.05	−0.02	−0.03	−0.02	0.15*	0.08	0.17	0.08
Size of organization (Ref. cat.=lower than 40)										
40–99	−0.14	−0.02	−0.38	−0.05	0.78***	0.24	−0.11	−0.02	0.27	0.03
More than 100	−0.02	0.00	−0.12	−0.02	0.08	0.02	−0.16	−0.04	0.07	0.02
Social contacts	−0.02	0.00	0.44***	0.09	−0.14	−0.04	0.36	0.07	−0.07	−0.01
Local political contacts (Ref. cat.=No contacts)										
One or two contacts	0.16	0.04	0.03	0.01	−0.58**	−0.17	0.40	0.09	0.42	0.08
Three or four contacts	0.40	0.09	0.60***	0.12	−0.29	−0.06	0.95***	0.22	0.54	0.10
Adjusted R^2	0.14		0.22		0.25		0.16		0.07	
N	929		1,297		314		695		601	

Notes
*** $P \leq 0.001$; ** $P \leq 0.01$; * $P \leq 0.05$; n.a. = not asked; Ref. cat. =≤Reference category.
b and Beta refer, respectively, to unstandardized and standardized regression coefficients.

Also among activists, income and education are strongly related to political empowerment. Just as was the case in the analysis of the citizens' sample, these two SES factors were by far the most important predictors of efficacy. Unexpectedly, neither length of membership nor time spent in the organization turned out to be related to political empowerment.

The most interesting variables are those referring to the contextual characteristics of organizational membership. As we indicated in the theoretical part of this chapter, we expected to find a relationship between the size and the linking capital of an organization and political empowerment. Our results indicate that size is unrelated to political empowerment. The amount of local political contacts, however, with the exception of the Netherlands, is related to political empowerment, indicating that activists who are members of an organization that is strongly connected to the local government feel more empowered than those who are members of an organization lacking these contacts.[16] Whether contacts with the local political arena are to be interpreted as a cause or a consequence of empowerment is a topic for further study. The effects of the organizational contacts on political empowerment, on the other hand, are much weaker and are not robust across countries.

4.6 Discussion

In this chapter we have focused on the role engagement in voluntary associations plays in the process of civic empowerment. Our main question was how engagement in civic associations is related to the subjective political empowerment of citizens. In our analysis, we focused first on different types of individual engagement (non-members; different types of membership). Our descriptive analysis shows that there is, as expected, a strong relationship between membership and activism on the one hand, and empowerment on the other. In particular, those involved in different types of political organizations feel more politically empowered. These results were confirmed in a multivariate analysis.

In a more focused analysis of activists, we also introduced some contextual variables. Size of the voluntary organization was unrelated to political empowerment. In most countries in the analysis, the amount of local political contacts was positively related to empowerment. Activists of an organization that has strong contacts with the local government feel more empowered than activists of an organization that lacks such contacts. Being a member of an organization with many contacts with other (non-political) organizations, on the other hand, did not have a similar positive effect.

Part of the mechanism relating organizational membership and activism to political empowerment is through the emergence of organizational efficacy, as discussed in the Chapter 3 of this volume. Including this factor in our model yields significant results, indicating that organizational efficacy and political efficacy are indeed related. At the same time, it does not dramatically change the overall properties of the model, or the specific relationships, indicating that the acquisition of organizational efficacy is only one of the mechanisms relating membership to political efficacy.

At first sight our main finding (namely, especially memberships in various types of political organizations are related to political efficacy) hardly comes as a surprise, and begs the question about the direction of causality. Is it membership in political organizations that breeds political efficacy, as 'Social Capital Theorists' have argued? Or are politically efficacious people simply more likely to join political organizations than other people, as has been argued by adherents to the 'Self-selection Argument' (see, for example, Hooghe 2008)? Although our data do not allow for a direct test of these arguments, on closer consideration our results nevertheless allow for some cautious conclusions about the issue of reciprocal causation. As we argued previously, the self-selection argument is more plausible for political organizations than for other organizations; indeed involvement in political organizations was the only type of membership that was positively related in both the citizen survey and amongst the organizational activists. This appears to be evidence in favour of the 'Self-selection Argument', and to be bad news for Social Capital Theory. However, we should not jump to conclusions too prematurely.

First, in the case of political organizations, even though the initial step towards involvement could very well be easier for people having at least a certain degree of political self-confidence (suggesting a process of self-selection), arguably a relatively self-confident person who joined a political organization might subsequently become (even) more politically self-confident. After all, political participation is likely to have educational effects, increasing people's political competences, opportunities and sense of political efficacy (see, for example, Pateman 1970). Hooghe (2008: 589) also argues that self-selection and socialization are likely to go hand in hand: 'actors do make a deliberate choice to join an interaction sphere, but subsequently are influenced by that sphere'.[17] Therefore, especially in the case of political organizations, we should in all likelihood interpret the relationship between organizational involvement and subjective political empowerment as a process of reciprocal causation, rather than as a one-way process.

Moreover, among both citizens and activists we found evidence that some forms of *non-political* organizational involvement were also related to political empowerment. Amongst citizens, for example, involvement in leisure organizations was as strongly related to political empowerment as engagement in political organizations. For leisure organizations as diverse as sports clubs and community choirs, it is hard to see why feeling politically efficacious would induce a person to join or become involved. For such organizations political efficacy is not likely to be a driving force in a process of self-selection, and the correlation between efficacy and membership is likely to be primarily the result of socialization in the organization (as argued by Social Capital Theory). That these relations are not as strong and not as consistent as the association between political memberships and political efficacy is perfectly understandable. The relative strength of the relationships of memberships in political organizations reflects the *combined* effects of self-selection and socialization, rather than an isolated socialization effect (as is the case for non-political organizations). The inconsistency of these socialization effects in the non-political organizations is understandable, when we consider Hooghe's observation that *socialization* in organizations is likely to be conditional. He argues that there is not 'a single indication that group interaction automatically lead to a more desired social value pattern', and that socialization effects 'will not be the same for all interaction contexts, but will be dependent upon context characteristics' (Hooghe 2008: 580).

Finally, we want to stress that we should neither overestimate nor underestimate the relationship between social activism and political empowerment. On the one hand, we have found that social activism is not a uni-dimensional phenomenon. Engagement in religious groups, for example, was only related to empowerment in the Spanish (and more weakly in the German) mass surveys. Although in some countries associational involvement indeed stimulates empowerment, going from no involvement to wide-ranging membership only adds a maximum of 2 points on an 11-point scale. On the other hand, none of the other variables in our models was equally meaningfully related to empowerment. This is even true for the powerful SES factors. Increasing education helps, but not as much as being a member of – for example – an interest organization. In this light, we may conclude that involvement in voluntary associations can be a resource for the legitimacy of large-scale democracy (cf. Dahl 1997; Vetter 2002), also at the EU level, as long as we bear in mind that the democratic effects of involvement are at best only modest and heavily depend on the characteristics of the interaction contexts provided by these organizations.

Notes

1 Ministry of Industry, Employment and Communications Stockholm, Sweden (June 2001) Presidency Summary of the Troika meeting on the occasion of the 7th European Conference on Social Economy (retrieved from http://ec.europa.eu/enterprise/entrepreneurship/coop/conferences/doc/troika-summary-en.pdf, dd. 15–02–2008).
2 It is for this reason that we leave out a CID item that refers to the perceptions of the actual responsiveness of political officeholders. We also set aside a CID item referring to the availability of opportunities to voice political opinions of *ordinary people*. In terms of personal political efficacy this item is ambiguous, because it is unclear whether or not individuals consider themselves to be 'ordinary'.
3 The section on data and research strategy features more information on these items. For their question wordings, see endnotes 10 and 11.
4 In addition, it is often hypothesized that participation in voluntary organizations produces trust and other types of democratic values (see for example; Stolle 1998: 498). Since we are focussing on antecedents of one aspect of human capital (political efficacy), this is not relevant for our line of argument.
5 Part of these mechanisms are also discussed in Chapter 3, where Herman Lelieveldt suggests a relationship between various individual and organizational characteristics and organizational efficacy – i.e. the feeling that one is able to affect the activities of social organizations. Organizational efficacy is expected to 'spill over' to political efficacy.
6 Teorell stresses the difference between the mere number of memberships and the dissimilarity of these memberships. He concludes that it is mainly the number of citizenships that matters (Teorell 2003).
7 Warren attributes part of the differences to the goals of the organization (as cited in

Hooghe 2008: 574). These differences, however, seem to be more relevant for the fostering of civic virtues than for the creation of human capital.
8 We distinguish two types of linking social capital: The first type refers to the social contacts of the organization in terms of the number of other voluntary associations they are in contact with. The second type refers to the linking capital in the political sphere, and is measured by the number of contacts the organization has with the following local political actors: municipal administration or local officials, the city council or members of the council, local parliament or local parliamentarians, and local political parties or politicians.
9 In addition to such personal characteristics, a sense of political efficacy might also be affected by the actual political opportunity structure in a particular locality. The size of the municipality, for example, might be an important factor. The size of the political system is likely to affect both participatory opportunities and the openness of the political system (see, for example, Dahl and Tufte 1973; Verba *et al.* 1978; Verba and Nie 1987; Oliver 2000) and important features of the network of voluntary associations in a locality (Dahl and Tufte 1973; Baglioni *et al.* 2007). Unfortunately, the design of our study is not appropriate for testing hypotheses relating to such effects of the local political opportunity structure.
10 The actual question wording of the variable is as follows: 'In your personal opinion: Do people like you have greater or smaller possibilities than others to present your opinions to politicians?' (Answering scale from 0=Much smaller to 10=Much greater).
11 The actual question wording of the variable is as follows: 'In your personal opinion: Do people like you have greater or smaller possibilities than others to make politicians take account of your opinions?' (Answering scale from 0=Much smaller to 10=Much greater).
12 Breadth of associational involvement refers to the number of associations respondent is involved in through membership, participation in activities, donations, doing voluntary work or having personal friends. The number of 'uninvolved citizens' is identical to the numbers in the second substantive row of Table 4.1. The variable was constructed by simply counting the 'involvement' in 23 associations.
13 In our theoretical argument we have introduced two additional organizational characteristics (size of the association and the association's linking capital), but these variables are only available for the activists and cannot therefore be used in the present analysis. The variables have been constructed as follows: for different sectors of organizations, 11 dichotomous variables have been constructed as a first step. These variables differentiate between respondents who participate in activities and/or do voluntary work in at least one of the organizations belonging to the specific sector, and those who do not. The 11 sectors and the organizations associated with them are as follows: Sports: sports or outdoor activities clubs; Family: youth or parents associations; Culture: cultural, musical, dancing or theatre societies; Community concerns: residents', housing or neighbourhood associations; Politics: political parties; New politics: peace organizations, associations for animal rights/protection or environmental organizations; General welfare: charity or social-welfare organizations or humanitarian aid/human rights organizations; Group-specific welfare: associations for patients, illnesses or addictions or associations for disabled; Economic interest: business/employers organizations or professional organizations; Religious: religious or church organizations; Other: pensioners/retired persons organizations, lodge or service clubs, farmers organizations, investment clubs, trade unions, consumer associations, hobby clubs/societies, automobile organizations, immigrants organizations, women's organizations, associations for war victims or veterans, other clubs/associations. These sectors (except for the category 'other') were then collapsed into four further categories as follows: Leisure organizations: sports, family and culture; Political organizations: community concerns, politics, and new politics; Economic organizations:

general welfare, group-specific welfare, and economic interest; Religious organizations were left as an individual category.

14 The construction of the control variables are as follows. For measuring income, we constructed a variable on the basis of both citizens' and activists' data files, with five values (consisting of quintiles) centred on the mean value (−2, −1, 0, 1, 2). In order to avoid an excessive loss of cases, missing values were recoded to the mean value (0). The variable education was constructed using the question on the highest level of education in each country. We collapsed this item into three categories, where −1 means less education than average, 0 means average level of education and 1 means level of education above average. In order to avoid an excessive loss of cases, missing values like 'other' and 'still being educated' were replaced with means. For marital status, a dichotomous variable was constructed on the basis of the question about the various ways in which one can live alone (single, divorced, widowed) or together with a partner (with or without being married). For children in household, a dichotomous variable was constructed on the basis of the question about whether people were having children or not. For employment status, a dichotomous variable was constructed on the basis of the question about whether people were working for more than 20 hours a week. In the gender variable, being male was coded 1. For these four variables, cases with missing values were left out of the analysis. Finally, we constructed an ordered age variable with five categories on the basis of the year in which people were born, with the help of which we later constructed dummies to check for non-linearity, whereas the median (in this case the agegroup born between 1950 and 1960) was taken as a reference category.

15 The additional independent variables for the activists' model were constructed as follows. The length of membership was measured by the question on the year of joining the organization. This was then subtracted from the year in which data were collected for each country. For the measurement of time spent for the organization, we used the direct question on the average time spent on participating in the activities of the organization in a month. To measure the size of the organization, we relied upon the independently administered organizational questionnaire sent to the board of the organization. We used the question on the number of active members, which we then recoded into three categories: less than 40, 40–99, and 100 and more active members. Since the data are categorical, we used dummies to analyse the effect of size, where the median (in this case, the group 'Lower than 40 members') was taken as the reference category. The variables 'social contacts' and 'local political contacts' represent the two types of linking social capital, and were also measured by using the organizational data. The variable 'social contacts' was measured by counting the number of organizational contacts with other associations/groups. For measuring local political contacts, a scale was constructed on the basis of the number of positive answers to the questions regarding whether the associations had contacted (a) the municipal administration; (b) the city council; (c) the local parliament; and/or (d) political parties. The resulting scale was then collapsed into three categories (no contact, one or two contacts, three or four contacts). We did not make a distinction between occasional and regular contacts. Due to the highly skewed distribution of frequencies, we created dummies to analyse the effects, whereas 'having no contacts' serves as the reference category.

16 The positive effects in East Germany and in the UK are not statistically significant.

17 Interestingly, Berry and colleagues (1993: 256–280) have looked into the issue of reciprocal causation in the relation between community participation and sense of political efficacy. They concluded that causation indeed appears to run in both directions (1993: 270).

5 Schools and schoolyards

The associational impact on political engagement

Jan W. van Deth

5.1 Introduction

Ever since Pericles delivered his famous funeral speech in the winter of 431–430 BC, the necessity of political engagement for the quality and stability of democracy has been stressed. For instance, Benjamin Barber (1984, 1995) argued strongly for a much more 'participatory' democracy, as an alternative for liberal 'thin democracy' or 'politics as zookeeping'. In this view, engagement in politics is not to be considered an optional activity, but as an integral part of social life and essential for every citizen. Debates hardly deal with the necessity of engagement as such, but focus directly on the question how much engagement is required for a vital democratic society. Or to put it even more strongly, and to reverse the argument: 'The thing called 'apathy' is democracy's version of original sin' (Minogue 1999: 8). Citizens' engagement, then, is a *condition sine qua non* for every democratic system.

Following the renaissance of Tocquevillean approaches in the 1990s, there has been widespread consensus that a revival of civic engagement (social capital, civil society) can compensate for many of the assumed deficiencies of modern democracies, including relatively low or decreasing levels of political engagement. While most voluntary associations[1] are not directly involved in political actions, they nevertheless function as 'schools for democracy'. Therefore, higher levels of engagement in voluntary associations will be matched by higher levels of political engagement. Although a positive relationship between both forms of engagement is – at least empirically – widely acknowledged, neo-Tocquevilleans too readily overlook rival interpretations. For instance, Theiss-Morse and Hibbing (2005: 227) warn against this tendency – 'Good citizens need to learn that democracy is messy, inefficient, and conflict-ridden. Voluntary associations do not teach these lessons' – while Armony (2004) goes further by speaking of 'The Dubious Link' when referring to the relationship between 'Civic engagement and democratization'. The degree of diversity and disagreement encountered in social contacts might be a strong disincentive to political engagement. As Huckfeldt and colleagues concluded: 'Political diversity within networks tends to reduce political interest without registering any effect on turnout' (Huckfeldt *et al.* 2001: 22). Furthermore, if social capital is accumulated, a more autonomous and resourceful citizen can be expected to be more inclined to rely on his or her own capacities to deal with the problems and challenges of everyday life.[2] Politics – as basically a collective affair with public outcomes – becomes less salient and turns out to be 'the politics of marginal issues' (Hardin 1999: 44). This also means that political engagement becomes less significant for individual citizens (van Deth 2000). Social and political engagement are not necessarily positively correlated.

In this chapter, the impact of membership in various voluntary associations on political interest will be analysed.[3] Special attention will be given first, to the question of whether active participation in voluntary associations has different consequences for interest in European politics as compared to interest in local, national and international politics. Since political engagement is only relevant in social contacts (when the participants speak about politics), a typology is created combining interest in European politics with the frequency of political discussions. The second question is whether organizational features of voluntary associations (size, formal structure, resources) are relevant for the development of political interest and willingness to take part in political discussions with others active in these organizations. Voluntary associations presumably function as Tocquevillean 'schools of democracy' where civic skills and competences are trained. By providing opportunities to meet people and to discuss all kind of topics, voluntary associations also offer a 'schoolyard' where political opinions are exchanged and tried out.

Debates regarding the consequences of associational engagement usually focus on individual features of participants or the perceptions of activists. Much less attention is paid to the *different opportunities provided by different organizations*. By analysing the combined impact of (i) individual features, (ii) the degree of engagement, and (iii) objective features of the specific associations concerned, the *organizational impact of voluntary activities on political interest and willingness to join political talks* can be assessed empirically. The main empirical basis for the analyses presented here is the Activists Study of the CID project in six communities (see Chapter 1 of this volume for information regarding the three parts of the CID project used).[4] By including the other parts of the CID project, the associational impact on interest in European politics and willingness to join discussions can be 'contextualized'; that is, the usual survey responses can be analysed by referring to objective features of specific organizational involvements.

5.2 Political interest in Europe

The early voting studies of the 1940s and 1950s depicted the average citizen as not being strongly interested in politics. More recent studies also highlight that the absolute levels of political involvement in most countries are rather low. On average, one out of every six European citizens frequently discusses politics with his or her friends, while every third citizen is completely unconcerned about politics (Inglehart 1970: 353–354; Topf 1995: 61; van Deth 1991: 204 and 1996:

386–387; van Deth and Elff 2004: 481). A second main conclusion from empirical research is that the level of political involvement clearly differs between various countries. We have the well-established democracies in North-western Europe that usually display high levels of interest, and younger democracies in Southern and Eastern Europe which tend to display less. Even if extensive statistical controls are implemented to neutralize compositional effects of crossnational variations, considerable differences can be observed in the levels of political involvement among citizens in various countries (van Deth and Elff 2004; van Deth 2008a).

Being engaged in voluntary associations usually is considered to have a positive impact on political interest.[5] Therefore, the simplest expectation to be tested empirically is that people engaged in voluntary associations show higher levels of political interest than citizens in general. This expectation should hold irrespective of the specific type of organization or the level of political interest in any given country. Furthermore, the object of political interest (local, national, international, European) should also be irrelevant. For an empirical test of these expectations, the CID data offer the following straightforward questions to measure political interest:

- In general, how interested in politics are you?
- People's interest sometimes varies across different areas of politics. How interested are you in each of the following areas? Local politics, national politics, European politics, and international politics.

For each of the five items mentioned, a four-point scale is offered to express the level of interest: very interested, fairly interested, not very interested, and not at all interested.

The mean scores for the various objects of political interest in various cities and countries are summarized in Figure 5.1. For each city, the average levels of interest among the activists in specific voluntary associations are represented by the (black) left-hand bars in the graphs. We know that this category of respondents is meaningfully involved in these organizations because they were selected by the organizations as being active members. In order to test our expectation of relatively high levels of political interest among organizational activists (the black bar in Figure 5.1), two additional groups of citizens from the population studies are also analysed: the socially actives from the population surveys who are active or volunteer in some voluntary association (the grey bar in Figure 5.1),[6] and the non-active respondents – i.e. citizens not involved in any associational activity (the white bar in Figure 5.1). On the basis of these data we can compute the levels of political interest among the socially actives and the nonactives. This information differs from the information about the activists in the CID Activists Study in two important ways: (i) the actual activities of socially actives are expressions of the respondents only and not based on information from the organization, and (ii) active citizens are drawn from the national samples, whereas organizational activists are from specific communities in each

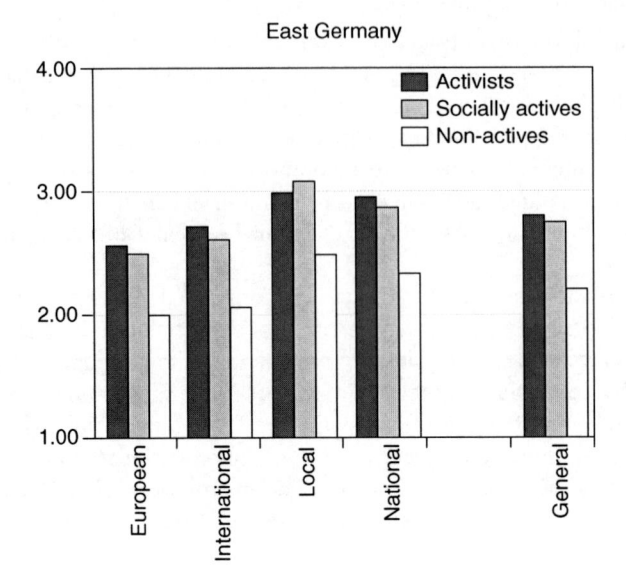

Figure 5.1a

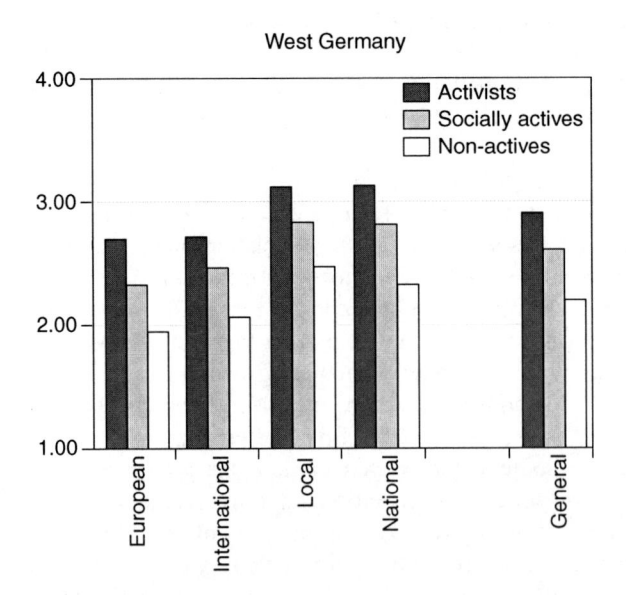

Figure 5.1b

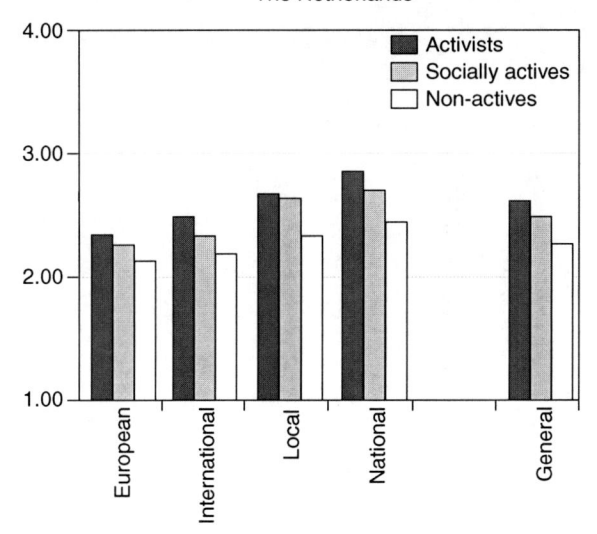

Figure 5.1c

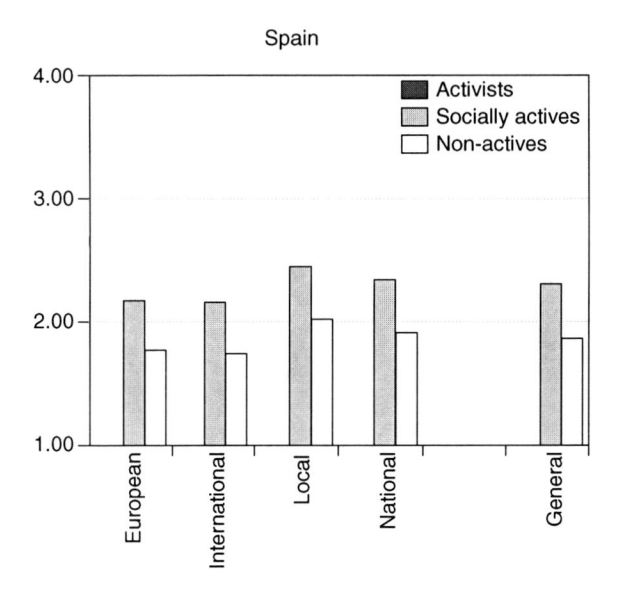

Figure 5.1d

continued

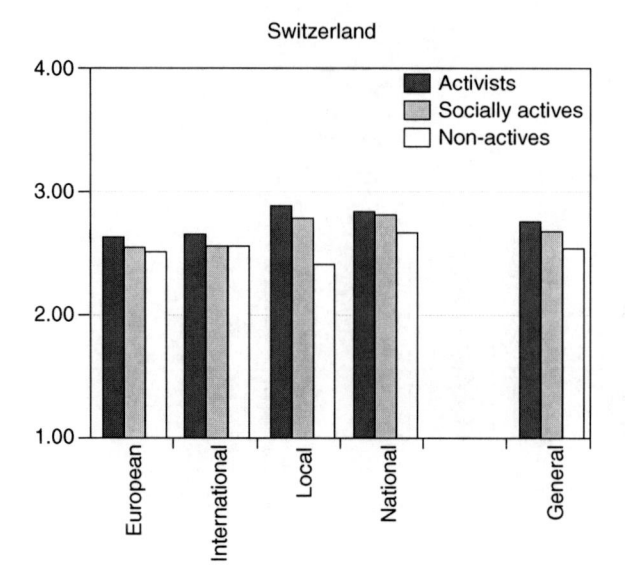

Figure 5.1e

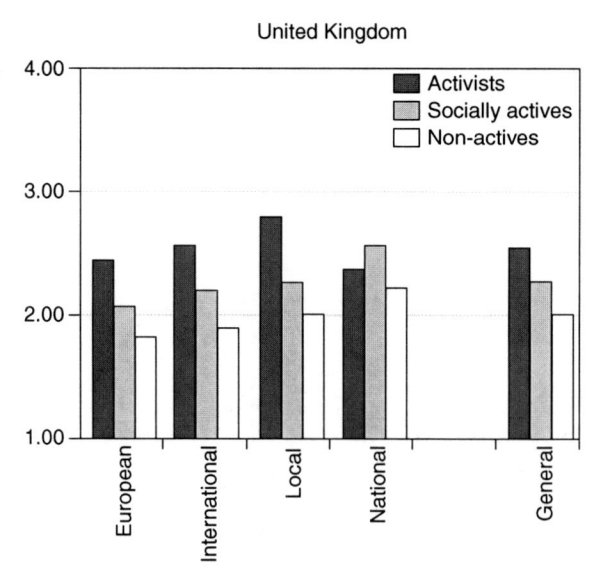

Figure 5.1f Political interest among activists, social actives and non-actives (averages).

country. The non-actives are added as the prime basis for comparisons: if involvement in voluntary association is accompanied by relatively high levels of political interest, then average levels should be higher among activists and socially actives than among the non-active parts of the populations. Since activists establish a 'hard core' of people engaged in voluntary associations, their average levels of political interest are probably higher than among socially active citizens.

Even from a cursory look at the results summarized in Figure 5.1 it is clear that activists and socially actives indeed show relatively high levels of political interest. With only two very minor exceptions (interest in local politics in East Germany, and interested in national politics in the UK), we find for each indicator in all six cities/countries that this expectation is corroborated. Furthermore, we see that the differences between activists and active citizens are also in the expected direction. For the five cities and countries for which we have data available,[7] the average levels of political interest are higher among activists than among active citizens. The effects of being active in some voluntary associations are especially clear in East and West Germany, Spain, and the UK, where the differences between the three groups compared are relatively large. Finally, the levels of interest in various objects or levels show a consistent pattern too, with local and national politics attracting the highest levels of interest in each city and country (with the UK exception already mentioned). European politics, on the other hand, is seen as the *least interested object everywhere*. This last result is remarkable, since the saliency of the European integration process and its consequences for citizens across Europe has increased considerably in the past decades. Yet European politics appears to be *even slightly less interesting* than international politics in all six cities/countries.[8]

Various authors have expressed their doubts about the existence of a positive relationship between social and political engagement (Theiss-Morse and Hibbing 2005; Armony 2004 or Eliasoph 1998). Furthermore, von Erlach (2005: 199) reported a negative correlation between active involvement in voluntary associations and interest in international politics. This scepticism is not supported by the empirical results presented here. In spite of the very different ways the activists were selected in each city, and the evident differences between the general levels of political interest in the five countries considered, *the average level of political interest among activists is (almost) always higher than among other groups*. Besides, both the activists and the socially active citizens show higher levels of political interest than can be found among the non-active parts of the populations of the six countries.

5.3 Interest in Europe and political discussions

The remarkably low levels of interest in European politics among organizational activists, active citizens and the populations do not necessarily establish a politically relevant factor. People can, of course, be stimulated to develop political orientations during their voluntary activities, and use these experiences in other contexts. For the associational impact on political orientations, the opportunities and challenges to be engaged in political discussions *offered within the associational context* seem to be very important.[9] If people frequently discuss politics with others, the likelihood of developing more articulated orientations increases. In addition to this, the question whether one is interested in specific political objects becomes much more intriguing when the frequency of political discussions is taken into account. For instance, an association where activists have little interest in Europe but regularly discuss political matters in general is unlikely to function as a 'school for European democracy'. The question, then, is how the level of interest in European politics and the frequency of political discussions are distributed among the voluntary associations in various cities and countries, and among different types of associations.

5.3.1 A typology of interest and discussion

In the CID project, the frequency of political discussions is measured by a straightforward question: How often would you say you discuss political matters with others? Often, sometimes, rarely, or never. In combination with the level of interest in European politics, a typology of engagement in European affairs can be constructed (see Figure 5.2).

This four-fold typology categorizes citizens according to their orientations towards politics, in particular towards European affairs. The most engaged citizens, who show both a high level of interest in European politics and discuss politics frequently, are labelled *Committed Multipliers*. These people are most likely to have an impact on the orientations of other people, because they will probably express their interest in discussions with others. The least involved citizens – those who are neither interested in Europe politics nor discuss politics – are labelled *Politically Unconcerned*. The impact of voluntary activities on the orientations of these individuals will be virtually non-existent. They do not engage in political discussions, and their lack of political interest will not be challenged. Those who have a high level of interest in European politics but rarely or never discuss politics are labelled *Silent Committers*. For this group, the consequences of voluntary activities are unclear, since their relatively high level of political interest is neither confirmed nor challenged in discussions with other people. Finally, individuals who frequently discuss politics but have a low level of interest in European politics are referred to as *Uncommitted Multipliers*. In the long run, they will probably benefit from the relatively high level of political interest among activists encountered in frequent political discussions. The distributions of these four types are summarized in Table 5.1.

In each city and country the largest group consists of the *Politically Unconcerned*. With the exception of the Swiss case, this group represents clear majorities among the total populations everywhere. Although not establishing a majority, the *Politically Unconcerned* is the largest group in Switzerland too. Among the activists, the picture is very different. In this group, the *Committed Multipliers* have a higher presence than those among the active and non-active

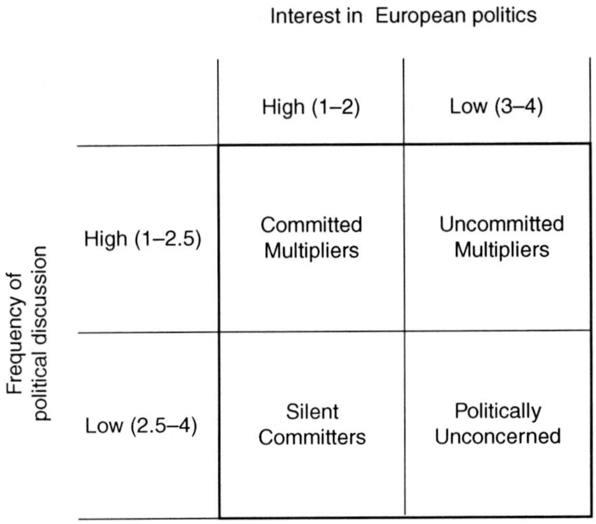

Interest in European politics

	High (1–2)	Low (3–4)
Frequency of political discussion High (1–2.5)	Committed Multipliers	Uncommitted Multipliers
Low (2.5–4)	Silent Committers	Politically Unconcerned

Figure 5.2 Typology of engagement in European affairs.

parts of the populations. In both parts of Germany and Switzerland we find large number of respondents belong to the *Committed Multiplier* category. In each city/country, the group sizes of the *Politically Unconcerned* are in the same order: largest among the non-active parts of the populations, smaller among socially actives, and smallest among activists. In a similar way, the *Committed Multipliers* are ordered consistently: smallest among the non-active parts of the populations, somewhat larger among active citizens, and largest among activists. Once again, we see that the relative positioning of the four groups is remarkably similar among activists, socially actives, and non-active parts of the populations, in spite of the huge cross-national differences in the distributions of the various groups. Apparently, the associational impact on engagement in European affairs is especially visible among activists.

5.3.2 Voluntary associations and engagement in European affairs

The relatively high levels of political interest and frequent discussions of activists and socially actives corroborate the general neo-Tocquevillean arguments. However, it is unlikely that each and every voluntary association will have a similar impact on the political orientations of their members. Previous empirical research draws a distinction between three broad types of organizations as being highly relevant for political involvement: sports/leisure-time associations, interest groups, and cultural organizations (Gabriel *et al.* 2002: 159–165). First, we examine the impact of various types of voluntary associations.

Voluntary associations are involved in numerous activities, concerns and tasks. In order to study different organizations systematically, a taxonomy of

Table 5.1 Distributions of types of people interested in European politics and engaging in political discussions (percentages)

	East Germany			West Germany			The Netherlands			Spain			Switzerland			United Kingdom		
	Non-actives	Socially actives	Activists	Non-actives	Socially actives	Activists	Non-actives	Socially actives	Activists	Non-actives	Socially actives	Activists	Non-actives	Socially actives	Activists	Non-actives	Socially actives	Activists
Committed Multipliers	12.5	29.8	45.3	9.1	22.0	47.6	15.6	21.6	29.3	6.4	18.6	n.a.	26.3	35.4	44.2	13.2	19.2	28.8
Uncommitted Multipliers	16.4	16.6	25.5	13.8	15.5	19.2	13.1	17.2	19.6	6.5	9.1	n.a.	12.7	17.4	13.4	13.3	18.7	14.8
Silent Committers	14.9	20.5	9.0	16.3	18.7	13.2	17.6	16.1	12.6	11.4	16.0	n.a.	24.6	17.8	16.8	10.3	12.2	21.8
Politically Unconcerned	56.2	33.2	20.2	60.8	43.8	20.0	53.8	45.2	38.5	75.7	56.4	n.a.	36.4	29.4	25.7	63.3	49.9	34.6
N	530	410	1,178	826	1,117	1,691	636	983	413	2,777	1,382	n.a.	552	873	853	2,154	937	749

different organizations is developed based upon the major issue concerns of each organization.¹⁰ Apparently, associational life in various cities is similarly structured. In order to deal with 'real world' peculiarities, several additions to the taxonomy appear to be necessary. The most important extension of the taxonomy concerns religion, which was included for its omnipresence and its importance within civil society. The final composition of the taxonomy used here represents the fuzzy empirical 'real world', and includes the following 11 categories:

1 Family
2 Sports
3 Culture
4 Community concerns
5 Politics
6 'New' politics
7 General welfare
8 Group-specific welfare
9 Economic interest
10 Religion
11 Other concerns

The relative numbers of *Committed Multipliers* among the activists and active citizens in these 11 types of voluntary associations are shown in Figure 5.3. In general, we find that the *Committed Multipliers* are much more clearly represented among the activists than among the active citizens – a finding that once again confirms the different levels of engagement in voluntary associations among distinct parts of the populations. More interesting, however, are the differences between the various types of organizations. The picture is very similar in each city/country in spite of the evident differences in the distributions of the four types of respondents distinguished (see Table 5.1). It is no surprise that *Committed Multipliers* are most prevalent among activists in associations concerned with political and 'new' political themes. At least two-thirds of the activists in political organizations appears to belong to this type! Since we are dealing with local associations, this widespread interest in European politics is remarkable. At the other end of the x-axes, we evidently find a-political associations in areas such as family affairs and sports. Due to the fact that the levels of *Committed Multipliers* do not differ greatly among voluntary associations at the right-hand side of the graphs, it is difficult to attribute much significance to the rank order of the various types of associations.

Broadly speaking, we see that *Committed Multipliers* (i) are strongly represented in political organization and interest groups (politics, 'new' politics, group-specific welfare, economic interest groups), (ii) somewhat less represented in public associations (welfare, culture), and (iii) clearly less visible in apolitical associations (sports, family). The fact that activists in political associations and interest groups have relatively high levels of political interest and willingness to

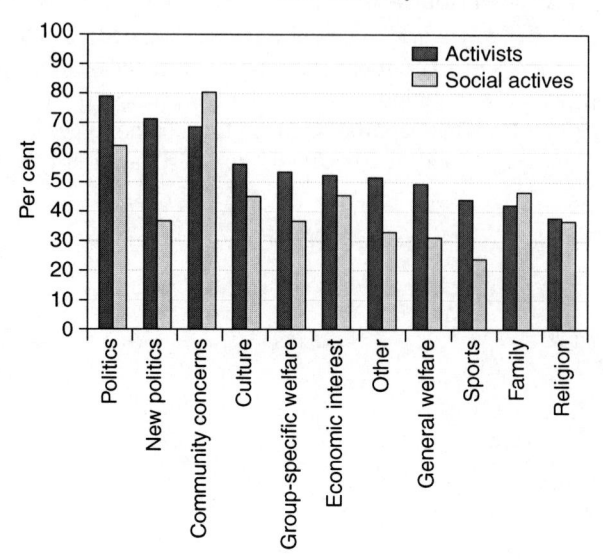

Figure 5.3a

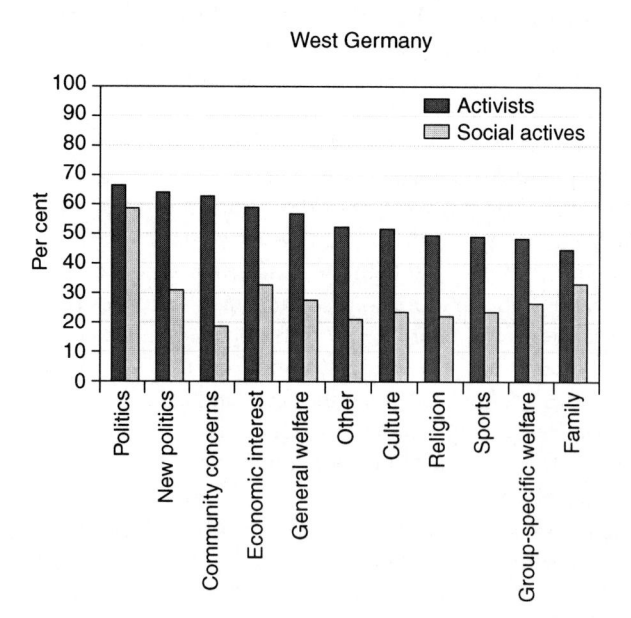

Figure 5.3b

The Netherlands

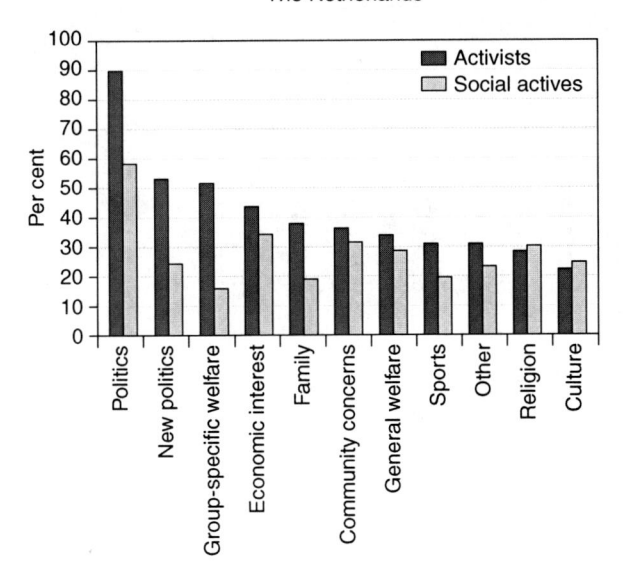

Figure 5.3c

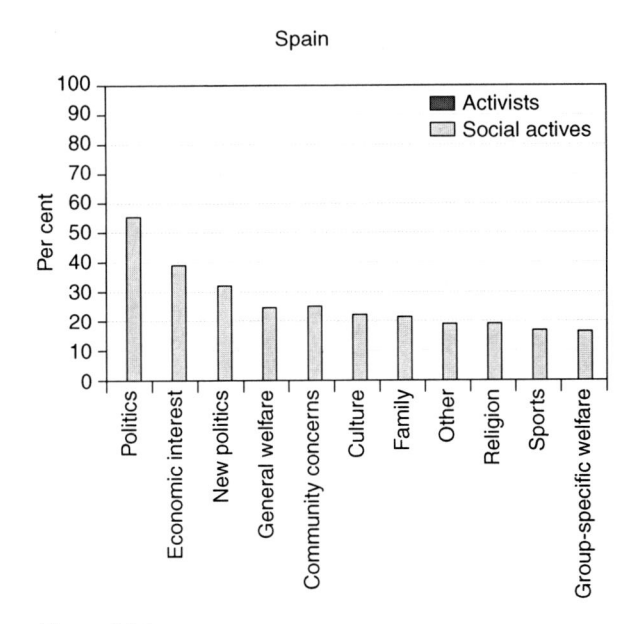

Spain

Figure 5.3d

continued

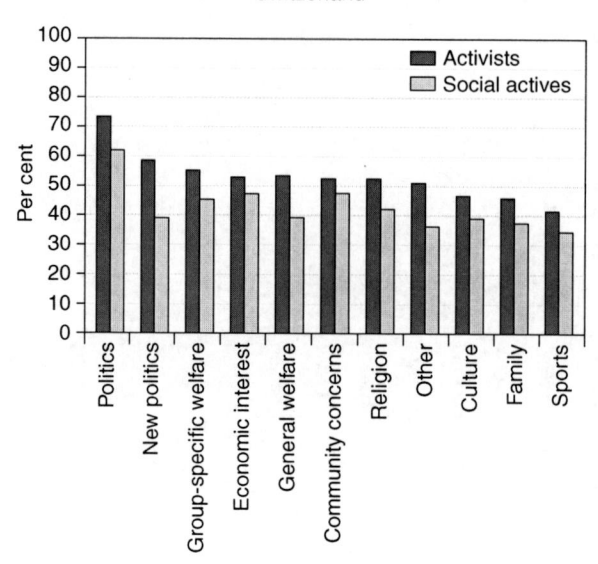

Figure 5.3e

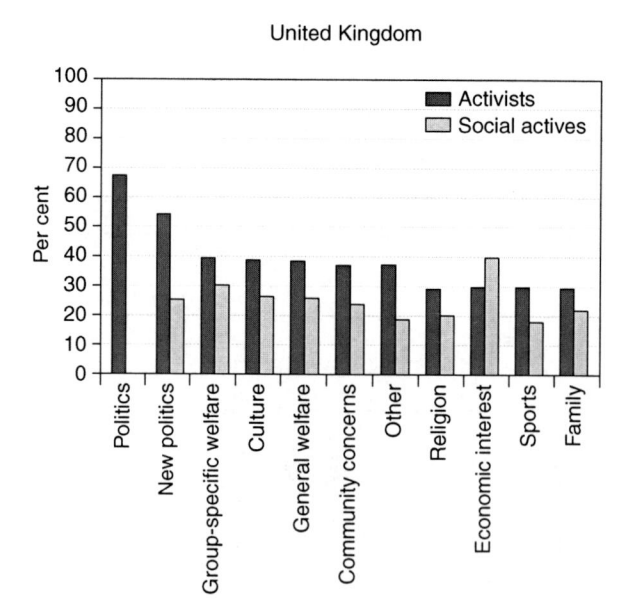

Figure 5.3f Distributions of *Committed Multipliers* in various types of associations (percentages).

join political talks is unsurprising. Nevertheless, a consistent pattern is found among very different associations in very different European cities and countries in spite of very large cross-national differences in the average levels of *Committed Multipliers* detected.

5.4 Contextualizing engagement in European affairs

In general, being active in a voluntary association is accompanied by relatively high levels of political interest and frequent discussions about politics. Yet this associational impact clearly differs between different types of associations. How should we account for these differences? On the one hand, *individual characteristics* seem to be relevant. Sports clubs mainly attract younger parts of the population, who are usually less interested in politics than older people are. Alternatively, differences between the opportunities for social engagement might vary between voluntary associations. Rotary and Lions clubs probably offer more opportunities for social engagement than do economic interest groups. Accurately assessing the impact of opportunities for engagement in voluntary associations requires drawing a distinction between the *actual engagement of individual activists* (intensity, duration, commitment of the activities, etc.) and the *associational context* (size of the organization, resources available, etc.). Information about these three distinct antecedents of associational impact is available in the CID Activists Study. Accordingly, the analyses are restricted to activists only. Multivariate analyses are carried out to estimate the relative impact of associational features, the nature of engagement in these organizations, and the individual characteristics on the likelihood of an activist belonging to one of the four engagement categories.

The results of an empirical search for the relative impact of associational features, engagement and individual characteristics are presented in Table 5.2. In the four parts of this table (5.2a–d), the likelihoods of becoming a *Committed Multiplier, Uncommitted Multiplier, Silent Committer* or *Politically Unconcerned* are compared. Several indicators are introduced for each of the three main explanatory variables. The *nature of the voluntary activities* performed by the respondent is indicated by the actual involvement (level of activities, time spent working for this organization), the degree of commitment reported, and the duration of the involvement in the activities of this organization. Furthermore, two attitudinal factors are added, indicating the importance the respondent attaches to clubs and voluntary associations in general and to the particular organization he or she is engaged in. Finally, the breath of engagement in voluntary associations is indicated by an additive index for the number of different types of organizational involvements.[11] Instead of constructing some general (latent) indicator for the concept 'associational engagement' or assessing the validity of each indicator separately, these seven indicators are introduced independently in the models. In this way, the empirical relevance of distinct aspects of associational engagement can be explored. A similar strategy is applied for the two remaining blocks of explanatory variables. *Associational features* are measured with indicators for the organizational size (number of members) and for the dependency on members' financial support (share of membership fees among budget). In addition, the degree of formalization of the association is measured by an additive index for a number of formal organizational aspects (written constitution, board of directors, treasurer, general assembly, etc.). A rather different indicator concludes this block. In order to explore the impact of the political character of the relevant association, an additive index is constructed for the organization's various political contacts.[12] For this set of organizational factors, too, no latent structure is explored. Instead, the various factors are included in the models in order to obtain information on the empirical relevance of the distinct organizational features. Finally, several indicators for *individual characteristics* are selected, which include general socio-demographic aspects (age, gender, education[13]) as well as a number of political orientations which might be related to the level of engagement in European affairs (satisfaction and trust; ideology, attachment to and confidence in Europe). The various blocks are included in the models stepwise, and the variance explained is computed for each block separately and for the complete models.

Although the specific coefficients vary, the overall picture of Table 5.2 is consistent. First, with the clear exception of the Dutch estimates, the models are not very successful in estimating the probability of being an *Uncommitted Multiplier* or a *Silent Committer*: the explained variances for these two mixed types are relatively low, and virtually no statistically significant coefficients are detected. More remarkable, however, is the fact that almost none of the factors indicating the (objective) features of the associations appear to have an impact on engagement in European affairs. The explained variances of the four indicators combined are generally low, and of the total of 80 coefficients no more than five reach an acceptable level of statistical significance (and these coefficients are not systematically distributed). The first conclusion, then, is that associational features are unexpectedly irrelevant – having no impact on citizens' interest in European politics or the frequency of political discussions.

A second conclusion is based on the impact of the various factors related to the associational engagement of the activists. Once again, the results indicate that these factors are largely irrelevant. Although the level of variances explained for this block is somewhat better than obtained for the associational features, only 17 out of 140 coefficients are statistically significant. For the two most interesting types – *Committed Multipliers* and *Politically Unconcerned* – the impact is clearly related to one factor only: the breath of associational activity. This means that individuals active in a number of different associations tend to be *Committed Multipliers*, whereas those with a narrower scope of engagement are much more likely to belong to the *Politically Unconcerned*. On the other hand, features of associational engagement (such as the level of activity or time spent on organizational tasks) have almost no relevance. Apparently, it is not the character or the degree of associational engagement that matters for political orientations of activists, but the number of organizational involvements. Thus, it is not associational activities per se that are relevant for the degree of engagement

Table 5.2a Antecedents of Committed Multipliers (activists only) (binary logistic regression; Nagelkerke R^2)

		East Germany		West Germany		The Netherlands		Switzerland		United Kingdom	
		Exp(b)	R^2	Exp(b)	R^2	Exp(b)	R^2	Exp(b)	R^2	Exp(b)	R^2
Associational engagement	Level of activity	0.82	0.12	0.89	0.09	0.81	0.12	1.00	0.10	1.01	0.09
	Time of participating	0.83		0.93		0.93		0.84		1.03	
	Commitment	1.32		0.70*		0.58		1.36		1.18	
	Duration of membership	1.00		1.00		1.01		0.99		0.99	
	Importance of clubs	1.00		1.04		0.95		0.92*		1.12	
	Importance of own org.	1.03		0.91		1.39		1.04		0.98	
	Breadth of engagement	1.14***		1.07***		1.11*		1.07**		1.09*	
Associational features	Number of active members	0.91	0.01	0.98	0.00	0.83	0.01	0.96	0.03	1.02	0.02
	Membership fees/budget	1.00		1.00		1.00		1.00		1.01	
	Degree of formalization	1.01		1.02		1.41		0.86		1.02	
	Political contacts	1.09		1.08		1.29		1.27**		1.22	
Individual features	Age	1.04***	0.06	1.02***	0.05	1.00	0.10	1.02	0.03	1.00	0.01
	Gender	1.33		0.83		1.15		1.66*		0.88	
	Education (tertiary)	1.27		1.48*		6.13***		1.48		0.76	
	Satisfied with democracy	1.29	0.03	1.39*	0.02	1.12	0.04	0.96	0.02	0.79	0.02
	Trust	0.90		1.02		0.90		1.05		1.08	
	Left–right placement	0.84**		0.96		0.77*		0.91		0.88	
	Attachment to Europe	1.26***	0.06	1.19***	0.04	1.65***	0.14	1.13*	0.04	1.17*	0.04
	Confidence in EU	0.99		1.03		1.11		1.11		0.99	
Nagelkerke R^2			0.28		0.20		0.41		0.22		0.18
N		444		691		223		452		251	

Table 5.2b Antecedents of Uncommitted Multipliers (activists only) (binary logistic regression; Nagelkerke R²)

		East Germany		West Germany		The Netherlands		Switzerland		United Kingdom	
		Exp(b)	R²	Exp(b)	R²	Exp(b)	R²	Exp(b)	R²	Exp(b)	R²
Associational engagement	Level of activity	1.07	0.04	1.03	0.02	0.52*	0.01	0.95	0.03	0.46*	0.08
	Time of participating	1.07		0.98		1.33		0.84		1.11	
	Commitment	0.79		1.33		1.65		0.81		0.39	
	Duration of membership	1.02		1.00		0.96		1.03		0.99	
	Importance of clubs	1.02		0.97		0.90		1.07		1.01	
	Importance of own organization	0.99		1.06		1.18		1.02		1.11	
	Breadth of engagement	0.95		1.02		1.02		1.00		1.10	
Associational features	Number of active members	1.07	0.01	0.93	0.01	0.96	0.10	1.14	0.02	1.32	0.09
	Membership fees/budget	1.00		1.01		1.01		1.00		1.01	
	Degree of formalization	0.87		0.98		0.92		1.11		0.60**	
	Political contacts	0.99		1.00		1.07		1.01		1.41	
Individual features	Age	1.00	0.00	1.00	0.00	1.02	0.06	0.98	0.01	1.00	0.02
	Gender	0.95		0.97		0.22***		0.63		0.49	
	Education (tertiary)	1.07		0.96		0.50		0.89		0.82	
	Satisfied with democracy	1.31	0.01	0.73	0.02	2.71*	0.02	0.62	0.02	0.77	0.02
	Trust	1.09		0.99		1.03		1.09		1.05	
	Left–right placement	0.97		1.07		0.90		1.14		0.84	
	Attachment to Europe	0.90*	0.05	0.92	0.02	0.65***	0.11	0.89	0.02	0.87	0.01
	Confidence in EU	0.87*		0.92		0.99		1.00		0.98	
Nagelkerke R²			0.11		0.07		0.30		0.10		0.22
N		444		691		223		452		251	

Table 3.2c Antecedents of Silent Committers (activists only) (binary logistic regression; Nagelkerke R^2)

		East Germany		West Germany		The Netherlands		Switzerland		United Kingdom	
		Exp(b)	R^2	Exp(b)	R^2	Exp(b)	R^2	Exp(b)	R^2	Exp(b)	R^2
Associational engagement	Level of activity	1.73	0.01	1.21	0.03	4.61*	0.13	1.13	0.03	1.09	0.04
	Time of participating	1.02		1.25		1.59		0.97		0.91	
	Commitment	1.34		0.76		0.44		1.18		1.37	
	Duration of membership	1.00		1.01		1.04		0.98		1.02	
	Importance of clubs	1.00		0.96		1.14		1.04		1.01	
	Importance of own org.	1.04		0.89		0.45*		0.99		0.93	
	Breadth of engagement	0.86**		0.96		1.14		1.00		0.91*	
Associational features	Number of active members	0.87	0.00	1.02	0.01	1.73	0.03	.98	0.01	0.80*	0.07
	Membership fees/budget	1.01		1.00		0.98		1.00		0.99	
	Degree of formalization	1.13		0.94		0.68		1.14		1.53**	
	Political contacts	1.05		0.90		1.41		0.95		0.85	
Individual features	Age	0.98	0.08	1.00	0.02	0.96	0.06	1.00	0.00	1.01	0.04
	Gender	1.07		1.95*		5.37		1.00		1.68	
	Education (tertiary)	1.38		1.10		0.63		0.65		2.03*	
	Satisfied with democracy	0.65	0.00	0.74	0.01	1.83	0.12	1.32	0.02	1.38	0.01
	Trust	1.01		0.90		1.03		0.91		1.01	
	Left-right placement	0.97		0.91		1.83**		0.98		1.10	
	Attachment to Europe	0.98	0.03	1.10	0.02	1.43*	0.04	1.12	0.02	0.96	0.01
	Confidence in EU	1.25*		1.16*		1.03		1.08		1.10	
Nagelkerke R^2			0.12		0.09		0.38		0.08		0.17
N		444		691		223		452		251	

Table 5.2d Antecedents of Politically Unconcerned (activists only) (binary logistic regression; Nagelkerke R^2)

		East Germany		West Germany		The Netherlands		Switzerland		United Kingdom	
		Exp(b)	R^2	Exp(b)	R^2	Exp(b)	R^2	Exp(b)	R^2	Exp(b)	R^2
Associational engagement	Level of activity	0.88	0.08	0.96	0.10	1.23	0.21	0.92	0.14	1.29	0.08
	Time of participating	1.15		0.99		0.67*		1.39*		0.95	
	Commitment	0.81		1.42		1.57		0.69		0.87	
	Duration of membership	0.98		1.00		1.01		1.00		1.00	
	Importance of clubs	0.94		1.00		1.05		1.03		0.89*	
	Importance of own org.	0.97		1.14		0.87		0.96		1.03	
	Breadth of engagement	0.95		0.90***		0.81***		0.91***		0.95	
Associational features	Number of active members	1.14	0.03	1.11	0.00	1.17	0.02	1.01	0.04	1.06	0.03
	Membership fees/budget	1.00		1.00		0.99		0.99		1.00	
	Degree of formalization	1.06		1.04		0.96		1.01		0.95	
	Political contacts	0.80		0.96		0.68*		0.73***		0.76	
Individual features	Age	0.97***	0.09	0.97***	0.08	0.99	0.05	0.99	0.01	1.00	0.01
	Gender	0.62		0.74		1.18		0.71		0.87	
	Education (tertiary)	0.55*		0.49**		0.34**		0.91		0.80	
	Satisfied with democracy	0.67	0.06	1.05	0.00	0.45*	0.05	1.18	0.01	1.16	0.03
	Trust	1.00		1.07		1.06		0.95		0.93	
	Left–right placement	1.32***		1.06		1.14		1.08		1.12	
	Attachment to Europe	0.85*	0.02	0.82***	0.06	0.83*	0.03	0.85**	0.09	0.91	0.01
	Confidence in EU	1.04		0.93		1.02		0.83**		0.94	
Nagelkerke R^2			0.28		0.24		0.36		0.29		0.16
N		444		691		223		452		251	

in European affairs, but individual involvement in voluntary associations in general.

The conclusion about the relevance of individual features is corroborated if we look at the results for the last block of factors in Table 5.2: the largest contribution to the explanations is provided by the socio-demographic variables – most notably age and educational attainment. *Committed Multipliers* are more prevalent among older than among younger people in Germany (Exp(b) 1.04 and 1.02 in both parts of Germany). Much stronger, however, is the positive impact of education on the chances to belong to this category in the Netherlands (Exp(b) 6.13). The reverse applies to the chances of being *Politically Unconcerned*, which appear to be clearly higher among younger Germans and among less-educated Dutch activists. (Exp(b) 0.97 and 0.34 respectively). Furthermore, for both groups attachment to Europe is unsurprisingly important: those more attached to Europe are more likely to be *Committed Multipliers*. After more than half a century of empirical research on political interest, these findings come as no surprise. What is remarkable, however, is the fact that *these factors remain highly relevant after the specific nature of the associational involvement of the respondent and the objective features of the specific organizations are taken into account*. Although virtually no coefficients smaller than 1.0 for the various aspects of associational involvement and associational features are reported, the general findings presented in Table 5.2 do not provide much support for the neo-Tocquevillean expectation of independent impacts of associational involvement or associational features on the political orientations of citizens. Irrespective of the nature of the activities or the type of association, being active in voluntary associations has little impact on citizens' orientations towards Europe.

5.5 Conclusion: associations as 'schoolyards for democracy'

In this chapter, the impact of membership in various voluntary associations on engagement with European affairs has been analysed by focusing on two questions. First, does active participation in voluntary associations have different consequences for interest in European politics as compared to interest in local, national, and international politics? Second, do organizational features have any effect on activists' level of interest or engagement with European affairs? By analysing the combined effects of associational engagement, associational features and individual characteristics, the organizational impact of voluntary activities on engagement in European affairs has been assessed empirically.

From a comparison of information obtained from activists, active citizens, and the total populations in East and West Germany, the Netherlands, Spain, Switzerland and the UK, it is clear that large cross-national differences in political interest still exist. These differences, however, do not militate against the emergence of a very consistent pattern of interest among the three groups considered here: the level of political interest is clearly highest among activists, somewhat lower among socially active citizens, and lowest among the non-active parts of the populations. Furthermore, interest in European politics is lower than interest in any other political object in the six cities/countries analysed. Combining these results with information about the frequency of discussing politics, we see that people who are interested in European politics and who are frequently involved in political discussions (*Committed Multipliers*) are more likely to be among activists than socially actives or non-active citizens. These findings all support the expectation that activities in voluntary associations can contribute considerably to the development and spread of civic orientations.

The general conclusion about the relevance of active engagement in voluntary associations, however, does not provide much insight into the specific factors accounting for this effect. In order to explore the possible alternative factors, engagement in European affairs in various types of organizations was analysed. Once more, previous findings were confirmed. Although voluntary associations in general have a positive impact on political interest and willingness to discuss political matters among their activists, political organizations and interest groups have the highest numbers of *Committed Multipliers*, whereas activists in welfare and culture organizations – especially sports and family organizations – are much less likely to be so politically enthusiastic. These rather trivial results are not remarkable, yet the consistent pattern found among very different associations in very different European cities and countries is surprising.

Finally, the relative impact of associational engagement, associational features, and individual characteristics of activists belonging to one of the four types of engagement categories was assessed empirically. By using the unique combination of information provided by the various parts of the CID project, a 'contextualization' of voluntary activities could be carried out. The results of these analyses show that individual factors (age and education, but also the breath of voluntary associational engagement of the respondent) are the most important determinants. When the individual characteristics of activists are taken into account, neither the nature of voluntary activity nor objective organizational features appear to be very relevant for engagement in European affairs. Differences in the impact of various associations on the average levels of political interest as reported in the first part of this chapter, then, should not be overestimated. The associational impact on European engagement seems to be mainly due to the fact that activists are relatively old, highly educated, and active in several different voluntary associations.

Voluntary associations, especially those that are unambiguously involved in political affairs, have activists with clearly higher levels of political interest and willingness to join political talks than is found among active citizens or the non-active parts of the population. Yet the associational impact is not as evident as those findings suggest. Although voluntary associations offer opportunities to develop civic skills and competences as the Tocquevillean metaphor of the 'schools of democracy' suggests, these opportunities appear to be selectively used by somewhat older, highly educated activists engaged in various types of organizations. For many activists, however, voluntary associations are not training institutes for civic skills and competences. By providing opportunities to discuss politics, these organizations seems to function more as 'schoolyards of democracy' rather than as Tocquevillean 'schools of democracy'. In these 'schoolyards' people meet other people and they use the opportunity to discuss politics and to try out specific opinions frequently. For a vital democracy, a lively 'schoolyard' provided by voluntary associations seems to be more important than the 'civic curricula' presumably offered by these organizations.

Notes

1 The terms 'associations', 'organizations' and 'clubs' are used synonymously.
2 For that reason 'social trust is the prerogative of the winners in the world' (Newton 1999b: 185).
3 I am grateful to Christian Schnaudt for his assistance with the preparation of the data and the empirical analyses presented here.
4 See the introduction to this volume for acknowledgements to the principal investigators and funding agencies for these studies.
5 For overviews of the extensive literature in this area, see van Deth (1997, 2008a).
6 Active citizens are those respondents in the population surveys who explicitly indicated that they 'participate in activities' and/or 'do voluntary work' in at least one of the 27 types of associations presented. By excluding passive members who are members only or donate money from this group, the active citizens selected are, in principle, similar to the activists interviewed in the local surveys.
7 For unknown reasons, the questions on political interest were not included in the Spanish CID Activists Study.
8 Given that our activists are all from local associations, it is not surprising that interest in local (and national) politics is relatively high. For these citizens, local and national policy-making will be more visible and have greater relevance than European politics has (van Deth and Maloney 2008).
9 Haug (2008: 5) distinguishes 'three levels of the public sphere' for social movements. Discussing politics belongs to 'Encounters', and requires only a 'low' degree of organization.
10 For a full description of the methodology and empirical results, see Roßteutscher and van Deth (2002). Because of the strong emphasis on non-political bodies in debates on the impact of associational activities, no a priori distinction between political and non-political bodies is used here. For an overview of the various arguments for such a distinction, see Morales (2004: 93–109).
11 This index is constructed by counting the number of different types of association the respondent is engaged in (being a member, volunteering, contributing money, etc.).
12 For this index, the responses to the four items include in the organizational questionnaire of the CID project (contact local officials, city council, local parliament, local political parties) have been dichotomized (contact/no contact) in a first step. The sum of these scores is used as an indicator for the political character of the association. For the UK, only three indicators are available.
13 Due to the complications of comparing levels of education cross-nationally, a dichotomy is used here between people reaching tertiary levels of education and those who did not reach that level.

6 Civil society organizations as 'little democracies'?

Patrick Bernhagen and William A. Maloney

6.1 Introduction

European and other advanced democracies appear to be suffering from a democratic squeeze. Voter turnout, partisan identification, party membership, and trust in politicians and government – all crucial to a healthy, functioning democracy – are declining (Mair 2006). Simultaneously, there has been a rise in supporter-based, memberless groups – that is, of tertiary associations or *protest businesses* – and more individualized participation (Jordan and Maloney 1997; Putnam 2000; Pattie *et al.* 2004). Against this backdrop, many political administrations, politicians, advocates of participatory democracy, and social capital enthusiasts have sought to find solutions to these democratic challenges. For example, the Commission of the European Union (EU) is aiming to tackle what it sees as a *democratic deficit* by encouraging a more meaningful political engagement of civil society in its attempt at 'bringing the institutions closer to citizens' (Commission of the European Communities 2004: 3). The contemporary democratic tenet is that '[u]nless citizens participate in the deliberation of public policy, and their choices structure government action, then democratic processes are meaningless' (Dalton 2008: 78).

While this view highlights the substantial benefits delivered by a vibrant associational universe, critics have voiced concerns about the lack of representativeness and accountability within many civil society organizations (Warleigh 2001; Jordan and Maloney 2007; Saurugger 2007). Indeed, high levels of non-democratic participation by unrepresentative groups can be seen as part of the 'dark side' of social capital formation (Fiorina 1999). Conversely, the democratic pathology of a lack of legitimacy associated with voluntary action may be partly alleviated if the voluntary activity is itself organized in a democratic fashion. This puts the degree of democracy *within* voluntary associations in the spotlight. It has been argued that in order to address the EU's democratic deficit, civil society organizations should be democratically wholesome and practise 'the principles of good governance' – that is, be open, accountable and responsive (Michalowitz 2004: 152). If groups are to contribute not only as intermediary associations, but also as participatory vehicles and even as Tocquevillian 'schools of democracy', it is possible that *internally democratic* groups make a bigger contribution to a democratic civic culture than groups that are not formally or practically democratic. It is this possibility that we explore in this chapter.

Many organizations that are commonly and unambiguously classified as civil society organizations are organized according to hierarchical business principles aimed at maximizing the efficiency of operations (Jordan and Maloney 1997, 2007). Research conducted by Warleigh (2001), Sudbery (2003), Michalowitz (2004) and Saurugger (2007, 2009) found many European NGOs lacking in terms of their internal democratic procedures. Moreover, it is not necessarily the case that internal democracy thrives in organizations where formal democratic procedures are institutionalized. Many organizations hold elections for office holders and have Annual General Meetings, but often only a miniscule proportion of the membership attend these gatherings.

A lack of internal democracy has at least three possible implications. First, it may undermine the legitimacy claims of supporter- or membership-based organizations that justify their involvement in public policy deliberations. Second, it may reduce the accountability and responsiveness of group leaders to their members. Third, it could diminish the ability of civil society groups to generate more and better democratic citizens. While the questions of legitimacy and accountability have been analysed elsewhere (Michalowitz 2004; Cram 2006), there is a lack of empirical research assessing the actual impact of groups' democratic procedures and practices – their constitutions and participatory opportunities – on the political behaviour of members. Civil society organizations can be characterized as 'little democracies' or 'venues of very little democracy' (Jordan and Maloney 2007: 26). This chapter seeks to assess the extent to which the difference between these two types matters for the democratic contribution of civil society.

The key question driving our analyses is: what impact does a vibrant intra-organizational democracy, or its absence, have on public-spiritedness and political participation? To address this question, we will first elaborate the role that internal organizational democracy plays for the ability of civil society organizations to perform as effective 'schools of democracy' according to the extant literature. We then outline our strategy for detecting the effects of democratic organizational features on the ability of associations to produce desirable outcomes in the area of democratic political participation. This leads us first to test the role that internal democracy plays for members' public-spiritedness and political participation directly. Second, we will investigate how internal democracy interacts with other factors that may affect the extent to which civil society engagement has desirable effects on members' public-spiritedness and political participation. These concern the length of membership and the intensity of participation, where intensity refers to the degree to which members engage actively in the running of their organization as reflected in office-bearing positions or time devoted to organizational involvement. After outlining our empirical strategy and how we measure democratic spirit, participation and intra-organizational democracy, we present the results of our empirical analysis. We conclude with a discussion of our findings on the role of democratic organizations in the light of the literature on civic engagement and the contribution of civil society to the democratic legitimacy of the European polity.

6.2 Schools of democracy

The argument that voluntary associational engagement serves to develop democratic beliefs and behaviour has been well rehearsed in many papers, articles and books. As early as 1835, Alexis de Tocqueville ([1835] 1969: 514–515) argued that associations act as 'learning schools for democracy' through which citizens learn to become *better democrats*. They achieve this by cultivating members' communicative skills and sense of community. A century later, Arthur Schlesinger reinforced the link between democracy and associational engagement:

> Considering the central importance of the voluntary organization in American history there is no doubt it has provided people with their greatest school of self-government ... they have been trained in from youth to take common counsel, choose leaders, harmonize differences, and obey the expressed will of the majority. In mastering the associative way they must have mastered the democratic way.
>
> (Schlesinger 1944: 24)

This link between an active citizenry and democracy implies many positive outcomes and spillover effects – as well as some negative externalities. At its core is the civic-minded *good citizen*. Many studies have shown that members of voluntary associations are 'better democratic citizens' (Hibbing and Theiss-Morse 2002: 171), and that 'associational membership facilitates individuals' involvement in public affairs' (Kwak *et al.* 2004: 643–644). Almond and Verba's (1963) seminal work discovered that associational members were more politically active, better informed about politics, and supportive of democratic norms. More recently, Howard and Gilbert (2008: 13, 26) have concluded that 'our results provide general support for the Tocquevillian argument. On average those persons with greater levels of involvement in voluntary associations also engage in more political acts'. Kwak *et al.* (2004: 648) argue that 'various forms of social associations contribute to participation in collective action', which they argue is 'consistent with prior observations that non-political *formal* associations function as an important channel by which citizens' traditional involvement in politics is increased' (see also Rosenstone and Hansen 1993). Following de Tocqueville, Olsen (1972: 318) argued that social involvement has a direct and positive effect on political participation for three main reasons: first, citizens develop a much greater interest in politics and see political issues as increasingly important; second, citizens are likely to have contact with a wider and more varied range of people and these relationships may draw citizens towards political engagement; and third, it increases citizens' information levels and facilitates the development of the civic skills required for effective political action.

Thus, a vibrant civil society is seen as facilitating and encouraging a vibrant political society.

The causal argument connecting democratic participation with associational engagement proceeds broadly as follows. Through associational involvement, citizens learn how to participate in a tolerant, understanding and civil manner. They develop skills such as effective letter writing and oral presentation, responsible argumentation and debate, as well as a variety of organizational abilities related to office-bearing positions. Furthermore, involved citizens may display higher levels of trust, be more tolerant and behave less opportunistically than their uninvolved peers. All this makes them more likely to act in a community- and politically-orientated way – for example, by voting in elections, signing petitions, contacting elected representatives, taking part in demonstrations and strikes, or donating to charities and exhibiting higher levels of interest and knowledge about political issues.

Many of the democratic benefits of civic engagement are claimed to stem from associations' important deliberative functions. However, if these functions are to be effective, they have to be utilized by members in a broadly equal fashion. In other words, citizens' involvement in associations itself would have to be democratic. Accordingly, for associations to qualify as schools of democracy they should be internally democratic. Elected office holders should be responsive to the rank-and-file membership, and fully accountable for their activities, policies, strategies and tactics. In other words, members must have the ability to exercise *voice* in addition to *exit* and *loyalty* (Hirschman 1970). Indeed, for scholars from de Tocqueville ([1835] 1969) to Barber (1984) and Putnam (2000), democracy is an important organizational feature. The deliberative dimension of collective decision-making is, though, perhaps most central to John Stuart Mill's notion of democratic and discursive engagement as a school of public spirit:

> It is by political discussion that the manual labourer, whose employment is a routine, and whose way of life brings him in contact with no variety of impressions, circumstances, or ideas, is taught that remote causes, and events which take place far off, have a most sensible effect even on his personal interests; and it is from political discussion and collective political action that one whose daily occupations concentrate his interests in a small circle round himself, learns to feel for and with his fellow-citizens, and becomes consciously a member of a great community.
>
> (Mill [1861] 1977: 469)

As this brief scan of the literature suggests, the schools of democracy thesis generates high expectations of what democratic groups can deliver for democracy. Can associations furnish these demands? Does *democratic civil society* participation breed *more democratic political* participation? Do democratic organizations contribute more to the development of democratic attitudes, political participation and public-spiritedness than non-democratic organizations? The following section investigates theoretically how organizations' internal characteristics might matter for the consequences they have for democratic political beliefs and participation.

6.3 Analysing the role of internal democracy for civic-spiritedness and participation

The claim that organizational internal democracy has desirable effects is contestable. To begin with, not everyone accepts the notion that more participation means better democracy. Schumpeter (1950) and Huntington (1981) did not view widespread participation as universally beneficial. However, even if one accepts that extensive citizen involvement in politics is desirable, or even essential, it is unclear just how the democratic structures of voluntary associations enhance democracy. The main factors emphasized by social capital theory, for example, are voluntary participation and overlapping membership, followed by the length and intensity of individual involvement and face-to-face communicative interaction. Whether or not an organization is internally democratic may feature on the social capital checklist, but ranks below these items. Indeed, the ambiguous theoretical status of intra-organizational democracy resembles earlier disputes in the context of pluralist theories. While some argued that all that matters for democracy is competition between parties, rendering internal democracy as irrelevant for political parties as it would be for a department store (Wilson 1962), others insisted that internal democracy is a necessary requirement for political parties (Ware 1971).

The CID data contain the full organizational spectrum, from groups that demand very little of ordinary members beyond writing an occasional cheque, possibly with little or no internal democracy, to organizations that involve members in a variety of activities, often entailing communicative face-to-face interaction. It is, of course, the latter that theorists such as Putnam expect to provide democratically beneficial effects. Following Putnam (1993), we can further distinguish between the horizontal and vertical dimensions of organizational governance. For Putnam, the horizontal dimension of civic engagement is of central importance for the generation of social capital. However, organizations can provide intense horizontal interaction among members, while simultaneously lacking rudimentary democratic features. The Salvation Army is an organization that offers plenty of opportunities for direct involvement of members, but its governance structures preclude ordinary members from having any say in policy or organizational decisions. Alternatively, many trades unions are organized in a bottom-up grassroots fashion, in effect constituting 'mini-democracies' (Edwards 2003: 83–84) that thrive in proportion to the democratic participation of their 'citizens'. However, it is not necessarily the case that internal democracy delivers external democracy, and expectations about the effects of intra-organizational democracy differ widely.[1]

Just how, then, are internally democratic organizations supposed to affect individual democratic engagement outside the organization? The logic of the 'schools of democracy' claim suggests that when citizens join groups they can be characterized as *democratic freshers* (democratic neophytes). Over time – through lessons – they develop pro-democratic values. The causal mechanism seems simple: citizens join groups and, through involvement, become better democrats. However, one does not have to be a disciple of the rational choice approach to political analysis to share the view that political actors usually know more or less accurately what they want, and only then go about getting it. At least at the micro-level of theory, attitudes and values are largely exogenous and precede action – with only the latter part being usually considered amenable to investigation by social scientists. But the idea of organizations as schools of democracy goes a step further and endogenizes people's identities and preferences: schools are places where individual actors are transformed. This transformation has a crucial attitudinal dimension.

Unlike Pavlovian dogs, citizens do not react mechanically to the stimulus of organizational engagement by, for example, turning out more frequently at elections. Instead, there has to be a change in the actors' mindsets. The civic effects of associational engagement concern the development of *public mindedness* or *civic-spiritedness*. This in turn may lead to a greater disposition toward democratic political participation. In the literature, the attitudinal link between civic engagement and political participation is usually seen as the degree to which citizens trust each other and/or their political institutions (Putnam 1995; Inglehart 1999; Uslaner 2002). While we agree that generalized trust is an integral part of a democratic political culture, its benefits are not specific to democratic participation. Like societal wealth or the absence of physical violence, generalized trust is claimed to contribute to a whole host of social goals, encompassing individual well-being, collective action and macro-economic performance, alongside political participation (Hooghe and Stolle 2003: 1–2). By contrast, civic-spiritedness is an attitudinal trait specifically related to democratic political participation: if individuals think that voting in elections, for example, is a citizen's duty, they can be expected to vote in an election themselves, if only to put their money where their mouth is. The concept is also at the core of Putnam's account of social capital, who writes that 'associations instil in their members habits of cooperation, solidarity, and public spiritedness' (Putnam *et al.* 1993: 89–90). Thus, when analysing the effects of citizens' democratic associational engagement on their political participation, we have to pay attention to the extent to which a civic spirit is fostered through associational activism and membership. Consequently, any pre-existing level of democratic commitment and skills that citizens possess at the point of joining an organization should be enhanced further through participation in democratic associations. This suggests a first hypothesis:

> *H1*: Membership in internally democratic organizations has a larger positive effect on members' public-spiritedness and political participation than membership in non-democratic groups.

However, we should not rely on the presence of formally democratic institutions per se to bring about desired democratic attitudes. Actual practice may be much more important, as many formally democratic organizations suffer from participatory sclerosis, apathy, and oligarchic tendencies (Michels [1911] 1959). Thus:

> *H2*: Membership in organizations characterized by high levels of actual democratic participation has a stronger positive effect on public-spiritedness and political participation than membership in other organizations.

A rival argument claims that associations attract people that are already *democratic graduates* (democratic veterans). According to this logic, rather than serving as schools of democracy, associations may simply be repositories for citizens who already possess civic and pro-democratic values. On the demand side, democratic graduates are predisposed to membership of groups. On the supply side, organizations seek to recruit these individuals because they are the most likely to join and, where required, to make a significant contribution to organizational maintenance – for example, through activity, time and possibly financial support. As Armingeon (2007: 361) argues, associations are 'self-selective. They do not educate citizens. Rather, politically educated citizens tend to join organizations to a much stronger extent than citizens without much interest in, or knowledge about, politics.' Stolle and Howard (2008: 3) note that 'it is not entirely clear whether those who score high on civic values and attitudes are the ones who might join voluntary associations disproportionately'.

Thus, the relationship between associational involvement and the possession of pro-democratic values may be spurious. We control for this possibility by comparing democratic freshers (new members) with democratic graduates (veteran members). If associations perform an educative function then we should detect differences between these sets of participants, allowing inferences about the actual impact of the associational socialization process. The implication of this for the school of democracy thesis is that:

> *H3*: The length of membership in internally democratic organizations affects members' public-spiritedness and political participation more positively than equal length of membership in non-democratic groups.

While the length of membership may be an important factor in generating pro-democratic values and enhancing societal integration, the intensity and level of involvement might be even more important. It is possible to join an association and to remain a member for many years while remaining continuously passive or simply participating in group activities such as playing badminton, cricket, football or chess, or choral singing, without being involved in policy or organizational decisions. While *H3* implies that passive membership is subject to spillover effects flowing from the activities of more *organizationally* active members, the regular participants in the local sports club (i.e. the badminton, cricket or football players) might simply not develop the same skills or public spirit as office holders – i.e. those at the top of the 'school of democracy' class. However, it is possible that the intensity of a person's involvement in democratic groups will itself be a contributory factor in the generation of democratic participation outside the perimeters of the group. The more members insinuate themselves into group activities and the greater the level and intensity of their involvement, the more likely they are to develop the civic spirit and democratic skills that the Tocquevillian view of voluntary engagement implies. According to the logic of internal democracy, this effect should be even stronger in democratic organizations. Therefore:

H4: The intensity of members' participation in democratic organizations has a stronger positive effect on their public-spiritedness and political participation than equally intensive participation in non-democratic groups.

6.4 Data, measurement, and empirical strategy

To test our four hypotheses, we use the CID data on national populations, local organizations and their members. As outlined in Chapter 1, we compare *activists* (those respondents who have been surveyed as members of specific organizations), *socially actives* (those in the general population who are supporters or members of organizations) and *non-actives* – (those who eschew organizational involvement – i.e. who do not report involvement with any group). To gain an initial overview of the extent to which internal democracy can affect members' external political disposition and engagement, we compare levels of public-spiritedness and participation between members in internally democratic and internally non-democratic organizations. For those cases in which the excepted relationship survives this initial test, we proceed further to controlling for a host of other factors that may affect civic-spiritedness and political participation. To this end, we add our measures of intra-organizational democracy to standard models of political participation.

Our first task is to measure the democratic dispositions and behavioural characteristics of civic activists and members of the general populations in the six countries. For the attitudinal dimension of citizens' civic disposition, we use a composite scale of civic virtues measuring how highly respondents rank the importance of four types of behaviour for being 'a good citizen'. The items capture the deliberative, discursive and participatory ideals underpinning a classic enlightenment understanding of democracy. They include 'voting in public elections', 'forming one's own opinion independently of others', 'being active in organizations', and 'subjecting one's own opinions to critical examination'. All four items load highly (>0.60) on a single factor extracted by principal-component analysis. Citizens are assigned high civic-spiritedness if they score 6 or higher on the averaged scale ranging from 0 to 10. This is the case for only 6 per cent of the non-active population of East Germany, while 52 per cent of Dutch non-actives display high levels of civic spirit.

To capture the full spectrum of political behaviour, we focus on electoral and non-electoral activities. To measure electoral participation, respondents were asked whether they had voted in the most recent general election. The reported turnout among non-actives in the six countries ranges from 58 per cent in Switzerland to 83 per cent in Spain. For the non-electoral forms of political participation, respondents were asked if during the past 12 months they had 'attempted to bring about improvements, or to counteract deterioration in society' by taking part in a public demonstration, a strike or an illegal protest. Other measures of non-electoral political participation have been used in the literature, frequently including more types of political action. Howard and Gilbert (2008), for example, combine seven items (contacting a politician or a local government official; wearing or displaying a campaign badge or sticker; signing a petition; taking part in a lawful demonstration; boycotting certain products; deliberately buying certain products for political, ethical or environmental reasons; and participating in illegal protest activities) to measure non-electoral political action. We consider such a wide variety of items to be problematic. In terms of Hirschman's aforementioned classification of political opportunities, some of these activities (for example, boycotting certain products; deliberately buying certain products for political, ethical or environmental reasons) involve a private refusal to consume certain goods; these actions are primarily exit-oriented. Other actions, such as taking part in a demonstration, are aimed to promote political views to a larger audience, and are therefore voice-oriented. As activities these adhere to a different logic of political engagement, they may also be subject to different causal mechanisms. Our smaller set of action modes (taking part in a public demonstration, a strike or an illegal protest) encompasses classic protest activities that are extra-representational and voice-oriented (Teorell *et al.* 2007). The percentages of non-active citizens claiming to have taken part in, for example, a demonstration varies between 2 per cent in the Netherlands and 9 per cent in Spain.

Internal democracy is measured both *institutionally* and *behaviourally*. In institutional terms, the most basic tenet of democracy in an association is the presence of a general assembly where members can voice their opinions, vote on matters of common concern, and elect chairs, secretaries and treasurers. While assemblies are not a ubiquitous feature, they are very common throughout the European associational universe: 14 per cent of activists in East Germany are in organizations that have an assembly – a figure that rises to 92 per cent in Spain. This wide variation is partly related to different registration and legal requirements in the various European countries.

Of course, members' opportunities to participate are not restricted to attending assembly meetings, and the extent to which such meetings provide opportunities for genuine democratic involvement in the organization can vary widely. Another way of tapping internal democracy is to ask members about their perceptions of it. Specifically, members were asked about the opportunities they believed they had to influence the decisions made in their organization. The responses were aggregated at the level of the organization, and the resulting indicator for participation ranges from 0 for very little opportunities to 10 for significant opportunities. We deem an organization *institutionally democratic* if either it has an assembly or it scores above 5 on members' ratings of internal opportunities to participate, or both.

Even in organizations with democratic constitutions and procedures, actual internal democracy may be atrophied. In such cases, formally democratic organizations may not be so far from organizations that do not possess such constitutions and procedures. Therefore, the question of internal democracy is not simply about the opportunities for such involvement, but also about the take-up rate. Even where democratic participatory opportunities exist, members may for various reasons fail to make us of them. Conversely, it is possible that organizations that lack formal democratic features practise democracy in an informal manner (see Jordan and Maloney 2007; Maloney 2008). To gauge the actual level of member participation inside an organization, we averaged responses to a question asking how often members participate in decision-making at a meeting. The responses ranged from 1 for the least participatory to 4 for the most participatory. Organizations are deemed to be *behaviourally democratic* if they score at least 2. As we do not know which of these measures – institutional democracy or behavioural democracy – best captures internal democracy, we test our expectations about internal democracy using all three indicators.

The length of membership in civil society organizations is simply the number of years a person had been a member of the organization in question at the time of the survey. The intensity of an individual's organizational engagement is the average of the self-reported frequency with which they participate in decision-making at a meeting, plan or chair a meeting, prepare or give a speech before a meeting, or write a text other than a private letter and at least a few pages long. The responses on all four items range from 1 for the least participatory ('never or almost never') to 4 for the most participatory ('a few times a week'). Lastly, the ingredients of the standard model of political participation used in the multivariate analysis are control variables. Their measurement will be explained in footnotes as we introduce the standard model.

6.5 Analysis and results

We begin by exploring the bivariate relationship between political involvement and intra-organizational democracy in each of the six countries. The first two columns in Table 6.1 compare average levels of civic-spiritedness, voter turnout, and taking part in demonstrations, strikes and illegal protests for activists with socially active and non-active citizens. In all countries, civic-spiritedness, voting and demonstrating are considerably higher among the socially active than among the non-active. In Spain, taking part in strikes and illegal protests is also significantly higher among the socially active than the non-active, and to a lesser extent this applies to East Germany and Switzerland as well. In the case of civic-spiritedness, the difference is as large 44 percentage points in West Germany (panel b). Voter turnout is also much higher among the socially active than the

Table 6.1 Civic-spiritedness, voter turnout, and protest participation among non-actives, socially actives and activists

a)

	East German population		East German activists			
	Non-actives	Socially actives	All organizations	Assembly	Opportunities to participate	High level of participation
Civic spirit	6	34*****	56	50	59***	56*
Vote	80	91*****	96	96	96	95
Demonstrate	8	18*****	20	10***	22*	23***
Strike	3	4***	4	5	4	4
Illegal protest	0	1	2	1	2	2

b)

	West German population		West German activists			
	Non-actives	Socially actives	All organizations	Assembly	Opportunities to participate	High level of participation
Civic spirit	25	69*****	84	84	84	84
Vote	80	91*****	96	96	97	96
Demonstrate	5	10****	17	17	19***	19***
Strike	4	4	5	5	5	4
Illegal protest	1	1	1	1	2	1

c)

	Dutch population		Dutch activists			
	Non-actives	Socially actives	All organizations	Assembly	Opportunities to participate	High level of participation
Civic spirit	52	72****	79	77	79	93
Vote	78	87****	95	94*	94	100
Demonstrate	2	4	6	6	6	0
Strike	2	2	3	3	3	0
Illegal protest	0	1	1	1	0*	0

d)	Spanish population		Spanish activists				
	Non-actives	Socially actives	All organizations	Assembly	Opportunities to participate	High level of participation
Civic spirit	35	57*****	–	–	–	–
Vote	83	87****	88	88	87*	87
Demonstrate	9	21*****	46	47**	48***	45
Strike	6	13*****	48	49*	50**	47
Illegal protest	1	3****	9	9***	9	9

e)	Swiss population		Swiss activists				
	Non-actives	Socially actives	All organizations	Assembly	Opportunities to participate	High level of participation
Civic spirit	39	58*****	65	65	66**	66
Vote	58	74*****	77	77	78	78
Demonstrate	5	8***	23	22	23	24***
Strike	1	2***	7	7	7	8**
Illegal protest	1	1	5	4	5	5*

f)	UK population		UK activists				
	Non-actives	Socially actives	All organizations	Assembly	Opportunities to participate	High level of participation
Civic spirit	–	–	78	78	77	76
Vote	77	82***	95	95	94	94
Demonstrate	–	–	10	11	9	9*
Strike	–	–	7	8	4**	5
Illegal protest	–	–	1	0	1	1

Notes
Cell entries are percentages of respondents classified as expressing public-spiritedness or having reported the respective political activity. *$P<0.10$, **$P<0.05$, ***$P<0.01$, ****$P<<<0.001$ (two-tailed Chi-squared test). The questions about civic duties and protest participation were not asked in the UK population survey.

general population. For example, 74 per cent of Swiss socially actives claimed to have voted at the most recent general election compared to 58 per cent of the socially inactive (panel e), and while 9 per cent of non-active Spaniards said they attended a demonstration, this figure rose to 21 per cent for their socially active compatriots.

The next four columns compare average levels of political activity for organizational activists according to the internal democracy of their organization. The baseline category is members in all organizations, whose political activism is then compared with that of members in organizations with a general assembly, extensive participatory opportunities, and high levels of actual internal democratic participation. The first noteworthy finding is that activists generally report even higher levels of political activism than citizens in the general population who claim to be engaged in civil society organizations (the socially active). Examining these data further allows a preliminary answer to our question about the impact of internal democracy: it appears to matter marginally, at best. For civic attitudes there are very few significant differences across organizational types. A noteworthy exception is East Germany (panel a), but even here the biggest difference between members in organizations with large opportunities for democratic engagement and all members is only 3 percentage points – compared with the considerable difference of 28 percentage points between non-actives and socially actives in that part of Germany.

As far as voting is concerned, there is no difference between members in democratic organizations and their non-democratic counterparts – regardless of whether internal democracy is measured institutionally or behaviourally. This is partly due to a ceiling effect: once turnout levels of 90 per cent or higher are reached, it is exceedingly difficult for any factor to increase activism levels further towards the maximum of 100 per cent. This is a simple reflection of a social reality: electoral turnout and public values are near-universal among activists, and the political constitutions of their organizations are then likely to have only a very limited impact.

Turning to non-electoral political activities, which on the whole engage far fewer participants. We see that democratic constitutions appear to make a difference, albeit only at the margins, to a varying extent in the different countries, and depending both on the measure of protest and on the measure of internal participation applied. In Germany (both East and West) and Spain, the likelihood of attending a demonstration is a few percentage points higher among members in organizations with ample opportunities for internal democratic participation. An assembly makes members more likely to demonstrate in Spain, but not in East Germany, where this democratic feature even seems to have the opposite effect. On the other hand, high levels of behavioural internal democracy seem to mobilize East German members but not their Spanish counterparts. In Spain, institutional democracy is also positively related to taking part in strikes. In Switzerland, too, demonstrating and striking are slightly higher among members of behaviourally democratic organizations. In the Netherlands and the UK, none of the expectations about the effects of internal democracy are borne out. In fact, in some instances, such as the relationship between internal opportunities to participate and striking in the UK, the opposite of what we hypothesized turns out to be the case.

Thus, our findings with respect to the effects of internal democracy on civic spirit and political behaviour are patchy at best. At the same time, we cannot report robust non-findings. It is therefore useful to subject those positive relationships that *did* appear to a multivariate analysis. It is possible that internally democratic organizations are particularly attractive to citizens that are already more politically active for reasons beyond the socializing effects of the associations: Dahl's (1961: 1348) claim that 'joining organizations and participating in politics are mutually reinforcing activities' describes a causal relationship in both directions. In order to ascertain whether the relationships between associational democracy, civic spirit and political participation are robust or merely artefacts of individuals' self-selection and/or other factors, we conduct a multivariate analysis using data on the activists in Germany (East and West), Spain and Switzerland. Because our expectations in the case of the Netherlands and the UK have already been falsified at the bivariate level, there is no need carry out multivariate analyses for activists in these countries. The remainder of the analysis controls for various individual-level characteristics commonly associated with higher propensity for political activism, as well as for the length and intensity of membership in democratic and non-democratic organizations. As only civic spirit and protest participation exhibited statistically significant differences depending on the type of association, we restrict the analysis to these modes of political activity, and omit voting from further analysis.

For the multivariate analysis, civic spirit is measured on the full 11-point scale.[2] In order to maximize the information available in the data on the three modes of protest participation (taking part in a public demonstration, a strike or an illegal protest), we combine our three protest activities into a dichotomous scale of non-electoral political participation. Respondents are coded 1 if they have reported at least one of these three activities, and 0 otherwise. Empirically, these items load highly on a single factor extracted by principal-component analysis and form a homogenous scale.[3] To estimate the effects of democratic organizational features on civic-spiritedness and protest participation, we first estimate standard models of political participation before adding our measures of intra-organizational democracy. Because we treat civic-spiritedness as part of a general proclivity toward democratic engagement, we apply the same set of predictors to a model of civic-spiritedness that feature in standard accounts of political participation.

Over the past 50 years, a plethora of research has confirmed a number of robust regularities of participatory behaviour throughout advanced industrialized democracies (Lipset 1960; Barnes and Kaase 1979; Verba *et al.* 1995). Age, education, income, gender and religion have all been found to be related to political participation (Topf 1995: 701; van Aelst and Walgrave 2001).[4] We expect protest participation – but not civic-spiritedness – to be lower among people who are, overall, fairly satisfied with the democratic system, and who believe that the political institutions are roughly working the way they should.[5] According to Putnam, 'trust and engagement are two facets of the same underlying factor – social capital' (Putnam 1995: 73). If trust is thus seen as a concomitant of civic engagement, the extent to which citizens trust other people should also be controlled for.[6] We expect politically active individuals to display higher levels of trust in others. There are also reasons to expect that alienation from mainstream political institutions makes adherents of extreme left or right ideologies more inclined toward engaging in protest activity (Gurr 1970). While in recent years there have been demonstrations by groups that are not easily categorized in terms of left–right ideological cleavages (for example, the petrol protest and the activities of Fathers 4 Justice in the UK), left-leaning anti-foxhunting and right-leaning pro-foxhunting campaigners continue to dominate the political landscape. We therefore control for left–right ideology, expecting a pronounced ideological attachment of either direction to have a motivating effect.[7] Because with strike action we have an item in our political action measure that is most clearly associated with the organized labour movement and therefore left-leaning ideology, we expect higher levels of protest participation among left-leaning respondents. Irrespective of their ideological orientation, those who are members of a trade union, express an interest in politics, identify strongly with a political party and believe that ordinary people have possibilities to present their opinions to politicians should display higher levels of political engagement.[8]

Furthermore, we know from earlier studies of political preference formation that the social environment can generate cross-pressures that may stimulate individual behaviour (Berelson *et al.* 1954). Drawing on this tradition, van Deth (1997: 9) suggests that interpersonal networks or discussion networks established or initiated in particular with family members, friends or neighbours have mobilizing effects on individuals' propensity to become politically active. Thus, people's civic spirit should be fostered through discussing politics with friends or within the family.[9]

The next ingredients we add at the level of the individual are membership duration and intensity of participation. If associational engagement activates people politically, rather than simply attracting people who are already politically active, individual political participation levels should increase with the amount of time spent as an organizational activist, as well as with the intensity of associational involvement. Positive effects of the length and intensity of membership on political activity would support the simple Tocquevillian notion that civic activism played out in any type of organization – democratic or other – enhances desirable participatory leanings in people. If, however, our hypotheses *H3* and *H4* about the effects of internal democracy are correct, length and intensity of membership should matter *even more* in democratic organizations. This would be indicated by a significant positive coefficient of a multiplicatory combination of membership or intensity, respectively, with the democratic organizational features of an assembly, participatory opportunities, and the general level of participation.[10] This leads to the inclusion of six interaction terms in the model. Finally, three organization-level variables are used to test hypotheses *H1*

'Little democracies'? 115

and *H2* concerning the effects of internal democracy: assembly, perceived internal opportunity structure, and internal participation levels.

The individual-level variables in the model measure characteristics of people grouped into organizations, creating the possibility of clustering along the higher-level units. To take into account that observations within organizations may thus not be independent, standard errors and tests of statistical significance are computed based on aggregate scores for the organizations (cluster-robust standard errors). To asses the explanatory contribution of internal democracy to political action and verify that our standard predictors of political behaviour work, we first run a general model of protest participation in each country, before adding indicators of internal democracy. To avoid problems of extreme multicollinearity, interactions of organizational characteristics with length and intensity of membership are included for each institutional characteristic at a time, leading to three separate interactive models for each country. Estimation of the civic spirit models is by least squares regression; the protest models are analysed by logit.[11]

Starting with East German activists, the baseline model of civic-spiritedness in the second column of Table 6.2 performs broadly as expected. Women and older people display higher levels of civic-spiritedness, as do those who place trust in the government and in other people. Not surprisingly, civic-spiritedness increases among people who are interested in politics, discuss political matters with others, and identify with a political party. By contrast, ideological orientation makes no difference for this attitudinal trait. Income, religion, union membership and satisfaction with the democratic process do not add to activists' civic orientation either. Perhaps surprisingly, university education seems detrimental to the development of civic-spiritedness. Both the length and intensity of associational membership are positively related to civic spirit, suggesting that organizational engagement might actually produce civic political orientations and engagement rather than merely reflecting these. In the next column, we add the three indicators of intra-organizational democracy to the equation. On its own, neither an assembly or other participatory opportunities nor behavioural internal democracy affects members' civic-spiritedness. Thus, the East German case offers no support for *H1* or *H2*. The only significant interactive effect is for length of membership in associations with an assembly. The fact that this effect is not replicated for the interaction of membership length and other participatory opportunities implies only modest support for *H3*. *H4* is not supported by the East German data.

Despite the considerable differences between East Germany and Switzerland, the picture looks quite similar for the determinants of civic spirit here and the role of internal organizational democracy in fostering it (Table 6.3). The main differences in the baseline model concern the role of religion, union membership and left-wing ideology, which matter in Switzerland but are irrelevant in East Germany. By contrast, party identification is positively related to civic-spiritedness in East Germany but not in Switzerland. While the intensity of membership boosts civic-spiritedness among Swiss activists, membership length

Table 6.2 Least squares regression estimates of organizational effects on civic spirit: East Germany

	Base model	Internal democracy	Interaction models Assembly	Interaction models Opportunities	Participation
Individual characteristics					
Age in years	0.01****	0.01****	0.01****	0.01****	0.01****
Female	0.42****	0.44****	0.42****	0.42****	0.43****
Income	−0.01	−0.02	−0.02	−0.01	−0.01
Education	−0.23***	−0.26**	−0.24***	−0.24***	−0.24**
Religiosity	0.02	0.03*	0.03**	0.02*	0.02
Discuss politics with others	0.24***	0.23**	0.21***	0.23***	0.26***
Discuss politics at home	−0.02	−0.05	−0.04	−0.03	−0.02
Union member	−0.06	−0.10	−0.04	−0.10	−0.10
Interest in politics	0.31****	0.35****	0.32****	0.31****	0.32****
Efficacy	0.01	0.03	0.02	0.01	0.02
Satisfaction with democracy	0.11	0.04	0.05	0.11	0.08
Left	0.02	0.05	0.05	0.02	0.03
Right	−0.20	−0.16	−0.15	−0.20	−0.22
Trust in others	0.07***	0.06**	0.07***	0.07***	0.06**
Trust in institutions	0.07****	0.08****	0.08****	0.07****	0.07***
Party ID	0.16*	0.15	0.17*	0.16*	0.14
Length of membership	0.01**	0.01*	0.00	0.00	0.01**
Intensity of participation	0.20***	0.15*	0.15**	0.20**	0.18*
Organizational characteristics					
Assembly		−0.17	−0.44		
Assembly × Length			0.02*		
Assembly × Intensity			0.03		
Opportunities for internal participation		0.04		0.09**	
Opportunities × Length				0.01	
Opportunities × Intensity				−0.07	
Internal participation level		−0.02			0.15
Internal participation × Length					−0.01
Internal participation × Intensity					−0.00
Constant	3.34****	3.49****	3.68****	2.82****	3.12****
N	914	775	851	914	835
Adjusted R-squared	0.20	0.20	0.21	0.21	0.20
F-test	10.84	7.74	9.31	10.40	8.42

Notes
Robust standard errors in parentheses; *p<0.10, **p<0.05, ***p<0.01, ****p<0.001 (two-tailed)). Two municipal dummies included in all models but not shown.

Table 6.3 Least squares regression estimates of organizational effects on civic spirit: Swiss municipalities

	Base model	Internal democracy	Interaction models		
			Assembly	Opportunities	Participation
Individual characteristics					
Age in years	0.02****	0.02****	0.02****	0.02****	0.02****
Female	0.24**	0.23*	0.23**	0.23*	0.23*
Income	−0.02	−0.03	−0.02	−0.02	−0.02
Education	−0.15	−0.14	−0.12	−0.16	−0.16
Religiosity	0.04***	0.04***	0.03**	0.05***	0.05***
Discuss politics with others	−0.03	−0.00	−0.02	−0.03	−0.02
Discuss politics at home	0.07	0.06	0.06	0.06	0.07
Union member	0.25*	0.26*	0.24	0.24	0.24
Interest in politics	0.22**	0.21**	0.20**	0.21**	0.22**
Efficacy	0.02	0.02	0.02	0.02	0.02
Satisfaction with democracy	0.07	0.05	0.06	0.08	0.05
Left	0.32**	0.39***	0.34**	0.34***	0.36***
Right	0.13	0.16	0.17	0.12	0.13
Trust in others	0.06*	0.05	0.06*	0.06	0.05
Trust in institutions	0.09***	0.10***	0.10***	0.09***	0.10***
Party ID	−0.04	−0.00	−0.02	−0.04	−0.03
Length of membership	−0.01	−0.01	0.01	−0.05****	−0.01
Intensity of participation	0.35***	0.40***	0.48	0.23	0.54***
Organizational characteristics					
Assembly		−0.46	0.01		
Assembly × Length			−0.16		
Assembly × Intensity			−0.01		
Opportunities for internal participation		0.06		−0.02	
Opportunities × Length				0.04****	
Opportunities × Intensity				0.12	
Internal participation level		−0.40**			−0.13
Internal participation × Length					0.01
Internal participation × Intensity					−0.17
Constant	3.95****	4.85****	3.96***	4.19****	4.20****
N	609	570	592	608	582
Adjusted R-squared	0.18	0.17	0.17	0.18	0.18
F-test	7.15	6.38	6.26	7.39	6.88

Notes
Robust standard errors in parentheses; *$p<0.10$, **$p<0.05$, ***$p<0.01$, ****$p<0.001$ (two-tailed). Seven municipal dummies included in all models but not shown.

has no positive effect. As in East Germany, however, hardly any of the organizational features make a positive difference, with only an interactive term of membership length and internal participatory opportunities suggesting that any positive effects from membership in associations are restricted to internally democratic ones. Thus, the Swiss case lends only weak support to *H3*, and does not support hypotheses *H1*, *H2* or *H4*.

Turning to protest behaviour in East Germany, we find a vaguely similar set of standard predictors at work as in the case of civic spirit (Table 6.4). The biggest differences in the baseline model concern age and gender: while in East Germany civic-spiritedness is more often found among women and elderly citizens, protest remains a domain of younger men. It is possible that strikes and illegal protests account for much of this age and gender bias. And while left–right ideology was irrelevant for the development of civic attitudes, people leaning toward the left of the political spectrum are significantly more likely to take part in protests and those with a right-wing orientation less so. The intensity of organizational involvement matters to an extent, but protest propensity is unaffected by how long a person is in a group. Most importantly for our research interest, however, few of the democratic associational features affect the extent to which members become politically active. The only organizational democratic characteristic that positively affects protest through length of membership is the presence of an assembly. In East Germany, long-standing members in institutionally democratic organizations protest more than others. An effect of membership in associations that are institutionally democratic in the sense of providing opportunities for participation is restricted to the interactive model and is therefore not robust. Thus, only *H3* receives a modicum of support from the East German case.

The picture looks broadly similar in West Germany (Table 6.5). With the exception of the male bias observed among East German members, the baseline model performs broadly as in the East German cities. As in the East, West German members are more likely to protest if they are left-wing, but, unlike in East Germany, being right-of-centre politically does not militate against protest participation. In addition, religiosity reduces protesting, while a sense of efficacy boosts participation. The length of membership has no bearing on protest propensity, while the intensity of participation boosts protest behaviour only in three of five models. None of our hypotheses are supported by the membership data from West Germany.

In Spain, too, the baseline model of protest participation behaves broadly as expected. With the exception of satisfaction with the way democracy works in the country, the patterns resemble those found among the Mannheim activists. The impression gained so far, that internal democracy matters very little, also receives further confirmation (Table 6.6). The protest behaviour of Spanish activists is unaffected by either the length or the intensity of their associational engagement. Crucially for our research question, the democratic constitution of the organization in which their engagement occurs is also irrelevant.

Finally, the Swiss activists' data tell an overall similar story about protest par-

Table 6.4 Logit estimates of organizational effects on protest: East Germany

	Base model	Internal democracy	Interaction models			
			Assembly	Internal democracy	Opportunities	Participation

	Base model	Internal democracy	Assembly	Opportunities	Participation
Individual characteristics					
Age in years	−0.03****	−0.03****	−0.03****	−0.03****	−0.03****
Female	−0.19	−0.03	−0.12	−0.20	−0.09
Income	−0.02	−0.01	−0.01	−0.02	−0.02
Education	−0.14	−0.25	−0.20	−0.10	−0.17
Religiosity	−0.03	−0.02	−0.03	−0.03	−0.02
Discuss politics with others	0.47***	0.62***	0.56***	0.47***	0.50***
Discuss politics at home	−0.12	−0.14	−0.12	−0.12	−0.14
Union member	0.92****	1.04****	0.99****	0.95****	0.96****
Interest in politics	0.18	0.13	0.14	0.16	0.18
Efficacy	0.05	0.06	0.04	0.04	0.07*
Satisfaction with democracy	−0.01	0.10	0.02	−0.01	0.08
Left	0.61***	0.59***	0.62***	0.61***	0.60***
Right	−0.31	−0.59	−0.47	−0.32	−0.37
Trust in others	0.03	0.04	0.04	0.03	0.01
Trust in institutions	−0.07	−0.11**	−0.08*	−0.07*	−0.10**
Party ID	0.48**	0.63***	0.56***	0.49**	0.53***
Length of membership	−0.00	−0.01	−0.01	0.01	0.01
Intensity of participation	0.19	0.06	0.23	0.26	−0.29
Organizational characteristics					
Assembly		−0.18	0.51		
Assembly × Length			0.04		
Assembly × Intensity			−0.79		
Opportunities for internal participation		−0.04		0.11	
Opportunities × Length				−0.03	
Opportunities × Intensity				−0.08	
Internal participation level		0.35			0.13
Internal participation × Length					−0.02
Internal participation × Intensity					0.38
Constant	−2.17***	−2.93***	−2.47***	−2.84***	−2.33***
N	917	777	854	917	837
Log pseudo-likelihood	−429.31	−356.93	−390.29	−426.84	−392.97
Pseudo R-squared	0.12	0.14	0.13	0.12	0.13
Wald Chi-squared	123.12	120.20	124.93	122.51	125.15

Notes
Robust standard errors in parentheses; *$p<0.10$, **$p<0.05$, ***$p<0.01$, ****$p<0.001$ (two-tailed). Two municipal dummies included in all models but not shown.

Table 6.5 Logit estimates of organizational effects on protest: West Germany

	Base model	Internal democracy	Interaction models		
			Assembly	Opportunities	Participation
Individual characteristics					
Age in years	-0.01*	-0.01	-0.01	-0.01	-0.01
Female	0.34*	0.35	0.34*	0.39*	0.29
Income	-0.04	-0.02	-0.04	-0.05	-0.02
Education	-0.08	-0.19	-0.09	-0.11	-0.14
Religiosity	-0.08***	-0.08***	-0.09***	-0.08***	-0.07**
Discuss politics with others	0.29**	0.27**	0.29**	0.26**	0.28**
Discuss politics at home	-0.09	-0.09	-0.09	-0.08	-0.09
Union member	0.99****	0.90****	0.95****	0.99****	0.93****
Interest in politics	0.38**	0.33*	0.42**	0.39**	0.29
Efficacy	0.05	0.07*	0.06	0.05	0.05
Satisfaction with democracy	-0.06	-0.03	-0.03	-0.05	-0.06
Left	1.02****	1.03****	1.00****	1.02****	1.04****
Right	0.01	-0.09	-0.01	0.01	-0.09
Trust in others	0.03	0.03	0.02	0.02	0.04
Trust in institutions	0.08*	0.07	0.08*	0.08*	0.07
Party ID	-0.17	-0.25	-0.17	-0.15	-0.26
Length of membership	0.00	-0.00	0.01	0.01	0.01
Intensity of participation	0.20**	0.16	0.21	0.25**	0.08
Organizational characteristics					
Assembly		-0.31	-0.08		
Assembly × Length			-0.02		
Assembly × Intensity			0.02		
Opportunities for internal participation		0.09		0.20***	
Opportunities × Length				-0.02	
Opportunities × Intensity				-0.11	
Internal participation level		0.06			0.08
Internal participation × Length					-0.01
Internal participation × Intensity					0.07
Constant	-3.62***	-4.14****	-3.74****	-4.99****	-3.66****
N	1,093	918	1,043	1,092	962
Log pseudo-likelihood	-472.96	-392.50	-449.44	-468.79	-413.89
Pseudo R-squared	0.16	0.15	0.16	0.16	0.14
Wald Chi-squared	153.15	131.96	153.86	155.74	130.06

Notes
Robust standard errors in parentheses; *$p<0.10$, **$p<0.05$, ***$p<0.01$, ****$p<0.001$ (two-tailed).

Table 6.6 Logit estimates of organizational effects on protest: Spain

	Base model	Internal democracy	Interaction models Assembly	Opportunities	Participation
Individual characteristics					
Age in years	−0.03****	−0.03****	−0.03****	−0.03****	−0.03****
Female	−0.01	−0.01	−0.03	−0.01	−0.01
Income	−0.06	−0.06	−0.07	−0.07	−0.05
Education	−0.20	−0.20	−0.20	−0.21	−0.21
Religiosity	−0.05	−0.03	−0.04	−0.05*	−0.03
Discuss politics with others	0.48****	0.47****	0.48****	0.47****	0.47****
Discuss politics at home	−0.03	−0.03	−0.03	−0.01	−0.05
Union member	0.66**	0.69**	0.75**	0.65**	0.63**
Interest in politics	0.46***	0.39***	0.44***	0.46***	0.42***
Efficacy	0.15***	0.15***	0.15***	0.15***	0.14***
Satisfaction with democracy	−0.56****	−0.53****	−0.55****	−0.55****	−0.51****
Left	1.07****	1.10****	1.06****	1.07****	1.11****
Right	0.40	0.27	0.40	0.38	0.29
Trust in others	0.09**	0.08*	0.08**	0.09**	0.08*
Party ID	−0.28	−0.29	−0.29	−0.27	−0.31
Length of membership	0.00	0.01	0.04	0.00	−0.03
Intensity of participation	0.12	0.11	0.34	0.11	0.35**
Organizational characteristics					
Assembly		0.30	1.26		
Assembly × Length			−0.04		
Assembly × Intensity			−0.22		
Opportunities for internal participation		0.14		0.03	
Opportunities × Length				0.00	
Opportunities × Intensity				0.08	
Internal participation level					0.07
Internal participation × Length					0.05
Internal participation × Intensity		−0.24			−0.23*
Constant	0.45	−0.05	−0.76	0.12	0.10
N	883	782	872	883	791
Log pseudo-likelihood	−424.89	−386.44	−420.27	−423.57	−388.93
Pseudo R-squared	0.26	0.25	0.26	0.26	0.25
Wald Chi-squared	193.93	203.16	194.29	191.76	204.46

Notes
Robust standard errors in parentheses; *p<0.10, **p<0.05, ***p<0.01, ****p<0.001 (two-tailed). Five municipal dummies included in all models but not shown.

Table 6.7 Logit estimates of organizational effects on protest: Swiss municipalities

	Base model	Internal democracy	Interaction models — Assembly	Interaction models — Opportunities	Participation
Individual characteristics					
Age in years	-0.00	-0.00	-0.00	-0.01	-0.00
Female	0.18	0.23	0.19	0.14	0.25
Income	-0.06*	-0.04	-0.06	-0.06*	-0.04
Education	-0.12	-0.29	-0.11	-0.12	-0.28
Religiosity	0.02	0.01	0.02	0.02	0.01
Discuss politics with others	0.51***	0.51**	0.59***	0.52***	0.44**
Discuss politics at home	-0.32**	-0.33**	-0.34***	-0.30*	-0.38***
Union member	1.20****	1.21****	1.20****	1.21****	1.15****
Interest in politics	0.23	0.24	0.24	0.25	0.23
Efficacy	-0.03	-0.03	-0.05	-0.02	-0.03
Satisfaction with democracy	-0.18	-0.28	-0.24	-0.14	-0.21
Left	1.16****	1.27****	1.23****	1.20****	1.19****
Right	0.05	0.09	0.10	0.10	-0.05
Trust in others	-0.06	-0.03	-0.03	-0.08	-0.07
Trust in institutions	-0.02	0.03	-0.01	-0.02	0.01
Party ID	0.56**	0.56**	0.49*	0.58**	0.61**
Length of membership	-0.01	-0.01	0.00	-0.03	-0.04
Intensity of participation	0.59***	0.46**	-0.60		0.84**
Organizational characteristics					
Assembly		-0.26	-2.83**		
Assembly × Length			-0.00		
Assembly × Intensity			1.21**		
Opportunities for internal participation		-0.31**		-0.18	
Opportunities × Length				0.03	
Opportunities × Intensity				0.56***	
Internal participation level		0.84**			0.53
Internal participation × Length					0.03
Internal participation × Intensity					-0.41
Constant	-2.48***	-1.91*	-0.02	-1.18	-3.29***
N	610	571	593	609	583
Log pseudo-likelihood	-289.55	-259.75	-277.51	-288.08	-272.19
Pseudo R-squared	0.22	0.25	0.23	0.22	0.23
Wald Chi-squared	154.52	180.40	171.09	150.42	162.67

Notes
Robust standard errors in parentheses; *$p<0.10$, **$p<0.05$, ***$p<0.01$, ****$p<0.001$ (two-tailed). †Trust in institutions omitted from model to ensure concavity.

Table 6.8 Summary of findings from multivariate analysis

Hypothesis		Internal democratic feature	Civic-spiritedness	Protest participation	Hypothesis supported?
H1	Institutional democracy matters	Assembly Opportunities for participation			No
H2	Behavioural democracy matters	Levels of internal participation		(✓)	No
H3	Membership length matters more in democratic organizations	Assembly × Length Opportunities × Length Internal participation × Length	(✓) (✓)		Weakly
H4	Membership intensity matters more in democratic organizations	Assembly × Intensity Opportunities × Intensity Internal participation × Intensity		(✓)	No

ticipation as do the data from the other countries (Table 6.7). Once again, the baseline model works well. Interestingly, socio-economic factors fade into insignificance against the important role that union membership, left-wing ideology and party identification play for protest participation. Furthermore, the intensity of membership – but not the length – is associated with increased protest behaviour. However, this increase is independent of the internal organizational features. There is a significant positive effect of behavioural democracy on the protest propensity of members, lending support to *H2*. There is also a significant interactive effect of the intensity of membership in organizations with large participatory opportunities, but this effect is not matched by equivalent associations involving the other measures of internal democracy. In Switzerland, actively participating members as well as those in vividly participatory groups protest more than others, but the two effects do not reinforce each other. Thus, only *H2* and *H3* find a modicum of support in the Swiss data, while *H1* and *H4* are not supported.

Table 6.8 summarizes the results with respect to the different operationalizations of each hypothesis. The ticks indicate which operationalizations of which hypotheses have generated positive findings. The parentheses around the ticks indicate that these findings only ever apply to a single country at a time. This overview suggests that *H3*, which states that the length of membership in institutionally democratic organizations affects members' external political behaviour, is the only hypothesis to receive some level of support for more than one indicator of internal democracy with regard to civic-spiritedness – but not for protest action. Overall, the analysis presented here generates at most very weak support for the idea that organizations' internal democracy affects their ability to contribute to democratic culture and behaviour outside their perimeters.

6.6 Conclusion

This chapter has examined differences in the types of organizations that people join, and has investigated whether the democratic credentials and institutional opportunity structures of organizations make a difference for the civic norms and political behaviour displayed by their members outside the organization. Put simply, to what extent can associations with internally democratic features be portrayed as better schools of democracy than organizations that lack such characteristics? Our analysis has found that, compared to the differences that associational activists display vis-à-vis the rest of the population, the democratic characteristics of their organizations are at best marginally related to individual political participation. In all six countries, activists display broadly similar levels of political participation regardless of whether they are members of institutionally or behaviourally democratic associations, or of non-democratic ones. The development of civic-spiritedness is somewhat increased by spending a length of time in institutionally democratic associations. However, these effects are rather weak as well as being restricted to East German and Swiss activists, while no support for these expectations comes from the West German or Spanish data.

'Little democracies'? 125

While it thus appears that the internal democratic constitution of civil society organizations is not something that should be of central concern to social scientists or policy-makers, neither is associational engagement in general. Only in East Germany does the length of associational membership have a modest effect on civic-spiritedness – but not on actual political participation. In Switzerland and East Germany, civic spirit seems to be fostered through intense participation. The intensity of individual associational engagement positively affects outside political behaviour in West Germany and Switzerland, but not in East Germany. The civic attitudes and political behaviour of Spanish activists seem utterly unimpressed by the length or intensity of their activism. These mixed findings do not allow us to refute the suspicion of spuriousness and the possibility that associations serve as receptacles for the virtuously active, rather than schools of participatory activity. This result should, as Gutmann (1998) suggests, temper the current enthusiasm for all things associational. However, to the small extent that associational engagement fosters citizens' democratic disposition and participation, it does so mainly regardless of whether the organizations in question are internally democratic or not.

This finding is of direct policy relevance. If political institutions such as the EU are interested in civil society as a means of addressing a democratic deficit, decisions about funding, cooptation and consultation involving voluntary groups do not need to bother discriminating between democratic and non-democratic organizations. Considerations of input legitimacy can of course provide independent reasons for supporting internally democratic organizations more than others.

Notes

1 In addition to questions about the link between internal democracy and individual political participation, it is at least theoretically possible that an organization that appears to be a paragon of participatory democracy – with formal and effective internally democratic procedures, an elected leadership constituting a microcosm of the membership, and where policy was developed in line with membership demands, values and goals – could seek objectives detrimental to democracy (or even to society generally).
2 As the civic spirit scale is an average of four 11-point scales, it can take on 44 different values in steps of quarter units, thus approximating the quantitative measurement assumed by OLS regression.
3 Factor loadings vary between 0.55 for attending a strike in the UK and 0.83 for attending a demonstration in Spain. In three of the four countries in which regression analysis of the combined scale is carried out, the protest participation scale satisfies Mokken's assumption of double monotonicity and yields high coefficients of scale homogeneity (H): 0.60 (East Germany), 0.47 (West Germany) and 0.62 (Spain). While this suggests that it is a strong scale measuring a single underlying trait of political activity, an exception occurs in Switzerland, where taking part in demonstration and illegal protests – but not strikes – forms a strong scale (H demonstration, illegal protests=0.69). To facilitate meaningful comparison across countries, we will use the same four-point scale for all countries despite its empirical weakness in Switzerland.
4 To facilitate cross-country comparison in spite of different education systems, education

is measured as the presence or absence of tertiary education. Income is household income in local currency. Religiosity is the self-reported importance of religion in respondents' life, ranging from 0 ('not important at all') to 10 ('very important').

5 For satisfaction with democracy, respondents were asked 'On the whole, are you very satisfied [4], fairly satisfied [3], not very satisfied [2] or not at all satisfied [1] with the way democracy works in [name of country]?' To gauge people's trust in institutions, they were asked how much they trusted seven government institutions or actors (city council, government, courts, civil service, police, politicians, European Union). Answers to these seven questions load strongly on a single factor extracted by principal component analysis. For ease of interpretation of the coefficients, rather than using the factor scores we have averaged the values of the seven items.

6 The interpersonal trust measure is based on the following question: 'Generally speaking, would you say that most people can be trusted or that you can't be too careful in dealing with people?' Answers on an 11-point scale range from 0 ('You can't be too careful') to 10 ('Most people can be trusted').

7 To capture political extremism on either end of the spectrum, we have created dummy variables based on an 11-point scale of left–right orientation. Respondents locating themselves on the lowest four points on the scale were classified as left-leaning, those on the highest four points as right-leaning.

8 Respondents' interest in politics is measured on a four-point scale ranging from 1 ('not at all interested') to 4 ('very interested'). For party identification, respondents were asked if they usually think of themselves as a supporter of a particular political party. For efficacy, respondents were asked, 'In your personal opinion: How large possibilities do ordinary people have to present their opinions to politicians?', ranging from 0 ('none at all') to 10 ('very large').

9 Respondents were asked, 'how often would you say you discuss political matters with others [your family]?' Answers on four-point ordinal scales range from 'never' (1) to 'often' (4).

10 To create multiplicatory terms with membership length and intensity, the dichotomous measures of internal democracy from the bivariate analysis are used.

11 We also estimated the protest models by negative binomial regression of the four-point count of protest activity, ranging from zero to three reported activities. As values above 1 become rare, very little additional information is utilized by that method and its results are very similar to the logit estimates. It could be argued that the difference between counts is of an ordinal kind (i.e. that reporting three protest items does not mean that a respondent is three times as active as someone reporting only one). Therefore, we have also estimated the model with the four-category count as the dependent variable using an ordered logit estimator. The results reported her are confirmed by that method as well.

Part II
European political orientations

7 Voluntary associations and support for Europe

Manuela Caiani and Mariona Ferrer-Fons[1]

7.1 Introduction

The increasing Europeanization of governance structures on the one hand, and the lack of a parallel development of an active European citizenship on the other – at the heart of the so called EU' 'democratic deficit' – is a crucial issue for current European politics. However, even before the popular rejection of the European Constitution in the French and Dutch referenda, there were indications that citizens' support for the European integration process was no longer self-evident. Since the beginning of the 1990s, the former 'permissive consensus' on the European integration has eroded (Sharpf 1999); trust in European institutions has strongly declined, as well as voter participation in European elections (Crepaz and Stenier 2007: 291). In addition, tendencies of a 'renationalization' of politics have been observable in many member states, such as the emergence of xenophobic and anti-European political parties and groups (Statham and Gray 2005).

The 'democratic deficit' and the legitimacy problems of the European Union (EU) have been often discussed in terms of institutional design and reform (for example, extending the powers of the European Parliament), or of a lack of interest in the EU among European citizens (for example, low participation in European elections) (Koopmans and Statham 2002: 4). More recently, however, scholars have begun to argue that the success of both institutional reforms and efforts to strengthen citizens' identification with Europe depend on the development of an European intermediary public sphere of civil society associations that can help bridge the gap between European policies and institutions, and the European citizenry (Koopmans and Statham 2002: 4). In Habermas' words, the debate about the future of Europe 'has to find resonance in a pan-European political public sphere, which presupposes a European civil society constitutes by interest groups, non governmental organizations and movements of citizens' (Habermas 2001: 103).

European institutions have recently joined the emerging and growing consensus that an active and vibrant civic engagement could greatly overcome the deficiencies of the EU. Since Delors' Social Dialogue, the EU has repeatedly emphasized the importance of a 'more open' and 'more transparent' dialogue with civil society, and has tried to reinforce its legitimacy by opening channels of access to the EU decision-making to civil society associations (Cotellessa 2005: 210–211). According to the White Paper on European Governance (Commission of the European Communities 2001b), Europe should constitute a 'platform' for a more active participation of citizens to the achievement of the objectives of the Union, offering structured channels for their reactions, critiques and protests (for example, the consensus forums set up by the commission to generate ideas; social dialogue on social policy; and the various possibilities opened by the Charter of Fundamental Human Rights and the Convention (Schmidt 2006: 105).

Following the Tocquevillian interpretation of voluntary associations as 'schools of democracy', associations are considered, both in some parts of the academy and beyond, as a vehicle for the promotion of a European identity and 'citizenship', by offering citizens opportunities for active participation in public debates and collective action concerning European politics and its institutions (Koopmans and Statham 2002). In particular, participation in voluntary associations offers citizens venues in which they can improve their social skills, pro-social norms and values such as trust, and get involved in social networks – all factors that are considered important for citizens' engagement and participation in democratic political life (Maloney and van Deth 2008a: 62). Given the 'beneficial' impact that associational participation is supposed to have on political orientations of members, there is no reason to assume that the same mechanisms cannot be at work when referring specifically to European politics.

In this chapter, we address such issues by investigating the associational impact on support for Europe. In particular, we focus on interest in European politics and trust in European institutions. The main questions driving our analyses are, first, does associational participation foster and enhance levels of trust in the European institutions and interest in European politics? Second, does greater participation in voluntary associations (more time spent, greater associational commitment, etc.) generate greater levels of trust in European institutions and interest in European politics? Third, do different associational contexts, namely voluntary associations characterized by different organizational features (size, resource, formal structure) and different concerns (politics, economy, etc.), impact differentially on the levels of trust in the EU and interest in European politics of their members?

Political scientists have extensively studied how the public forms its opinions about European integration, utilizing a variety of techniques and data sets, as well as focusing on different units of analysis (e.g. party manifestos and elite surveys, national economic performances, institutional performances of national vs European institutions, etc.; Brinegar and Jolly 2005: 156). Expanding on these studies, other research stresses that the best way to analyse support for European integration is to combine multiple levels of analysis, examining multiple causal factors (for example, individual as well as socio-political and economic factors) (Steenbergen and Jones 2002; Marks and Hooghe 2004; Brinegar and Jolly 2005). Accordingly, we pay attention to both micro-level (individual) and meso-level (associational) factors for understanding support for Europe. By analysing the combined impact of (a) the individual characteristics of the activists, (b) the degree of their actual associational engagement and (c) the objective features of the voluntary associations in which they are involved, this chapter examines the organizational impact of associational activities on (European) political attitudes by novelly combining two levels of analysis.

The data for the empirical analysis comes from the Citizen, Involvement and Democracy (CID) project, which offers a unique database that combines information about individual characteristics of activists with associational features of the specific organizations in which they are involved for six different European countries and cities (East Germany, West Germany, The Netherlands, Switzerland, Spain and the UK; see Chapter 1 of this volume).

7.2 The associational impact on European attitudes

The issue of citizens' support for the EU and its institutions has became more salient in recent years, which have witnessed the deepening of European integration, seemingly accompanied by the increasing detachment of European citizens. Opinion polls (such as the Eurobarometer)[2] have repeatedly confirmed a growing dissatisfaction with European institutions among European citizens (with an approximately 50 per cent dissatisfaction rating; Pache 2001). This trend is also evident within the new member countries (for example, in the low voter turnout in the 2004 European election; Crepaz and Steiner 2007: 291). Qualitative research on the ways in which ordinary citizens conceive Europe have stressed that the EU is largely perceived as opaque, distant, non-responsive and inefficient (Díez Medrano 2003: Chapter 2). Furthermore, the levels of (and reasons for) support for Europe vary greatly from country to country. British citizens tend to look at Europe in terms of a loss of national identity; conversely, Spaniards see Europe as a mechanism for 'normalizing' their country, while in Germany Europe projects a more positive image of the country as a corrective to its Nazi past (Díez Medrano 2003: 203).

However, citizens' political orientations are also considered to be influenced by their participation in associational activities. Accordingly, we begin by examining the question: *does associational participation foster pro-European feelings? Namely, does it favour interest in European politics and trust in European institutions?* The CID question concerning interest in European politics is:

> People's interest sometimes varies across different areas of politics. How interested are you in each of the following areas? Local politics, national politics, European politics and international politics.[3]

Trust in the EU is captured by a question asking:

> Listed below are several institutions such as the police, government, civil service, the European Union etc. (...) Please, indicate your level of trust in each of these institutions?[4]

If associational participation can positively contribute to the promotion of European support, our simple expectation to be verified here is that associational activists are more interested in European politics and trustful in European institutions than are citizens in general. Obviously, a self-selection bias problem might exist – that is, those who hold (positive) attitudes and orientations might join associations, so organizational contexts have little impact on the development of these attitudes. However, we cannot test this alternative explanation with the data available. What we can do to test this hypothesis is contrast associational activists with other two categories of 'ordinary' citizens – namely, the 'socially actives', who are respondents from the population surveys saying that they 'are active or volunteer in some voluntary associations', and the 'non-actives', who are interviewees in the general population who state that they are not active in any association. If our expectation of a positive impact of associational participation on trust and interest in Europe is confirmed, we should also find that activists can be considered as the 'hard-core' (of civically engaged people), characterized by higher levels of interest in European politics and trust in European institutions than socially actives. Simultaneously, activists and socially actives are characterized by higher levels of interest and trust in Europe than are citizens who are less active. Finally, if associational participation proves to impact positively on European attitudes, then we should find that it matters regardless of the context (more Euro-sceptic or more pro-European) of the countries in which activists and associations are inserted. In other words, we should find that activists (and socially actives) are more trustful and interested in Europe than are the less active citizens in all the countries under examination.

When considering interest in European politics (see Figure 7.1a), our first expectation is confirmed. Indeed, the data show that in general, in the six European countries (and local contexts) under study,[5] the average levels of interest in European politics are higher among associational activists and socially actives than among non-actives. Moreover, the ranking between activists and socially actives confirms our expectations, with the level of political interest in Europe being on average, in all countries, higher among activists than among socially actives. The influence of associational participation on interest in European politics is particularly evident in West Germany and the UK, which are the countries where there are greater differences between activists, socially active and non-active citizens.[6] Considering cross-country differences, finally, it is not surprising to see that the UK (traditionally considered one of the most Euro-sceptic European countries) shows the lowest levels of interest in European politics in comparison to other countries. In spite of the consistency across countries with regard to (European) political interest, when we look at trust in European institutions, the picture is somewhat different (see Figure 7.1b). Our findings even indicate some less positive perceptions of European institutions from activists in some countries. In line with our expectations, Swiss and the British activists are slightly more trustful of European institutions than are non-actives (and socially actives).[7] However, the opposite is true in West and East Germany, where activists are more critical of Europe than non-actives (and socially actives are more

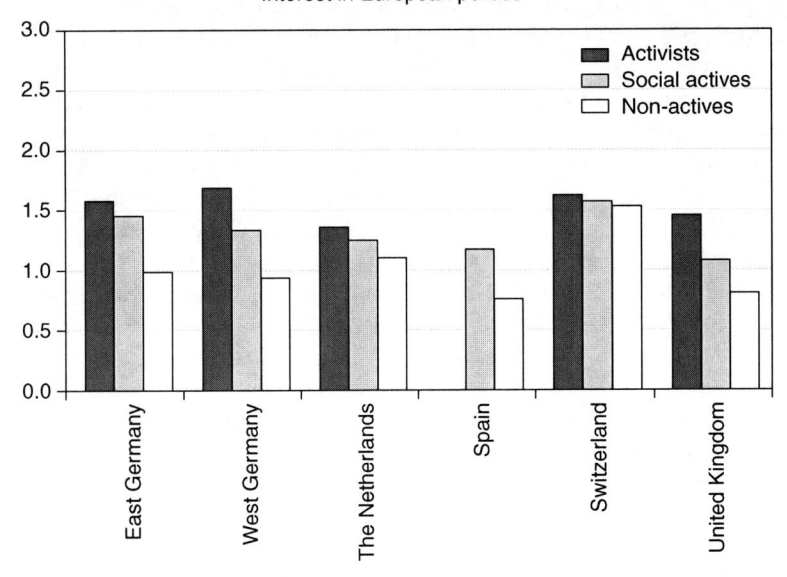

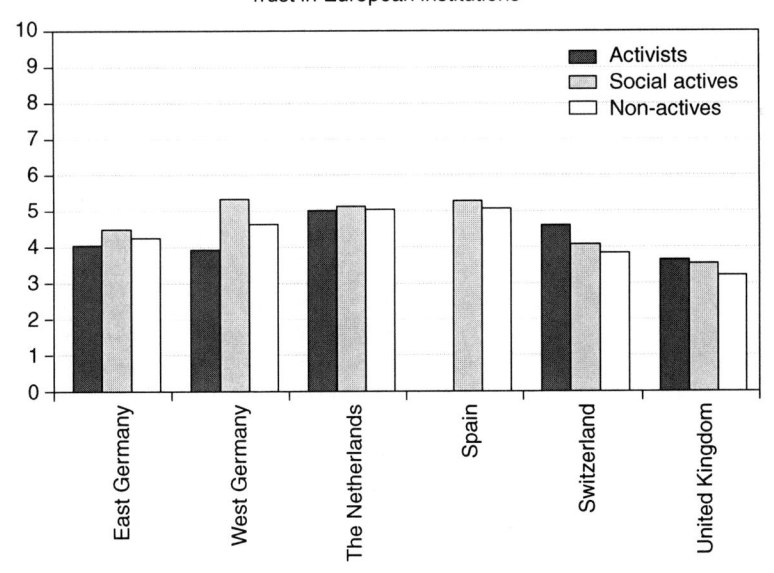

Figure 7.1 Interest in European politics, and trust in European institutions among activists, social actives, and non-actives (means).

trustful than activists!). Finally, in the Netherlands, there are no differences between the three groups. Overall, looking at cross-country differences, the United Kingdom (for the three types of citizens in terms of associational involvement) and, to lesser extent, Switzerland show the lowest levels of trust in European institutions, while the Netherlands and Spain emerge as the most trustful.

Our results concerning trust in European institutions could be seen as evidence of a 'negative', instead of a 'positive', impact of associational activities for political support, at least as far as attitudes towards European institutions are concerned. In fact, these findings raise some doubts about the existence of a positive relationship between social participation and political trust. This relationship has been challenged by some studies which demonstrated that highly socially engaged people can also be characterized by high levels of mistrust toward political institutions (see Tarrow 2000; Caiani 2003; Maloney and van Deth 2008a). However, mistrust towards political institutions is not necessarily a signal of the decline of the political commitment of citizens (Tarrow 2000). On the contrary, it is a common trait within Western democracies, with many exhibiting a general decline of citizens' trust towards governments, that there is an increasing social and political commitment, even if in contentious forms such as protests (Tarrow 2000, 273). How can we make sense of our findings? Does associational participation have a 'positive' or a 'negative' impact on support for Europe? A more refined reflection on the meaning of European support is required.

7.3 A typology of support for Europe

The findings presented above stress that associational participation affects European attitudes and orientations. However, it depends on which indicator of Europeanization we are considering: it has a positive impact on interest in European politics; and works in the opposite direction with regard to trust in European institutions. Is that enough to conclude that associational participation does not foster pro-European attitudes or – even worse – that it favours Euro-scepticism?

Recent insights from the literature on public opinion and Europe suggest that some caution should be exercised when using the 'Euro-scepticism' concept. It is a very complex concept, which can indicate different degrees and types of opposition to Europe (Cotta et al. 2005; della Porta and Caiani 2006: 63). Drawing on Easton's distinction between specific and diffuse support, we would argue that low 'specific support' for European institutions does not necessarily imply an absence of 'diffuse support' for Europe (Díez Medrano 2007: 143). In this sense, the low level of trust in European institutions found among activists does not necessarily signify their rejection of European integration per se. In fact, with the increasing politicization of European matters among public opinion (Cotta 2005), one can be 'supportive' of the European integration project but simultaneously very critical towards Europe in terms of the content of its policies (for example, the lack of 'European social protection'; Sharpf 1999) or in terms of the current performances of its institutions (for example, lack of substantial democracy). In any case, this type of criticism of Europe raises questions about the support for the construction of a 'supranational' polity (della Porta 2006).[8]

Following these reflections, we deepen our analysis by differentiating *support for Europe* by combining the level of interest in European politics (considered as a proxy of a *diffuse support for the idea of European integration*) and the level of trust in European institutions (taken as a proxy of a more *specific support for the practices of the integration process*). In this way, and taking into account some suggestions deriving from the pertinent literature on Europeanization, we can distinguish several discrete profiles of 'European' citizens: (a) the 'Euro-enthusiasts' (Cotta *et al.* 2005), in favour of both the practices and the ideals of the European integration (high levels of trust in European institutions and interest in European politics); (b) the 'Euro-pragmatics' (Kopecky and Mudde 2002), who approve the practices (high trust in European institutions) but do not believe in the project of European integration (low interest in European politics); (c) the 'critical Europeanists' (della Porta and Caiani 2006), who are critical towards the practices (low trust in European institutions) but not the ideals (high interest in European politics); and, finally, (d) the 'Euro-disaffected', who are critical of both (see Figure 7.2).

Following from this, the starting point of our analysis is: What kinds of 'support for Europe' are associations more likely to foster and enhance? If associational participation has a positive impact on European attitudes, we should find the most supportive type of European citizens (namely the 'Euro-enthusiasts') most prevalent among activists (and among socially actives) and less so among general citizens. On the contrary, we should find a larger portion of the Euro-disaffected among general citizens than among activists (and socially actives), since the former do not participate in associational activities and cannot exploit the associational context in order to meet people, discuss politics, develop civic and democratic skills, etc. By analysing the distribution of our four

		Interest in European politics	
		+ High (2–3)	– Low (0–1)
Trust in European institutions	+ High (Individual value in the 0–10 scale > the country mean)	Euro-enthusiasts	Euro-pragmatics
	– Low (Individual value in the 0–10 scale < the country mean)	Critical Europeanists	Euro-disaffected

Figure 7.2 A typology of 'support for Europe', combining interest in European politics and trust in European institutions. [9]

types of support for Europe among activists, socially actives and non-actives, we might discover that some organizational contexts are more conducive to the development of positive European attitudes among their members in a way that resonates with the general Tocquevillean vision of a consensual supporting role (for the political system) of voluntary associations in liberal democracies. In other words, some associations may foster mainly 'Euro-enthusiast' activists. Conversely, other organizations might be closer to the idea of the social movement paradigm, fostering 'critical Europeanists' – namely, activists who are highly engaged in European politics (showing a high level of interest) but simultaneously disappointed by the functioning of the European institutions (exhibiting low trust). However, in terms of legitimacy it should be noted that this type of critical support can be considered as a beneficial type of 'critical social capital' (Tarrow 2000: 289). According to this vision, the normatively 'bad social capital' would be those represented by associations that foster 'Euro-disaffected' activists (people detached from the political system, not interested and not trustful in politics).

Table 7.1 shows the distribution of the four types of 'European support' among activists, socially actives and non-actives in the six countries and cities. Focusing on non-active citizens, we see that the Euro-disaffected represent the largest group in the majority of the countries (with the exception of Switzerland and West Germany, where they represent the second largest group).[10] The Euro-disaffected account for at least one-third of the non-actives (in the case of the UK, and Spain they constitute the majority of the non-actives). Moreover, in all countries the percentage of Euro-disaffected is higher among non-actives than among activists and socially actives. Among non-actives, in all countries (with the exception of Switzerland), the critical Europeanists are the smallest group (circa 10 per cent of the population).

Among the activists (and the socially actives), a very different picture emerges. Here, the Euro-enthusiasts are more heavily represented than among the non-actives. This is true especially in West Germany and Switzerland, where the Euro-enthusiasts are the largest group among activists and socially actives (accounting for around 32–40 per cent). The second more conspicuous type of activists in all the locales (with the exceptions of the Netherlands and East Germany) are the 'critical Europeanists'. In all countries, however, the critical Europeanists are more numerous among the activists and socially actives than among non-actives. Among activists, the Euro-disaffected are less represented than among the non-actives. The difference concerning the presence of Euro-disaffected among activists and among non-actives is especially evident in the UK. This last finding can be interpreted as further confirmation of the positive relevance of associational participation on political orientation towards Europe. Not only do associational members display greater support for Europe than the non-actives, but the beneficial effect of taking part in associational activities is also stronger where the country context is less conducive towards positive attitudes toward Europe – i.e. in the traditionally Euro-sceptic UK.

Table 7.1 Distribution of types of support for Europe among activists, socially actives and non-actives (percentages)

	East Germany			West Germany			The Netherlands			Spain			Switzerland			United Kingdom		
	Activists	Non-actives	Socially actives	Activists	Non-actives	Socially actives	Activists	Non-actives	Socially actives	Activists	Non-actives	Socially actives	Activists	Non-actives	Socially actives	Activists	Non-actives	Socially actives
Euro-enthusiasts	30.1	18.2	32.0	32.3	18.3	31.8	21.9	20.9	22.9	n.a.	12.5	21.1	40.2	36.9	40.2	25.0	13.6	19.7
Euro-pragmatics	18.5	33.6	22.4	14.2	41.4	40.5	24.3	27.9	27.1	n.a.	27.1	25.3	18.4	15.7	18.9	18.3	22.4	21.1
Critical Europeanists	23.6	9.5	19.0	28.3	7.5	9.1	20.7	14.2	15.8	n.a.	7.8	15.6	20.5	19.2	20.5	25.9	12.0	13.4
Euro-disaffected	27.8	38.7	26.5	25.2	32.7	18.6	33.1	37.0	34.2	n.a	52.6	38.0	20.4	28.1	20.4	30.8	52.0	45.9
N	1,204	545	415	1,748	823	1,121	411	584	935	–	2,358	1,286	908	542	826	804	1,838	868

Note
n.a., not available.

7.4 Voluntary associations and European orientations: are all associations alike?

An important aspect of the democratic potential of voluntary organizations with regard to Europe is the analysis of differences in fostering different types of European support between different types of organizations. In other words: Do different types of associations have a differential impact on support for Europe among activists?

As our analysis has so far shown, associational participation is relevant for attitudes towards Europe. However, it is unlikely that all associations (e.g. sport clubs, cultural associations or political groups) have a similar impact on the European political orientations of their members. Indeed, in terms of associations as (more or less) conducive contexts for developing pro-European attitudes, it is important to note that the European integration process strongly affects the relative distribution of power among collective actors (associations, interest groups, etc.), opening up new opportunities for some, but also providing new constraints and challenges for others (della Porta and Kriesi 1999; Bartolini 2002). Consequently, scholars have argued that collective actors' attitudes and positions towards Europe might reflect the degree to which they profit (or stand to lose) from the European integration process (Koopmans 2008). Civil society associations in each country differ greatly in their goals, concerns and tasks, and for this reason they are affected differently by the European integration process (some more positively, other more negatively, and others not affected at all). Thus, there is no reason to suppose that such different groups will have the same influence on the orientations and attitudes of their members towards Europe.

In particular, our expectation is that activists from market and political organizations will be more interested in European politics than are other types of organizations (such as leisure and sport groups), because the EU is mainly a process of economic and political building. In the case of trust, however, political organizations might show some variation, as members can be either Euro-enthusiasts or critical Europeanists, depending on the type of political groups (politics and new politics) and, in particular, their perceptions regarding the functioning of European institutions. In order to analyse the impact of various types of voluntary associations on European support, we apply our typology of forms of support for Europe to a sectoral taxonomy distinguishing associations under study in 11 associational sectors (e.g. welfare, politics, culture, etc.).[11]

Figures 7.3a and 7.3b show the distribution of the two extreme types, the Euro-disaffected and the Euro-enthusiasts, among the activists and socially actives across the sectors and the countries under study. First of all, our data show a consistent pattern between these two different types of European support across associational sectors. This finding can be interpreted as additional confirmation of the relevance of the impact of active associational engagement on political orientations, which appears greater among the 'hard-core' of socially engaged people (i.e. activists). Focusing on the Euro-disaffected (see Figure 7.3a), it emerges that this category is most prevalent among activists from 'non-political' organizations, such as family, sports and religion groups. This is true in all countries and cities,[12] and specifically the Netherlands, East Germany and Switzerland; the Euro-disaffected are also largely present among activists from economic interest groups. On the contrary, overall, voluntary associations concerned with politics and new politics are those in which Euro-disaffected activists are the least present (or not present at all, in the case of the Netherlands). In East and West Germany, the Euro-disaffected are the least present among activists from associations working on community concerns.[13] For the remaining associational types, there is a high cross-country variation in the relative presence of the Euro-disaffected among activists (and among socially actives as well), and a common pattern cannot be detected, apart from the fact that in welfare and culture associations they are slightly more present than in non-political associations and, to some extent, less common than in strictly 'political' groups.

Concerning the Euro-enthusiasts (see Figure 7.3b), first of all, our data display a consistent pattern of distribution across countries among different associational sectors. In general, we find that Euro-enthusiasts are more heavily represented among activists than socially actives. However, this pattern is less evident than the one found for the Euro-disaffected between the two categories of socially engaged people. Everywhere, Euro-enthusiasts tend to belong to political organizations, such as politics and new politics groups, representing over one-third of their activists.[14] Contrary to what we might expect, they are not so prevalent in economic interest groups. Indeed, Euro-enthusiasts are more concentrated in some countries (such as West Germany and Switzerland) than in others.[15]

For the others two types of 'supporters' of Europe, namely the critical Europeanists and the Euro-pragmatics, the picture is more scattered, and no common pattern can be discerned among countries and associational sectors.[16] Nevertheless, it is worth noting that critical Europeanists have a greater presence among activists from associations dealing with 'new political' themes (in East and West Germany and Switzerland), politics and community concerns (in East Germany and the UK), and welfare (in the Netherlands and West Germany).

The fact that activists in associations concerned with politics show relatively high levels of both interest in European politics and trust in EU confirms, at least for this type of association, the positive relation between social and political engagement and political trust. Furthermore, this pattern has been found consistently among different specific voluntary associations and different cities and countries in Europe. Finally, our findings about the relatively large presence of critical Europeanists within associations working on new politics and social issues are in line with results of other recent studies. Indeed, social movements organizations dealing with 'new politics' (such as environmental groups, women' groups, etc.) and NGOs (working on migrants, humanitarian and social issues, etc.) are often the most protest-driven and critical civil society groups targeting European institutions (for example, raising social protection concerns; Balme 2008). Most social movement organizations, however, proclaim their own Europeanism, stressing their general orientation towards supranational multilateralism and cosmopolitanism (Tarrow 2005).

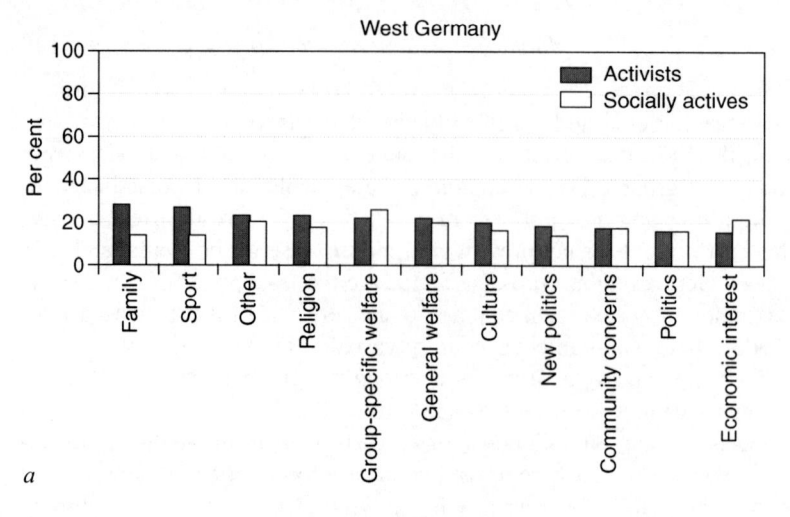

West Germany

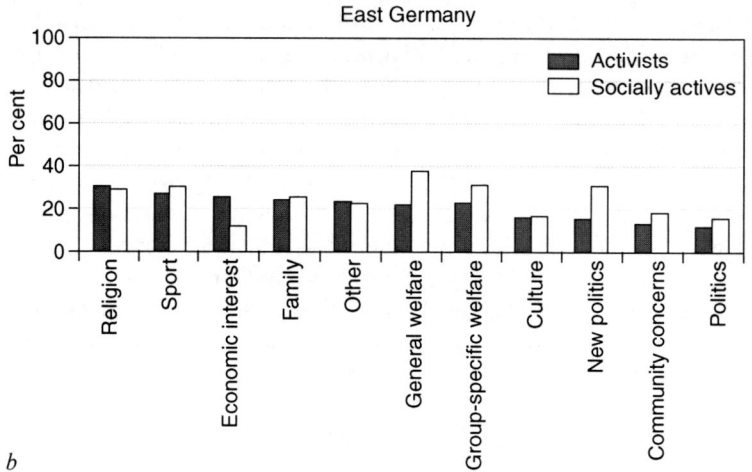

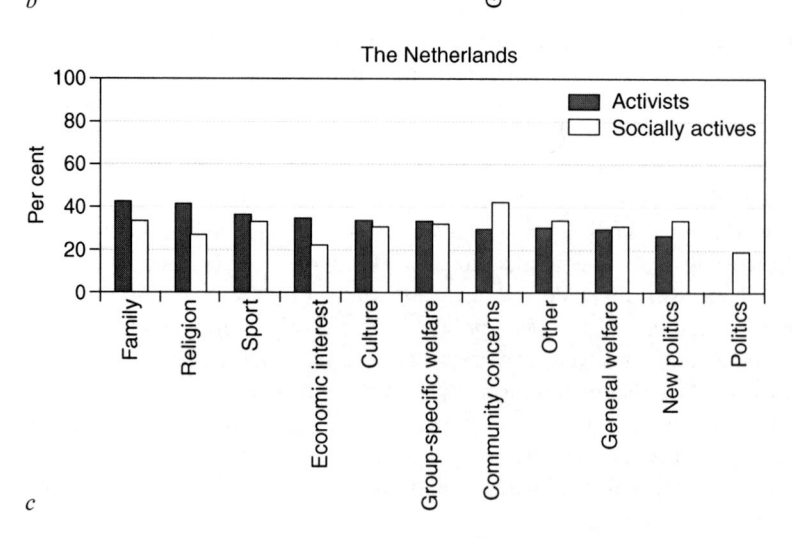

a

East Germany

b

The Netherlands

c

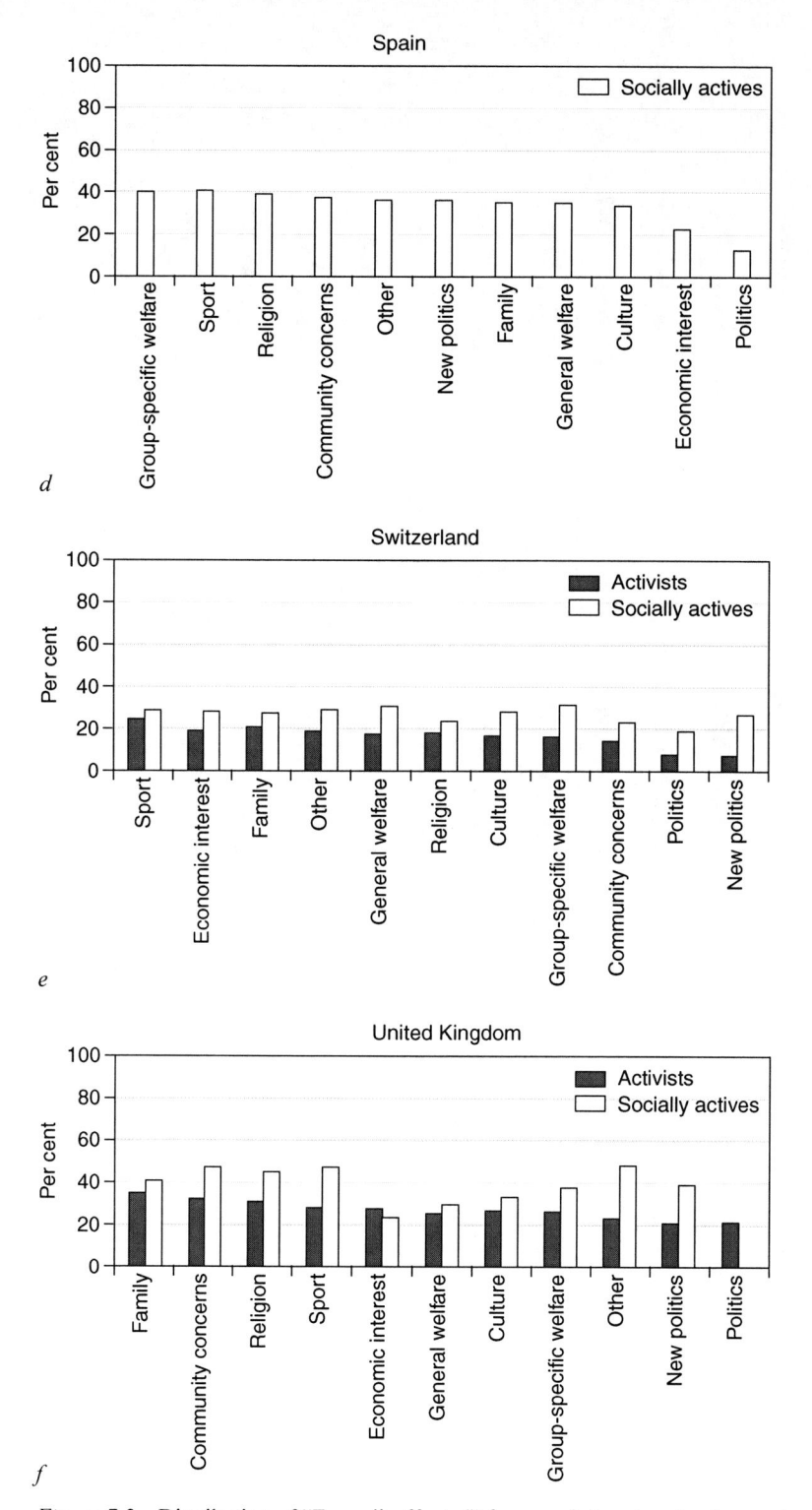

Figure 7.3a Distribution of "Euro-disaffected" for associational sector (percentages).

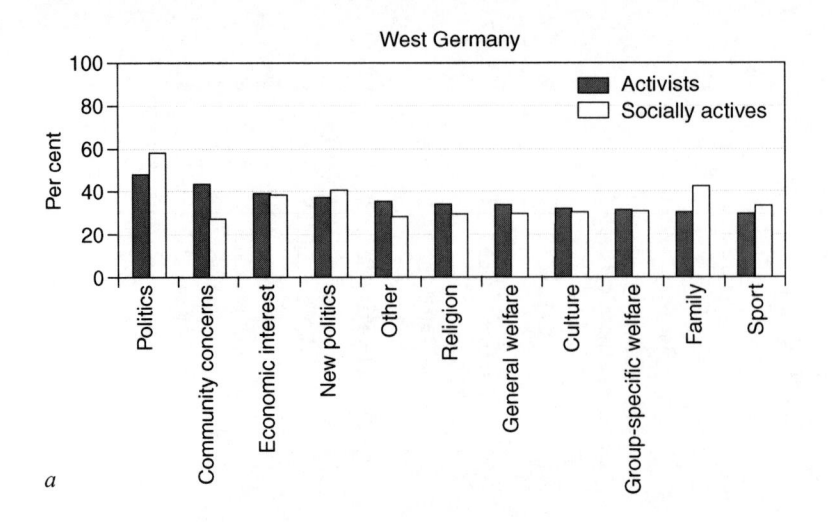

a

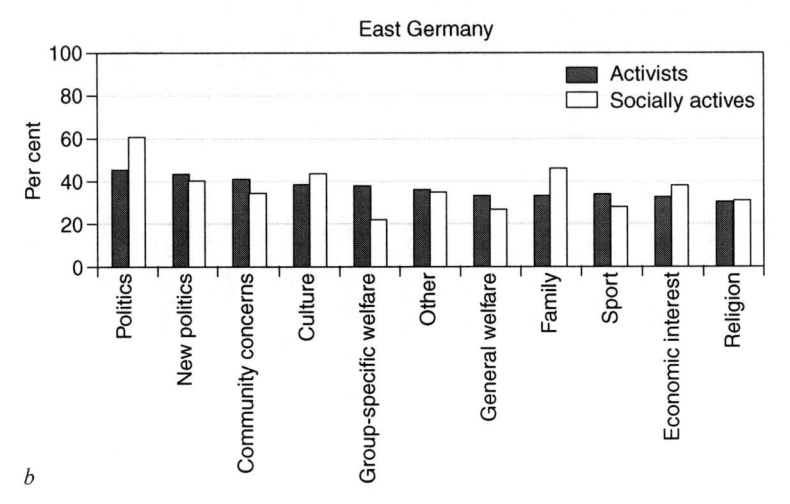

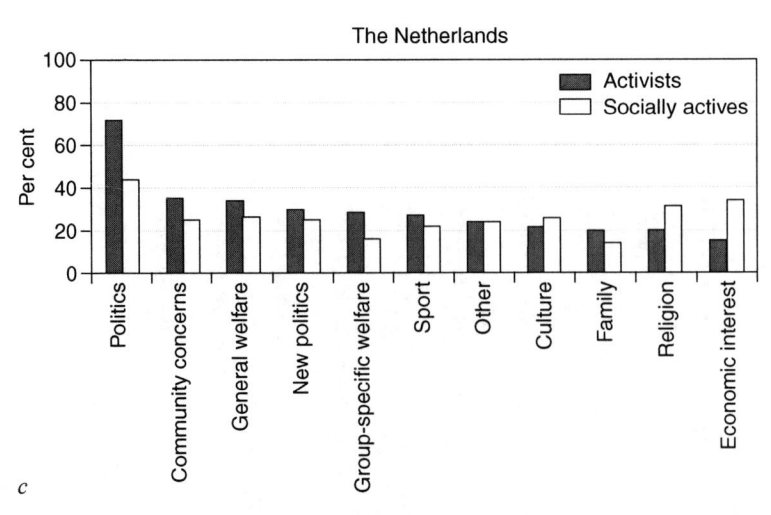

West Germany

b

East Germany

c

The Netherlands

Spain

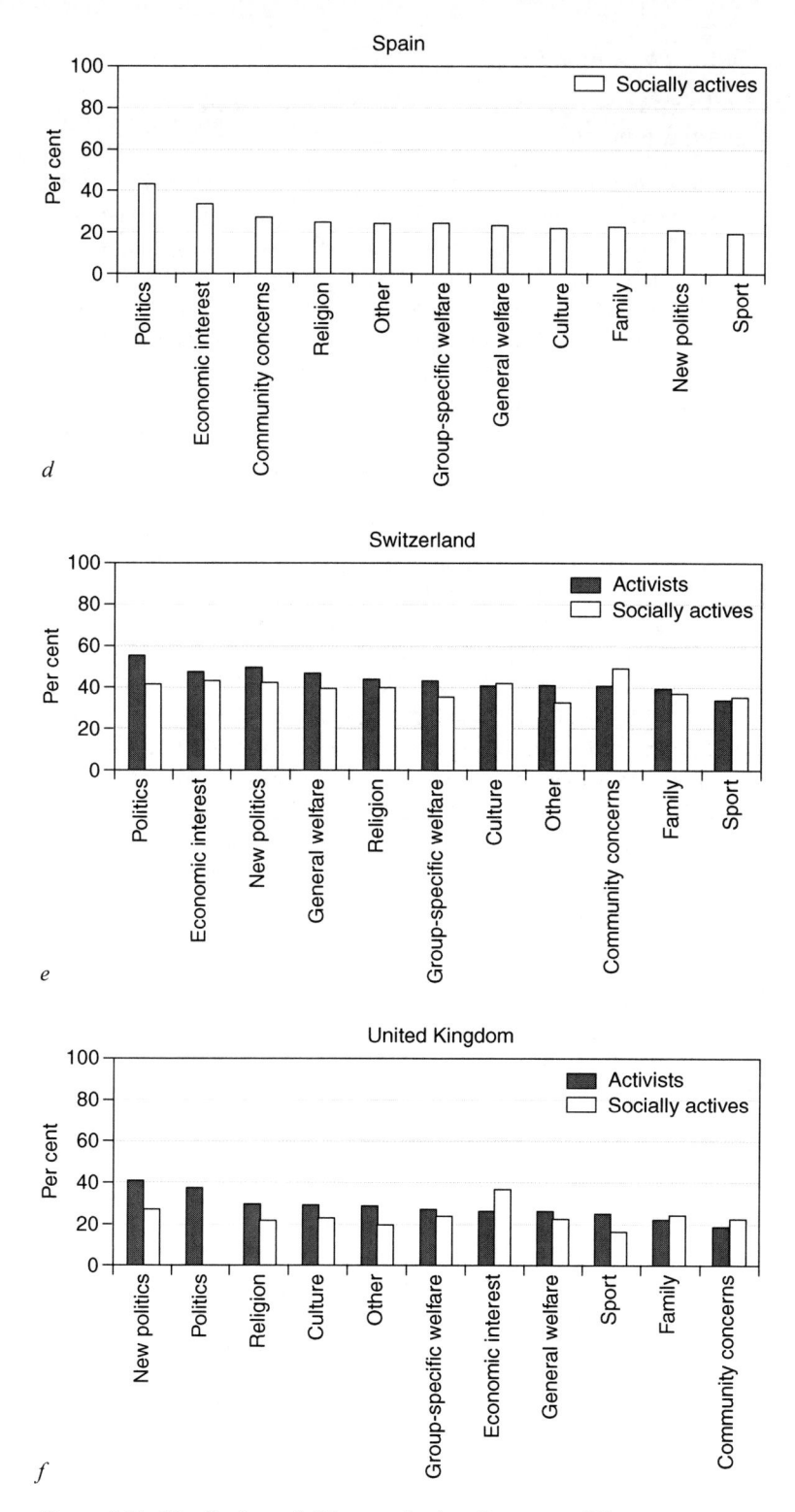

d

Switzerland

e

United Kingdom

f

Figure 7.3b Distribution of "Euro-enthusiasts" among different types of associations (percentages).

7.5 Individual features, associational context and actual associational engagement

In general, associational participation seems to have a positive impact on political orientations towards Europe. Although voluntary associations sometimes might be a place for the development of a more critical type of European support (the critical europeanists), they are not, in any case, settings for the development of the most challenging citizens for European democracy: the Euro-disaffected. However, as we have seen, the associational impact also differs strongly between different types of associations. How can we comprehend these differences? Is it a matter of individual characteristics of associational members, or are different opportunities offered by different associational contexts crucial? Or, ceteris paribus, is it a matter of differences in the levels of associational engagement within associations? What mechanisms lie behind support for Europe?

In this section, we analyse the relevance of three sets of explanatory variables on support for Europe between activists.[17] In particular, multivariate models are carried out to estimate the relative impact of the individual characteristics, the associational features of the organizations in which they are active, and the nature of their engagement, on the likelihood of activists belonging to one of the four types of support for Europe. For each set of variables we have introduced several indicators. On the one hand, at the *individual* level, there is a long tradition of research that utilizes Eurobarometer data to identify variables affecting citizens' attitudes toward Europe (see, for example, Carey 2002; Brinegar *et al.* 2004; Gabel and Anderson 2004). First and foremost, the standard socio-demographic variables (age, gender and level of education) are considered important in explaining support for Europe. With regard to education, much of the public opinion literature suggests that low-educated and low-skilled workers are likely to have a more negative evaluation of European integration, being less competitive in an integrated market, and being on the side of the 'losers' in the process (Gabel 1998; Hix 1999). Furthermore, a number of political orientations are considered to be related to the level of support for Europe. A good level of political information, for example, is considered particularly important for European support (Statham 2007). Otherwise, the EU is perceived by citizens as distant and obscure, and the risk of citizen detachment from European affairs is greater (see, for example, the case of ratification of the EU Constitution, Machill *et al.* 2007). Left–right placement is also considered a relevant factor for explaining European support. Scholars have hypothesized that the existence of a curvilinear relationship (the so-called 'inverted U-curve') between ideological position and support for Europe which is likely to generate Euro-scepticism is more likely among citizens located at the peripheries/extremities of the left–right continuum, whereas citizens at the core of the political spectrum are expected to be less critical toward Europe (see, for example, Szczerbiak and Taggart 2000).[18] Support for Europe is also related to the attachment of citizens to their nation, and trust in national institutions. Here, there are two contrasting 'schools'. Some scholars present support for Europe as compensating for low trust in national institutions (Sánchez-Cuenca 2000), while identification as Europeans is considered to be undermined by a strong and exclusive national identification (Carey 2002). For these reasons, they expect a negative relationship between high trust and attachment to national-level institutions, and support for Europe. On the other hand, Europe can be seen as a complement to the nations, and a positive relationship between strong national identities and trust in national institutions and support for Europe is predicted (Duchesse and Frognier 2007).

In our analyses we included several *indicators of individual characteristics*, which comprise general socio-demographic features (age, gender, education)[19] as well as political orientations (political information,[20] left–right placement,[21] trust in national institutions and attachment to the country[22]).

However, citizens' attitudes towards Europe can also interact with meso-level agents of socialization such as voluntary associations that are very different contexts in terms of opportunities they provide for social engagement.[23] Furthermore, with regard to European support, if resourceful organizations are considered to be endowed with more material and organizational resources to deal with the shifts in power toward the supranational-European level (Balme 2008), one could expect that bigger and richer organizations would provide a more conducive context to foster pro-European attitudes. With regard to *organizational contextual features*, we include in our analyses indicators for the size and financial strength of an association (the variable 'size', measured as the number of total members, and the variable 'budget', measured through the total annual operating budget of the organization). In addition, the participatory capacity of an organization is measured by the presence of a general assembly.[24] Finally, we take into account the scope of associational activities,[25] arguing that support for Europe requires enlarging the scope of one's own identification and trust towards a supranational sphere. The larger the geographical scope of activities of an association, the more likely it is to generate a context that fosters cosmopolitan feelings and positive orientations towards Europe.

In order to assess the impact of associational features, we need to distinguish between the associational context and the actual engagement of activists. The distinction between these two aspects of associational participation (features of organizations and nature of associational engagement) is required in order to take into account the difference that exists between the (potential) context of an association and the actual degree of engagement of an activist (and thus the actual level of 'exposure' to its potential 'effects'). The *actual associational engagement* has been measured by the 'length of the membership' in the association (the number of years active in the association), the 'time spent' in associational activities (the number of hours active in the association on a monthly basis)[26] and the (perceived) 'commitment' to the association (using the question 'how committed do you feel to this organization?').[27]

The results of the multivariate analyses and the relative impact of the three sets of independent variables are presented in Tables 7.2–7.5. In each table, a binomial logit equation for predicting Euro-disaffection, Euro-enthusiasm, Euro-pragmatism and critical Europeanism is estimated as a function of these three sets of variables.

Overall, the empirical evidence presented in Tables 7.2–7.5 shows that among the three blocks of explanatory variables, the strongest contribution to explanation for the four types of European support – after comparing the level of variance explained by each block – is provided by the individual-features variables. The effects of associational engagement and of associational features are limited.

With regard to the influence of *individual-features variables* on support for Europe, the results confirm most of the theoretical expectations. As Table 7.2 shows, trust in national institutions (and, to a lesser extent, attachment to the country), political information, and being in the extreme left versus being ideologically moderate are positively related to the likelihood of being a Euro-enthusiast, whereas the impact of socio-demographic variables is almost negligible (with the exception of West Germany). This means that individuals more trustful in national institutions (and attached to their country), more informed about politics and located on the extreme left in terms of ideology are more likely to be Euro-enthusiasts. The fact that trust in national institutions (and partly attachment to the country) has a positive relation with Euro-enthusiasm seems to support the 'school' that sees support for Europe as cumulative rather than exclusive to the national one (Carey 2002). On the contrary, the result of the impact of left–right placement on European support goes partly against the expectation that relates the ideological extremism to Euro-scepticism. When comparing the results concerning Euro-enthusiasm with the determinants of Euro-pragmatism (see Table 7.3), the most interesting finding is that in the latter case, those individuals with lower levels of education and political information are most likely to be Euro-pragmatics.[28] This result is relatively unsurprising, because it seems reasonable that people with low levels of political information and low levels of educational attainment express a type of support for Europe that can be distinguished as rather pragmatic – that is, a type of support for Europe that is based more on instrumental considerations about Europe (such as the contingent 'benefits' of the EU integration for ones own country) than on abstract reflections about the 'normative' aspects of the European project per se. This type of pragmatic European support implies nevertheless a positive attitude towards Europe, among citizens, that European political elites can claim as a legitimate basis for proceeding further with the European integration process. Looking at Euro-scepticism (Table 7.4), we find some consistent trends concerning the relevance of individual features on European support; however, this time a very different picture of the 'European citizen' emerges. The likelihood of being a Euro-sceptic is greater among those who are less trustful of national institutions, less attached to their country, less politically informed and ideologically moderate. Once again, left–right placement is the only variable that seems to work differently on European support than expected. Neither people located on the extreme left (in East and West German cities) nor those located on the extreme right (in Enschede and Aberdeen) tend to be Euro-

Table 7.2 Prediction of euro-enthusiasts (activists only)

	East Germany		West Germany		The Netherlands		Switzerland		United Kingdom	
	Coef.	R^2	Coef.	R^2	Coef.	R^2	Coef.	R^2	Coef.	R^2
Individual features										
Age	0.00		0.01		−0.01		0.02**		−0.01*	
Gender	−0.19		−0.30**		0.05		0.01		−0.26	
Tertiary education	−0.01		0.29**		−0.01		0.14		0.17	
Trust in national parliament	0.43****		0.49****		0.38***		0.34****		0.47****	
Attachment to the country	0.06*		0.09***		−0.01		−0.02		0.10**	
Political information	0.26****		0.25****		0.79****		0.31****		0.40****	
Extreme left (vs moderate)	0.52***		0.40**		0.11		1.07****		0.35	
Extreme right (vs moderate)	−0.25	0.23	−0.32	0.27	−1.01	0.19	−0.47	0.19	0.02	0.26
Associational features										
Scope	−0.06		0.04		−0.18		0.06		0.00	
Size	0.00		−0.02		0.43****		0.00*		−0.02	
Budget	−0.09		0.04		0.00*		0.00		0.11	
Assembly	−0.28	0.00	−0.15	0.00	−0.18	0.09	−0.23	0.01	0.11	0.00
Associational engagement										
Commitment	0.29		0.13		−0.66***		0.12		0.10	
Time of participating	−0.08		−0.07		−0.05		−0.08		0.01	
Duration membership	−0.01	0.00	−0.01*	0.00	0.00	0.03	−0.03***	0.02	−0.01	0.00
Intercept	−4.28		−5.27		−5.06		−3.75		−5.06	
Nagelkerke R^2		0.24		0.28		0.32		0.23		0.27
N	1,001		1,425		279		552		548	

Notes
Entries are maximum likelihood logit estimations. *$P<0.10$, **$P<0.05$, ***$P<0.01$, ****$P<0.001$.

Table 7.3 Prediction of Euro-pragmatics (activists only)

	East Germany		West Germany		The Netherlands		Switzerland		United Kingdom	
	Coef.	R^2	Coef.	R^2	Coef.	R^2	Coef.	R^2	Coef.	R^2
Individual features										
Age	−0.02***		−0.02****		0.00		−0.01		0.00	
Gender	0.41**		0.62****		0.31		0.09		0.20	
Tertiary education	−0.39***		−0.36***		−1.25****		−0.45*		−0.05	
Trust in national parliament	0.36****		0.34****		0.75****		0.24****		0.65****	
Attachment to the country	−0.08*		−0.06*		0.17*		−0.07		−0.03	
Political information	−0.41****		−0.54****		−0.57****		−0.56****		−0.67****	
Extreme left (vs moderate)	−0.34		−0.66**		−0.75		−0.45		−1.33**	
Extreme right (vs moderate)	−0.14	0.23	0.67**	0.19	0.76	0.30	−0.28	0.18	−0.50	0.28
Associational features										
Scope	−0.08		0.03		0.34**		0.20		0.17*	
Size	0.00		0.12**		0.04		0.00		0.12	
Budget	0.03		−0.01		0.00		0.00		0.02	
Assembly	−0.22	0.00	−0.31	0.00	−0.14	0.02	0.61	0.00	−0.71**	0.02
Associational engagement										
Commitment	−0.07		−0.16		−0.34		−0.19		0.03	
Time of participating	0.08		−0.06		−0.14		0.01		0.01	
Duration membership	0.01	0.00	0.01*	0.00	0.00	0.01	0.02	0.00	0.01	0.00
Intercept	−0.80		−0.74		−4.52		−1.40		−4.93	
Nagelkerke R^2		0.23		0.20		0.33		0.19		0.31
N	1,001		1,425		279		552		548	

Notes
Entries are maximum likelihood logit estimations. *$P<0.10$, **$P<0.05$, ***$P<0.01$, ****$P<0.001$.

Table 7.4 Prediction of Euro-disaffected (activists only)

	East Germany		West Germany		The Netherlands		Switzerland		United Kingdom	
	Coef.	R^2	Coef.	R^2	Coef.	R^2	Coef.	R^2	Coef.	R^2
Individual features										
Age	0.00		0.00		0.00		−0.03***		0.02***	
Gender	−0.10		−0.14		−0.15		−0.21		0.22	
Tertiary education	−0.16		−0.66****		−0.05		0.39		−0.28	
Trust in national parliament	−0.37****		−0.36****		−0.50****		−0.29****		−0.39***	
Attachment to the country	0.00		−0.05*		−0.18**		0.08		−0.01	
Political information	−0.18***		−0.22****		−0.12		−0.36****		−0.54****	
Extreme left (vs moderate)	−0.80****		−0.49**		0.36		−1.34****		−0.71	
Extreme right (vs moderate)	−0.09	0.18	0.16	0.20	−2.40***	0.21	0.57	0.18	−0.29	0.27
Associational features										
Scope	0.02		−0.07		−0.23*		−0.11		−0.27***	
Size	0.00		−0.02		−0.06		0.00		0.06	
Budget	0.12*		0.10**		0.00		0.00		−0.04	
Assembly	0.46*	0.00	0.21	0.00	0.96*	0.02	−0.29	0.00	0.11	0.02
Associational engagement										
Commitment	−0.32**		−0.19		0.62***		−0.18		0.08	
Time of participating	0.07		0.01		0.16		0.02		−0.01	
Duration membership	0.01	0.01	−0.01	0.00	−0.01	0.04	0.04***	0.02	−0.01	0.00
Intercept	1.72		2.61		1.71		3.04		1.35	
Nagelkerke R^2		0.20		0.21		0.28		0.21		0.29
N	1,001		1,425		279		552		548	

Notes
Entries are maximum likelihood logit estimations. *P<0.10, **P<0.05, ***P<0.01, ****P<0.001.

Table 7.5 Prediction of critical Europeanists (activists only)

	East Germany		West Germany		The Netherlands		Switzerland		United Kingdom	
	Coef.	R^2	Coef.	R^2	Coef.	R^2	Coef.	R^2	Coef.	R^2
Individual features										
Age	0.02****		0.01*		0.04**		0.00		0.00	
Gender	0.04		0.23*		−0.06		0.13		−0.09	
Tertiary education	0.63****		0.46****		1.60****		−0.16		0.23	
Trust in national parliament	−0.36****		−0.31****		−0.32****		−0.34****		−0.33****	
Attachment to the country	0.03		−0.01		−0.06		0.02		−0.05	
Political information	0.36****		0.46****		0.30*		0.66****		0.54****	
Extreme left (vs moderate)	0.37**		0.37**		−0.43		−0.23		0.43	
Extreme right (vs moderate)	0.25	0.23	−0.24	0.16	1.27**	0.15	0.23	0.19	0.40	0.20
Associational features										
Scope	0.14		0.00		0.17		−0.16		0.06	
Size	0.00		−0.01		−0.39****		0.00***		−0.11	
Budget	−0.07		−0.11**		0.00**		0.00		−0.08	
Assembly	0.04	0.00	0.13	0.00	−0.68	0.12	0.42	0.01	0.26	0.01
Associational engagement										
Commitment	0.19		0.15		0.15		0.22		−0.28	
Time of participating	−0.11		0.09		−0.09		0.05		0.05	
Duration membership	−0.01	0.00	0.01	0.00	0.01	0.00	−0.01	0.00	0.01	0.00
Intercept	−2.82		−2.23		−1.36		−3.27		1.24	
Nagelkerke R^2		0.24		0.17		0.28		0.22		0.22
N	1,001		1,425		279		552		548	

Notes
Entries are maximum likelihood logit estimations. *$P<0.10$, **$P<0.05$, ***$P<0.01$, ****$P<0.001$.

disaffected. Finally, as Table 7.5 shows, the chances of being a critical Europeanist are higher among older people in West Germany and the Netherlands, who do not trust national political institutions (similarly to what we have seen for Euro-disaffected people) and who (different than Euro-disaffected!) are characterized by higher levels of political information and education. In terms of left–right placement, critical Europeanists tend to be located on the extreme left (in West and East Germany), but they can also be located on the extreme right (in the Netherlands).

Turning to the impact of *organizational features*, the explained variances of the four indicators combined are generally low, with the exception of the Netherlands (most notably, for Euro-enthusiasts and critical europeanists). Out of a total of 80 coefficients, only 18 reach acceptable levels of statistical significance. We find some variation in the direction of the coefficients depending on the type of support for Europe. First, in all cities (excluding Swiss municipalities) having an assembly is positively related to the chances of being Euro-sceptics, whereas for the likelihood of being Euro-enthusiasts the reverse applies. This means that, apparently, taking part in an association characterized by a more 'participatory' context is not conducive to the development of positive attitudes toward Europe. Perhaps activists who have more opportunities to be involved in discussions within their organizations, and possibly discussions on European matters, have more occasions to weigh up the pros and cons of European politics, and might be more likely to form some negative attitudes towards Europe. Second, the budget, size and scope of the organizations have an impact on some specific types of support for Europe and in some European municipalities. In particular, in line with our expectations, the more international in scope an association is, the less likely activists are to be Euro-disaffected. The pattern moves in the opposite direction from Euro-pragmatists. Budget actually contradicts the expectation that resourceful associations should be a more conducive context for the development of positive attitudes towards Europe. Activists in associations with larger budgets tend to be Euro-disaffected at least in the two German cities, while the opposite is true for critical Europeanism. Nevertheless, size has clearer effects than budget. Activists from larger organizations tend to have less critical attitudes towards Europe (in Enschede and Swiss cities they tend to be Euro-enthusiasts, whereas in Mannheim they tend to be Euro-pragmatics).

A final conclusion based on the impact of the various aspects related to the *associational engagement* (commitment, time of participating, duration of membership variables) of activists can be drawn. On the one hand, the empirical findings indicate that these factors are largely irrelevant to the likelihood of being Euro-pragmatics and critical Europeanists. For these two mixed types, the level of variances explained for this block are very low and only one coefficient out of 30 is statistically significant. On the other hand, for the two most extreme types – Euro-disaffected and Euro-enthusiasts – the levels of variances explained are somewhat better (six coefficients out of 30 are statistically significant), most notably in the Netherlands and, to a lesser extent, in Switzerland and East Germany. More specifically, the level of commitment in one association seems to be positively related to being Euro-disaffected, while the duration of membership tends to be negatively related to the likelihood of being Euro-enthusiasts. The latter finding is contrary to the expectations of social-capital type arguments that would suggest that the duration of membership should be positively related to Euro-enthusiasm. Apparently, a higher level of involvement in an association is not conducive to the development of positive attitudes towards Europe.

7.6 Conclusion

In this chapter, the impact of membership in various voluntary associations on support for Europe has been analysed by addressing two main questions: first, whether the associational participation fosters and enhances trust and interest in European politics; and second, whether different types of associations impact differentially on the levels of trust and interest in European politics exhibited by activists. By using these two indicators to measure support for Europe, and by comparing information about these attitudes coming from three groups of citizens at a different level of engagement in voluntary associations (the activists, the socially actives and the non-actives) in six European countries, we have empirically tested the impact of voluntary activities on European support.

In spite of the huge variation in the cross-national context specificities with regard to support for Europe among the countries studied (some of them among the most pro-European founding fathers, other among the most traditional Eurosceptic countries), apparently the findings that emerged from our descriptive analyses support our expectation that activities in voluntary associations can contribute to the development of a more engaged European citizen. Associational participation emerged, with a consistent pattern across countries, as relevant for European political interest, which is clearly highest among activists as opposed to the other two groups of citizens (socially actives and non-actives). Furthermore, taking into account the complexity of the concept of European support (as a 'polymorphic' term that might refer to different concepts and processes; della Porta 2006) and constructing a more refined typology of it by combining interest in European politics and trust in European institutions, we have seen that the most supporting type of citizens (the Euro-enthusiasts) has a greater presence among activists than among socially active and non-active citizens. Moreover, everywhere, Euro-enthusiasts are more heavily concentrated in 'political organizations' such as 'politics' and 'new politics' groups. Yet associational participation in some sectors (such as 'new politics' and welfare–social issues) also appears conducive to the development of a more contentious and challenging type of European support – that is, the critical Europeanist. Evidently, associational activities offer opportunities for increasing, if not unconditional support for Europe, at least attention to Europe and European affairs, fostering in this way an active 'European citizenship'. Indeed, in the case of critical Europeanists we have to take into account the positive role that they can play in European democracy. As Thomas Risse underlines:

contestation is a crucial pre-condition for the emergence of a European public sphere rather than an indicator for its absence. If political issues are not contested, if European politics remains the business of elites, the attention level for Europe and the EU will remain low. European issues must become salient and significant in the various public debates so that a European public sphere can emerge.

(Risse 2003: 6)

That is to say, the support for Europe and the European integration process cannot be simply measured in terms of 'permissive' consensus to European decisions and institutions (della Porta and Caiani 2006: 208). On the contrary, contestation, accompanied by a commitment to the project of the European integration process (demonstrated, for instance, by interest in European affairs) is a possible road toward the creation of a supranational democracy (Risse 2003: 6).

When the relative impact of associational engagement, associational features and individual characteristics of activists on different types of support for Europe are empirically assessed, it is the individual features that appear most relevant for explaining support for Europe. Neither objective features of associations nor the levels of actual engagement of activists appear to be important.

Some characteristics of the organizations seem to matter for European support. Associations with a more international scope appear to provide a better context for the development of positive orientations toward Europe. Surprisingly, the opposite trend emerges with regard to more 'participatory' associations (better contexts for fostering Euro-scepticism). The characteristics of organizations often display different results depending on the country, and, in most of cases, are not statistically significant. The associational impact on European support seems to be mainly due to the fact that activists have some specific political orientations of their own – for example, with regard to the two most extreme and interesting types (the Euro-enthusiasts and the Euro-disaffected) of trust in national institutions, attachment to the country, and political information. In other words, from our study it emerges that it is the individual features of the active citizens that account for the impact of the associations, and not the associations as such. Indeed, associations attract people with specific individual features, and that explains the associational impact on attitudes towards Europe. It is also worth noting for future research that our empirical findings concerning (left) extremism challenge some of the common hypotheses in the literature about its association with Euro-scepticism (see section 7.5). In sum, the associational impact is weak after controlling for the individual features of activists.

Notes

1 This chapter was planned, thought about and discussed jointly by the two authors. To this common work, Manuela Caiani contributed the final writing of sections 7.1–7.3, while Mariona Ferrer-Fons contributed sections 7.4–7.6.
2 See http://ec.europa.eu/public_opinion/archives/eb_arch_en.htm.

3 More specifically, at the empirical level, interest in European politics was measured on the basis of a four-point scale question; from 0 ('not at all interested') to 3 ('very interested').
4 An 11-point scale was used to measure the answer, ranging from 0 ('not attachment/ trust at all') to 10 ('very strong attachment/high trust').
5 These questions are not included in the Spanish Activists Study. Hence, for Spain we will show only descriptive results from the population sample.
6 In West Germany and the UK, the difference between activists and non-actives on the mean of interest in European politics is relatively large (accounting for 0.7 and 0.6, respectively), whereas in Switzerland and the Netherlands it is smaller (0.1 in both countries). The difference in the level of interest in European politics between socially actives and non-actives is notable particularly in Spain and East Germany.
7 Furthermore, in these two countries the ranking between activists and socially actives corroborates our expectation, with the former expressing higher levels of trust in Europe than the latter.
8 In fact, many studies have underlined that today a simple distinction among people who are pro and against Europe is of little usefulness in understanding citizens' positions towards Europe (Marks and Steenbergen 2004; Cotta et al. 2005; della Porta and Caiani 2009). Indeed, the criticism towards Europe is not only regarding the dimension of the polity (namely, on the issue of the boundaries of the political community opposing traditionally nationalists vs Europeanists) but also, and above all with politicization of the EU, regarding the content of the European policies and on the European politics (namely, on the institutional structure of the EU – for example, more power to the Parliament vs the Council of Ministers) (Cotta et al. 2005: 29; della Porta and Caiani 2006, Chapter 2). This means that support for Europe does not necessarily imply 'trust' for its institutions and policies, and that one can support the project of European integration per se (the ideal), being, for instance, very interested in and committed to European matters but criticizing (or distrusting), at the same time, some specific European policies or institutions. In sum, this means that it is important to consider 'support' for Europe as a complex concept worth measuring with several indicators.
9 In order to categorize the variable 'trust in European institutions', low-trust citizens are those who show a mean lower than their country mean (calculated through the population representative sample only) on the 0–10 scale. High-trust citizens are those who show a score higher than this mean. The empirical strategy to compare country means is used as a point of reference to differentiate between high and low trust in European institutions and construct the typology. In the case of interest, we have directly recoded the level of interest in European politics in two categories: those who have very (high) interest and those who have none or very little (low interest).
10 In all the countries under study, the second largest group among non-active citizens is represented by the Euro-pragmatics. Everywhere, they represent about one-quarter of the non-actives (although they reach more than 40 per cent in West Germany).
11 For details on the construction of this taxonomy, see Roßteutscher and van Deth (2002).
12 In such mentioned types of associations, from 20 per cent to 30 per cent of activists are 'Euro-disaffected'.
13 Associations concerned with politics are also those in which Euro-disaffected socially actives are the least present, whereas for what concerns associations working on 'new politics' this is true only in some countries. In the Netherlands, East and West Germany and Switzerland, Euro-disaffected citizens are also largely present among socially actives from welfare and economic groups.
14 However, in some countries the presence of Euro-enthusiasts belonging to political organizations goes far beyond the proportion of one-third of all activists. This is the case, for instance, in the Netherlands (where Euro-enthusiasts represent 70 per cent of

all activists) and in associations concerned with 'new politics' in Switzerland (where they are 50 per cent of all activists).
15 In West Germany and the Netherlands, Euro-enthusiasts are also significantly present among activists from associations working on community concerns.
16 These data are not shown here, but they are available from the authors. The Euro-pragmatics are mainly present among activists from non-'strictly' political associations. They are present (a) in associations working on family, sport, culture, religion and community concerns in Switzerland, West and East Germany and the Netherlands; (b) in economic groups in the UK; and (c) in welfare associations in the Netherlands and in West and East Germany.
17 These analyses concern activists only, since information about two of the three distinct antecedents of associational impact (actual engagement and organizational features) is only available in the CID Activists Study.
18 Parties in the ideological mainstream are generally supportive of the integration process, as they have often been part of governing coalitions throughout Western Europe and have therefore been largely responsible for the course of integration. Left-wing and right-wing extremist parties, however, most strongly oppose European integration (Szczerbiak and Taggart 2000). Furthermore, a distinction is made between extreme left and extreme right positions, the latter being considered more likely to be Euro-sceptics for the traditional nationalistic ideology of these forces that would oppose the idea of a loss of sovereignty of the nation-state (Hooghe *et al.* 2004).
19 Age is measured in number of years; gender is a dichotomy where being female takes the value 1 and being male 0; and for the level of education a dichotomy between people reaching tertiary levels of education and those not doing so is used. The use of a dichotomy for tertiary education is due to the lack of equivalence between countries, and the relatively high level of tertiary education among activists. In general, building on the traditional hypotheses of participation research, regarding what concerns these individual levels variables, we could expect in our analyses to find more support towards Europe in older people than younger, in men than in women, and in people with a higher level of education.
20 Political information is measured on an ordinal scale ranging from 0 (for those who declare they never read the political content of a newspaper) to 4 (for those who declared they read the political content of a newspaper every day).
21 Left–right placement is measured with a variable composed of three categories: extreme left (0 to 2), moderate (3 to 7), and extreme right (8 to 10).
22 Attachment to the country is measured through on an ordinal scale from lower (0) to higher (10) attachment. Trust in national institutions is evaluated through trust in parliament (0–10). The choice of 'trust in the national parliament' as a measure of 'trust in national institutions' is not unproblematic, yet among the different indicators of institutional trust available we considered this to be the most comparable between different societies.
23 And thus in terms of opportunities for the promotion of democratic competences and orientations of individuals through transmission of information, developing of political skills and civic virtues, trust, etc. (Warren 2001: 77).
24 This is a dummy variable, measured by 1 if there is an assembly and 0 if not.
25 The scope of the association is measured on an ordinal scale that ranges from 1 (local), through 2 (regional) to 3 (national or international).
26 The time spent in associational activities is measured on a five-point scale where 1 is 'less than one hour per month' and 5 is 'more than 20 hours' per month.
27 The perceived commitment is measured in a four-point scale where 1 is 'not all committed' and 4 is 'very committed'.
28 There are also similarities in the determinants of Euro-enthusiasm and Euro-pragmatism – for instance, the positive effect of being trustful in national institutions on both pragmatic and enthusiast support for Europe.

8 EU legitimacy and social capital
Empirical insights into a complex relationship

Sonja Zmerli

8.1 Introduction

Despite its recent fiftieth anniversary and an impressive record of successful economic and political integration, the European Union (EU) is increasingly being confronted with debates questioning its legitimacy. More precisely, this development started with the ratification of the Maastricht Treaty, a milestone in the history of European integration, which is also described as the end of the 'permissive consensus' (Kohler-Koch *et al.* 2004: 206). In fact, it is exactly the EU's success story itself, with its breathtaking processes of economic and political integration, which seems to challenge most Europeans' willingness to accept and adapt to these major changes (de Vries and van Kersbergen 2007; Eichenberg and Dalton 2007; McLaren 2007). As van Deth (2008b) observes, European citizens do not only show a lack of interest in EU affairs and a lack of EU related knowledge; they are also rather distrustful of the EU and do not feel particularly attached to it (compared to other mainly national political objects of reference).

Many scholars attribute this alarming development to a democratic deficit which is inherent in the institutional arrangements of the EU (Benz 1998; Abromeit 2000; McLaren 2007). Pundits criticize the lack of fundamental rights of the European Parliament as the only elected representative body of the European citizenry, the absence of both a European party system and a European public sphere, the disproportional representation of the European societies in the European Parliament, the introduction of majority votes in the Council of Ministers, a lack of transparency of the decision-making processes within the EU, and a lack of an all-embracing European identity that would bring about the emergence of a European demos (Schmalz-Bruns 1997; Benz 1998; Eder *et al.* 1998; Abromeit 2000; von Bogdandy 2002; Loth 2002; Sbragia 2002; Kielmansegg 2003; Sudbery 2003; Knodt and Finke 2005; Maurer 2006; Zürn 2006; Green 2007). In view of these manifold deficiencies and their consequences, the European Commission has been attempting to counter any further loss of legitimacy by developing and applying a number of measures, one of which pertains to the opening up of the European policy cycle to civil society actors (Kohler-Koch *et al.* 2004).[1] Whether these actions are appropriate to increase the legitimacy of the EU is still an open question. Some political scholars raise serious doubts about the effectiveness and even the legitimacy of these well-intentioned measures unless a European demos becomes a reality (Kielmansegg 2003; Sudbery 2003). From this perspective, however, any of these outlined EU measures seem to lack substance and would, therefore, presumably be bound to fail.

A more optimistic outlook on the future of the EU can be drawn from social capital theory. In a nutshell, this theory claims that vital civil societies contribute significantly to the performance, stability and legitimacy of political systems. According to its line of argument, civil society actors instil in their members a regard for the public interest, encourage cooperation, and facilitate collective behaviour. As a result, citizens are politically more interested and active, and also more inclined to abide by the law. Consequently, the performance of political institutions in democratic political systems is enhanced, and results in stronger support for institutions and increases the legitimacy of the political system as a whole (Putnam et al. 1993; Putnam 2000). From this perspective, the White Paper on European Governance, published by the European Commission in 2001, undoubtedly represents an important step towards integrating civil society actors and their preferences, interests and expertise into the EU policy cycle.[2] As recent studies suggest, however, this strategy could also induce negative rather than favourable orientations towards the EU amongst social activists. In particular, strong social engagement at the local level appears to impede the development of pro-European orientations (van Deth 2008b). These findings not only contrast the social capitalists' common wisdom of benevolent effects resulting from vital civil societies, but also stress the relevance of discriminating the *levels* of social involvement. Civil society actors operating at the EU level might indeed contribute significantly to an improvement of the EU's input and output legitimacy. Being socially active on the local level, by contrast, could rather induce a strong local attachment at the expense of favourable orientations towards the EU, as Sudbery (2003) demonstrated in her informed study on the role of civil society in bridging the legitimacy gap in the EU. The flow of communication and support between NGOs in Brussels, their national member organizations and the individual members is neither necessarily mutual nor encompassing. What is worse, 'it appears that neither members nor supporters see themselves as having a role to play in policy formulation: this is considered to be a matter for the [associational] specialists in Brussels' (Sudbery 2003: 94).

Apart from the importance of the operational level of civic organizations, the diversity of associational features and its impact on individual orientations should likewise be the subject of empirical scrutiny. There are a number of organizational characteristics that are assumed to exert a direct impact on members' degree of activism or volunteering and, consequently, on their individual political orientations. As Maloney and Roßteutscher (2007) comprehensively sketch in their edited volume, voluntary associations can differ remarkably in terms of their size and concerns, spectrum of activities, degree of professionalization, internal decision-making procedures and networking activities with other organizations, as well as their political role in the community. While some associational features have already been demonstrated to be effective on

158   S. Zmerli

individual orientations (van Deth and Maloney 2008), others are perceived to be less so. To which extent social capital in general and associational characteristics in particular affect citizens' perception of the legitimacy of the EU will be the main focus of this chapter.[3] For this purpose, the subsequently presented analyses draw on unusually rich data. This data set is based on five European population surveys on one hand, and social activists' data and features of their organizational context on the other.

At first, linear regression analyses based on the survey data show the impact of social capital indicators such as social involvement and social trust on confidence in the EU, which is conceived of as a proxy of EU legitimacy. In a second step, the peculiarities of socially active individuals' orientations towards the EU will be scrutinized. To this end, their proclivity to trust the EU will be compared to that of less socially active and non-active people. Scrutinizing the extent to which associational features and different types of trust impact on activists' EU-related orientations will complete the analysis of the role of social capital as one potential root of EU legitimacy. Accordingly, the empirical findings should provide some suggestions about whether welcoming opportunity structures and providing resources to civil society actors can be a remedy or an obstacle to increasing the legitimacy of the EU.

8.2 Theoretical foundation

Inquiring about the legitimacy of the European Union and its roots is not a straightforward task. The EU certainly represents more than just an institutionalized coordination of political processes between a diversity of countries, and it is less than a state, not to mention a nation. Instead the EU is often described as a 'system sui generis', with no comparable institutional equivalent worldwide (Pfetsch 1997: 112). Nevertheless, during the course of its existence the EU has extensively adopted governance structures which make it in many respects comparable to governance structures in nation-states. Given these similarities, but also bearing these differences in mind, we draw on Gilley's concept of the meaning and measure of state legitimacy which he applied to more than 70 countries.[4] According to his definition, 'a state is more legitimate the more that it is treated by its citizens as rightfully holding and exercising political power' (Gilley 2006: 500). As such, this concept 'admits of degrees' and can therefore be perceived as a continuous variable (Gilley 2006: 501). The rightfulness of holding and exercising power arises from three different sources that are also considered as sub-types of legitimacy. These sub-types are views of legality, views of justification and acts of consent (Beetham 1991: 15–19). Citizens' common views about laws, rules and customs lie at the heart of their views of legality, which, in modern societies, are substantiated in written laws. Views of justification, moreover, are 'based on conformity to shared principles, ideas and values' (Gilley 2006: 502). The citizens' evaluation of the state's moral reasoning for holding and exercising power is at the core of this sub-type of legitimacy. It can also be described as a '"vertical social contract" of shared beliefs between states and citizens' (Gilley 2006: 503; original emphasis). Finally, the notion of acts of consent 'refers to positive actions that express a citizen's recognition of the state's right to hold political authority and an acceptance, (...), to be bound to obey the decisions that result' (Gilley 2006: 503). In an attempt to operationalize these three sub-types of legitimacy, Gilley distinguishes between attitudinal and action-related indicators of legitimacy. Several attitudinal indicators in the realm of the 'views of justification' sub-type of legitimacy link this concept with late social capital research. These refer particularly to indicators of political support, such as political trust (Gilley 2006: 505).

As social capital theory argues, social trust and norms of cooperation should be important precursors of the stability and legitimacy of democratic systems. They are said to sustain a cooperative social climate, to facilitate collective behaviour, and to encourage a regard for the public interest. In particular, social trust between citizens makes it easier, less risky and more rewarding to participate in community and civic affairs, and helps to build the social institutions of civil society upon which peaceful and stable democracy rests. Democracy and good government may then reinforce the conditions in which social and political trust can flourish, enabling citizens to cooperate effectively in community and public affairs for their common good (see, among many others, Putnam *et al.* 1993; Putnam 2000; Seligman 1997; Braithwaite and Levi 1998; Warren 1999; Uslaner 2002; Rothstein and Stolle 2003).

The prerequisites of political trust have been analysed in great detail before (Zmerli 2004; Gabriel and Zmerli 2006; Denters *et al.* 2007; Zmerli *et al.* 2007).[5] Recent studies reveal a strong and consistent relationship between political confidence and social trust throughout Europe (Zmerli and Newton 2008). For social capitalists this finding is not surprising, since it reflects empirically what is described theoretically (Putnam 1993, 2000).

If social trust was one of the main pillars of the social capital concept at the beginning of its triumphant advance in the political sciences in the early 1990s, subsequent research contributed to an essential differentiation of this theoretical tool (Putnam 2000; Zmerli 2008). As a result, social networks, as the structural component of social capital, are now classified according to their bonding or bridging capacities. Homogeneous groups bond along similar socio-economic or social characteristics, which lead to a reinforcement of exclusive group identities, personalized trust and specific norms of reciprocity. Heterogeneous networks, on the other hand, cut across social cleavages, thus bringing together people with different socio-economic or social backgrounds. These networks are considered to be socialization agents that foster all-embracing identities, mutual recognition, social tolerance, social trust and generalized norms of reciprocity. This late differentiation resonates in terms such as 'bonding' or 'exclusive social capital', and 'bridging' or 'inclusive social capital' (Putnam 2000: 19–22). An alternative approach to differentiate the concept of social capital focuses on processes of social influence within groups such as voluntary associations. It starts from the basic assumption that the characteristics of the contextual setting (i.e. associational goals) in which individuals regularly and voluntarily come together and form a social group exerts an independent and decisive impact on the group members' behaviour and orientations. Drawing on Warren's (2001) concept of associational constitutive goods associations can be discerned according to their potential to foster either inclusive social capital with social trust as one constitutive component or exclusive social capital with personalized trust as another characteristic feature (Zmerli 2008). In this line of reasoning, even homogeneous groups can enhance social trust as long as they pursue goals which are conducive to it. Although these outlined theoretical approaches differ in terms of explaining the mechanisms of inclusive and exclusive social capital formation, both concepts assign similar societal and political effects to these two different forms of social capital. As Putnam observes, both types perform important functions for any society. Nevertheless, it is bridging or inclusive social capital which is assumed to be more conducive to stabilizing democratic political systems as well as increasing any society's common goods, while bonding or exclusive social capital has the potential to exert illiberal effects (Putnam 2000: 19–22). As pointed out above, the assumption about the importance of social trust is indeed supported empirically. On the other hand, the nature of the impact of personalized trust, as one element of bonding or exclusive social capital, on trust in the EU has not been subject to empirical scrutiny before.

Even though, in the past, numerous studies have mostly failed to establish firm and convincing empirical links between social and political trust on the individual level (Kaase 1999; Newton and Norris 2000; Newton 2001b; Uslaner 2002). Recent research has unambiguously revealed strong and consistent relationships throughout Europe (Jagodzinski and Manabe 2004; Zmerli *et al.* 2007; Zmerli and Newton 2008). In addition, the authors demonstrate that the lack of these relationships in former studies can mainly be attributed to inadequate measurement. Moreover, as principal component analyses revealed, in most European countries confidence in national as well as in supranational or international political institutions are part of the same underlying trust dimension (Zmerli *et al.* 2007; Zmerli and Newton 2008).[6] Given the uni-dimensionality of this multitude of political trust items and the relevance of social trust as one of their predictors, the latter can be assumed to be a prominent determinant of confidence in the European Union. Personalized trust, by contrast, as part of the bonding or exclusive social capital concept, is said to potentially exert illiberal effects in democratic societies (Putnam 2000: 19–22). Therefore, personalized trust is not expected to relate significantly and *positively* to confidence in the EU. On the contrary, personalized trust might even impede the development of trust in the EU, because strong attachment to well-known others and the local surrounding might strengthen at the expense of more abstract entities. However, the true nature of the relationships between different types of trust and confidence in the EU has not yet been scrutinized systematically and in detail. While an ever-increasing number of studies focus on the specific links between social and political trust, appropriate and reliable data which would uncover the relationship between personalized and political trust is difficult to retrieve (Zmerli 2004; Gabriel and Zmerli 2006; Zmerli *et al.* 2007).

Whether and, if so, in which way the *structural* component of social capital is related to confidence in the EU shall also be addressed in this chapter. The impact of social involvement is going to be examined from two different angles. First, the individual degree of associational activity will be taken into consideration. Assuming that voluntary associations act as 'schools of democracy', a higher individual degree of associational activity strengthens an activist's civic skills, which results in an increase of political confidence. Second, the effect of social involvement on confidence in the EU can also be triggered by the specific associational characteristics. Aspects to be considered in this regard include the geographical scope of associational activity. A wider geographical radius of associational activities implies that activists are not exclusively concerned with their immediate surrounding, but relate to more distant entities. Thus, it is plausible that a wider geographical scope of associational concerns positively affects members' orientations towards the European Union. Moreover, social activities based on and guided by an association's written constitution, as well as attending associational general assemblies, are expected to impact on activists' political skills, orientations and interest, and should also induce higher political trust. Likewise, initiating and maintaining political contacts on the behalf of one's association or simply being socially engaged in an organization which is politically active has the potential to positively affect individual political orientations such as confidence in political institutions. All these associational activities can certainly be better performed if a sufficient number of individuals are in charge of these tasks. Accordingly, a higher degree of associational professionalization (i.e. the number of paid staff) should be another associational predictor of political confidence. Finally, the sector in which the association is predominantly active might also exert an impact on activists' orientations. In particular, politically active groups or associations which deal with EU-related topics or policies, such as economy, environment or welfare, could influence activists' confidence in the EU.

Finally, as one recent study suggests, it might be predominantly the *type* of association which matters, and not the associational context or the intensity of individual involvement (van Deth and Maloney 2008). Given the importance of the differentiation between social and personalized trust, an additional research focus shall address the question of whether and to which extent associational features impact on these two types of trust.

8.3 EU legitimacy and social capital: empirical sketches of a complex relationship

Before turning to the analysis of the causes of confidence in the EU, a depiction of the average levels of confidence in the EU and social trust will provide first insights into potential cross-national differences.[7] Assuming that the degree of social activism fosters the propensity to trust unknown others as well as political institutions, three different categories of social activism are discerned: non-actives, socially actives, and activists.[8]

8.3.1 Cross-national perspectives on confidence in the EU and trust

As Table 8.1 unveils, British citizens in each and every category of social activism appear less willing to trust the EU than are the citizens of the other countries. This comes as little surprise, given the prevailing Euro-sceptic attitudes. Most remarkably, however, they even fall below the averages of Switzerland, whose citizens, as non-EU members, are presumably not particularly inclined or motivated to trust a political entity whose decisions are neither directly aimed at Swiss politics nor can be directly influenced by Swiss citizens. Notwithstanding, the citizenry in East and West Germany, the Netherlands and Spain are not very enthusiastic about the EU either. This reservation holds true for each and every degree of social activity. At first, however, a comparison of the non-actives with the socially actives confirms by and large the assumption that socially active people show a stronger inclination to trust political institutions. Although we can detect cross-national differences between the average confidence levels in the EU, the described pattern of the non-actives vs the socially actives is mostly consistent, with the exception of the Netherlands, where these two categories do not differ from each other. The findings based on the Activists' Study, however, deviate strongly from this detected pattern. In particular, East and West German activists' confidence in the EU ranges from below the mean values of the German non-actives. So too do Dutch activists', albeit to a considerably smaller extent. By contrast, the Swiss as well as the British activists, relatively speaking, exhibit the highest means of confidence in the EU. Accordingly, these findings already partly allude to a rather ambiguous relationship between the EU and highly socially active members of societies.

Analysing levels of social trust, on the other hand, provides, in each and every country, results that are completely in accordance with social capital theory. As Table 8.2 shows, non-actives are the least inclined to be socially trustful. Even though socially actives in the Netherlands and the UK differ only marginally from the group of non-actives, the German, Spanish and Swiss categories of

Table 8.1 Mean values of confidence in the EU amongst non-actives, socially actives and activists

	Non-actives M	Socially actives M	Activists M	F-Test
East Germany	4.3	4.6	4.1	7.3***
West Germany	4.7	5.3	4.1	119.7****
The Netherlands	5.2	5.2	5.1	0.9
Spain	5.1	5.3	n.a.	9.7***
Switzerland	3.9	4.2	4.6	12.5****
UK	3.3	3.6	3.8	119.7****

Notes
Spanish data weighted.
$*P<0.050$, $**P<0.010$, $***P<0.001$, $****P<0.000$.

EU legitimacy and social capital 163

socially actives reveal, just as expected, more pronounced differences compared to the non-active parts of their populations.

Moreover, in their average level of social trust, associational activists range consistently higher than those socially actives whose degree of social engagement is assumed to be less pronounced. Only in Switzerland can no difference be identified. Comparing the average levels of social trust from a cross-country perspective reveals another interesting pattern. With regard to the group categories of non-actives and socially actives, the Spanish and East Germans range the lowest, followed by the West Germans. The British, on the other hand, show the highest average levels of social trust for all three categories of social activism. The Dutch and Swiss group categories take on mean values which range between the British ones, on one hand, and the Spanish as well as the East and West Germans on the other.

The activists' data sets contain numerous trust items which, at first sight, seem to represent the two underlying trust dimensions of social and personalized trust respectively. By means of principal component analysis, however, a threefold dimensionality is identified for most countries (Table 8.3).[9] Although a social trust as well as a personalized trust dimension are revealed, the existence of a third dimension suggests that individuals distinguish between generally unknown others (social trust), others they know personally (personalized trust) and others whom they do not know personally but whom they relate to specific groups of people (group-related trust). Apparently, the latter can be based either on criteria of the geographical context or on some social characteristics. Moreover, in each and every country the goodness of fit of the principal component analyses is stressed by a respectable KMO coefficient.

In a next step, and based on the presented findings of the principal component analyses, three trust indices (Table 8.4) are constructed.[10] As the within-country comparisons depict, personalized trust ranks (not surprisingly) always highest among the three trust indices. This consistent ranking across countries also applies to the two remaining trust dimensions, with social trust taking on the second position and group-related trust the third. Despite this consistency, a

Table 8.2 Mean values of social trust amongst non-actives, socially actives and activists

	Non-actives M	Socially actives M	Activists M	F-Test
East Germany	4.3	4.6	6.0	157.7****
West Germany	4.8	5.7	5.9	111.7****
The Netherlands	5.9	6.1	6.6	33.7****
Spain	4.1	4.7	6.0	474.1****
Switzerland	5.4	6.3	6.3	63.1****
UK	6.4	6.5	6.7	8.8****

Notes
Spanish data weighted.
*$P<0.050$, **$P<0.010$, ***$P<0.001$, ****$P<0.000$.

Table 8.3 Principal component analysis of different types of trust amongst activists

	East Germany			West Germany			The Netherlands				Switzerland			UK		
	F1	F2	F3	F1	F2	F3	F1	F2	F3	F4	F1	F2	F3	F1	F2	F3
People in region	0.880			0.897			0.876				0.912			0.822		
People in country	0.886			0.890			0.886				0.910			0.839		
People in municipality	0.852			0.860			0.894				0.818			0.789		
Ethnic minorities	0.795			0.819			0.809				0.643			0.883		
Lesbian/homosexual	0.648			0.578			0.695							0.800		
Members of this organization			0.707		0.782				0.896			0.772				0.823
People who run this organization			0.714		0.769				0.864			0.771				0.816
Family members			0.595		0.647					0.750		0.717				0.591
Your friends					0.616			0.412		0.752		0.652				0.605
Your neighbours										0.735						
Your colleagues		0.852	0.552		0.520							0.620				
People try to be helpful		0.841				0.856		0.841					0.741		0.829	
People try to take advantage of you		0.790				0.848		0.841					0.812		0.816	
Most people can be trusted						0.788		0.828					0.815		0.723	
Eigenvalue	5.11	1.44	1.30	5.34	1.61	1.53	6.03	1.82	1.47	1.04	4.92	1.57	1.46	5.68	1.67	1.11
Explained variance in %	42.6	12.0	10.8	41.1	12.4	11.8	46.4	14.0	11.3	8.0	41.0	13.0	12.2	47.3	13.9	9.2
KMO	0.849			0.860			0.768				0.840			0.852		

Notes
Only factor loadings greater than 0.400 are depicted, varimax rotation.

Table 8.4 Mean values of group-related, social and personalized trust amongst activists

	Group-related trust M	Social trust M	Personalized trust M	Paired T-Test
East Germany	4.9	6.0	8.3	−17.9****
West Germany	5.0	5.9	8.0	−19.4****
The Netherlands	6.3	6.6	8.2/8.5	−4.7****
Switzerland	5.2	6.3	8.1	−17.5****
UK	6.3	6.7	9.2	−6.2****

Notes
The first Dutch factor of personalized trust=neighbours, second factor=family, friends. Paired T-Test (group-related with social trust): ****$P<0.000$.

cross-country analysis reveals, first, that the respective mean values show some variation, and, second, that British activists rank highest on each and every trust dimension, closely followed by Dutch activists. By contrast, and with the exception of personalized trust, East and West German activists exhibit the lowest trust averages.

Whether or not activists' trust indices show higher mean values compared to non-actives and socially actives must remain unanswered here, since relevant population data are hitherto not available. Nevertheless, activists are higher with respect to social trust (Table 8.2), and could also be so in terms of group-related trust. Even their personalized trust could exceed the respective means of non-actives and socially actives. This is for two reasons; first, because this trust dimension also encompasses trust in associational executives and co-members; and second, because activists should have a higher number of *strong* ties, the cornerstone of personalized trust.

8.3.2 Confidence in the EU and social capital: disentangling a complex relationship

After having scrutinized differences and commonalities in a cross-country perspective among non-actives, socially actives and activists, we will now turn to the analysis of the origins of confidence in the EU inasmuch as they relate to the concept of social capital. For the analyses based on the population surveys, this approach takes account of social trust and a dummy variable for social involvement. As discussed in Section 8.2, higher social trust and social engagement are perceived as promoters of confidence in the EU. The analyses based on the activists' data sets allow us to identify the effects of the three trust dimensions together with the activists' degree of associational involvement. Again, social trust and a higher degree of social activity should be conducive to higher trust in the EU. Despite the fact that group-related and social trust clearly represent distinct trust dimensions, it can be assumed that group-related trust should also positively influence EU confidence. Given that this latter type of trust expresses the respondents' orientations towards people they do not know personally, it certainly represents an element of *inclusive* social capital. Personalized trust, on the other hand, relates to people with whom one maintains strong relational ties, and can be conceived of as an element of exclusive social capital. Personalized trust is, therefore, not necessarily expected to relate significantly and *positively* to confidence in the EU. In addition, several organizational features are included as predictors, which are outlined in Section 8.2 together with their assumed impact on activists' orientations towards political institutions in general and the EU in particular. These are the geographical scope and the sector in which the association is active, whether it organizes general assemblies, has a written constitution or maintains political contacts and employs staff.[11]

Apart from the described social capital indicators and associational features, several other variables are of major importance for the explanation of political confidence (Zmerli 2004; Gabriel and Zmerli 2006; Zmerli *et al.* 2007; Zmerli and Newton 2008). According to these studies, besides the standard socio-demographic variables satisfaction with democracy in one's own country, political efficacy, life satisfaction, length of residence and attachment to one's neighbourhood, left–right placement as well as political interest should be included as predictors in models of political confidence.[12] A strong impact on political confidence is particularly exerted by one's satisfaction with democracy, one's sense of being politically efficacious, and high political interest. These predictors certainly reflect citizens' generally positive orientations towards the political system. Even though a respondent's placement on the left–right scale represents another expression of political orientation, its effect on confidence in the EU might deviate in accordance with the country-specific setting. Satisfaction with one's own life, a strong attachment to one's neighbourhood and a longer time of residence at one place usually go along with higher political confidence. These indicators of personal happiness and important personal bonds are also a basis for continuity rather than radical change in the political realm.

Tables 8.5 and 8.6 depict the results of the same linear regression models which differ only in terms of the database used. While Table 8.5 presents results based on the population surveys, Table 8.6 unveils the nature of relationships amongst European activists. Interestingly, the main findings derived from the two different data sets are quite similar.

Social trust is, in each and every country, significantly and positively related to confidence in the EU. Moreover, within-country comparisons reveal, for most cases, that the impact of social trust on confidence in the EU is considerable. As predicted, interest in the EU and political efficacy are very powerful determinants of confidence in the EU. Interestingly, satisfaction with democracy in one's own country is also an influential determinant of EU confidence. Despite this consistently identified cross-national pattern, the detected relationship between EU confidence and satisfaction with democracy in one's own country should not be as self-evident as the strength of the coefficients suggests. Rather, one would expect it to be strongly and positively linked to political trust in *national* institutions instead of supranational or international ones. The influence of the left–right placement variable is quite mixed. While right-leaning political orientations exert a moderate and significant impact in the Netherlands and Spain, left-leaning orientations matter in Switzerland and the UK, where Euroscepticism prevails. In East Germany, right-leaning orientations are influential amongst the population, while left-leaning orientations are effective amongst activists. In addition, and contrary to expectations, only in West Germany and Spain is life satisfaction significantly and positively related to confidence in the EU. Interestingly, this predictor also attains statistical significance in the case of Switzerland (the non-EU member state). However, it is *dissatisfaction* with one's own life that strengthens EU confidence amongst the Swiss citizenry; moreover, the same is true for the East German population survey findings. Social involvement, included as a dummy variable in the regression models based on the population surveys, does not clearly meet the EU's expectations. Where this predictor attains statistical significance, it turns out that *non-actives* show a higher likelihood to be politically trustful. Length of residence and attachment to neighbourhood are not detected as relevant predictors of EU confidence. Length of residence has a moderate though negative impact only in East Germany and Switzerland. Similarly, attachment to neighbourhood is influential only in East Germany, the Netherlands and Spain. For these few cases no clear pattern can be discerned, since it appears to promote EU confidence in East Germany and Spain, and impede it in the Netherlands. Moreover, the socio-demographic predictors included in the explanatory models show no consistent tendency across the countries. Finally, in most cases the explained variances of the regression models point to an appropriate model specification and do not differ considerably from each other.

We now turn to the analyses of the impact exerted by the differentiated social capital indicators, such as the three different trust dimensions and the individual degree of associational activity. In addition, the associational features outlined in Section 8.2 will also be included in the explanatory model. In order to trace the ways in which integrating additional trust dimensions and organizational features affect the relationships depicted so far, the models described above will be expanded by these predictors.

Scrutinizing, at first, the impact of the three different trust dimensions reveals astonishing insights. In line with the assumptions, group-related trust fosters confidence in the EU and in some countries exerts the strongest influence on the dependent variable (Table 8.7). Interestingly, the findings for social trust mostly contrast its relevance depicted in Tables 8.5 and 8.6. With the exception of West Germany, social trust is no longer statistically significant. The effects of personalized trust, on the other hand, are in accordance with expectations. In none of the countries is it significantly and positively related to confidence in the EU; on the contrary, the Dutch results suggest that personalized trust can even impair political confidence. The individual degree of associational activity, however, does not figure as a prominent determinant of EU confidence. As the Swiss finding shows, a higher associational involvement can even be to the detriment of trust in the EU. With regard to the relevance of the included associational

Table 8.5 Predictors of confidence in the EU amongst European citizens, OLS regressions, beta coefficients

Predictors	East Germany	West Germany	The Netherlands	Spain	Switzerland	UK
Gender[a]	0.05	−0.06**	0.13****	0.05***	0.07**	−0.02
Age	−0.02	0.03	−0.12****	0.01	−0.05	−0.12****
Level of education	−0.04	−0.02	−0.06**	−0.08****	0.01	0.01
Life satisfaction	−0.07**	0.06**	−0.01	0.09****	−0.06*	−0.02
Time of residence	−0.08**	−0.03	0.01	−0.01	−0.07**	n.a.
Attachment to neighbourhood	0.17****	0.03	−0.03	0.06***	0.02	−0.02
Political efficacy	0.12***	0.19****	0.24****	0.20****	0.12****	n.a.
Satisfaction with democracy	0.28****	0.16**	0.18****	0.18****	0.14****	0.21****
Left–right placement	0.06*	−0.02	0.06**	0.12****	−0.11***	−0.13****
Interest in the EU	0.15****	0.18****	0.19****	0.23****	0.29****	0.33***
Social involvement	−0.07*	0.03	−0.04	−0.05***	−0.01	0.02
Social trust	0.14****	0.15****	0.14****	0.09****	0.09***	0.15****
Constant	7.05	0.64	1.96****	0.10	1.32*	0.71
Adj. R² in %	19.7	19.0	23.3	23.8	19.7	20.6
N	741	1,471	1,310	2,507	903	1,135

Notes
In Spain, years of education;
a Reference category male; Spanish data weighted.
*$P<0.050$, **$P<0.010$, ***$P<0.001$, ****$P<0.000$.

Table 8.6 Predictors of confidence in the EU amongst activists, OLS regressions, beta coefficients

Predictors	East Germany	West Germany	The Netherlands	Switzerland	UK
Gender[a]	0.03	−0.01	0.00	0.05	0.00
Age	−0.01	0.02	−0.11**	0.03	−0.09**
Level of education	−0.08**	−0.01	−0.16****	0.01	0.00
Life satisfaction	0.05	0.10***	0.13**	−0.01	0.01
Time of residence	−0.03	−0.03	0.02	−0.03	n.a.
Attachment to neighbourhood	0.10***	0.00	−0.10**	0.04	−0.01
Political efficacy	0.21****	0.20****	0.42****	0.13***	0.31****
Satisfaction with democracy	0.22****	0.20****	0.13***	0.23****	0.22****
Left–right placement	−0.06*	0.02	0.13***	−0.18****	−0.07*
Interest in the EU	0.18****	0.18****	0.13***	0.13***	0.11***
Social trust	0.10***	0.20****	0.11***	0.10***	0.07*
Constant	3.96	−1.65***	2.55***	0.14	1.62**
Adj. R² in %	22.2	25.2	32.0	19.5	25.2
N	855	1,108	338	661	663

Notes
a Reference category male.
*P<0.050, **P<0.010, ***P <0.001, ****P<0.000.

Table 8.7 Predictors of confidence in the EU amongst activists, OLS regressions, beta coefficients

Predictors	East Germany	West Germany	The Netherlands	Switzerland	UK
Gender[a]	0.04	-0.01	-0.11	0.05	0.00
Age	0.02	0.02	0.07	0.04	-0.10*
Level of education	-0.07	0.01	-0.06	0.04	-0.03
Life satisfaction	0.08*	0.05	0.33**	-0.02	-0.02
Time of residence	-0.07	-0.03	0.11	-0.03	n.a.
Attachment to neighbourhood	0.08*	0.01	-0.17	-0.01	0.03
Political efficacy	0.18****	0.18****	0.24**	0.19****	0.23****
Satisfaction with democracy	0.19****	0.18****	0.05	0.21****	0.31****
Left–right placement	-0.09**	0.01	0.05	-0.17****	-0.05
Interest in the EU	0.13***	0.19****	0.26**	0.08*	0.08
Group-related trust	0.22****	0.20****	0.33**	0.20****	0.13**
Social trust	0.00	0.15****	-0.16	0.07	0.01
Personalized trust[c]	-0.06	-0.03	0.28*/-0.36***	0.01	0.01
Degree of associational activity	0.00	0.01	-0.11	-0.08*	0.04
General area of associational activity	0.07	0.05	n.a.	n.a.	0.10*
General assembly	-0.11*	0.02	0.33**	0.02	0.04
Written constitution	0.15***	-0.04	-0.17	0.01	0.01
Professionalization	-0.03	0.04	0.05	-0.02	0.01
Political contacts with					
City councillors	-0.03	0.02	0.41*	-0.10*	0.00
Officials city council	-0.05	0.00	-0.37*	-0.04	-0.07
Local parties	0.03	-0.05	0.14	-0.03	0.02
Mayor and aldermen	0.04	0.00	-0.13	0.05	n.a.
Sectorial type					
Family[b]	0.00	-0.02	0.19	-0.01	-0.03
Sports	0.00	-0.04	-0.03	-0.02	0.07
Culture	-0.05	0.01	0.00	-0.02	0.04

Community concerns	−0.02	0.02	0.21*	0.03
				−0.01
Politics	−0.07	0.04	0.27*	0.05
				−0.02
New politics	−0.01	−0.08**	−0.08	0.05
				−0.01
General welfare	−0.08*	−0.06*	0.15	−0.07*
				−0.04
Group-specific welfare	0.12***	0.00	−0.11	0.05
				0.02
Economic interest	0.02	−0.02	−0.10	−0.09**
				0.00
Religious	−0.03	0.00	−0.02	−0.04
				0.02
Constant	−4.10	−1.43	2.82	0.16
				−0.86
Adj. R^2 in %	25.9	28.2	44.4	25.6
				28.5
N	475	841	78	519
				323

Notes
a Reference category male;
b Reference category: other associations;
c The first Dutch coefficient refers to trust in organizational members, the second to trust in family and friends.
*$P<0.050$, **$P<0.010$, ***$P<0.001$, ****$P<0.000$.

features, the results are rather sketchy, even though we can observe statistically significant coefficients for the scope of associational activity, organizing general assemblies, having a written constitution, maintaining political contacts and the sectoral typology of associations. None of these predictors impacts on EU confidence in a cross-nationally consistent manner. The same also holds for the influence of gender, age and education, where no meaningful *systematic* pattern can be discerned. The inspection of determinants unrelated to social capital reveals no surprises compared to the results presented in Tables 8.5 and 8.6. Again, in most countries, political efficacy, satisfaction with democracy in one's own country and interest in the EU are particularly important promoters of EU confidence. Political orientations, however, figure only twice as significant determinants in the explanatory models. Finally, the explained variances of the regression models point to an appropriate model specification, and do not differ considerably from each other.[13]

8.3.3 The interrelationship between trust, social involvement and features of associations

As the presented analyses suggest, trust is certainly an important prerequisite of confidence in the EU. However, not every type of trust matters similarly. Group-related trust seems to be far more important than social trust. Personalized trust, by contrast, can even be an impediment to EU confidence. In this regard, the aforementioned assumptions about the deviating effects of inclusive and exclusive social capital are confirmed. But do different degrees of social involvement in voluntary associations or specific associational characteristics impact differently on processes of trust formation? Given the extraordinary richness of the activists' data sets, one can attempt to explain whether and to what extent social involvement and associational features affect the three trust dimensions. The relevance of the subsequent analyses pertains particularly to group-related and personalized trust, since both trust dimensions were identified as predictors of confidence in the EU, though with opposing effects.

To this end, several associational characteristics that are expected to be influential are selected as determinants of the three dependent variables. The duration of associational membership in years, for instance, should certainly be positively related to all three types of trust, since trust formation is perceived as being subject to long-term associational processes of socialization. A higher degree of associational activity is likewise assumed to go along with frequent individual social contacts, which should promote all three forms of trust. In addition, it is plausible to expect that the individual strength of associational attachment could favour processes of trust formation. In particular, trust in closely related others (i.e. personalized trust) might be affected by this predictor. Creating bridging or inclusive social capital by means of maintaining associational contacts with other organizations, on the other hand, should particularly enhance social and group-related trust. A larger geographical scope of associational activities where geographically more distanced and possibly more abstract concerns are taken

EU legitimacy and social capital 173

into account could also be a promoter of both social and group-related trust. Furthermore, regularly organized general assemblies are assumed to provide ideal training grounds for establishing trustful social relationships in general.

Apart from the associational characteristics outlined above, recent studies reveal several other individual traits as important predictors of social trust (see, for example, Zmerli 2004; Zmerli *et al.* 2007). Most importantly, life satisfaction is pivotal for the formation of social trust. In addition, stronger attachment to one's neighbourhood and a longer time of residence at one place have previously been detected as promoters of social trust (Zmerli *et al.* 2007).

At first, Table 8.8 depicts the results for the group-related trust model and provides some rather unexpected findings. Overall, however, it has to be conceded that the explanatory power of this regression model is rather limited, which indicates its under-specification.[14] For the explanation of group-related trust, *none* of the organizational features exerts a cross-nationally consistent predictive power. Only stronger associational attachment as well as a higher degree of associational activity (both are individual traits) meet, in few instances, the expectations. A longer duration of associational membership amongst East German activists impedes the development of group-related trust. These rather sketchy results contrast with the consistent patterns which can be attributed to the strong effects exerted by life satisfaction and attachment to one's neighbourhood. Length of residence, on the other hand, does not figure as a noteworthy predictor of group-related trust.

In terms of the impact of associational characteristics on social trust formation, the empirical results do not differ significantly from the ones described before (Table 8.9). Again, none of the organizational features demonstrates any consistent influence. In accordance with the assumptions outlined above, more years of associational membership strengthens social trust only in the UK, while stronger associational attachment is a modest positive predictor in East Germany and Switzerland. The broadly accepted assumption that bridging organizations should foster social trust is also contested by the empirical findings, with only one single detected significant coefficient in West Germany. A rather contradictory picture is drawn by the geographical scope of associational activity. While a significant and positive coefficient in the Netherlands confirms the assumption, the West German finding suggests that an associational focus on geographically *closer* concerns fosters social trust. The effect of regularly organized general assemblies, moreover, clearly contrasts the expectations in West Germany and Switzerland. With the exception of the Netherlands, however, the only cross-nationally consistent impact is exerted by life satisfaction. A stronger attachment to one's neighbourhood, on the other hand, seems to be much less important for the explanation of social trust than for the prediction of group-related trust. Similar to the explanatory power of the group-related trust models, the adjusted R^2 coefficients for social trust indicate, by and large, an under-specification of the linear regression models.

These impressions are clearly contrasted by the predictive power of most personalized trust models that can certainly be attributed to the relevance of one

Table 8.8 Predictors of group-related trust amongst activists, OLS regressions, beta coefficients

Predictors	East Germany	West Germany	The Netherlands	Switzerland	UK
Gender[a]	−0.06	−0.02	0.33***	0.01	0.01
Age	−0.03	0.04	−0.05	0.01	0.01
Level of education	0.01	0.08**	0.17	0.06	0.01
Life satisfaction	0.20****	0.17****	0.32***	0.12***	0.17***
Time of residence	−0.01	0.04	−0.12	−0.04	n.a.
Attachment to neighbourhood	0.15****	0.14****	0.26**	0.22****	0.13**
Years of joining association	−0.08*	−0.05	0.13	0.02	0.04
Degree of associational activity	0.02	0.07*	−0.04	0.00	0.02
Strength of associational attachment	0.03	0.03	0.24**	0.09*	0.04
Contacts with other associations	0.06	0.00	−0.05	−0.04	0.01
General area of associational activity	−0.01	0.01	−0.03	n.a.	0.03
General assembly	0.03	0.05	−0.08	−0.04	0.01
Constant	10.54	1.09	−0.93	3.19****	3.32****
Adj. R² in %	6.9	7.2	26.4	7.2	3.9
N	723	962	81	598	402

Note
a Reference category male.
*P<0.050, **P<0.010, ***P<0.001, ****P<0.000.

Table 8.9 Predictors of social trust amongst activists, OLS regressions, beta coefficients

Predictors	East Germany	West Germany	The Netherlands	Switzerland	UK
Gender[a]	0.04	−0.10***	0.10*	0.07*	−0.04
Age	−0.07*	0.07*	0.10	0.13***	0.09*
Level of education	0.01	0.09***	0.09	0.15****	0.06
Life satisfaction	0.24****	0.20****	0.09	0.11***	0.25****
Time of residence	−0.04	0.05	−0.01	−0.04	n.a.
Attachment to neighbourhood	0.00	0.08***	0.10	0.03	0.12**
Years of joining association	−0.06	−0.01	−0.01	0.00	0.10*
Degree of associational activity	0.05	−0.01	0.03	0.00	0.08
Strength of associational attachment	0.07*	0.03	0.07	0.11**	0.01
Contacts with other associations	0.06	0.08**	−0.09	0.02	0.00
General area of associational activity	−0.04	−0.07**	0.12**	n.a.	0.01
General assembly	0.03	−0.06*	−0.04	−0.09**	0.06
Constant	19.39	2.53	3.26***	4.15****	1.68*
Adj. R² in %	8.1	9.0	5.3	7.8	13.2
N	767	1,030	296	626	408

Note
a Reference category male.
*P<0.050, **P<0.010, ***P<0.001, ****P<0.000.

Table 8.10 Predictors of personalized trust amongst activists, OLS regressions, beta coefficients

Predictors	East Germany	West Germany	The Netherlands[b]		Switzerland	UK
Gender[a]	0.07*	−0.06*	0.02	0.01	0.02	0.00
Age	−0.11****	0.12****	0.14	−0.05	0.04	0.14***
Level of education	−0.02	0.01	0.06	0.06	0.04	0.08
Life satisfaction	0.23****	0.22****	0.33***	0.16	0.25*****	0.18*****
Time of residence	−0.05	0.01	0.12	0.07	−0.02	n.a.
Attachment to neighbourhood	0.17****	0.17****	0.18*	0.07	0.11***	0.20****
Years of joining association	−0.06	−0.08**	−0.10	0.06	−0.08*	0.00
Degree of associational activity	0.08**	0.09***	0.00	−0.13	0.01	0.10**
Strength of associational attachment	0.16****	0.19****	0.20*	0.09	0.19****	0.13**
Contacts with other associations	0.04	−0.04	−0.05	0.02	0.04	−0.11**
General area of associational activity	0.02	−0.02	0.11	0.02	n.a.	−0.08*
General assembly	0.06	0.00	−0.06	−0.01	−0.05	0.12**
Constant	23.11	3.91	0.24	6.87****	5.38*****	5.86*****
Adj. R^2 in %	17.9	18.4	24.3	−7.3	13.3	20.2
N	763	1,033	89	92	628	414

Notes
a Reference category male;
b The first Dutch coefficient column refers to trust in organizational members, the second one to trust in family and friends.
*$P<0.050$, **$P<0.010$, ***$P<0.001$, ****$P<0.000$.

particular determinant (Table 8.10). It is strong associational attachment which impacts considerably on the formation of personalized trust.[15] In addition, a strong associational attachment does not necessarily go along with a positive effect of long-term associational membership as the West German and Swiss findings suggest. On the other hand, a higher degree of associational activity is, indeed, in most countries positively related to the dependent variable. Admittedly, the remaining associational features confirm the aforementioned assumptions only for the British case. Less bridging organizational contacts, a restricted geographical scope of associational activities, as well as organizing associational general assemblies foster the development of personalized trust. Apart from these associational related effects, the personalized trust models show some interesting similarities with the group-related trust ones. Again, life satisfaction and a stronger attachment to one's neighbourhood exert considerable effects on the dependent variable. Gender and age, by contrast, do not allow for any consistent insights. The overall lack of statistical significance for the level of education indicates, however, that the development of personalized trust is largely independent of individual educational achievements.

8.4 Conclusion

Starting from the assumption that the European Union is increasingly being confronted with debates questioning its legitimacy, the main focus of this chapter was to enhance the knowledge regarding whether social capital could be a remedy to increase the legitimacy of the European Union. The presented analyses provided mixed results at best.

At first, and without taking all three identified trust dimensions into consideration, social trust mainly supported the findings of former empirical studies by depicting a consistently significant and positive relationship with confidence in the EU. This pattern was true for both the population and the activists' surveys. Turning to the impact of all three identified trust dimensions, though, disclosed some rather unexpected relationships. As the results showed, the assumption that group-related and social trust would affect the dependent variable in a likewise manner was not supported empirically. Overall, group-related trust appeared to be a strong predictor of confidence in the EU, while social trust did practically not impact EU confidence at all anymore. The positive effects of social trust disappeared when group-related trust was also included in the explanatory model as a predictor of EU confidence. Certainly, these findings put Putnam's general arguments about the importance of social trust into perspective. Nevertheless, conceding that group-related trust is part of the inclusive social capital concept, they also confirm the assumption about the latter's relevance for society at large. In the same vein, the fact that personalized trust, as a component of exclusive social capital, was either not effective or a negative predictor of confidence in the EU substantiates Putnam's expectations about possible negative effects resulting from exclusive social capital. Moreover, as the analyses revealed, neither individual aspects of social involvement nor associational features figured as cross-nationally consistent predictors of EU confidence, even though some statistically significant effects could be detected.

This striking irrelevance of features of social engagement disappeared, however, when precursors of the three identified trust dimensions were traced. As it turned out, the strongest and most consistent link exists between personalized trust and the strength of the individual attachment to one's association. Group-related and social trust, however, seem to be by and large unaffected by features of social involvement. These findings, together with the notion that group-related trust is one potential source of EU legitimacy (in contrast to social and personalized trust), allow for a rather critical evaluation of the EU strategy to find its cure in strengthening and involving civil society actors. In addition, they also confirm van Deth's (2008b) insight that strong social engagement at the local level potentially impedes the development of pro-European orientations. This contribution adds to van Deth's research inasmuch as the pivotal relationship between personalized trust and associational attachment, and its link to the legitimacy of the EU, was disclosed.

Even though broad civic engagement and social capital do not seem to be an effective remedy for the EU's ills, several other prerequisites of EU legitimacy were detected that have their origins in a national rather than a transnational or supranational context. In this regard, Kielmansegg's (2003) widely shared argument about the necessity of the existence of a threefold European community which would provide the basis for a collective European identity and finally result in an increase of EU legitimacy was contradicted. Interestingly, the extent to which one is willing to trust the EU is clearly related to one's satisfaction with democracy in one's own country. This consistent finding is rather surprising, since it is not self-evident that the perception of the way democracy is working nationally should affect one's orientations towards supranational institutions to such a degree. Moreover, political efficacy and a high interest in European affairs figured consistently prominently amongst the predictors of EU legitimacy. In conclusion, the impact of national system performance, together with national politicians' sense of responsiveness and accountability, on the legitimacy of the EU should certainly be assessed anew. However, the high relevance of group-related trust for confidence in the EU also suggests that even the trustworthiness of social entities *within* nations can shape citizens' positive evaluations of the European Union at large.

Notes

1 Other measures relate to an extension of the rights of the European Parliament, the institutionalization of an EU citizenship and, most importantly, the framing of the elaboration of a European Constitution (Kohler-Koch 2004).
2 With this White Paper, the Commission seeks to increase the legitimacy of the EU 'through procedures of representative democracy' (Hurrelmann 2007: 27). By this means, the Commission follows a so-called logic of complementarity which 'justifies the legitimacy of the EU by pointing to the systematic differences between European and national institutions, arguing that their specific capacities supplement each other

in an effective way' (Hurrelmann 2007: 24). Two other strategies to increase the legitimacy of EU institutions can be discerned. One is based on the logic of analogy, which presumes that 'the legitimacy of the EU institutions is justified by pointing out that EU institutions conform to the same principles that underlie the legitimacy of the Member States' (Hurrelmann 2007: 23). European and national institutions are perceived to be 'more or less "alike"' (Hurrelmann 2007: 24; emphasis in original). The other pursues the logic of derivation which 'treats one level as normatively superior to the other. In the European context, most arguments grant this privilege to the nation-state' (Hurrelmann 2007: 24).

3 Apart from the relevance of social capital as a potential promoter of EU legitimacy, a number of other factors, such as the interplay between supranational and national politics, a nation's security and trade interests in EU membership, the partisan context of integrated reforms as well as utilitarian consequences of integrative policy, already proved to be influential in empirical studies (Anderson 1998; Gabel 1998; Gabel and Palmer 1995; Sánchez-Cuenca 2000; Rohrschneider 2002; Kritzinger 2003). The research focus of this chapter, however, will predominantly scrutinize the predictive power of a variety of social capital indicators as well as associational features.

4 Pursuing strategies to increase the legitimacy of the EU which follow the logic of analogy is based on similar assumptions (see endnote 2).

5 In a number of studies, political confidence is operationalized as a composite index embracing trust in national institutions as well as in the EU or the European Parliament and the UN.

6 See endnote 5.

7 Based on principal component analysis results, we constructed an index of social trust. The index was constructed by summing up each individual's responses on the 11-point rating scales (0=lowest, 10=highest) and dividing the total sum by the number of valid responses. The questions referred to trust in general, helpfulness and fairness. Confidence in the EU is also measured on an 11-point rating scale.

8 See Chapter 1 for a detailed explanation.

9 The Dutch activist data set provides a four-factor solution with the personalized trust dimension split into two parts which represent very close contacts, such as with friends and family, on one hand, and contacts in voluntary associations on the other.

10 The indices are based on the sum of the items measured on an 11-point rating scale and divided by the number of the respective items belonging to the specific trust dimension. If respondents did not answer to some of the trust questions, the sum of the items was divided by the number of valid answers. For the Dutch activists, four trust indices were constructed.

11 The sectoral typology of associations is not included as a predictor in the analyses based on the population surveys because we focus, at first, on the effects of social involvement as such.

12 For the subsequent analyses, we include interest in the EU. The predictor 'political efficacy' encompasses external political efficacy (i.e. the perception that politicians really care about citizens' interests and needs) and internal political efficacy (i.e. a subjective sense of being able to influence political decision-making processes). Unfortunately, the British population survey lacks data on the respondents' sense of political efficacy, which impairs the cross-national comparability of results.

13 The Dutch model, with its clearly higher adjusted R^2 coefficient, deviates from this overall pattern; this can be attributed to the small number of cases here.

14 With the exception of the Dutch model – but see also endnote 13.

15 It is also plausible that associational attachment does not affect trust in family, members or friends, as the Dutch example stresses.

9 The relational basis of attachment to Europe

Hajdeja Iglič

9.1 Introduction

The expansion of the membership and dramatic changes in the extent of integration of the European Union (EU) over the past 15 years – the single European currency, increased primacy of European law and partial elimination of border controls between EU members – has heightened the need for a more stable and deeper basis of political support for the EU project. Such support should be less dependent on everyday economic and political considerations among citizens of the EU countries, and more so on the elements of social solidarity and reciprocity, similar to those found in the relation of citizens to their nation-states, regions and municipalities. Although some authors argue that the type of attachment which characterizes the nation-state is neither necessary nor desirable for the post-national, federal unity of the EU (Koslowski 1999; Shaw 1999), the empirical studies clearly show that collective sentiments contribute in an important way to support for European integration. In fact, attachment to Europe is as strong a predictor of the individual-level support for European integration as are more utilitarian concerns, such as different kinds of benefits stemming from EU membership (Laffan 1996; Carey 2002).

The general level of identification with the EU is at present moderate, with stable differences between countries: in most comparative surveys, citizens of the UK show low levels and citizens of Germany and Spain high levels of European identification. For this reason, the European policy-makers have long been aware of the need to put more effort in building the European identity. However, this is a very difficult endeavour, because EU member states lack the commonalities that usually underlie collective identities, such as common origin myths, language, religion and history (Smith 1992). In order to compensate for the apparent weaknesses of primordial sentiments among Europeans, the solution has been to seek a more constructivistic approach that focuses on the building of European identity through strengthening the notion of European citizenship. There was a clear expectation that allowing for free movement and residence of people, establishing the common legal framework of citizens' rights and duties, and promoting political and civic participation would, in the long run, produce the feeling of collective belonging.

The Maastrich Treaty (1992) institutionalized the Citizenship of the Union, which was further elaborated in the treaties of Amsterdam (1997) and Nice (2001) and, most recently, in the Treaty of Lisbon (2007). In these documents, the meaning of citizenship has been gradually broadened from passive to more active forms, which include various forms of civic and political participation of European citizens at different levels of the European institutional system. The aim of the system of multi-level governance is the empowerment of European citizens vis-à-vis the institutions of EU.

Civic organizations are considered to be one of the cornerstones of this European multi-level governance system. Their role is to provide the organizational framework for the participation of citizens in decision-making processes. The expectation is that civic participation will enhance the feelings of political efficacy and confidence in European institutions, thereby strengthening identification with the European polity. In particular, larger associations which are involved in wider networks of contacts are seen as very likely to have a positive impact on the attitudes of their members towards Europe because they help to bring together people from different countries and regions. However, smaller associations, which nurture face-to-face interpersonal relations and help to develop solidarity that reaches beyond the private and family-centred social existence, might also be crucial for the development of large-scale identification of any kind.

So far, the positive effects of civic engagement on European identity are more an assumption than established fact. There is very little empirical evidence about the actual impact of involvement in voluntary associations on the identification with Europe and what kinds of associations are especially important in this respect. The notable exception is van Deth and Maloney (2008), which explicitly analyses the link between local associations, their members, activists and volunteers, and EU institutions. By comparing the local associational life in two cities, Aberdeen and Mannheim, the authors conclude that commitment to Europe depends on the sector of associational activities. In the context of Aberdeen, it is supporters of family and general welfare groups that are among the most committed Europeans, while in Mannheim it is supporters of community concerns, general welfare and politics groups. In both cities, very weak attachment to Europe is found among supporters of religious groups.

In this chapter, I continue the discussion about the role of voluntary associations in forming commitment to Europe by comparing a larger number of countries (cities) and observing more dimensions on which associations differ. Associations vary in scope, sector, size, degree of formalization, engagement patterns, and social relations among their members. As other studies have already suggested, associations are diverse social contexts with potentially different impacts on the attitudes of their members.

The focus of the analysis is on the strength of social integration and the quality of social relations within associations. To what extent do members of organizations help each other when facing problems? To what degree do they engage in political discussions during their meetings? And to what extent do members feel they can influence the decisions made by the group as a whole? We are interested in the question of whether strong social integration within the associations contributes to the identification with large-scale entities such as Europe, or whether, under certain conditions, high social integration achieved within predominantly locally-based associations strengthens local and regional identities rather than more abstract and distant ones, and even stymies the development of the latter. The generalization of attachment from lower- to higher-level identities is a process that needs to be subjected to concrete empirical analysis.

The chapter is divided into four parts. In the first section, I discuss the theoretical difference between relationally based and imagined collective identities, and present arguments about the relationship between associations and identification with Europe. In the second section, I examine whether the relationship between voluntary associations and attachment to Europe is indeed supportive in a larger number of European countries, as has been suggested by the proponents of active European citizenship; I do this by comparing different groups of citizens – activists, socially actives and non-actives – with respect to their average degree of attachment to Europe. In the third section, I propose a new approach to the analysis of standard indicators of attachment to territories in order to make a distinction between different social mechanisms that lie behind the identification with Europe. Finally, in the fourth section, I examine how different characteristics of associations and their members jointly determine the level of attachment to Europe, paying special attention to the issue of social integration and social relations within associations.

9.2 The relational and categorical basis of collective attachment

The discussion of attachment to different territorial entities is historically rooted in theories of nationalism and the rise of the nation-state. National identity is often considered as an example of imagined community, which is, as the label suggests, to a large extent constructed and imagined rather than rooted in primordial solidarities (Anderson 1983). Despite the criticism that all social relations and identities are imagined and constituted by symbolic means, even the closest ones, the concept of imagined community gained a large prominence in social theory. One of the reasons for this, as noted by Calhoun (1991), was that it was built on the crucial distinction made by the process of modernization – namely, a distinction between direct face-to-face relations of small worlds and indirect symbolically constituted relations among anonymous citizens who share a common institutional framework but have no personal experience and knowledge of each other. The historical analysis by Anderson (1983) shows that, in the latter case, the presentation of similarities through the mass media and standardized curriculum in the educational system was crucial for the creation of national identities. Although the construction of national identities went hand-in-hand with the actual broadening of the geographical scope of social relations caused by the rise of the market society and the formation of the nation-state, these social relations were too weak, sparse and indirect to bring about a strong sense of solidarity by themselves. What was needed was an intense ideology which helped to stabilize the social borders between 'us and them' on a larger scale – borders that were only vaguely delineated by changing social relations in the economic and political spheres. The symbolic presentations served to assign people to national categories by emphasizing similarities among those within the category of the nation, and dissimilarities to those outside it.

Relational solidarities based on direct social relations, and imagined communities, which are constructed around indirect ties and perceptions of similarities, present two contrasting cases of collective identities. In most situations our collective attachment combines the two kinds of identification, which is what is captured by the concept of 'catnets' proposed by White (1992) and Tilly (2005). A catnet is a set of persons who share both categorical commonality and relational connectedness. Due to the dual system of collective identification, this kind of collective identity has a very strong mobilization potential, as has been shown in various historical studies of collective action (Tilly 1978; Gould 1995). The efforts to deliberately build European civil society through heightened social mobility of citizens and creation of different kinds of regional and European-wide social networks should be understood along the lines of catnet theory – namely, that raising solidaristic sentiments among European citizens imply the symbolic construction of European identity as well as community-building.

What about social networks that are local and do not reach across regional and national boundaries, such as networks established in voluntary associations? Can they contribute to European identity, or do they actually prevent its formation by strengthening local identities? Since most social relations and loyalties that are born within voluntary associations are limited in scope, their role in building European identity deserves special attention. Existing theories offer three different hypotheses regarding the likely contribution of associations with strong relational and locally bounded solidarities to the formation of large-scale identity. The first sees the relationship as supportive, the second sees it as as competitive, and the third sees it as potentially supportive or competitive, depending on the specific social and political conditions.

Shils (1991) perceives the relationship as supportive despite the fact that the large-scale community, in our case Europe, does not coincide with relational solidarities formed in face-to-face social relations. According to Shils, the theory of imagined communities misses the important point by neglecting the role of local networks and by not making the distinction between 'knowledge that is identically possessed by individuals and knowledge that is collectively possessed' (Shils 1991: 129). The difference is crucial, since it tells us that in order to have collectively possessed knowledge of commonalities that is shared by larger numbers of people, knowledge should be mediated through social networks regardless of how limited they are in scope. People identify with an abstract community only if collective identification is shared and reinforced by other members of their social networks. Shils (1991) thus offers an explanation why we should expect voluntary associations to be important promoters of European identity. These are social spaces in which people interact, establish social ties of various strength and discuss politics, including the issues related to European integration, which all lead to the creation of 'collectively possessed knowledge' as opposed to knowledge that individuals can acquire by reading political news in their homes. Shils (1991) also reminds us about the limits of a pure constructionist approach in which there is no place for the interplay between social relations and symbolic imagination of commonalities.

On the other hand, some authors argue that the two ways of building identity – the one based on connectedness and the other on categorical commonalities – are incompatible with one another, and that strong local networks in which voluntary associations are important actors can jeopardize integration within large-scale entities. This is the argument regarding 'terminal community' (Deutsch 1966), which is defined as the highest political unit to which people feel attached. If identification with a lower-level territorial unit is such that it achieves the status of terminal community, the action aimed at integration within a larger community will be met by negative feelings and objection. Inglehart (1970, 1977a), building on the work of Deutsch, argues that the choice of the terminal community is limited by the cognitive competence of people. Cognitive competence refers to the inferences that people make regarding the terminal community, either on the basis of direct social relations and the social networks to which they belong, or through the abstract processes of categorization and knowledge acquisition. Inglehart shows that education and cognitive mobilization – for example, knowledge about EU affairs – raise the cognitive competence of individuals, and thereby contribute to their identification with Europe. These findings were later supported by Janssen (1991).

Based on his theory of cognitive competence, Inglehart also predicted a negative relationship between identification with Europe and identification with entities smaller than nation-states, such as regions. The reason for this lies in the profoundly different levels of cognitive competence that are required for the relationally based identification with region, and more abstract ways of identity-building in the case of nation-state and supranational identities. Inglehart and, latterly, Duchesne and Frognier (1995) indeed found a negative relationship between regional and European identity.

Finally, the work done in the conceptual framework of 'nested identities' has opened the way for the elaboration of different territorial entities in terms of compatibility as well as competition. Nested identities are lower- and higher-level identities that encompass one another. The concept is particularly useful for understanding the relationship between territorial identities, such as European identity versus national and regional identity (Díez Medrano and Gutiérrez 2001). In the work of Calhoun (1994) and Brewer (1993, 1999), it has been suggested that whether nested identities are compatible or competitive depends on how well they serve two very different kinds of identity claims: for Calhoun, these are differentiation and equivalence; for Brewer, differentiation and inclusion. The lower-order identity is supposed to differentiate individuals within groups, while the higher-order identity should allow for inclusion and feelings of equality. If identities successfully perform these two functions, they can coexist and be equally salient for individuals. Applied to the case of the EU, this means that a higher level of identity, such as Europe, can coexist with strong national identities as long as it is perceived by citizens as embodying the constitutional principles that guarantee their equal rights and freedoms. Díez Medrano and Gutiérrez (2001) describe such coexistence of national and European identity in the case of Spain; however, they also warn that under some conditions the higher-order identities might be perceived as threatening the survival of local identities. This is when citizens have a low level of confidence in European institutions, or when they have a high distrust of other people, which McLaren (2002) discusses under the notion of cultural threat. Similarly, the proponents of the rational approach to European identity (Gabel and Palmer 1995; Gabel 1998) argue that attachment to a higher-level identity is stronger if individuals perceive it as important for their life, meaning that it provides certain benefits for the individuals and social groups to which they belong.

To conclude, this chapter has presented three lines of argument regarding the relationship between higher- and lower-level territorial identities. The first, proposed by Shils, talks about the supportive role the relationally based solidarities have in the process of construction of higher-level, abstract identities. Locally based social networks, such as those formed in voluntary associations, are sites of interpersonal communication in which collectively shared knowledge about Europe is produced. The second argument, elaborated by Inglehart, suggests that higher-level abstract identities and lower-level relationally based identities are inherently incompatible, due to the processes of modernization and increasing cognitive mobilization. These processes cause some people to think along the lines of more parochial and relationally based identities, while others build their identities under the impact of strong symbolic imagination and categorization. Yet the third argument, formulated within the 'nested identities' theory, searches for the factors that contribute to the compatibility of identities at various levels. Even national and European identities, which, according to Inglehart, both belong to the class of categorical or abstract identities, can be competitive if they do not perform the functions of differentiation and inclusion effectively, or when one of them is functionally less important than the other.

Below, I examine the processes of identification with Europe at the individual level by considering all three arguments. Special attention will be paid to factors that can be characterized as relationally based attachments, such as involvement in associations and other kinds of informal social networks; the strength and type of relationships people maintain in associations; and associational features, which define the context within which interpersonal interactions take place. I anticipate that the analysis will deliver some evidence on whether and/or how civil society contributes to the creation of European identity.

9.3 Attachment to municipality and Europe

In this study, I draw upon the Citizenship, Involvement, Democracy (CID) project (CID).[1] The combined CID data set, with the information on citizens, activists and associations, allows us to examine the effects of individual as well as contextual variables on the identification with Europe. We do this for different subsets of citizens: those who are uninvolved in any kind of associational activity (non-actives), socially active citizens (socially actives), and organizational activists (activists). The information about non-actives and socially actives is drawn from the Population Study, while the information about activists has been obtained by the Activists' Study and the Organization Study (see Chapter 1).

The question of attachment to territorial entities was formulated in the following way: 'How attached are you to the place in which you live?' The respondents were asked to rate the intensity of their attachment to different objects, from neighbourhood to municipality, city, region, country, Europe, and humanity as a whole, on a scale from 0 (not at all) to 10 (very attached).[2] The cross-national comparison of the levels of attachment to Europe in six countries[3] gives the expected results: the attachment to Europe is the lowest in the UK, and highest in West Germany and Spain.

In the next step, respondents were classified into four types of attachment with respect to where they stand on two variables: the first is attachment to municipality, which is considered as a lower-level and relationally based identity, and the second is attachment to Europe as a higher-level, abstract identity. The four groups correspond to what Marks (1999) calls multiple identity, exclusive identity and 'un-attachment', while exclusive identity can refer either to lower- or higher-level identity.

The selection of variables for classification purposes is closely related to the central question of this chapter regarding the relationship between associational involvement and attachment to Europe. Since associational activity is the strongest at the municipal level, the attachment to municipality seems to be the right choice for the lower-level identity. The classification was carried out in such a way that individuals were classified into four cells according to whether they have a high or low level of attachment on the selected variables. All scores equal to or greater than 6 were considered to indicate a high level of attachment, while scores equal to or less than 5 were considered to indicate a low level of attachment (see Figure 9.1).

The results of the classification confirm the view that a large proportion of citizens today hold multiple identities that are equally salient for the individual (see Figure 9.1). This means that both attachment to municipality and attachment to Europe are at high levels. The percentage of multiple identifiers is higher in West Germany, East Germany and Spain. In these countries, high levels of attachment to Europe have been successfully combined with various lower-level identities. In all countries, those who hold high attachment to global identity but low attachment to local identity are in the minority (ranging from 6 per cent in the East Germany to 17 per cent in Switzerland). Thus, holding a global identity

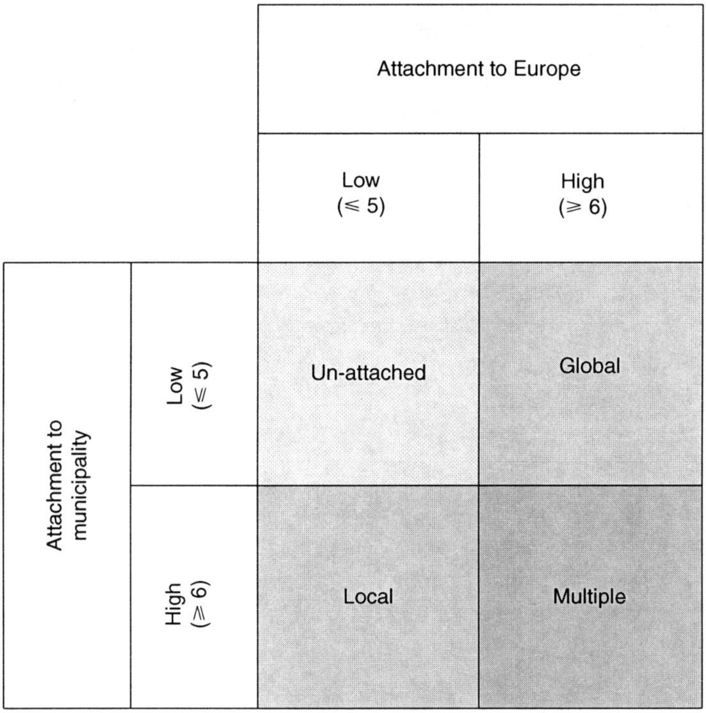

The relational basis of attachment to Europe 187

	Attachment to Europe	
	Low (⩽ 5)	High (⩾ 6)
Attachment to municipality — Low (⩽ 5)	Un-attached	Global
Attachment to municipality — High (⩾ 6)	Local	Multiple

Figure 9.1 A typology of attachment: municipality and Europe.

which would not be supported by a low-level identity is rather rare. In general, a higher proportion of people fall into the category of having both identities either strong or weak (about 60 per cent across different countries) than into the category of having exclusive identity, either global or local. The exception is the UK, where local identity is the most frequent one.

In the next step, we show the distribution of four types of attachment across the three categories of respondents – uninvolved citizens (non-actives), citizens who are involved in associations (socially actives) and activists – who were surveyed by the Activists Study. The comparison of socially actives and activists across different characteristics of their engagement shows that although both are actively involved in associations, activists are significantly more likely to play a central role in decision-making processes in the organizations. For example, they are more likely to participate in meetings, to plan or chair a meeting, to prepare of give a speech before a meeting, and to write a text other than a private letter. On the other hand, socially actives differ from uninvolved citizens in that they participate in the activities or carry out voluntary work for associations. Respondents who declare themselves as members of associations but show no activity are considered as uninvolved.

Table 9.1 Distribution of types of attachment across countries (percentages)

Types of attachment	East Germany	West Germany	The Netherlands	Spain	Switzerland	United Kingdom
Multiple	48	53	31	53	28	22
Local	32	28	25	27	24	46
Global	6	8	14	8	17	7
Un-attached	14	11	30	12	31	25
N	989	1,979	1,623	3,977	1,492	2,875

Table 9.2 Distribution of types of attachment among activists, socially actives and non-actives (percentages)

Types of attachment	East Germany			West Germany			The Netherlands			Spain			Switzerland			United Kingdom		
	Activists	Socially actives	Non-actives	Activists	Socially actives	Non-actives	Activists	Socially actives	Non-actives	Activists	Socially actives	Non-actives	Activists	Socially actives	Non-actives	Activists	Socially actives	Non-actives
Multiple	44	51	45	49	61	44	31	33	29	n.a.	53	53	37	30	25	35	24	22
Local	31	34	30	23	25	33	28	28	21	n.a.	27	27	25	27	19	43	44	47
Global	8	6	7	11	7	9	14	13	16	n.a.	8	8	11	16	18	6	8	6
Non-attached	17	9	19	17	8	14	27	26	34	n.a.	12	12	27	27	38	16	24	25
N	2,181	422	567	1,728	1,134	845	428	984	639	n.a.	1,328	2,649	925	906	586	802	910	1,965

The distributions of attachment types within three groups of citizens in Table 9.2 show some similarities across the countries.[4] Most generally, we can say that activists and socially actives tend to have multiple identities or strong local identities, while non-actives are more likely to be unattached or feel attached only to global identity. The exceptions are Spain, where the differences between activists and non-actives are non-significant, and West Germany, where socially actives are the most likely to have multiple identities. Among respondents who are active in voluntary associations, we find higher percentages of those who are strongly attached to local identity or who combine local identity with the global one, than among the non-involved respondents. Associations seem to support the development of local identification and multiple identifications where local identity is combined with higher-level identities.

9.4 Two dimensions of attachment to territorial entities: the strength and direction of attachment

In order to understand the processes behind the formation of different types of attachment we need to first reduce the data to find the relevant underlying dimensions. The principal component analyses of attachment to various objects in all countries reveals two dimensions: the *strength* of attachment and the *direction* of attachment (see Tables 9.3a and 9.3b). The strength of attachment component tells us that those who are high identifiers tend to identify strongly with different objects, regardless of whether these are lower-level and relationally based identities, or higher-level, abstract identities. In this case, the relationship between identities at different levels is supportive. On the other hand, the second dimension suggests that the relationship between global and local communities can also be competitive. Those who identify highly with more distant communities, such as the nation-state, Europe and the world, tend to reject more proximal and relationally based identities, such as neighbourhood, town and region. The two dimensions were identified in all countries, separately for citizens and activists.

In line with Inglehart's (1977a) argument of a crucial gap lying between the region and the nation-state, the principal component loadings for the second dimension, the direction of attachment, have negative signs in the case of region and territorial entities smaller than region. On the other hand, the signs are positive for the country and entities larger than country. However, the results confirm the argument about the incompatibility of two fundamentally different ways of constructing collective identity.

In terms of eigenvalues, the strength of attachment is a much clearer component than the direction of attachment. This suggests that attaching to different collective identities is possible. The most probable explanation for this finding is Shils' (1991) theory about the supportive role of relationally based identities in the creation of imagined communities. The involvement in social networks endowed with social solidarity allows for the generalization of feelings of solidarity beyond the borders of local communities, through the experience of jointly shared knowledge of group similarities and distinctions.

Table 9.3a Two dimensions of attachment to territories among citizens (principal component analysis of attachment)[a]

Principal components	East Germany	West Germany	The Netherlands	Spain	Switzerland	United Kingdom
Strength of attachment						
Attachment to neighbourhood	0.80	0.78	0.61	0.70	0.76	0.77
Attachment to town	0.80	0.81	0.74	0.77	0.84	0.83
Attachment to region	0.79	0.82	0.79	0.74	0.81	0.84
Attachment to country	0.76	0.76	0.74	0.71	0.70	0.67
Attachment to Europe	0.69	0.60	0.71	0.71	0.47	0.25
Attachment to world	0.62	0.48	0.56	0.56	0.33	n.a.
Eigenvalue	3.36	3.10	2.92	2.95	2.75	2.54
Direction of attachment						
Attachment to neighbourhood	−0.45	−0.46	−0.62	−0.48	−0.37	−0.12
Attachment to town	−0.48	−0.44	−0.51	−0.45	−0.31	−0.08
Attachment to region	−0.27	−0.17	−0.11	−0.20	−0.14	−0.08
Attachment to country	0.20	0.12	0.27	0.22	0.07	−0.02
Attachment to Europe	0.59	0.68	0.46	0.47	0.73	0.97
Attachment to world	0.63	0.75	0.56	0.59	0.80	n.a.
Eigenvalue	1.29	1.47	1.25	1.19	1.43	0.96
N	989	1,979	1,623	3,977	1,492	2,875

Note
a Entries are principal component loadings.

Table 9.3b Two dimensions of attachment to territories among activists (principal component analysis of attachment)[a]

Principal components	East Germany	West Germany	The Netherlands	Switzerland	United Kingdom
Strength of attachment					
Attachment to neighbourhood	0.65	0.60	0.47	0.71	0.72
Attachment to town	0.74	0.70	0.72	0.80	0.85
Attachment to region	0.82	0.82	0.78	0.83	0.85
Attachment to country	0.80	0.80	0.75	0.78	0.63
Attachment to Europe	0.79	0.76	0.73	0.61	0.44
Attachment to world	0.67	0.56	0.65	n.a.	0.47
Eigenvalue	3.36	3.05	2.90	2.81	2.87
Direction of attachment					
Attachment to neighbourhood	0.51	−0.53	0.61	−0.58	−0.34
Attachment to town	0.41	−0.47	0.41	−0.40	−0.32
Attachment to region	0.30	−0.23	0.29	0.18	−0.30
Attachment to country	−0.13	0.15	−0.09	0.35	0.33
Attachment to Europe	−0.48	0.50	−0.53	0.49	0.72
Attachment to world	−0.59	0.60	−0.52	n.a.	0.60
Eigenvalue	1.11	1.19	1.18	0.99	1.24
N	1,259	1,728	428	925	802

Note
a Entries are principal component loadings.

The relational basis of attachment to Europe 193

The partial deviation from this pattern is shown in the cases of the UK and Switzerland, which have lower loadings on the component 'strength of attachment' with respect to Europe and world. This suggests that the outcome of the process of generalization of solidarity from lower- to higher-level collective identity, which is suggested by Shils, can be jeopardized when the perception or image of the higher-level identity is not positive (as in the case of the UK), or when higher-level identity is much less relevant for the life of citizens than lower-level identity (as in the case of Switzerland).

Thus, the empirical analysis supports all three theories about the relationship between the lower- and higher-level identities. With the help of Shils' (1991) argument, we can understand the generally positive relationship between the two levels – municipality and Europe – which is expressed in the first component, in the strength of attachment. The authors who use a rational approach to European identity (Gabel and Palmer 1995; Gabel 1998), according to which attachment is lower if a collective entity is not a source of significant benefits, can be invoked to explain the case of Switzerland, and the argument about the importance of positive image (Díez Medrano and Gutiérrez 2001) can be applied in the case of the UK. Finally, Inglehart's (1977a) argument explains the dynamics behind the second component, the direction of attachment, and the reversed relationship between the lower- and higher-level identities.

9.5 Predictors of strength and direction of attachment to Europe

We now turn to the central question of this chapter: namely, what is the impact of associational involvement on the attachment to Europe? In the previous section we showed that the relationship between lower- and higher-level identities can be both supportive and competitive. Two processes can be at work simultaneously. The first implies that people either identify or do not identify with the communities, regardless of the type of community. The second implies that those who identify with relationally based communities do not identify with abstract ones. The aim of this section is to show which factors stand behind these two very different mechanisms of forming attachment to Europe. To this purpose, regression analyses will be performed for two dimensions of attachment to Europe, separately for the population and activists' data.[5]

The variables which are most often used to explain the attachment to Europe can be placed in several groups. Special attention will be given to associational activity variables. Thus, the first group of variables measure different aspects of associational engagement, from involvement in associations to strength of social integration and political communication. *Involvement* is a dichotomous variable indicating if someone is involved in the association through participating regularly in the activities of the organization or doing voluntary work for the organization. Declaring oneself as a member is not enough to be considered as active. This variable is used only in the analysis of the citizens' data, where a distinction is made between social actives and non-actives. The *strength of social integration* is operationalized with a variable 'how often members of associations help each other with practical matters outside organizational life', and *political communication* with a variable 'how often members of associations discuss politics'. In the analysis of activists, two additional variables of associational engagement are available; both are included in the model. These are the *level of activity*, measured on a scale from not at all active to very active, and the *level of commitment*, which ranges from very committed to not at all committed to the organization.

The second group of variables is also related to associations, but instead of individual engagement we now look at associations as social contexts within which the activity takes place. These variables are available in the organizational audit. Among the relevant organizational variables are: the *size* of the organization measured with the number of active members; *institutionalization*, measured as whether the association has written constitution or not; the *proportion of membership fees* in the overall budget of the association; the *scope of the activity*, which refers to the geographical area in which organization is active and can range from a part of the town, to the town in general, the region and the country; and a variable of *democratization*, measured as perceived opportunities for influencing the decisions made regarding the range and type of activities the organization undertakes and its management structure.

The third group of variables includes 11 measures of *associational type*, defined according to the sectors in which the association has been active during the last year. Associational type was an important predictor of identification with Europe in the study by van Deth and Maloney (2008). The reason for this is that people involved in certain types of association share interests, and view Europe as more or less beneficial environment for the realization of these interests. Among the associational types are family, sports, culture, community concerns, politics, new politics, general welfare, group-specific welfare, economic interests, religion, and the residual category of 'others'.[6] The information about associational type is available for citizens and activists.

The fourth group of variables refers to other forms of local community integration apart from voluntary associations; namely, involvement in the *church* and *neighbourhood* community. The former is measured by the frequency with which the respondent attends religious services, and the latter by the number of years the respondent has been living in the given municipality. Together with the variables of associational engagement these variables should tell us whether social integration at the local level promotes pro-European attitudes, as suggested by Shils (1991).

The fifth set of variables is defined according to Inglehart's (1977a) theory of cognitive competence. Cognitive mobilization is operationalized with variables measuring *education* (more precisely, whether the respondent has achieved tertiary education or not), and how often he or she follows *political news* in the newspapers, on the radio and on the TV.

The sixth group of variables consists of measures of *institutional confidence*, including the confidence in municipal boards and European institutions. These

The relational basis of attachment to Europe 195

variables measure the perceptions of people about European and local institutions, and are in line with the argument of Díez Medrano and Gutíerrez (2001) that attachment to Europe depends on how the EU is portrayed in public and perceived by the citizens. European integration can be perceived either as a process threatening local and national identities or, conversely, as a process that benefits individuals and nations. The lack of confidence in European institutions means that any increase in the prerogatives of the EU is understood as a threat to the integrity of the nation-state. If we agree that future of the EU lies in the identification of citizens with its constitutional principles rather than common culture (Habermas 1996), then raising confidence in the European institutions presents a crucial step towards achieving this goal.[7] Finally, the variable *generalized trust* is added to the group of variables on institutional confidence, since it indicates whether other people (other European nations, other cultures), rather than European institutions, are perceived as threats. The notion of perceived cultural threat and its importance for understanding the attitudes towards Europe has been emphasized by McLaren (2002).

9.5.1 Explaining attachment to Europe among citizens

Table 9.4 reports the bivariate correlation coefficients and the multiple regression coefficients for citizens in six societies, including West and East Germany, the Netherlands, Spain, Switzerland and the UK. Large numbers of variables in the model turn out to be significant predictors of strength of attachment. Those who are involved in the associations, frequently discuss politics with their co-members and are socially integrated to the extent that they help each other with practical matters outside organizational life identify more with Europe than do the uninvolved part of the population. However, the effects of these variables are stronger in the bivariate than in the multiple regression analysis, which includes larger number of variables. Involvement in associations loses its explanatory impact when we include variables like generalized trust and duration of residence in the model. People who have higher levels of generalized trust and have been living in the municipality for a longer time are more likely to be members of associations and at the same time to feel strongly attached to Europe, which causes a spurious relationship between attachment and associational involvement in the bivariate analysis. Also, the associational type shows a significant relationship with attachment to Europe in bivariate but not in multiple regression analysis. The reason is that the impact of associational type depends very much on what kind of citizens are involved in the associations, which is why the multiple regression analysis included individual variables such as institutional confidence, church attendance and age.

Different forms of community involvement are important predictors of European identification as well. Living for a longer period in the municipality strongly increases the attachment to collective entities in general, and to Europe in particular.

The perception of threat is the strongest prediction of the strength of attachment. The crucial role here is played by the confidence people have in local

Table 9.4 Predictors of strength of attachment among citizens

Predictors		East Germany		West Germany		The Netherlands		Spain		Switzerland		United Kingdom	
		r	Beta	r	Beta	r	Beta	r	Beta	r	Beta	r	Beta
Associational engagement	Involvement in associations	0.13****	0.01	0.18****	−0.03	0.10***	−0.02	0.02	0.01	0.10****	−0.01	−0.02	−0.03
	Political discussion co-members	0.07**	0.01	0.16****	0.06**	n.a.	n.a.	0.05***	0.06***	0.13****	0.07**	n.a.	n.a.
Associational type	Helping each other	0.12****	0.11***	0.23****	0.10*****	0.07***	0.02	0.00	0.02	0.06***	−0.01	n.a.	n.a.
	Family	0.01	0.01	0.02	0.01	−0.02	−0.04	−0.03	−0.01	0.00	−0.03	−0.00	0.03
	Sports	0.00	−0.03	0.07***	0.02	0.07***	0.07**	−0.04*	−0.01	0.06**	0.04	−0.04*	−0.01
	Culture	0.03	0.01	0.13****	0.02	0.03	0.01	−0.04**	−0.03*	0.07**	0.03	−0.02	−0.03
	Community concerns	0.03	0.04	0.00	−0.03	0.08***	0.06**	0.02	0.02	0.04	−0.00	0.03*	0.05
	Politics	0.07**	0.02	0.03	−0.03	0.06**	0.02	0.00	0.01	0.08***	0.00	n.a	n.a
	New politics	0.01	0.00	0.05**	0.02	0.07***	0.05**	−0.05***	−0.02	0.05*	0.03	−0.04**	−0.03
	General welfare	−0.01	−0.06**	0.03	−0.04*	0.03	−0.02	0.01	0.03*	0.05*	−0.02	0.01	0.01
	Group-specific welfare	0.01	−0.02	0.02	0.01	0.08***	0.03	0.01	0.01	0.04	0.04	−0.00	0.05
	Economic interests	0.02	0.02	0.02	−0.01	−0.02	−0.03	−0.03	−0.01	−0.00	−0.02	−0.03	−0.01
	Religious	0.04	−0.05	0.10****	−0.02	0.08***	0.03	0.02	0.01	0.04	−0.01	0.02	−0.00
	Others	0.13****	0.03	0.12****	0.00	0.06**	0.03	0.05**	0.05**	0.09***	0.03	−0.01	−0.02
Community involvement	Duration residence	0.25****	0.20****	0.30****	0.16****	0.11****	0.07**	0.15****	0.09****	0.15****	0.09***	0.21****	0.08**
	Church attendance	0.15****	0.04	0.20****	0.03	0.10****	−0.02	0.17****	0.03*	0.16****	0.08***	n.a.	n.a.
Cognitive mobilization	Political news in media	0.16****	0.06**	0.20****	0.09****	0.11****	0.06**	0.00	0.01	0.17****	0.07***	0.13****	0.07**
Perception of threat	Education (tertiary)	0.02	0.00	−0.02	−0.06**	−0.05**	−0.08**	−0.14****	−0.10****	−0.15****	−0.03	−0.04*	−0.07**
	Confidence municipal board	0.41****	0.28****	0.44****	0.27****	0.21****	0.07**	0.29****	0.17****	0.29****	0.26****	0.25****	0.12****
	Confidence EU	0.30****	0.16****	0.27****	0.12****	0.21****	0.15****	0.28****	0.20****	0.15****	0.08***	0.11****	0.00
	Trust in people	0.14****	0.09***	0.21****	0.13****	0.18****	0.11****	0.04**	0.02	0.09****	0.01	0.29****	0.24****
Demographic variables	Age	0.24****	0.13****	0.29****	0.16****	0.11****	0.09***	0.21****	0.13****	0.15****	0.01	0.28****	0.13****
	Gender (male)	−0.06**	−0.03	−0.03	−0.04*	−0.12****	−0.10****	−0.10****	−0.07****	−0.12****	−0.16****	−0.05****	−0.05
Total variance explained (adjusted) R²		0.28		0.32		0.12		0.18		0.16		0.15	
N		886		1,833		1,412		3,292		1,166		1,022	

Notes
Levels of statistical significance: **** 0.00; *** 0.01; ** 0.05; * 0.10
Entries are Pearson's correlation coefficients and standardized multiple regression coefficients.

institutions like the municipal board, followed by confidence in European institutions. As expected, cognitive competence matters as well. Strength of attachment to different territorial entities depends on how often people follow political news in the media. The impact of education is, contrary to expectations, negative. To identify with Europe through generalization of collective attachment from local to European level is characteristic for people with lower than tertiary education, but who have high cognitive mobilization and show interest in politics by frequently following the political news.

Also, demographic variables are important predictors of strength of attachment, with women and, especially, older people being more attached than men and younger people. Women are usually considered more integrated into various kinds of informal social networks than men, especially in personal and support networks (Iglič and Font Fábregas 2007), which contributes to their stronger collective attachments of all sorts. This is similar for older people, who have in general a more collectivistic political culture than do younger generations (Inglehart 1997, Inglehart and Welzel 2005).

As can be seen in Table 9.5, the opposite is true for the second dimension, direction of attachment. On this dimension, younger and higher-educated people have more positive feelings towards the Europe than do older and less-educated individuals. To be high on the dimension of direction of attachment (i.e. to have strong attachment to Europe) does not depend on the integration into the community of any kind. Community involvement is even negatively related to the direction of attachment. The same is true for the confidence in the municipal board. People who are not integrated in local communities and do not have confidence in local institutions, but have a high level of confidence in European institutions, are people who are highly attached to Europe. The strongest effect of institutional confidence is found in the UK, which expresses a country-specific effect. A strong public contention over the image of the EU assigns the issue of institutional confidence a central place in determining individuals' attachment to Europe.

The positive orientation to Europe, which is built on a clear distinction and even conflict between lower- and higher-level identity, is more often found among the citizens involved in associations active in the sector of new politics than any other associational type. These citizens are placing hope in the EU to promote policies which have been traditionally disregarded by local institutions, and see Europe as part of the global society about which they are particularly concerned. Citizens involved in associations which are active in the fields of economic interests, conventional politics and sports tend not to be high on this dimension of attachment to Europe.

9.5.2 Explaining attachment to Europe among activists

Now we turn to the Activists Study and the Organization Study, which provides information about what kinds of associations present particularly fertile ground for the strengthening of European identity. Table 9.6 shows the antecedents of

Table 9.5 Predictors of direction of attachment among citizens

Predictors		East Germany		West Germany		The Netherlands		Spain		Switzerland		United Kingdom	
		r	Beta	r	Beta	r	Beta	r	Beta	r	Beta	r	Beta
Associational engagement	Involvement in associations	-0.05	0.03	0.08***	0.05	-0.03	0.06*	0.06****	0.03	-0.04*	0.03	0.04*	-0.01
	Political discussion co-members	-0.03	0.00	0.03	-0.04	n.a.	n.a.	-0.04***	0.02	-0.05*	0.01	n.a.	n.a.
Associational type	Helping each other	-0.06*	0.01	0.03	-0.03	0.04	-0.01	-0.05***	0.02	-0.07***	-0.04	n.a.	n.a.
	Family	0.01	-0.01	0.04*	-0.00	-0.05***	-0.06**	0.04**	-0.01	0.01	0.01	0.09****	0.07**
	Sports	0.00	-0.01	0.08****	-0.03	-0.02	-0.03	0.04**	-0.00	-0.08***	-0.06**	0.02	-0.03
	Culture	0.05	0.05	0.04*	0.02	-0.02	-0.02	0.06****	0.04**	-0.01	-0.01	0.04**	0.00
	Community concerns	0.00	0.02	0.01	0.00	-0.05***	-0.03	-0.03	-0.03	-0.01	-0.03	0.01	0.00
	Politics	-0.02	-0.02	0.00	-0.01	-0.08***	-0.09***	-0.01	-0.03*	-0.03	-0.01	n.a.	n.a.
	New politics	0.02	0.04	0.07***	0.04**	0.05*	0.05*	0.02	-0.02	0.03	0.03	0.04**	0.06**
	General welfare	-0.04	-0.02	0.00	-0.01	-0.05***	-0.03	0.06****	0.03	0.04	0.04	0.03*	0.03
	Group-specific welfare	-0.02	0.00	0.02	0.02	0.00	-0.03	0.04**	0.01	-0.01	-0.02	0.04**	0.00
	Economic interests	-0.03	-0.04	-0.03	-0.05**	-0.04	-0.03	0.04**	0.01	-0.02	-0.02	0.04**	-0.03
	Religious	-0.03	0.00	-0.03	0.00	-0.02	0.02	0.02	0.02	-0.00	-0.00	-0.02	-0.03
	Others	-0.05	-0.04	0.03	0.05**	-0.08***	-0.09***	0.02	0.03	-0.10***	-0.04	0.00	-0.03
Community involvement	Duration residence	-0.22****	-0.16****	-0.30****	-0.21****	-0.14****	-0.14***	-0.16****	-0.12****	-0.18****	-0.10***	-0.07****	-0.01
	Church attendance	-0.05	0.00	-0.13****	-0.02	-0.05*	-0.06*	-0.07****	-0.03*	-0.06**	-0.00	n.a.	n.a.
Cognitive mobilization	Political news in media	0.06**	0.01	0.05**	0.06***	0.06**	0.07**	0.10****	0.07****	0.00	0.06**	0.04**	0.09***
	Education (tertiary)	0.05	0.05	0.11****	0.04**	0.09****	0.08***	0.14****	0.06***	0.12****	0.03	0.12****	0.01
Perception of threat	Confidence municipal board	-0.08***	-0.16****	-0.10****	-0.16****	-0.03	-0.09***	-0.11****	-0.18****	-0.11****	-0.21****	-0.16****	-0.14****
	Confidence EU	0.14****	0.20****	0.25****	0.29****	0.11****	0.16****	0.18****	0.25****	0.42****	0.44****	0.62****	0.67****
	Trust in people	0.10****	0.07**	0.16****	0.09****	-0.04	-0.06**	0.05***	0.00	0.06**	0.04	0.05**	-0.04
Demographic variables	Age	-0.15****	-0.08**	-0.30****	-0.17****	0.03	-0.04	-0.13****	-0.09****	-0.16****	-0.08**	-0.11****	-0.03
	Gender (male)	0.07**	0.04	0.03	0.02	-0.02	-0.03	0.01	-0.01	-0.08**	-0.07**	0.01	0.01
Total variance explained (adjusted) R^2		0.09		0.22		0.07		0.10		0.25		0.41	
N		881		1,833		1,412		292		1,166		1,022	

Notes
Levels of statistical significance: **** 0.00; *** 0.01; ** 0.05; *0.10
Entries are Pearson's correlation coefficients and standardized multiple regression coefficients.

the strength of attachment, which are now expanded with two variables of associational engagement – the level of activity and commitment to a specific association – and a whole group of variables illustrating different associational features, from the number of active members to perceived opportunities for influence and scope of activity. The variables of political discussion and social relations among co-members are now contextualized in the sense that they measure these relations within the specific association to which the activist belongs.

Most explanatory variables show the same relationship with the dependent variable as in the citizens' model. The variables of associational engagement are important predictors of the strength of attachment. Apart from helping each other and discussing politics with co-members, the level of commitment to association also shows a positive relationship with the dependent variables. Those activists who are highly committed to the specific association are more likely to identify strongly with territorial identities in general. The objective pattern of participation indicated by the level of activity is much less important in this respect than the social integration and subjective identification with the association.

Associational features are not particularly strong predictors of collective attachment, especially when compared to variables of individual engagement and other individual variables. Two associational features stand out in this respect: the geographical scope of the associational activity, and the level of internal democratization. Associations which are limited in their activity to very local environments seem to be better promoters of this kind of European identity than those who reach wider in the town, region or country. In all countries, local associations represent the majority of all associations surveyed in the CID Study. Associations that are active in the region, nation or in an even wider field are much rarer.

The second associational feature which has significant impact on the strength of attachment is activists' perception of how much they can influence the decisions made in the association. The more democratic the associations, the higher is the strength of attachment to territorial entities in general. Empowerment contributes to the subjective engagement with the association as a community, which helps raises attachment to higher-level entities.

As far as associational type is concerned, the pattern is less clear, and the role of associations varies across countries. The same associational type has a positive relationship with strength of attachment in one country, and a negative one in the other, which calls for more country-specific analysis of the specific sectors of associational activity.

The second dimension of identification with Europe, the direction of attachment, is again best explained by the perceptions of threat, education, age and residence (see Table 9.7). All other variables are relatively weak predictors of attachment in this case. Confidence in European institutions is a very important promoter of identification with Europe. On the other hand, identification with Europe is again negatively related to confidence in local institutions. Activists who are high on this dimension of attachment to Europe do not trust municipal

Table 9.6 Predictors of strength of attachment among activists

Predictors		East Germany		West Germany		The Netherlands		Switzerland		United Kingdom	
		r	Beta	r	Beta	r	Beta	r	Beta	r	Beta
Associational engagement	Level of activity	0.08**	-0.01	-0.02	-0.03	0.00	-0.06	0.06*	0.10*	0.01	0.02
	Commitment	0.18****	0.11***	0.18****	0.08**	0.20****	0.22***	0.06*	0.06	0.14****	0.14**
	Political discussion co-members	0.08**	0.08**	0.15****	0.04	0.14***	0.17**	0.04	-0.09**	0.10**	0.14**
	Helping each other	0.07**	0.04	0.06**	0.05	0.18***	0.12**	0.12***	0.02	0.12**	0.05
Associational features	Number of active members	-0.02	0.00	0.00	-0.02	0.07	0.12*	0.01	-0.04	-0.05	-0.14**
	Written constitution (yes)	0.00	-0.01	0.03	0.05	-0.06	-0.07	0.09***	0.06	0.02	0.06
	Membership fees/budget	0.03	-0.01	0.02	0.03	-0.01	-0.01	-0.07*	-0.04	0.02	0.00
	Opportunities for influence	0.10***	0.05	0.14****	0.10**	0.09*	0.05		0.07	0.14***	0.06
Associational type	Scope of activity	-0.06**	-0.04	-0.17****	-0.07*	-0.03	0.00	n.a.	n.a.	0.04	-0.02
	Family	-0.04	-0.06*	-0.03	-0.06	-0.01	-0.07	-0.02	0.01	-0.02	0.00
	Sports	0.00	-0.01	0.05*	0.08*	-0.04	-0.08	0.02	-0.00	0.02	-0.08
	Culture	0.07**	0.03	0.03	0.03	-0.08	-0.06	0.02	-0.05	0.01	-0.07
	Community concerns	0.09***	0.08**	0.08**	0.06	-0.06	-0.13*	0.06*	0.03	0.06	-0.03
	Politics	0.02	0.01	0.06*	-0.01	0.09*	0.04	0.07*	0.03	-0.05	0.00
	New politics	0.02	0.01	-0.07*	0.00	0.09*	0.04	-0.10***	-0.11***	0.00	-0.01
	General welfare	-0.01	-0.02	0.03	-0.03	0.08	-0.03	0.01	-0.04	0.07*	0.05
	Group-specific welfare	-0.01	-0.04	-0.02	0.04	0.05	0.20***	0.02	-0.01	0.02	-0.03
	Economic interests	0.04	0.07**	-0.01	-0.01	-0.09*	-0.04	0.07**	0.07*	0.05	0.00
	Religious	-0.01	0.02	0.06**	-0.04	-0.12**	-0.00	0.03	-0.00	0.09*	0.04
	Others	0.07**	0.01	0.06*	0.08*	0.02	0.03	0.05	0.02	0.16*	0.08
Community	Duration residence	0.12****	0.10***	0.21****	0.13***	0.22****	0.20***	0.13****	0.04	0.23****	0.15***

		(1a)	(1b)	(2a)	(2b)	(3a)	(3b)	(4a)	(4b)	(5a)	(5b)
involvement	Church attendance	0.05*	0.10***	0.14***	0.08*	0.06	0.09	0.12****	−0.04	n.a.	n.a.
	Media political news	0.15****	0.06	0.17****	0.08*	0.23****	0.05	0.17****	0.08*	0.10***	0.00
Cognitive mobilization	Education (tertiary)	−0.04	−0.09**	−0.06*	−0.05	−0.03	−0.02	0.01	−0.05	0.00	−0.04
Perception of threat	Confidence municipal board	0.33****	0.23****	0.35****	0.24****	0.15***	0.10	0.41****	0.35****	0.07*	0.03
	Confidence EU	0.32****	0.23****	0.27***	0.09*	0.21****	0.27****	0.21****	0.07	0.07*	0.11*
	Trust in people	0.13	0.00	0.16****	0.05	0.11*	0.08	0.19****	−0.01	0.13**	0.20****
Demographic variables	Age	0.14****	0.09**	0.19****	0.05	0.30****	0.25****	0.27****	0.13***	0.14****	0.14**
	Gender (male)	−0.05*	−0.07*	0.03	−0.01	0.14***	−0.24***	0.04	0.10**	0.05*	0.05
Total variance explained (adjusted) R²		0.28		0.21		0.34		0.25		0.12	
N		739		571		201		532		359	

Notes

Levels of statistical significance: **** 0.00; *** 0.01; ** 0.05; * 0.10. Entries are Pearson's correlation coefficients and standardized multiple regression coefficients.

Table 9.7 Predictors of direction of attachment among activists

Predictors		East Germany		West Germany		The Netherlands		Switzerland		United Kingdom	
		r	Beta	r	Beta	r	Beta	r	Beta	r	Beta
Associational engagement	Level of activity	0.00	−0.04	0.02	−0.06	0.03	0.04	−0.06*	0.02	0.07**	0.06
	Commitment	0.02	0.04	−0.06**	0.11**	−0.15***	−0.22***	0.07**	0.03	0.03	0.07
	Political discussion co-members	0.04	0.01	0.07**	0.02	0.03	0.04	−0.08**	0.07	0.11***	0.08
	Helping each other	0.02	0.00	0.01	0.05	0.02	0.07	−0.08**	0.04	0.07*	0.07
Associational features	Number of active members	−0.04	0.05	−0.02	−0.02	0.12**	−0.04	0.03	0.07	−0.10**	−0.10*
	Written constitution	0.01	0.00	0.04	0.08*	0.06	0.10	0.05	0.00	0.03	0.04
	Membership fees/budget	0.00	−0.03	0.04	0.00	0.03	0.06	0.05	0.05	−0.06	−0.02
	Opportunities for influence	0.01	0.03	0.01	−0.01		0.03	−0.04	0.01	0.00	0.03
Associational type	Scope of activity	0.04	0.05	0.19***	0.08*	0.19***	0.17**	n.a.	n.a.	0.00	0.01
	Family	0.02	0.01	0.01	0.01	−0.04	−0.21***	−0.01	0.07	0.02	0.07
	Sports	−0.03	−0.03	−0.03	−0.01	−0.09	−0.11	−0.02	0.00	0.02	−0.05
	Culture	0.06**	0.03	−0.01	−0.01	0.12**	0.08	−0.05	−0.04	0.10**	0.10*
	Community concerns	−0.02	0.02	−0.03	−0.01	−0.12**	−0.01	−0.10***	−0.07	−0.04	−0.12**
	Politics	0.05*	0.01	0.02	−0.04	0.08	0.18**	−0.05	−0.01	0.10**	0.17**
	New politics	0.08**	0.02	0.07**	0.04	−0.03	−0.11	0.02	0.01	0.09**	0.05
	General welfare	0.05	0.02	0.04	−0.04	0.00	−0.03	0.01	0.05	0.05	0.02
	Group-specific welfare	0.08**	0.03	0.01	0.04	0.00	0.01	−0.06*	−0.07	0.06	0.06
	Economic interests	0.03	0.02	0.08**	0.00	0.04	0.01	−0.04	0.04	0.04	−0.06
	Religious	0.00	0.00	−0.03	0.02	0.00	0.02	−0.00	0.01	−0.02	−0.06
	Others	0.05*	0.05	0.03	0.03	0.06	0.11	−0.02	−0.05	0.00	0.02
Community involvement	Duration residence	−0.12***	−0.08**	−0.24***	−0.16***	−0.32***	−0.11	−0.14***	−0.19***	−0.24***	−0.16***
Cognitive mobilization	Church attendance	−0.05*	0.02	−0.07**	−0.03	−0.07	−0.20**	0.02	0.02	n.a.	n.a.
	Political news in media	0.00	0.09**	−0.02	0.01	0.16***	0.13*	0.04	0.00	0.02	0.01

		(1) r	(1) β	(2) r	(2) β	(3) r	(3) β	(4) r	(4) β	(5) r	(5) β	(6) r	(6) β	(7) r	(7) β	(8) r	(8) β	(9) r	(9) β	(10) r	(10) β
Perception of threat	Education (tertiary)	0.03	−0.10***	0.05	−0.18****	0.12****	−0.13****	0.09**	−0.14****	0.06	−0.05	0.12*	−0.18**	−0.01	−0.05	0.01	−0.15***	0.16****	0.05	0.02	0.03
	Confidence municipal board	0.21****	0.30****	−0.24****	0.30****		0.23***	0.17		0.24*****		0.11***		0.06	
	Confidence EU	0.04	−0.03	0.10***	0.08*		0.01	0.00		−0.03		0.10***		0.14**
	Trust in people	−0.10***	−0.07	−0.09****	−0.06	−0.05	0.01	0.02	−0.11**	−0.16****	−0.13**
Demographic variables	Age	0.00	−0.03	0.01	0.12	−0.06	0.06	0.24	0.04	0.01	0.07	0.04	0.00	0.11	0.03
	Gender (male)																				
Total variance explained (adjusted) R²		0.08		0.12		0.24		0.07		0.11		
N		739		571		201		532		357		

Notes

Levels of statistical significance: **** 0.00; *** 0.01; ** 0.05; * 0.10. Entries are Pearson's correlation coefficients and standardized multiple regression coefficients.

boards in the localities in which they live but do have confidence in European institutions. They are also younger, have a higher level of education, tend not to have lived very long in the present municipality, and are not integrated in local networks.

Associational features and individual engagement do not show any significant relationship with the direction of attachment variable. The only exception is scope of activity, which shows a reversed relationship compared to the strength of attachment dimension. While in the previous model the scope of activity was negatively related to the dependent variable, this time its effect is positive, although it shows up in only two countries: West Germany and the Netherlands. This means that the process of attachment to Europe which is indicated by the direction of attachment dimension depends on involvement in associations with wider networks, and those that are active beyond the local boundaries.

The associations active in the fields of conventional and new politics, and culture, have a positive impact on the direction of attachment, while the effects of other associational types are less clear. Most of the significant effects become weaker and non-significant in the multiple regression analysis due to the impact of various individual variables, which means that the effect of associational type that shows in the bivariate analysis is largely due to the composition of associational members.

9.6 Conclusion

Identification with Europe is seen as one of the most important elements in achieving support for various projects of European integration. Its importance lies in the stabilization of feelings of belonging to Europe which can, when necessary, counterbalance the negative attitudes that rise with respect to concrete measures and policies that often divide the citizens into 'losers and winners'. Although the studies of support for the EU are numerous, much less is known about the factors that contribute to the development of attachment to Europe. This chapter contributes to this gap in our knowledge.

The weak primordial basis and cultural homogeneity of European citizens makes it very difficult to construct the strong version of identification with Europe along the lines of ethnic identities. Instead, efforts have been made in building a European identity based on the notion of political citizenship, which consists of inclusion in the common institutional framework enhanced by different forms of political and social participation. It is the voluntary associations that are considered to be the main building blocks of European civil society due to their ability to act as vehicles of political and social empowerment of European citizens.

Because of the high expectations vested in the concept of European civil society and voluntary associations, it is very important to examine their actual role in constructing a European identity. Are voluntary associations an appropriate vehicle to enhance citizens' identification with Europe? The analysis presented in this chapter suggests that associational involvement of citizens supports the creation of a European identity. There are actually two different mechanisms of how attachment to Europe is formed, and voluntary associations are particularly important in promoting the first mechanism: strength of attachment. According to this process, all voluntary associations that allow for frequent political communication and strong social integration of their members help to build European identity. This is very much in line with Shils' argument that imagined communities, which aim to build feelings of attachment on common knowledge of social and political affairs, can do so only if this common knowledge is also collectively possessed. With respect to associational characteristics, associations which are limited in their activities to smaller areas, like neighbourhoods or parts of the bigger city, are more likely a source of strong pro-European attachment than are associations with larger scope and wider networks. The same is true for associations where members have high levels of commitment. Associational type is also relevant here; sports, culture, community concerns, politics, new politics, and religious type of associations promote identification with Europe, but the effects of associational type are shown mainly in the bivariate analysis, which means that they are due to different compositions of their memberships.

However, the analysis has also revealed an inverse relationship between the identities that are based on social relatedness, such as regions and municipalities, and those based on categorization and symbolic imagination of commonalities, such as the nation-state and Europe. This process is described by the second dimension, called direction of attachment to Europe. It can best be explained in terms of cognitive mobilization, described by Inglehart (1970, 1977a). Cognitive mobilization that occurs through education and informal acquisition of knowledge means that some people are more able or likely than others to identify with the abstract or imagined communities. This distinction is reinforced by confidence in more global as opposed to local institutions. Citizens who are not strongly embedded in social networks of any kind (associational, neighbourhood or church-related networks), who are younger, more highly educated and, most importantly, have high levels of confidence in European institutions, show high levels of this kind of attachment to Europe. At the same time as they hold high confidence in European institutions, they reject local institutions. They probably perceive local institutions as less able to deal with the most pressing issues of today, which are global rather than local in their nature (for example, the environment, global inequalities, protection of human rights, etc.). Associational characteristics are less relevant for the activists and citizens that follow this route to identification with Europe. They are somewhat more likely to be found among the members of the new-politics type of associations, and associations that are active not only locally but also more broadly.

Throughout the analysis, associational factors emerged as important predictors of European identity. This is true for the individual engagement variables, which describe the kind of associational members and how they are integrated into the associations, as well as associational characteristics, such as scope of activity and level of internal democratization. Both kinds of associations – locally bounded associations with a high level of internal democracy, high social integration and commitment of their members, on the one hand, and associations which are part of wider networks and have a scope of activity that reaches beyond the local boundaries, on the other – promote attachment to Europe, but in very different ways and to different extents. The impact of associations is stronger in the case of the mechanism 'strength of attachment', where the social integration aspect of associational life is especially important. On the other hand, there are citizens and activists, especially younger and more educated ones, whose attachment to Europe is driven primarily by their confidence in European institutions. We can conclude that in order to enhance European identity and pro-European attachment, the two strategies, which have both been mentioned in EU documents, should be followed simultaneously. First, make the European institutions highly accountable to European citizens to enhance citizens' confidence. Second, promote the development of the civil society, even at the most local level.

Notes

1 The network 'Citizenship, Involvement, Democracy' (CID) was funded by the European Science Foundation; see www.mzes.uni-mannheim.de/projekte/cid. The CID project produced two edited volumes (van Deth *et al.* 2007, and Maloney and Roßteutscher 2007) and Chapter 1 of the present volume. Data can be obtained from the Zentral Archiv in Cologne (Study number 4492; http://info1.za.gesis.org).
2 The measure used in our study, which combines the question of identification with the rating scale, shows the highest level of external validity among the many varieties of measures of collective identification, judged on the basis of the relationship with relevant attitudinal variables, such as national pride, support for EU integration, confidence in the EU, etc. (Sinnott 2005).
3 These are East and West Germany, the Netherlands, Spain, Switzerland and the UK.
4 For Spain and East Germany we have no data on the attachment to territorial entities among activists.
5 The variables 'strength of attachment' and 'direction of attachment' to Europe are regression scores obtained by principal component analysis.
6 For a full description of the methodology on how the 35 different sectors in which the associations have been active during the last year were reduced to 11 associational types, see Roßteutscher and van Deth (2002), and Maloney *et al.* (2008).
7 Since our goal is to explain attachment to Europe, as distinct from social support for European integration, we do not include in the model the variables of social position of individuals. The variables like income or occupation are usually meant to indicate the benefits and gains one can expect from the increased level of integration, and are assumed to influence the level of social support jointly with non-economic considerations such as identification with Europe.

10 Political trust in the EU

Active idealists and rational non-actives in Europe?

Silke I. Keil

10.1 Introduction

In December 2007, the results of a published Eurobarometer survey about the trust of citizens in the EU boosted discussions about the possible consequences of a lack of trust. According to the findings of the survey, the institutions of the EU had suffered a major loss of citizens' trust within the previous six months – most notably in Germany (–17 per cent), the Netherlands (–16 per cent), the UK (–11 per cent) and Spain (–7 per cent). A decrease within a six-month period could be regarded as a blip. However, this snapshot can be regarded as the continuation of a long-term trend. The European Social Surveys[1] from 2002 to 2006 highlight that the decline in trust has some longevity.[2] A clear distinction also emerges regarding the attitude of Germans separated according to old and new Federal States. East German citizens have no trust in the European Parliament. A gradual decline can also be observed in the UK; however, the base level is considerably higher. While more than half of the respondents had no trust in the institution in 2002 (59.3 per cent), the proportion increased to almost 64 per cent in 2006. The changes in Switzerland and the Netherlands are less acute. Between 2002 and 2004, the proportion of respondents who expressed little or no trust at all in the European Parliament rose from 39.5 percent to 41.6 percent in Switzerland, and from 37.7 percent to 40 per cent in the Netherlands. In 2006, however, trust levels returned to those of 2002. An opposing trend is apparent in Spain. There are more people who have trust in the European Parliament than have little trust or none at all. In addition, the proportion of people who have little or no trust decreased in the observed period (2002–2006) from 36.5 per cent to 32.7 per cent.

Taking into account the results of both the European Social Survey and the Eurobarometer, a long-term decline in trust can be observed. How can this development be interpreted?

It is indisputable that it is an essential basic requirement that the people who are governed trust the institutions of democracy. However, the 'required level' of trust is debatable. The relevance of this decrease in trust is therefore a subject for discussion. However, there is the almost unanimous perspective that a constant decrease in trust would have negative effects on democracy. According to this, the question about the reasons for the regressive trend arises. The question about the reasons for the decline is subordinate to the question about the general determinants of citizens' trust in the EU.

In the tradition of social capital theory (Putnam 1993, 2000), social capital generates political trust. Accordingly, citizens who support values and norms relating to the community, who trust other people and who are involved in voluntary associations are likely to exhibit relatively high levels of political trust.

The prominence of the concept of social capital is mainly based upon Putnam's (1993, 2000) work. In his comprehensive study *Making Democracy Work*, he analyses the conditions for the effectiveness of newly implemented regional governments in Italy in the 1970s (Putnam 1993: 3–7). Putnam identifies the extent of a civil society as the most important explanatory factor for the vast differences of otherwise identical political institutions: 'By far the most important factor in explaining good government is the degree to which social and political life in a region approximates the ideal of the civic community'. In *Bowling Alone*, Putnam (2000) analyses the reasons for, and consequences of, a broad decline of civic engagement in the USA. Civil society builds on 'civic virtues', which, according to Putnam (2000: 19), only take effect in the close interaction of social relationships.

For Putnam, 'social capital refers to connections among individuals – social networks and the norms of reciprocity and trustworthiness that arise from them' (Putnam 2000: 19). In their interplay they enforce one another and generate a close network of socio-cooperative ties, whose basis is participation in voluntary associations (Kunz 2006: 335). Participation in voluntary associations, such as clubs and citizens' initiatives, engenders common norms and values, and fosters social trust. In addition, people are better able to reach common and individual goals because transaction costs are lowered due to reciprocity (Gabriel 2002: 25). Voluntary associations reduce the distance between the citizen and the state (Gabriel 2002: 20), and are widely considered as 'schools of democracy' (Putnam 2000: 338; Armingeon 2007: 360).

In what way do the different components of social capital affect political trust? A positive correlation between both concepts is plausible, because trust also plays an important role within the concept of social capital. Social trust, as well as norms of reciprocity and cooperation, is strengthened by participation (Gabriel 2007: 87). This can be related to the political system in two ways. Putnam (2000: 338) speaks of 'external' and 'internal' effects on the functioning of a democracy. Externally, individuals are better able to express their interests and to make demands towards politics through associations and organizations; and internal, as 'schools of democracy', since the involvement of citizens teaches them cooperative norms of behaviour and fosters individual skills that will facilitate participation in public life (Putnam 2000: 338).

Three sources of political trust can be identified within social capital theory. Social trust, whose generation is enforced by social capital, can be transformed into political trust via generalization processes (Gabriel 2002: 175). This generalization results from the implicit assumption that social norms and values, on

Political trust in the EU 209

which social trust is based, are also valid in the political system. However, citizens who have access to high levels of social capital are more likely to experience the political system in a positive way by playing a part and interacting with other social actors on equal terms – even though divergent interests exist. This experience can also be generalized, and can therefore add to trust in the political system (Morales and Geurts 2007: 135). It is further argued that in societies characterized by a high degree of social capital, responsiveness is increased and governance is made more efficient by the orientation towards the community and norms of reciprocity, such as solidarity (Putnam 2000: 347; Gabriel 2002: 175; Uslaner 2002: 218). This also leads to increased trust in the political system as well.

According to this, social capital can be regarded as a production factor of political trust, which can generate political trust in three ways: first, through the generalization of social trust; second, through the generalization of positive experience from horizontal interactive relationships with the political system; and third, through a positive evaluation of improved government work.

How does social capital influence the generation of political trust in institutions? As far as political trust in institutions is concerned, Hardin (1998, 1999) is critical. He defines trust as 'encapsulated interest' (Hardin 1999: 26), which means that the trusting person can assume that the person who is trusted in is interested in considering the interests of the trusting person. The trusting person cannot make this assumption with regard to political institutions, such as the EU, because he or she has neither sufficient knowledge of the individuals within the institution in whom he could put such trust, nor of the structures and processes within the institution which determine the framework for the actions of individuals within that institution (Hardin 1999: 29). The relationship between citizens and the EU does therefore not depend on trust, but on inductively derived expectations (Hardin 1999: 39). Braithwaite (1998) integrates this criticism into a concept of trust which assumes two different forms of trust – 'communal-based trust', which refers to a collective and mutual understanding and is therefore community-orientated, and 'exchange-based trust', which refers to predictability and can be interpreted as a trade-off (Braithwaite 1998: 51, 65.). Both forms of trust can coexist, but they have a different meaning depending on the object of trust, as Braithwaite (1998) has demonstrated empirically.[3]

This chapter aims to test and clarify to what extent people of varying social commitment trust the EU. As shown by Braithwaite, trust in institutions is not one-dimensional but has to be broken down into two components. And it seems plausible to assume that Braithwaite's distinction between exchange-based trust and communal-based trust corresponds to different intensities of participation. That means it can be assumed that for people who are actively participating, rationalistic motives are less decisive for their trust in the EU than idealistic and emotional reasons. This in turn means that trust is communal-based. For people who are not actively participating, it can be assumed that it is exactly the other way round – trust is created because performance is evaluated positively, and because a person is integrated into a system via different factors. This is a matter of exchange-based trust. Thus, whether trust in the EU is based on exchange or on the community has implications for the explanation. Depending on the form of trust, different determinants may be responsible for its generation.

According to this line of argument, the question for the present chapter is: Do activists, socially actives and non-actives differ with respect to political trust in the EU? (See Chapter 1 for the characteristics of these three groups of citizens.) This question can be specified on the basis of Braithwaite's differentiation: Can political trust of activists in the EU be explained with social capital theory because it emphasizes the community-orientated dimension of political trust? On the other hand, does the exchange-based dimension most notably play an important role for non-actives? And is political trust in the EU the product of a state's achievement in terms of integration and of the evaluation of a state's performance?

In the following section, the corresponding theoretical concepts and their relationships are presented. After that, the derived hypotheses will be presented, as well as the indicators which are relevant for the study and the applied regression analyses. Section 10.3 gives an account of the level of trust in the EU, whereas in Section 10.4 the correlations between the components of the explanatory approaches are analysed and discussed. Section 10.5 discusses the importance of contextual features of voluntary associations for trust in the EU. The chapter closes with a summary of the main findings.

10.2 Theoretical foundation and research design

10.2.1 Institutionalist approach vs. culture-based approach: political trust based on exchange and political trust based on the community

As noted above, this chapter follows Braithwaite's differentiation between communal-based and exchange-based trust. Figure 10.1 summarizes the underlying assumptions and consequences. Different norms form the basis of these two forms of trust: communal-based trust refers to understanding and esteem for the needs of others as well as mutual respect. This form has its roots in shared views, common objectives and social responsibility. In contrast, exchange-based trust emphasizes predictability and procedural accuracy and aims to reach an aspired advantage (Braithwaite 1998: 52, 65). Braithwaite assigns harmony values to communal trust and security values to exchange trust (Braithwaite 1998: 51).

The following analysis focuses on the question of how citizens' trust in the EU is created. It is not the trust of citizens in general that is of interest, but rather the various levels of trust among citizens with varying social commitments. Some people are actively involved, others are involved to only a limited extent, and others again do not participate at all – why?

Social capital theory emphasizes the culture-based[4] and communal-based dimension of political trust. Its explanatory power therefore refers particularly to people who are involved in social activities. However, do people who participate to a small extent or do not participate at all trust the EU as well?

	Exchanged-based = rational, cognitive perspective	Community-based = emotional, non-cognitive perspective
Assumption	A trusts B to do X	A trusts B
Precondition	Knowledge about competence	Identity and loyalty
Orientation/ consequence	**Results-oriented**/little stability	Less **results-oriented**, therefore more stable and more **effective**

Figure 10.1 Two perspectives on political trust.

The generation of political trust in a culture-based perspective is expressed by Rohrschneider as 'ideological values shape support for existing institutions' (1999: 14). In contrast to this perspective, Di Palma argues from an institutionalist standpoint: 'genuine democrats need not precede democracy' (1990: 30). The supportive output thus results from the rational evaluation of the performance of democratic institutions such as the EU. From an institutionalist perspective, the generation of trust can therefore be explained by the performance of institutions on the one hand and by the integration of people via institutions on the other. Following the argument of performance, it is assumed that the performance of the EU itself creates political trust. However, centring on the assumption of integration, it is assumed that the EU is able to better integrate citizens into the system and with it to influence their attitudes as well. As a consequence, better integration into the system generates political trust. Regardless of which line of argument is followed, both make it clear that the institutionalist perspective emphasizes the exchange-based dimension of political trust. A person trusts the EU because he or she is convinced by its performance and/or because the EU as an institution contributes to that person's feeling of being better integrated, and this integration generates political trust. Thus, trust in the EU can be based on different factors – either exchange-based or communal-based. It is plausible to assume that this varying quality of political trust can be observed among people of varying social commitment. People involved in social activities differ from those who are not involved in such activities. Therefore, it is plausible to check whether people of varying social commitment trust the EU more or less. The analysis will show whether these presumptions are empirically valid.

10.2.2 Hypotheses

This chapter does not analyse the importance of determinants of trust for all citizens, since it does not primarily serve the purpose of comparing two competing approaches. Rather, it explores patterns of explanations for citizens with varying levels of social commitment. Accordingly, the following hypothesis forms the basis of this chapter.

Basic hypothesis:

Activists' trust in the EU is influenced more strongly by the indicators of social capital theory, whereas non-activists' trust in the EU is better explained by the institutionalist approach.

Hypotheses 1–3 refer to social capital theory, and hypotheses 4 and 5 test the relevance of the institutionalist approach. In doing so, it has to be emphasized that the competing approaches do not exclude one another. Since political trust consists of an exchange-based and a communal-based component, both approaches have a significant effect on political trust.

Social capital hypotheses

H1: The stronger the trust in other people, the stronger the trust in the EU.

H2: Individuals who support communal-based values and norms rather trust in the EU.

H3: If people are socially active, their trust is more pronounced.

Institutionalist hypotheses

H4: If citizens are confident with the overall performance of the system, they trust in the EU more strongly.

H5: If citizens are integrated into the system by institutions (identifying with a certain party, going to the polls or to church and increasingly consuming media respectively), they rather trust in the EU.

The clarification of reasons for the different degrees of individuals' activities must not stop short of the level of individual characteristics. We know from social capital theory that it has positive effects because of the experiences and interactions taking place within voluntary associations (Armingeon 2007: 366). Since voluntary associations vary with regard to goals and organization, it is unlikely that all voluntary associations exert the same influence. The influence of contextual factors will therefore be tested after testing determinants on the micro-level.

10.2.3 Operationalization and strategy of analysis

To assess the effects of the independent variables (social capital and institutional factors) on the dependent variable (trust in the EU among activists, socially actives and non-actives), they have to be operationalized via the items surveyed in the CID questionnaire. To measure the independent variable, the respondents were asked whether they trusted the EU. The following wording was used:

> I will now read out names of different institutions such as the police, government, civil service, etc. Please tell me how strongly you personally trust each of these institutions.

Respondents could give their answer on a scale from 0 to 10.

The explanatory power of social capital theory for the citizens' trust in the EU will be tested using the three components social trust, networks and norms of reciprocity. Social trust is measured by the use of three standard items consisting of 11 points: general trust in fellow citizens, trust in their helpfulness and trust in their fairness. Communal-based norms and values, as a second element of the cultural component of social capital, are measured by the use of the standard question blocs 'Good citizen' and 'Ideal society'. An index created out of these variables combines the data into a bundle, and a further index summarizes the norms of reciprocity.[5] The significance of the structural component – integration into networks – can be tested via the respondents' participation in different organizations.[6]

The relevance of the institutionalist line of explanation for the trust of citizens of varying social commitment in the EU was tested by means of the following variables. The question about the evaluation of the system's performance, which uses a four-point scale, is of particular importance.[7] With it, it is possible to test those effects that are purely based on performance. The second category underscores the argument of integration by institutions via the variables 'party identification', 'voting', 'media consumption' and 'church attendance'. Each of these constructs contributes to the citizens' integration on its own, and both constructs produce stronger involvement, which in turn generates citizens' trust in the EU.

Socio-demographic variables (gender, nationality, religious affiliation, income) and other variables which are important for the generation of trust (satisfaction with life, political discussions and political interest) are included as control variables.

To test the hypotheses formulated above, the effects have to be estimated by means of OLS regression analyses. The underlying data for these analyses are the data sets for citizens and activists, where the activist data set is relevant for the group of activists and the citizen data set is relevant for the groups of socially actives and non-actives (see Chapter 1). The dependent variables make up the trust of activists, socially actives and non-actives in the EU, each with a regression of its own.[8] This means that three models are estimated for each country to test the effects of social capital factors. In a further step, again three models are estimated, in which institutionalist factors of explanation are included. In a last step, an integrated model is tested; this model includes social capital variables *and* institutionalist factors of explanation *and* control variables.[9]

10.3 Levels of political trust in the EU

In the introduction to this chapter, declining trust in the EU over time was noted. However, what picture do the CID data paint? It should be emphasized that a comparison with the data from Spain is only possible to a limited extent, since Spanish activists were not asked about trust in the EU. This means that questions about the level of trust and questions about the determinants of trust in the EU can only be answered referring to Spain's socially actives and non-actives.

A first examination of the proportion of individuals who trust or strongly trust the EU and individuals with little or no trust (percentages not specified) shows a slightly different picture than that presented in the introduction. In 2001, one year before the first European Social Survey was conducted, the atmosphere was relatively positive. In West Germany (55.9 per cent), in the Netherlands (48.7 per cent) and in Spain (42.0 per cent), the proportion of people who had some or strong trust in the EU outweighs the proportion of people who had little or no trust in the EU (West Germany 31.2 per cent; the Netherlands 26.9 per cent; Spain 26.7 per cent). In the other countries, however, an atmosphere of mistrust predominates: mistrust outweighs trust in the UK, a country that is traditionally Euro-sceptic, in Switzerland, which does not belong to the EU, and in East Germany (little trust and no trust at all: East Germany 49.6 per cent, Switzerland 46.1 per cent, UK 50.3 per cent).

In a cross-country comparison of activity groups – as Figure 10.2 indicates – a systematic pattern is not evident. The differences between the groups in the individual countries turn out to be generally moderate. Activists do not trust the EU most, and non-activists do not trust the EU the least. This pattern can only be observed in two countries. Interestingly, one of these cases is a country that is traditionally Euro-sceptic – the UK – and the other case is the non-member Switzerland. Both in Switzerland and in the UK, activists are more trusting than non-activists. Regarding the differences between the groups in other countries, it can be established that in both parts of Germany socially actives possess the highest degree of trust, whereas activists have least trust in the EU. In the Netherlands, people trust the EU regardless of the extent of social commitment.

A comparison between the countries results in the following ranking. By far the largest proportions of individuals who trust the EU live in Spain. More than half of the active, but also of the non-active Spanish population trusts the EU. In the Netherlands, the proportion is half of the population, followed by West Germany. The lowest degree of trust can be found in the UK, followed by East Germany and Switzerland. However, within this comparison it has to be added that the differences are relatively small. The difference is only significant between the countries of the opposite poles – Spain and the UK.

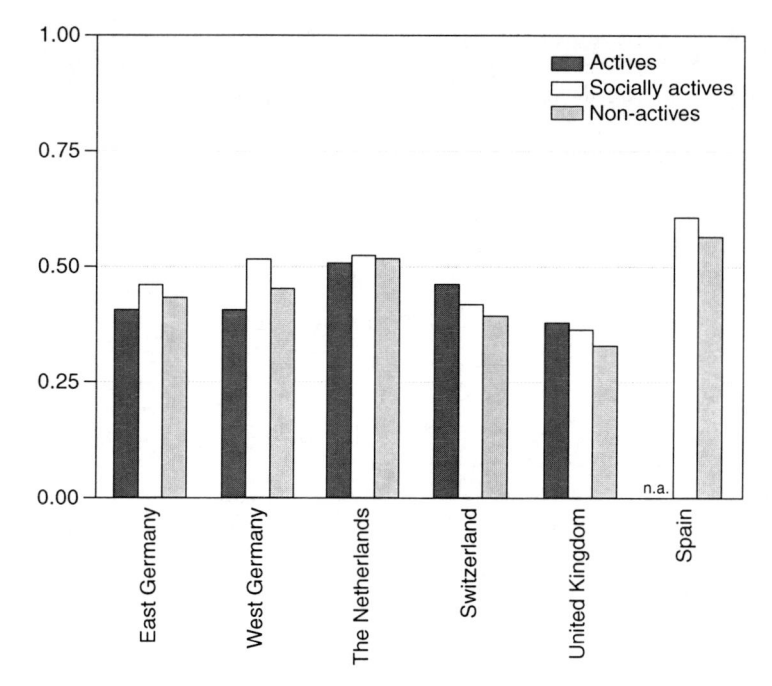

Figure 10.2 Means of trust in the EU.

10.4 Determinants of political trust in the EU

10.4.1 Active idealists and rational non-actives in Europe?

Figure 10.2 made clear that people of varying social commitment show a different degree of trust in the EU, with the exception of the Netherlands. How can this be explained, and what determinants are responsible for these developments? As outlined previously, it can be assumed that there exist other cause–effect relationships for activists than for non-actives. Accordingly, the basic hypothesis will be tested: i.e. is communal-based trust of activists more strongly affected by indicators of social capital theory, and is the exchange-based trust of non-activists better explained by variables of the institutionalist approach?

Figure 10.3 shows that the assumption of active idealists and rational non-actives is not supported by the data, as measured by adjusted R^2 comparison. The theoretically established pattern that trust of activists in the EU can best be explained by social capital theory and trust of non-actives can best be explained by variables of the institutionalist approach[10] appears in none of the countries. That means the basic hypothesis could not be verified in the presented form. It has to be pointed out, however, that the explained variance of all models is moderate, with the adjusted R^2 range between 0.01 and 0.16.[11]

If, in a first comparison, varying involvement is considered, the following pattern emerges: the trust of socially actives is best explained by the institutionalist

216 S.I. Keil

R²: Actives		
East Germany: 0.10		
West Germany: 0.14	R²: Social actives	
The Netherlands: 0.05	East Germany: 0.05	R²: Non-actives
Spain: n.a.	West Germany: 0.07	East Germany: 0.14
Switzerland: 0.10	The Netherlands: 0.08	West Germany: 0.11
United Kingdom: 0.04	Spain: 0.11	The Netherlands: 0.11
	Switzerland: 0.03	Spain: 0.11
	United Kingdom: 0.03	Switzerland: 0.04
		United Kingdom: 0.02

Culturalist explanatory factors/social capital → Community-based Trust in the EU

Institutionalist explanatory factors → Exchange-based

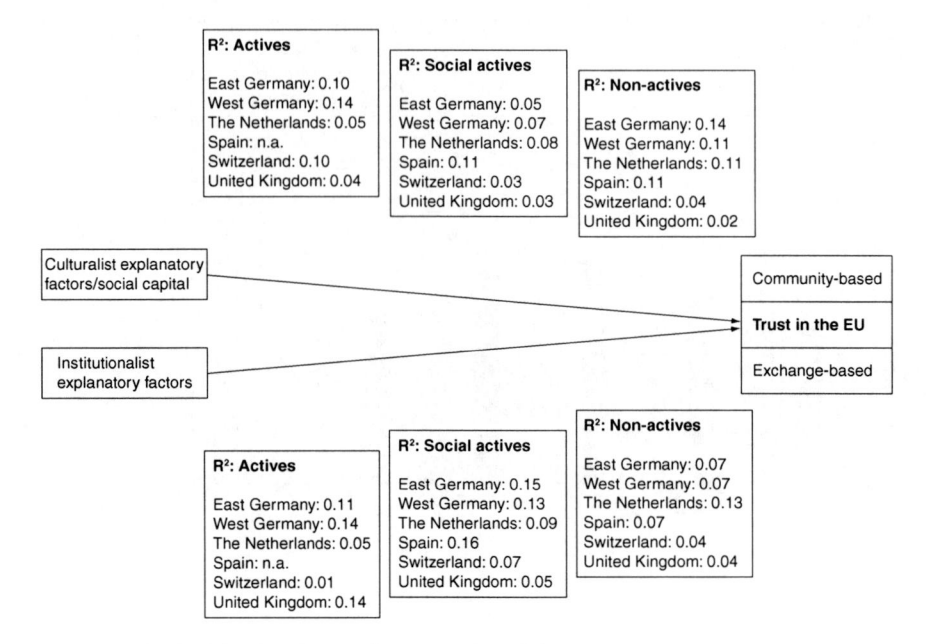

R²: Actives	R²: Social actives	R²: Non-actives
East Germany: 0.11	East Germany: 0.15	East Germany: 0.07
West Germany: 0.14	West Germany: 0.13	West Germany: 0.07
The Netherlands: 0.05	The Netherlands: 0.09	The Netherlands: 0.13
Spain: n.a.	Spain: 0.16	Spain: 0.07
Switzerland: 0.01	Switzerland: 0.07	Switzerland: 0.04
United Kingdom: 0.14	United Kingdom: 0.05	United Kingdom: 0.04

Figure 10.3 Explained variance of two tested models.

approach. People who report that they are involved in social activities are less likely to be doing so because they trust other people and have internalized norms of reciprocity. It is more likely that they are convinced by the state's performance, and because they are integrated via institutionalist mechanisms. Exchange-based trust is therefore the basis of this correlation.

The examination of activists does not reveal a systematic pattern. Thus, contrary to the *basic hypothesis* formulated above, trust of activists cannot be explained primarily by social capital variables. Rather, both approaches are equally powerful as far as the explanation of trust in the EU is concerned. The trust of active citizens in Switzerland can better be explained by social capital variables than by institutionalist factors – consistent with the basic hypothesis. Only in Switzerland it is therefore possible to talk of communal-based trust. In the other countries, both communal-based trust and exchange-based trust coexist.

Regarding the determinants of trust in the EU of non-actives, social capital theory proves to have a greater explanatory power in more than half the analysed countries. For this reason, part of the basic hypothesis has been refuted. Basically, the trust of the non-active population in the EU can be explained best (with the exception of Switzerland) – independent of the chosen explanatory approach.

In a second step, the comparison of countries is the centre of attention. As already mentioned, the explained variance is moderate. As Figure 10.3 shows, the tested models work best for both parts of Germany and worst for Switzerland

Political trust in the EU 217

and the UK. As far as the basic hypothesis is concerned, the trust of active and non-active citizens as well as activists cannot be explained in the expected way in any of the countries. Only in Switzerland do the social capital variables hold some explanatory power for activists. However, the second component of the basic hypothesis – that institutionalist factors play the most important role for non-actives – cannot be verified. In the other countries, differences in explanatory power are relatively small. There are almost no differences in the Netherlands.

Since the basic hypothesis could not be verified, how robust do the other hypotheses appear? The results can be seen in Tables 10.1–10.6. Hypothesis 1 can be considered as verified, because the results show that the more strongly individuals trust in other people, the more strongly they trust the EU. It also turns out that support for communal-based values and norms fosters trust (i.e. Hypothesis 2 is verified). No correlation can be identified for the intensity of participation and trust, which means that Hypothesis 3 is not verified. It further turns out that – as expected, according to Hypothesis 4 – the positive evaluation of the system's performance strongly influences trust in the EU. If, however, the second dimension of the cultural approach – integration – is analysed, a less clear picture is produced. Church attendance (especially in West Germany and in Spain), media consumption, voting (especially in the UK and Switzerland) and party identification influence trust in the EU, although nowhere nearly as strongly as the evaluation of performance, and not in all countries either (Hypothesis 5).

10.4.2 Communal-based and exchanged-based explanatory approaches compared

Until now, explanations have only referred to the testing of the hypotheses. It has become clear thereby that both explanatory approaches add to the explanation of political trust in the EU – even if not as exclusively as formulated in the basic hypothesis. Moreover, as already mentioned in the introduction, the question regarding determinants of political trust in the EU is generally relevant for this chapter. The following explanation therefore highlights determinants which are responsible for the generation of political trust. Which of the approaches and/or variables possess the greatest explanatory power?

Tables 10.1–10.6 make it clear that there are two factors that are continuously important for all examined types of activities in all countries: social trust, and the positive evaluation of the state's performance. According to this, political trust in the EU is generated if people trust other people and generalize this trust. This generalization results from the implicit assumption that social trust is converted into political trust, and is therefore also valid in the political system, relating to the EU. In this context, we can, according to Braithwaite, speak of communal-based trust. Communal-based trust and exchange-based trust do not exclude one another. The generalized evaluation of the government's performance considerably influences the degree of trust in the EU in all countries. The

Table 10.1 Determinants of political trust in EU, East Germany (beta coefficients)

	Activists	Socially actives	Non-actives	Activists	Socially actives	Non-actives	Activists	Socially actives	Non-actives
Social capital									
Network	0.05*	−0.11**					0.04	0.00	0.76**
Trust	0.17****	0.18****	0.19****				0.10****	0.15****	0.14****
Community	−0.14****	0.07	0.05				0.17****	0.12**	0.07
Reciprocity	0.12****	0.06	0.30****				0.07**	−0.02	0.22****
Institutional factors									
System's performance				−0.31	−0.37****	−0.23****	−0.27****	−0.36****	−0.14***
Party identification				−0.03	0.00	−0.03	0.00	−0.04	−0.04
Voting				0.05*	−0.06	−0.06	0.07**	−0.02	0.01
Media consumption				0.01	−0.37	−0.10**	0.03	0.06	−0.03
Church attendance				−0.05*	0.00	−0.03	−0.02	−0.07	−0.06
Control variables									
Gender							0.00	0.02	−0.05
Citizenship							−0.03	−0.03	−0.10
Religion							−0.02	0.14****	−0.02
Income							0.00	n.a.	n.a.
Life satisfaction							0.09***	−0.05	0.02
Political discussions							−0.01	0.17****	0.19****
Political interest							0.00	−0.12**	−0.15**
Adj. R²	0.10	0.05	0.14	0.11	0.15	0.07	0.18	0.21	0.15
Constant	0.31	3.06	1.12	6.26	6.65	6.32	2.22	5.39	2.90
N	1,195	391	505	1,027	373	424	987	356	401

Notes
*$P<0.10$; **$P<0.05$; ***$P<0.01$; ****$P<0.001$.

Table 10.2 Determinants of political trust in EU, West Germany (beta coefficients)

	Activists	Socially actives	Non-actives	Activists	Socially actives	Non actives	Activists	Socially actives	Non-actives
Social capital									
Network	0.03	−0.01					0.03	0.02****	
Trust	0.24****	0.17	0.20****				0.15****	0.19	0.04
Community	0.15****	0.14	0.06**				0.12****	−0.01****	0.13****
Reciprocity	0.14****	0.06	0.21****				0.18****	0.07****	0.18****
Institutional factors									
System's performance				−0.35****	−0.34****	−0.27****	−0.30****	−0.25	−0.18****
Party identification				0.05**	0.00	0.00	0.03	−0.02***	−0.05
Voting				0.02	0.01	−0.02	0.06**	0.08	0.05
Media consumption				0.01	0.06**	0.03	0.03	0.05	0.00
Church attendance				−0.08****	−0.06***	0.01	−0.01	0.02	0.05
Control variables									
Gender							0.01	−0.01	−0.03
Citizenship							0.01	0.01	−0.04
Religion							0.00	0.02*	0.03
Income							n.a.	−0.05***	0.03
Life satisfaction							0.03	0.08****	0.03
Political discussions							0.05	0.12****	0.07*
Political interest							−0.04	−0.19****	−0.12***
Adj. R²	0.14	0.07	0.11	0.14	0.13	0.07	0.23	0.17	0.13
Constant	−0.29	2.55	1.68	5.96	6.52	5.53	1.18	3.06	2.88
N	1,728	1,463	1,299	1,723	1,488	1,284	1,636	1,115	762

Notes
*$P<0.10$; **$P<0.05$; ***$P<0.01$; ****$P<0.001$.

Table 10.3 Determinants of political trust in EU, The Netherlands (beta coefficients)

	Activists	Socially actives	Non-actives	Activists	Socially actives	Non-actives	Activists	Socially actives	Non-actives
Social capital									
Network	0.10**	-0.03					0.10*	-0.03	
Trust	0.15****	0.19****	0.24****				0.14***	0.15	0.20
Community	-0.02	0.01	-0.04				-0.02	0.03	-0.06
Reciprocity	0.14***	0.19****	0.20****				0.10*	0.13	0.15
Institutional factors									
System's performance				-0.21	-0.28****	-0.36****	-0.18****	-0.24	-0.22
Party identification				-0.11	-0.01	0.02	-0.11**	-0.02	0.05
Voting				0.03	0.03	0.04	0.07	0.10	0.06
Media consumption				0.01	0.02	-0.01	0.01	0.02	0.05
Church attendance				-0.11	-0.14****	-0.07	-0.12**	-0.11	0.02
Control variables									
Gender							0.06	-0.12	-0.11
Citizenship							-0.02	-0.02	0.12
Religion							-0.14***	-0.03	0.03
Income							0.03	0.01	-0.03
Life satisfaction							0.14***	0.00	0.04*
Political discussions							0.05	-0.04	-0.07
Political interest							0.04	-0.01	-0.05
Adj. R^2	0.05	0.08	0.11	0.05	0.09	0.13	0.12	0.15	0.17
Constant	2.66	2.39	2.31	6.30	6.44	6.55	2.65	4.35	3.78
N	401	910	562	401	908	544	369	825	459

Notes
*$P<0.10$; **$P<0.05$; ***$P<0.01$; ****$P<0.001$.

Table 10.4 Determinants of political trust in EU, Spain (beta coefficients)

	Activists	Socially actives	Non-actives	Activists	Socially actives	Non-actives	Activists	Socially actives	Non-actives
Social capital									
Network	n.a.	−0.02		n.a.			n.a.	−0.04	
Trust	n.a.	0.18	0.17****	n.a.			n.a.	0.13****	0.09****
Community	n.a.	−0.03	0.05**	n.a.			n.a.	0.01	0.03
Reciprocity	n.a.	0.29	0.25****	n.a.			n.a.	0.16****	0.23****
Institutional factors									
System's performance				n.a.	−0.33****	−0.20****	n.a.	−0.25****	−0.12****
Party identification				n.a.	−0.08**	−0.09****	n.a.	−0.04	−0.02
Voting				n.a.	−0.07**	−0.03	n.a.	−0.03	−0.01
Media consumption				n.a.	−0.03	0.05*	n.a.	−0.02	0.08****
Church attendance				n.a.	−0.11****	−0.09****	n.a.	−0.05	−0.07****
Control variables									
Gender							n.a.	0.01	0.07**
Citizenship							n.a.	n.a.	n.a.
Religion							n.a.	−0.01	0.02
Income							n.a.	0.11****	0.04
Life satisfaction							n.a.	0.04	0.07***
Political discussions							n.a.	0.07*	0.01
Political interest							n.a.	−0.13****	−0.16****
Adj. R²	n.a.	0.11	0.11	n.a.	0.16	0.07	n.a.	0.23	0.16
Constant	n.a.	1.80	1.24	n.a.	7.52	6.61	n.a.	3.77	2.30
N	n.a.	1,221	2,111	n.a.	894	1,321	n.a.	843	1,180

Notes
*P<0.10; **P<0.05; ***P<0.01; ****P<0.001.

Table 10.5 Determinants of political trust in EU, Switzerland (beta coefficients)

	Activists	Socially actives	Non-actives	Activists	Socially actives	Non-actives	Activists	Socially actives	Non-actives
Social capital									
Network	−0.02	−0.03					−0.04	0.00	
Trust	0.15****	0.12****	0.15****				0.15****	0.09***	0.17
Community	0.18****	0.09****	0.09**				0.17****	0.11****	0.13
Reciprocity	0.12****	0.08**	0.04				0.09**	0.07*	0.03
Institutional factors									
System's performance				0.02	−0.24****	−0.18****	0.00	−0.19****	−0.13
Party identification				−0.05	0.00	−0.06	−0.02	0.03	−0.05
Voting				0.06*	0.16****	0.10**	0.05	0.09**	−0.01
Media consumption				−0.05	−0.03	−0.02	0.00	−0.03	0.01
Churchgoing				−0.09***	−0.02	0.07*	0.02	0.00	0.12

Notes
*P<0.10; **P<0.05; ***P< 0.01; ****P<0.001.

Table 10.6 Determinants of political trust in EU, United Kingdom (beta coefficients)

	Activists	Socially actives	Non-actives	Activists	Socially actives	Non-actives	Activists	Socially actives	Non-actives
Social capital									
Network	0.00	n.a.					−0.02	n.a.	
Trust	0.07*	0.18****	0.14****				0.03	0.18****	0.27****
Community	0.18****	n.a.	n.a.				0.12**	n.a.	n.a.
Reciprocity	0.00	n.a.	n.a.				−0.07	n.a.	n.a.
Institutional factors									
System's performance				−0.36****	n.a.	n.a.	−0.33****	n.a.	n.a.
Party identification				0.07**	n.a.	n.a.	0.09*	n.a.	n.a.
Voting				−0.02	0.06*	0.00	0.03	0.47**	−0.03
Media consumption				0.05	−0.08**	−0.07****	0.00	−0.11**	n.a.
Church attendance				n.a.	n.a.	n.a.	n.a.	n.a.	n.a.
Control variables									
Gender							−0.06	−0.01	0.08
Citizenship							n.a.	n.a.	n.a.
Religion							−0.03	n.a.	n.a.
Income							n.a.	n.a.	n.a.
Life satisfaction							0.06	n.a.	n.a.
Political discussions							−0.04	−0.03	−0.08****
Political interest							−0.03	n.a.	n.a.
Adj. R²	0.04	0.03	0.02	0.14	0.005	0.04	0.12	0.04	0.02
Constant	1.29	1.88	2.21	5.31	3.72	3.50	4.40	1.95	2.14
N	770	865	1,817	775	852	1,782	423	843	1,770

Notes
*P<0.10; **P<0.05; ***P<0.01; ****P<0.001.

evaluation of performance is bound to the long-term performance of political institutions. That is why an exchange-based relationship must be assumed, and trust exists in an exchange-based form.

Examining the models separately, the following picture emerges. The variables of social capital theory all play an important role, whereas social trust normally exerts the strongest influence. It has to be pointed out that integration into networks is not important (with the exception of activists in the Netherlands). In other words, contrary to Putnam's assumptions, the cultural aspect – and not the structural component of social capital – exclusively influences trust in the EU. Participation in voluntary associations does not exert a significant influence. This result is not surprising, since all previous empirical research shows the same picture as identified in the present analyses – a non-significant correlation between political trust and membership in networks (Gabriel and Kunz 2002; Job 2005; Evans and Letki 2006; Newton 2006; Denters *et al.* 2007; Newton 2008; Rothstein and Stolle 2008).

As mentioned, all variables of social capital theory (with the exception of networks) play an important role for the explanation of trust in the EU. This is different if trust is to be explained via the institutionalist approach. The role of the evaluation of performance on the part of the population is central. In addition, the assumption that political trust is generated by integration is supported by the importance of the variables 'church attendance' and 'voting'. However, two further components which are theoretically important for the integration into a political system and its institutions, such as party identification and media consumption, exert influence sporadically.

The importance of the variables 'social trust' and 'evaluation of performance' is demonstrated exemplarily by the analyses of the integrated models. The influence remains the same even when checking for important control variables. As a rule, the evaluation of performance exerts a stronger influence than does trust. However, both variables are significant. This shows that the two explanatory approaches do not exclude but complement each another. A further interesting result is that, when checking for control variables, almost all social capital variables remain important. However, the variables of the institutionalist approach do not. As a rule, only the positive evaluation of performance remains relevant.

10.4.3 The basic hypothesis – once again: do active idealists and rational non-actives exist after all?

In the first test of the basic hypothesis, the adjusted R^2 values of both basic models were analysed. As a result, the hypothesis in total has to be considered as falsified. In a second step, the determinants of both explanatory approaches have been explored with regard to the question of what the individual variables could add to the explanation of trust in the EU. In doing so, it became clear that both approaches contain variables that are relevant for the generation of political trust in the EU. In a last step, it will now be discussed, on the basis of Tables 10.1–10.6, whether the basic hypothesis has still to be considered falsified when regarding the individual determinants. Which attitudes and behaviours cause different levels of activity in each case?

Concerning activists, all variables of social capital theory prove to be significant in the analysed countries (with the exception of networks). The variables of the institutionalist approach, however, are not significant. In the Netherlands and in East Germany, these variables have no significant influence on trust of activists in the EU. Regarding the integrated models – the models in which the influence of both variables of social capital theory and of the institutionalist approach are estimated allowing for control variables – the importance of social capital theory for the explanation of political trust of activists in the EU is emphasized once again. Social trust and norms and values of reciprocity predominantly exert influence among activists. In East Germany and in Switzerland, these are the only factors that are of consequence. The evaluation of performance is more important in only two countries. However, besides this component, even in these cases the variables that play a role are those of social capital theory.

It was possible to revise the original result of the unverified basic hypothesis related to activists by taking a differentiated look at the analyses. According to that, active idealists exist. With regard to non-activists, however, the result remains the same. The variables of the institutionalist approach *do not* explain the trust of this group in the EU. Quite the contrary: for non-actives, too, the variables of social capital theory normally exert a stronger influence. Finally, the socially actives differ from the other two groups in the fact that a lot of different variables are important. These are both institutionalist variables and trust and norms of reciprocity, as well as – in addition and in contrast to activists and non-actives – control variables such as political interest, political discussions, life satisfaction, etc., which carry a relatively strong weight. In West Germany, only the control variables influence trust of socially actives in the EU.

10.5 Trust in the EU: a matter of context?

As noted above, voluntary commitment plays an important role in the tradition of social capital theory. Participation in voluntary associations is in turn theoretically related to social trust and to the acceptance of norms and values. They can then influence political trust in institutions via generalization processes. So far, the importance of voluntary associations has been analysed on the micro-level. The results showed that – in general – voluntary associations can add very little to an explanation of political trust in the EU. However, this could be due to the fact that the micro-model acts on the implicit assumption that all organizations are equal. This is obviously not the case. There is a wide range of voluntary associations that differ with regard both to content and to organization. Below, voluntary associations are therefore controlled with regard to two important macro-features: size and institutionalization. There are several important issues. Does it makes a difference for trust in the EU if activists are involved in small or large organizations? What are the effects when activists are involved in more institutionalized or less institutionalized organizations? Does the context in which activities take place play a role? These issues are not addressed for all population groups, but only for actives.

Contextual factors, such as size and institutionalization, can heavily influence involvement. And it seems plausible to assume that more variance can be explained in small and little institutionalized organizations than in large and institutionalized ones. A corresponding analysis will show if this is the case.

Multi-level analyses seem to be the most appropriate method for the analysis of these contextual characteristics, but they cannot be applied here because the number of cases is too small. Therefore, the issue of contextual features is addressed by means of group comparisons. For this purpose, a typology is presented which results from a combination of the characteristics 'size' and 'institutionalization'.[12]

To assess the impact of contextual characteristics, the adjusted R^2 values, as indicated in Table 10.7, are compared to those obtained for activists, which have been estimated on the micro-level on the basis of the entire model.[13] In doing so, it becomes clear that the contextual factors have additional explanatory power in all countries except Switzerland. In other words, context matters. In most cases, trust in the EU is better explained with the chosen indicators when the organizations are differentiated according to their size and the degree of institutionalization. The increase in explanatory power is extensive. The increase is most prominent in the Netherlands, being up to 20 per cent for the large and institutionalized organizations. In East Germany the models adds 9 per cent more variance, and in West Germany it adds between 0 and 7 per cent. In Switzerland, however, there is no improvement, and in the UK the explanatory power improves as a general rule. However, variance turns out to be half as low for small and not very institutionalized organizations.

These results show that characteristics on the macro-level, and thus the context in which voluntarily active members are involved, have a significant

		Professionalization	
		Low	High
Size	Small	Type 1: small – largely unprofessionalized organizations	Type 2: small – highly professionalized organizations
	Large	Type 3: large – largely unprofessionalized organizations	Type 4: large – highly professionalized organizations

Figure 10.4 Typology of voluntary associations, differentiated according to size and degree of professionalization.

Table 10.7 Determinants of political trust, differentiated by professionalization and size of organizations (beta coefficients)

	East Germany				West Germany				Switzerland				The Netherlands				United Kingdom			
	Type 1	Type 2	Type 3	Type 4	Type 1	Type 2	Type 3	Type 4	Type 1	Type 2	Type 3	Type 4	Type 1	Type 2	Type 3	Type 4	Type 1	Type 2	Type 3	Type 4
Social capital																				
Network	0.16**	1.27	−0.37	−0.245	0.88	0.38	−0.08	0.38	2.24	0.55	0.78	6.35	−1.28	−0.13	−2.22	−0.08	2.37	−0.61	0.74	−0.98
Trust	0.120	0.24***	0.17**	−0.033	0.33	0.12*	0.25***	0.28****	0.30***	0.08	0.33*	−0.01	0.30**	0.18*	0.23	0.23***	−0.04	0.12	0.04	−0.03
Community	0.16*	0.08	0.19***	0.535****	0.24	0.14**	0.15**	0.11*	0.02	0.04	−0.32*	−0.16	0.21	0.13	0.33	0.22***	−0.08**	0.07	0.06	0.44***
Reciprocity	0.22***	−0.05	0.12*	−0.004	0.05	0.22***	0.06	0.22***	−0.06	0.09	0.45****	0.01	0.10	0.08	0.18	0.12	0.40***	−0.29*	0.23	−0.22
Institutional factors																				
System's performance	−0.99****	−0.77****	−0.74****	−1.16****	−1.38	−1.05****	−1.06****	−1.18****	−0.77**	0.22	−0.67**	−0.15	−0.76**	0.28	−0.14	0.05	−1.26***	−1.39****	−0.84***	−1.20****
Party identification	0.36	−0.38	−0.18	−0.12	0.01	0.07	−0.56**	−0.13	0.19	−0.71**	−0.66**	−0.89**	−0.13	−0.59	−0.64	0.04	0.04	−0.01	−0.52	−0.09
Voting	0.98**	0.99*	−0.39	1.21**	−0.42	0.90*	0.58	0.59	−1.47	0.98	0.85	2.02***	0.44	0.45	−0.15	0.55	0.47	−1.01	1.87	−2.42***
Media consumption	0.15	0.03	0.12	−0.02	0.02	−0.04	−0.05	0.25	0.01	0.05	−0.33*	0.51**	−0.44*	0.20	−0.41	0.05	0.03	0.16	−0.08	0.28
Church attendance	−0.11	0.04	−0.05	−0.23*	0.130	0.04	−0.08	−0.02	−0.09	−0.18*	−0.02	−0.01	0.31**	−0.16	0.51*	0.00	n.a.	n.a.	n.a.	n.a.
Control variables																				
Gender	0.06	−0.08	−0.26**	0.79	−0.04	0.49**	−0.11	−0.24	0.35	0.92	−0.12	0.17	0.39	−0.10	2.26**	−0.36	0.83*	−0.12	0.24	0.44
Citizenship	−0.07	0.02	−0.05	−0.03	−0.98	−0.20	−0.16	−0.09	1.54	0.88	n.a.	n.a.	0.52	0.97	−2.59	1.72***	n.a.	n.a.	n.a.	n.a.
Religion	−0.23	−0.23	0.20	−0.34	0.40	0.13	−0.85**	0.06	0.38	−0.94**	−0.82**	−0.26	1.81	0.87	−0.15	−0.02	0.27	0.33	−0.26	−0.74
Income	0.78	−1.38	0.95	n.a.	−0.03	−0.04	−0.05	−0.02	0.03	0.23***	−0.04	−0.08	0.01	0.09*	−0.07	0.07*	n.a.	n.a.	n.a.	n.a.
Life satisfaction	0.13***	0.05	0.04	0.12*	−0.17	0.17***	0.14*	−0.07	0.06	0.31*	0.26	0.47***	−0.04	−0.01	−0.22	−0.05	−0.00	0.06	0.45***	−0.06
Political discussions	−0.38*	0.22	0.01	0.00	−0.18	−0.22	0.72**	0.23	0.09	0.18	−0.03	−0.25	−0.02	−0.17	−0.03	0.09	0.05	−0.38	−0.38	−0.12
Political interest	0.17	0.42*	−0.02	0.47	0.01	0.02	−0.16	−0.26	−0.02	0.46**	0.71**	−0.92**	0.15	−0.18	0.28	−0.30	0.11	−0.32	−0.77**	0.27
Constant	1.19	3.55	2.24	2.53	2.78	0.50	2.41	2.54	2.45	−0.79	1.57	3.62	0.99	0.92	0.21	0.27	1.23	6.91	−0.28	5.05
N	244	23	328	17	258	36	231	421	10	98	78	65	92	244	56	33	93	12	95	129
Adj. R²	0.27	0.14	0.14	0.27	0.23	0.23	0.30	0.26	0.19	0.24	0.28	0.32	0.12	0.09	0.10	0.12	0.06	0.16	0.21	0.23
Adj. R² b)	0.18	0.23	0.12	0.11	0.12															

Notes

*P<0.10; **P<0.05; ***P<0.01; ****P<0.001.

influence on how levels of trust in the EU can be explained. What can be gathered from this result? At a first glance, it is astonishing that the explanatory power improves to this extent – after all, the same individuals are involved. However, in the micro-models, as indicated in Tables 10.1–10.6, these individuals form a unit, whereas in Table 10.7 the attitude patterns of these individuals are differentiated according to organizational size and the degree of institutionalization. Since the differences between the R^2 values are relatively large, it can be assumed that individuals within groups have more similar attitudes than individuals of different groups. Consequently, context plays a key role.

However, although context does play a role, it is not in the expected way. It is not possible to explain more variance in small and not very institutionalized organizations. On the contrary, the biggest R^2 differences are observed in the Netherlands among large and institutionalized organizations, in West Germany and the UK among large organizations, and in East Germany among large and institutionalized as well as small and not very institutionalized organizations. Accordingly, there is no consistent pattern which occurs in all countries.

The group comparison has made clear that context normally exerts a significant influence. However, on this basis, it is not possible to make a statement about the direction of this influence. Further analyses are necessary in order to make assumptions about the direction of change. Clarification is only possible when more sophisticated methods such as multi-level analyses can be applied.

10.6 Conclusion

This chapter focuses on the question of political trust in the EU. It distinguishes between exchange-based trust and communal-based trust. Different norms form the basis of both forms of political trust. However, both forms exist simultaneously, but have a differential impact depending on citizens' varying social commitments. Thus, it can be assumed that for very active citizens communal-based trust is predominant, and for non-active citizens exchange-based trust is predominant. As a consequence, the question arises of whether different determinants are responsible for these different forms of trust. This question is examined on the basis of two different explanatory approaches – which do not exclude one another – whereas the theoretical approaches correspond with the two forms of trust. The analysis of communal-based trust is carried out via the culture-based social capital theory, and exchange-based trust is tested via the institutionalist approach. The following basic hypothesis has been tested: activists' trust in the EU is most strongly influenced by indicators of social capital theory, whereas non-activists' trust can be better explained by the institutionalist approach.

The multivariate analyses verified this hypothesis only to a limited extent. A differentiated examination of the approaches and their determinants leads to the conclusion that, in the analysed countries, trust of activists can best be explained by the indicators of social capital theory. The existence of social trust, but also values and norms of reciprocity, positively influence the generation of trust in the EU. This result remains the same when checking for control variables. Thus, activists convert social trust into political trust mainly via generalization processes. This generalization is based on the assumption that social norms and values are also valid in the institutions of the political system. It becomes evident that in this case mutual trust is due to reference to common norms and values, and is therefore best understood as communal-based trust.

While this part of the basic hypothesis could be verified, the situation of non-actives turns out differently. The expectation that institutionalist explanatory factors are relevant for non-actives could not be confirmed by the analyses. Although the generalized evaluation of the government's performance plays an important role, the variables of social capital theory seem to exert a stronger influence breadth-wise.

Regardless of the importance of social capital theory for the explanation of political trust of activists and – in weakened form – of non-actives, the analyses have revealed that both approaches are important for the explanation of trust in the EU. Continuously, two indicators exert significant influence in all countries: evaluation of performance and social trust. This emphasizes that the two approaches do not exclude one another but are complementary and explain different types of trust. The analysis of socially actives, however, has shown that a purely exchange-based relationship is crucial. Only institutionalist determinants continuously influence trust in the EU.

In a final step, the influence of contextual features was explored. Social commitment does not take place in a vacuum but in informal and formal networks. Following social capital theory, participation in voluntary associations, in particular, positively influences political trust via generalization processes. Whether the contextual features 'size' and 'degree of institutionalization' exert influence was therefore tested. The group comparisons have shown clearly that context matters. If voluntary active individuals are differentiated – from individuals who are involved in small and not very institutionalized organizations up to individuals who are involved in large, highly institutionalized organizations – there are huge differences as far as the explanation of political trust in the EU is concerned.

The introduction to this chapter referred to a decrease in trust in the EU. Considering these results, and keeping in mind that trust in political institutions is an essential basic requirement, the present chapter has addressed the question of how trust in the EU can be explained. Thereby, it has become clear that it is not only social capital which makes us 'smarter, healthier, safer, richer, and better able to govern a just and stable democracy' (Putnam 2000: 290); other factors play a role as well, especially the generalized evaluation of the government's performance. Different mechanisms have a differential impact on citizens' varying social commitment.

Notes

1 The European Social Survey measures trust in the European Parliament with an 11-point scale from 'complete trust' to 'no trust at all'.

2 Especially in Germany, a dramatic decline in trust can be observed. In 2006, more than half of the respondents (54.8 per cent) had little or no trust at all in the European Parliament, whereas in 2002 less than half of the respondents (44.6 per cent) had little or no trust at all in the European Parliament.

3 The affirmation of the validity of both approaches was confirmed by empirical analyses of other authors (see, for example, Rohrschneider 1999; Mishler and Rose 2001, 2005, Pollack et al. 2003; Torcal et al. 2006; Denters et al. 2007).

4 Within the culture-based explanatory approach there exist explanations in the tradition of social capital theory on the one hand and in the tradition of value change theory on the other hand (Inglehart 1977b). In the following empirical analysis, only explanations of social capital theory will be used.

5 *Mutual trust* consists of the variables 'Trust in people: general', 'Trust in people: helpfulness' and 'Trust in people: fairness'. *Norms of Reciprocity* consists of the two indices *community values* and *norms of reciprocity*. Community values consist of the variables 'Good citizen: show solidarity' and 'Good citizen: think of others'. 'Good citizen: vote', 'Good citizen: obey laws' and 'Good citizen: not evade taxes' form the index *norms of reciprocity*.

6 The network variable consists of an index of the variables 'Family sectoral typology: family', 'Sport sectoral typology: sports', 'Culture sectoral typology: community concerns', 'Political sectoral typology: politics', 'General welfare sectoral typology: general welfare', 'Group-specific welfare', 'Econint sectoral typology: economic interest', 'Religious sectoral typology: religious' and 'Others sectoral typology: other'.

7 'Evaluation of system's performance' is operationalized via 'Satisfaction with democracy'.

8 In Spain it is not possible to perform corresponding analyses of activists, because trust in the EU was not asked for in the Activists Study.

9 Analyses for UK are only possible to a limited extent because a lot of relevant variables are only available in a non-comparable form.

10 This conclusion is the result of the following comparison: if the adjusted R^2 of activists in a country is higher when testing for social capital theory than the adjusted R^2 of activists in a country when testing for the institutionalist approach, part of the basic hypothesis is verified. Accordingly, the hypothesis for non-actives is considered verified if the explained variance is higher when testing for the institutionalist approach than for non-actives in consideration of social capital theory. The adjusted R^2 values presented in the figure are the result of analyses conducted separately in each case (social capital theory on the one hand and institutionalist approach on the other hand, in each case together with the corresponding variables); thus, they are *not* the result of an analysis of the complete model including control variables.

11 Only the integrated models (i.e. those models that take into account both social capital variables and variables of the institutionalist approach as well as control variables) can explain between 11 and 23 per cent of variance.

12 Size is operationalized by the variable 'total number of member, precise'. The variable is enumerated via count and split at the median. The value 1 is assigned to values below the median, and the value 2 is assigned to values above the median. Institutionalization is operationalized by the variable 'organizational structure'. In this variable it is asked if the respective organization has a Chair and/or a board of directors and/or an executive committee and/or a secretary and/or a treasurer and/or committees for specific tasks and/or a general assembly and/or a written constitution. Again, the variable is enumerated via count and split at the median. The value 1 is assigned to values below the median, and the value 2 is assigned to values above the median. The typology is the result of all four combinations.

13 Social capital model plus institutionalist explanatory approach plus control variables – see Tables 10.1–10.6 and Table 10.7, last rows.

11 Conclusion

Activists, active people and citizens in European communities

William A. Maloney and Jan W. van Deth

11.1 Introduction

The quality of contemporary democracy and the threat to its survival are the shared concerns of several leading scholars (Putnam 1995, 2000; Dalton 2004; Stoker 2006a, 2006b; Hay 2007). These academics maintain that civic and political disengagement, declining levels of political trust, confidence and attachment, and growing citizen disenchantment and scepticism (possibly even cynicism) about politics, politicians, political institutions and political processes represent a *clear and present* danger to democracy. At times the language is dramatic – part poetic licence, but mostly genuine concern – and an important component of the remedy for this pathology is the greater involvement of citizens in voluntary associations. Such involvement is seen as inculcating citizens with pro-democratic values, enhancing their civic and democratic skills and making them better democrats.

While such democratic concern is widely shared, empirical evidence is in somewhat short supply. The authors in this volume sought to assess what impact active participation in voluntary associations actually has on citizens. Our research design pre-empted the problems subsequently identified by Glanville (2004: 487) at the conclusion of her own research – namely:

> Voluntary association membership is unlikely to have a uniform influence on other outcomes, such as trust and political participation ... Therefore, instead of combining all association memberships into one measure, researchers should consider voluntary association type and other organizational characteristics when examining the impact of membership on a variety of outcomes.

This approach has been implemented in the contributions herein. In fact, we moved one crucial step further by not restricting our analyses to different types of organizations and organizational characteristics. We also considered distinct types of associational involvement among different parts of several European citizenries. In this way, we are able to avoid the Achilles' heel of treating all (civically-oriented) associations and all citizens alike.

The complex research design was necessary to meet our dual comparison requirements – that is, distinguishing between associational types and between three main categories of citizens (see below). This allows us to locate citizens (as members) of a wide and diverse variety of voluntary associations. In addition to this, it provides for a more nuanced and robust analysis of how specific associational types and varying organizational features affect the contribution these entities make to democracies. The obvious and significant appeal of this approach is that a direct link between the precise organizational context and the actual activist can be established. Our inventive research design permitted (European) country and organizational-type comparisons as well as comparisons of activists (respondents surveyed as members of identifiable organizational-types), socially actives (individuals in the general population who are supporters or members of organizations) and non-actives (citizens who are not involved in formally organized groups). Accordingly, the key questions driving our analyses include:

- To what extent can these organizations deliver for democracy in the ways that scholars such as Putnam (1995, 2000), Dalton (2004) and Stoker (2006a, 2006b), among many others, envisage?

- Should we be championing and valorizing *all* types of civic and pro-democratic groups within the associational universe?

- Alternatively, are specific organizational features more conducive to producing better democrats than others?

- To what extent is the nature, scope or degree of organizational involvement relevant for the apparent benevolent democratic consequences of engagement in voluntary associations?

11.2 Towards a brief synthesis

While the contributions to this volume deal with diverse aspects of democratic citizenship, the main findings reflect more general underlying patterns. Below we discuss the most salient results, and our analysis largely follows the same structure as the contributions to the volume. First, we examine the associational impact on democratic political attitudes, and second, we focus on European orientations. In these concluding discussions we touch on the various aspects of associational life that affect the quality of democracy in several European countries. The main questions can be summarized accordingly:

1   What impact do *organizational characteristics*, such as size or the institutionalization of democratic procedures and practices, have on members or democracy more generally? For example, are small groups likely to be greater generators of active participation and social capital than their larger

counterparts? Are internally democratic groups better schools of democracy than their non-democratic counterparts?

2   To what extent is there a *self-selection* bias in the associational universe? Do citizens already richly infused with pro-civic and pro-democratic attitudes have a greater predisposition towards joining voluntary associations? Or do voluntary organizations conform to the school of democracy thesis, and inculcate citizens with positive values and attitudes? In summary, is the societal stock of pro-civic and pro-democratic values and attitudes generated largely beyond the associational sector – i.e. are civically wealthy citizens delivering this to groups rather than vice versa? Could there be reciprocal effects?

3   The associational universes examined in this volume are drawn largely from medium-sized European cities. Does this generate any specific *locality effects*?[1] These organizations are in close geographical proximity, and have (potentially) greater ease of access and more frequent interaction opportunities with local or regional political institutions. Accordingly, do organizational members exhibit higher levels of trust and confidence in (or attachment to) local or regional political institutions and objects, than national or transnational ones?

4   To what extent is the encompassing *associational context* a crucial explanatory factor in the democratic orientations generated by voluntary associations?

These questions are addressed in several chapters in this volume. However, other issues are also discussed in detail in the various contributions, and this concluding chapter provides a relatively brief synthesis and critical commentary on the main findings to further enhance the volume's coherence. Finally, we will draw some general conclusions on the four main questions set out above.

11.3 Democratic political attitudes

The impact of associational features on democratic political attitudes, as well as the relevance of the nature, scope and degree of associational involvement, has been demonstrated in each of the contributions to this volume. A synthesis of these results can be obtained by focusing on: (i) participatory habits, (ii) efficacy and empowerment, (iii) volunteering, and (iv) various European orientations.

11.3.1 Schools of democracy

The neo-Tocquevillean model is most closely associated with claims about the civic and democratic educational effects of voluntary associations – i.e. associations as 'schools of democracy'. In Chapter 6, Patrick Bernhagen and William Maloney assessed the impact (or absence) of a vibrant intra-organizational democracy on activists' public-spiritedness and political participation; and how internal democracy interacts with other factors (e.g. length of membership and the intensity of participation) that may also affect such spiritedness and participation. In short, they examined the extent to which associations with internally democratic features can be portrayed as better schools of democracy than organizations devoid of these characteristics. Berhagen and Maloney discovered that length of membership of institutionally democratic associations increased civic-spiritedness slightly. However, their main finding is that the democratic characteristics of associations are *at best* marginally related to individual political participation. The political participation levels of activists were comparable irrespective of whether they were members of formally or behaviourally democratic associations, or of non-democratic groups. Clearly, the 'school of democracy' thesis faces some challenge from these findings. It may be that associations can act as civic and democratic educational institutions, but the democratic aspects of the curriculum appear to be largely irrelevant. Thus, if voluntary associations act as 'schools of democracy', inculcating and enhancing participatory habits and civic attitudes, then non-democratic organizations are as efficient (or inefficient) as their democratic counterparts. Based on similar findings, van Deth (Chapter 5) suggested that it would be more accurate to consider associations as 'schoolyards of democracy' rather than 'schools of democracy'. If we view the apparent irrelevance of internal democratic procedures for the development of democratic attitudes from a policy-relevant perspective, then if political institutions such as the EU are keen to foster civil society as a means of addressing the 'democratic deficit', it need not bother discriminating between democratic and non-democratic organizations.

11.3.2 Efficacy and empowerment

Associational involvement is most likely to have an impact on attitudes directly related to activities within these organizations. Herman Lelieveldt (Chapter 3) and Bengü Dayican, Bas Denters and Henk van der Kolk (Chapter 4) investigated the impact of various associational characteristics on members' intra-organizational efficacy (Lelieveldt) and their sense of political efficacy – or *subjective political empowerment* (Chapter 4). Lelieveldt examined the participation of members in organizational management and decision-making processes, and the extent to which the organizational context (e.g. size, professionalization, budget, institutional structure) affects such involvement and intra-organizational efficacy – i.e. the extent to which members felt they could affect organizational decision-making. Lelieveldt initially speculated that members who feel most able to affect decisions are also more likely to exhibit higher participation levels in decision-making processes. His results demonstrated that there is a substantial amount of participation in organizational management and decision-making among activists and socially actives; hence, unsurprisingly, efficacy and participation are strongly related. However, individual-level background variables and organizational factors appear to have very little impact on participation rates. As Lelieveldt concludes, this leads 'to the somewhat sobering conclusion that the most important factors are also the

Conclusion 235

least surprising ones'. Individuals heavily involved in running the organizations are also most likely to possess the highest levels of intra-organizational efficacy, and those on the organizational margins the lowest. With regard to professionalization, Lelieveldt noted that the efficacy scores of highly engaged members are lower in larger and more professionalized associations. Accordingly, it may well be the case, as Lelieveldt concludes, that if we are keen to preserve 'the essence of associational democracy, small may indeed be beautiful'.

Dayican, Denters and van der Kolk identified a strong relationship between membership and activism and empowerment. They also discovered that citizens involved in different types of political organizations feel more politically empowered and (somewhat unsurprisingly) that membership in various types of political organizations is related to political efficacy. This led them to consider the question about the direction of causality: i.e. does such membership increase political efficacy (the social capital model), or are politically efficacious citizens more likely to join political organizations (the self-selection thesis)? They concluded that self-selection was most likely for political organizations. In his earlier research, von Erlach (2006: 19) drew a similar conclusion: 'Differences in political involvement between association members and nonmembers are probably attributable in large measure to self-selection effects.' However, Dayican, Denters and van der Kolk are sagely circumspect and advocate caution. They argue that there is likely to be a process of reciprocal causation. While it may be the case that relatively self-confident individuals are more likely to join political organizations, there still remains the distinct possibility that, through membership, they may further enhance their politically self-confidence. As La Due Lake and Huckfeldt (1998: 573) have argued:

> Citizens who choose to join organizations and voluntary associations have an opportunity to meet more people, to develop more extensive systems of social relationships, and hence to become more fully engaged in civil life (Verba *et al.*, 1995). At the same time, however, some individuals are more like to be organizationally engaged than others.

11.3.3 Volunteering

Complex mechanisms also seem to underlie the mobilization of volunteers. In Chapter 2, Tobias Schulz investigated the relationship between welfare policy and volunteering, in particular, the *crowding-out* thesis – i.e. do high levels of welfare expenditure drive out or engender volunteering? The two main questions he examines are: To what extent is the amount of volunteering dependent upon organizational type? And to what extent is volunteering related to local government funding, or is it a result of the strong ties between organizations and the local elite? Schulz's results are mixed. He finds that, on balance, money is more predictable in its impact than contacts: local government subsidies have a largely positive (and some times statistically significant) impact on volunteering. Among the organizational factors that demonstrate a largely consistent positive effect is the associational share of *local subsidies*. This finding presents some challenge to the 'crowding-out' thesis, because it suggests that it is important to differentiate between subsidies received from different governmental levels. Finally, Schulz found that organizational characteristics are not particularly important for the mobilization of volunteers. What appear to be more crucial are organizational tasks – which in many cases are directly related to the actual design of welfare policies and programmes. Finally, Schulz's empirical analyses also imply that we should be cautious about drawing parsimonious conclusions on volunteering. He discovered that the mobilization of volunteers does not depend on associational features; rather, it is the local context that matters.

11.4 European orientations

Various European orientations appear to be related to features of voluntary associations and active citizens in similar ways. In Chapter 10, Silke Keil investigated how political trust in the EU is generated among activists, socially actives and non-actives. Can activists' trust be explained by references to social capital theory? That is, is it community orientation that generates such trust? Does the trust of non-actives differ from activists and relate more to exchange-based dimensions (institutionalist approaches)? Keil found that while both forms of political trust (exchange-based and communal-based) exist concurrently, they nevertheless have 'a differential impact depending on citizens' varying social commitments'. She found that social trust and values and norms of reciprocity have a positive impact on trust in the EU. However, Keil discovered that two indicators exert significant influence in all countries – evaluation of performance and social trust. Thus, exchange-based (*institutional*) and communal-based (*social capital*) trust can be seen as complementary in that both generate trust, albeit different types. Trust can be earned or lost depending on the nature of governmental performance. However, features of associations and differences in the nature, scope and degree of volunteering appeared to be much less relevant for political trust in the EU.

Jan van Deth (Chapter 5) and Manuela Caiani and Mariona Ferrer-Fons (Chapter 7) have addressed the issue of political interest in the EU. Van Deth analysed the specific impact of membership in various voluntary associations on political interest; in particular, whether active participation has a differential effect on interest in European politics (compared to interest in local, national and international politics), and if organizational characteristics (size, formal structure, resources) are relevant for the development of political interest and willingness to engage in political discussions. Caiani and Ferrer-Fons assessed whether associational involvement per se, higher participation levels, or different associational characteristics (size, resources, formal structure) and concerns (welfare, politics, environment) affect citizens' levels of interest and trust in European politics. Van Deth found that while large cross-national differences in political interest were prevalent, there remained a consistent pattern of interest among the three groups of respondents (activists, socially actives and non-actives). The level of political interest is highest among activists, a bit lower in the socially active category, and lowest among the non-active group. In line with other recent research that van Deth (2008b) has conducted, he demonstrated that interest in European politics is lower than interest in any other political object in all the cities/countries examined. He also discovered that the willingness to discuss political matters among activists was greatest in political organizations and interest groups – activists in welfare and culture organizations (most notably, sports and family organizations) were much less likely to be politically enthusiastic. Caiani and Ferrer-Fons found some evidence that while associational activity contributed to a more engaged European citizenry, it did not always generate fully supportive Euro-enthusiasts, but also more critical Europeanists. However, when they assessed the relative impact of associational characteristics, engagement levels and individual features of activists on different types of support for Europe, they discovered that engagement levels and organizational features were unimportant. The crucial aspect that explained support for Europe was at the individual level. Accordingly, Caiani's and Ferrer-Fons' key finding buttresses the results of Dayican, Denters and van der Kolk (Chapter 4) with regard to the self-selection hypothesis. As Caiani and Ferrer-Fons argue, 'Associations attract people with specific individual features and that explains the associational impact on attitudes towards Europe.' Self-selection can be an important explanation for the reciprocal relationship between voluntary associations and their active members.

In Chapter 8, Sonja Zmerli examined the affect of social involvement on trust and confidence in the EU from two different perspectives: the extent of individual associational involvement, and specific associational characteristics. The former is predicated on the 'schools of democracy' thesis – i.e. the deeper the degree of involvement, the higher the level of an activist's civic skills and the greater the likelihood of increased political confidence. The latter focuses on the impact of organizational characteristics, such as the geographical reach of group concerns or the impact of the association's written constitution, that may engender greater social involvement and increased confidence in the EU. Zmerli initially found that social trust exerted 'a consistently significant and positive relationship with confidence in the EU' for both the general population and the activists'. When she assessed the impact of the various trust dimensions, Zmerli found that group-related trust was a strong predictor of confidence in the EU, while social trust had almost no impact on confidence. Akin to van Deth (2008b), Zmerli also discovered that while active *local* social engagement may hinder the development of pro-European attitudes; positive European orientations have roots in national rather than transnational/supranational associational contexts – i.e. citizens' level of trust in the EU is directly related to their satisfaction with democracy in their nation-state. She concluded that, 'The high relevance of group-related trust for confidence in the EU suggests that even the trustworthiness of social entities *within* nations can shape citizens' positive evaluations of the European Union at large'.

The findings presented by Zmerli raise some challenge to Schulz's results in Chapter 2 with regard to the importance of local subsidies and the irrelevance of national patronage. However, the solution to this conundrum is relatively clear: in both studies it is the *relevance of a specific context* that matters. Schulz demonstrates that the content of specific programmes makes local subsidies relevant, and Zmerli emphasizes that national orientations are relevant for trust and confidence in Europe.

Finally, Hajdeja Iglič's analysis (Chapter 9) focused on 'the strength of social integration and quality of social relations within associations'. Do associations characterized by high levels of social integration facilitate identification with bodies such as Europe? Alternatively, do these types of organizations bolster more locally-based identities and possibly even thwart more far-flung identifications? Iglič found that associational involvements did fortify European identity – organizations that had frequent political communication and high levels of social integration built European identity. She also found that organizations that were smaller in scope, such as neighbourhood- or locally-based groups, also generated strong pro-European attachment – more so than bigger groups engaged in wider networks (labelled *strength of attachment*). Iglič's analysis demonstrated an inverse relationship between locally or regionally-based identities and more geographically expansive identities such as the nation-state or Europe. Citizens who are not strongly embedded in any type of organized social network but who are younger, more highly educated and have higher levels of confidence in European institutions also exhibit higher levels of attachment to Europe. These individuals have relatively little confidence in local institutions (labelled *direction of attachment*). In conclusion, Iglič offered the following prescription for European architects. The enhancement of European identity and attachment can be achieved via two main strategies, 'First, make the European institutions highly accountable to European citizens to enhance citizens' confidence. Second, promote the development of the civil society, even at the most local level'.

The 'locality effect' detected by Iglič is also reported by Dayican, Denters and van der Kolk (Chapter 4). They found that the number of local political contacts had a positive impact on political empowerment. We should also recall that Schulz highlighted the relevance of local subsidies for volunteering, and Zmerli also identified locality effects. Once again, we see that while the general associational context is not an important determinant of associational engagement, a specific context can be crucial to an explanation of particular effects and outcomes.

11.4 Do organizations matter?

In this concluding section, we discuss the first principle social capital question: *Do organizations matter?* Generally speaking, our empirical results – linking empirical information about associations, activists and citizens in several cities and countries – will make disappointing reading for those championing the pivotality of associations for democracy. In Chapter 4, Dayican, Denters and van der Kolk noted that 'none of the other variables in our models was equally meaningful related to empowerment (including SES factors) ... [and] that the democratic effects of involvement are at best only modest'. Arguably, van Deth's key finding is that it is individual factors (age and education and the breath of voluntary associational engagement) that are the most important determinant for engagement in European affairs. Neither the nature of voluntary activity nor objective organizational features are relevant. As he concludes, 'The associational impact on European engagement seems to be mainly due to the fact that activists are relatively old, highly-educated, and active in several different voluntary associations'. It appears that empirical reality is shaking the foundations of the neo-Tocquevillean gospel. The challenge to the neo-Tocquevillean model from our findings can be summarized as follows.

1. **Organizational characteristics.** Discriminating between democratic and nondemocratic associations is irrelevant for the development of democratic attitudes among active members of these organizations. Membership of any organizational type will do.
2. **Self-selection.** Clearly, citizens with high levels of self-confidence are more likely to be active in voluntary associations, but the associational impact cannot be fully discounted. There is likely to be a reciprocal relationship between features of activists and associations, and mono-causal explanations are inadequate.
3. **Context.** The general or overarching associational context does not appear to be an important explanatory factor with regard to democratic orientations, but in particular cases the impact of specific germane contexts can be crucial – for example, on certain issues the local context of voluntary associations can be important.[2]

To date a few authors have presented critical views on social capital/neo-Tocquevillean approaches, and the findings in this volume do not make us a wholly lone sceptical voice. Several benevolent consequences of associational involvement have been detected but, in general, these effects do not seem to follow the simple pattern implied in many explanations. Furthermore, our empirical evidence points to other, apparently more important, factors for the development of civic attitudes among associational activists.

Several studies have also challenged the notion that voluntary associations are key generators of social capital (see, for example, Frietag 2003; La Due Lake and Huckfeldt 1998; Stolle 2001, 2003; Mayer 2003; Wollebæk and Selle 2003, 2007; Wollebæk and Strømsnes 2008). While these studies are largely restricted to surveys of volunteers or citizens, and lack the direct information about the associational contexts that our study has, their findings clearly support the results presented in the contributions to this volume. For instance, Wollebæk and Selle (2003: 84) found no evidence that active compared to passive participation 'broadens social networks or strengthens civic engagement', and passive membership appeared to have a positive impact on civil engagement. Furthermore, in 2007 they stated that they 'found no relationship between the extent of face-to-face interactions in organizations and social capital' (Wollebæk and Selle 2007: 2).

Frietag (2003) also challenged the necessity of face-to-face contacts within voluntary associations as the dominant way to create trust. In line with our finding that individual factors are relatively important for the development of civic orientations in organizations, and associational features are relatively unimportant, Freitag (2003: 957) stresses the fact that his results provide 'little support for the thesis that activist membership in various kinds of associations fosters social trust (the so-called Tocqueville model)'.[3] Several other empirical studies have challenged the relevance and importance of the organizational impact for social capital. La Due Lake and Huckfeldt (1998: 582) argued that their results questioned the 'excessive focus on organizational involvement and its consequences for the production of social capital'. Wollebæk and Selle (2007), while supporting that argument, stressed that the contribution voluntary associations make to democracy cannot be discarded. They argued that the organizational contribution has been misconstrued: 'Voluntary organizations are crucial to the sustenance of social capital – not mainly as agents of socialization, but as institutions within which social capital is embedded' (Wollebæk and Selle 2007: 2).[4] Irrespective of such a judicious and prudent proposition, it is difficult to resist the conclusion that associations do not generate democratic orientations among active citizens to anywhere near the extent the social capital/neo-Tocquevillean thesis suggests.

The presumed benevolent consequences of associational engagement for the development of democratic orientations among citizens have been overstated by neo-Tocquevilleans and social capitalists. The main reason for the endurance of these ideas has been a lack of relevant empirical evidence. In the Citizen, Involvement, Democracy (CID) project, a very large collective 'we' – beyond the contributors to this volume – have generated data that have allowed the contributors herein to combine information about associations, activists and the general population in a number of countries and assess the relative impact of various factors. The extraordinary investments in the various parts of the CID-project, and the integration of data, have enabled us to draw some highly relevant conclusions on the associational contribution to the development of a vibrant democracy. Associations do matter for democracy, but their contribution is more limited than assumed in much of the literature – and teasing out how much and in what ways voluntary associations enhance democracy is a much more complex task than previously thought.

Notes

1 However, as we argued elsewhere, the organizational universe is the *primary context* for our analyses. The various associational universes comprise the full and diverse range of associative forms and activity. 'In summary, the research context is predicated upon the assumption that these cities provide much variation of organizational types, albeit within varying historical, institutional and cultural settings. The primary research object and unit of analysis is the organization universe, not the city' (Maloney *et al.* 2008: 264).

2 These findings are in line with the results of the CID Organization Study published earlier (cf. Maloney and Roßteutscher 2007; Maloney et al. 2008).
3 Wollebæk and Selle (2007) also noted that Stolle (2001, 2003) found that active associational participation had no impact on trust over time, and that the role ascribed to organizations as trust producers has been exaggerated.
4 Wollebæk and Strømsnes (2008: 250) argue that Putnam has over-emphasized the degree of socialization that occurs with voluntary associations and 'that the primary contribution of voluntary organizations … lies not in socializing individual active members but in institutionalizing social capital'.

Bibliography

Abromeit, H. (2000) 'Kompatibilität und Akzeptanz: Anforderungen an eine integrierte Politie', in E. Grande and M. Jachtenfuchs (eds), *Wie problemlösungsfähig ist die EU?* Baden-Baden: Nomos, pp. 59–75.

Almond, G.A. and Verba, S. (1989 [1963]) *The Civic Culture: Political Attitudes and Democracy in Five Nations*, Newbury Park, CA: Sage.

Anderson, B. (1983) *Imagined Communities: Reflections on the Origin and Spread of Nationalism*, London: Verso.

Anderson, C.J. (1998) 'When in doubt, use proxies: attitudes towards domestic politics and support for European integration', *Comparative Political Studies*, 31(5): 569–601.

Armingeon, K. (2007) 'Political participation and associational involvement', in J.W. van Deth, J.R. Montero and A. Westholm (eds), *Citizenship and Involvement in European Democracies: A Comparative Analysis*, London: Routledge, pp. 358–383.

Armony, A.C. (2004) *The Dubious Link. Civic Engagement and Democratization*, Stanford, CA: Stanford University Press.

Baglioni, S., Denters, B., Morales, L. and Vetter, A. (2007) 'City size and the nature of associational ecologies', in W. Maloney and S. Roßteutscher (eds), *Social Capital and Associations in European Democracies. A Comparative Analysis*, London: Routledge, pp. 224–243.

Balme, R. (2008) *European Governance and Democracy: Power and Protest in the EU*, Lanham, MD: Rowman and Littlefield.

Barakso, M. (2005) 'Civic engagement and voluntary associations: reconsidering the role of the governance structures of advocacy groups' *Polity*, 37: 315–334.

Barber, B.R. (1984) *Strong Democracy*, Berkeley, CA: University of California Press.

—— (1995) *Jihad vs McWorld*, New York, NY: Times Books.

Barnes, S.H. and Kaase, M. (1979) *Political Action: Mass Participation in Five Western Democracies*, London: Sage.

Bartolini, S. (2002) 'Lo stato nazionale e l'integrazione europea: un'agenda di ricerca', *Quaderni di Scienza Politica*, 9(3): 397–414.

Becker, Gary S. (1964) [1993, 3rd edn] *Human Capital: A Theoretical and Empirical Analysis, with Special Reference to Education*, Chicago, IL: University of Chicago Press.

Beetham, D. (1991) *The Legitimation of Power*, London: Macmillan.

Benz, A. (1998) 'Ansatzpunkte für ein europafähiges Demokratiekonzept', *Politische Vierteljahresschrift*, Special Issue 29: 345–368.

Berelson, B.B., Lazarsfeld, P.F. and McPhee, W. (1954) *Voting: A Study of Opinion Formation in a Presidential Campaign*, Chicago, IL: University of Chicago Press.

Berry, J.M., Portney, K.E. and Thomson, K. (1993) *The Rebirth of Urban Democracy*. Washington, DC: The Brookings Institution.
Bowler, S., Donovan, T. and Hanneman, R. (2003) 'Art for democracy's sake? Group membership and political engagement in Europe', *Journal of Politics*, 65: 1111–1129.
Braithwaite, V. (1998) 'Communal and exchange trusts norms: their value base and relevance to institutional trust', in V. Braithwaite and M. Levi (eds), *Trust and Governance*, New York, NY: Russell Sage Foundation, pp. 46–74.
Braithwaite, V. and Levi, M. (1998) *Trust and Governance*, New York, NY: Russell Sage Foundation.
Brewer, M.B. (1993) 'Social identity, distinctiveness, and in-group homogeneity', *Social Cognition*, 11(1): 150–164.
—— (1999) 'Multiple identities and identity transition: implications for Hong-Kong', *International Journal of Intercultural Relations*, 23(2): 187–197.
Brinegar, A. and Jolly, S. (2005) 'Location, Location, Location', *European Union Politics*, 6(2): 155–180.
Brinegar, A., Jolly, S. and Kitschelt, H. (2004) 'Varieties of capitalism and political divides over European integration', in G. Marks and M.R. Steenbergen (eds), *European Integration and Political Conflict*, Cambridge: Cambridge University Press, pp. 62–89.
Caiani, M. (2003) 'Capitale sociale e partecipazione politica: associazioni e attivisti a Firenze', *Polis*, 17(1): 61–92.
Calhoun, C. (1991) 'Indirect relationship and imagined communities: large-scale social integration and the transformation of everyday life', in P. Bourdieu and J.S. Coleman (eds), *Social Theory for a Changing Society*, Boulder, CO: Westview Press: 95–120.
—— (1994) 'Social theory and the politics of identity', in C. Calhoun (ed.), *Social Theory and the Politics of Identity*, Cambridge, MA: Blackwell Publishers, pp. 9–32.
Campbell, A., Gurin, G. and Miller, W.E. (1971) [1954] *The Voter Decides*, Westport, CT: Greenwood Press.
Cappellari, L. and Turati, G. (2004) 'Volunteer labour supply: the role of workers' motivations', *Annals of Public and Cooperative Economics*, 75(4): 619–643.
Carey, S. (2002) 'Undivided loyalties: is national identity an obstacle to European integration? *European Union Politics*, 3(4): 387–413.
Commission of the European Communities (CEC) (2001a) *European Governance: A White Paper*, 25.07.2001 COM(2001) 428 final (Brussels: CEC).
—— (2001b) *Communication from the Commission to the Council, European Parliament, Economic and Social Committee, the Committee of the Regions on a New Framework for Co-operation on Activities Concerning the Information and Communication Policy of the European Union*, COM(2001) 0354 final (Brussels: CEC).
—— (2004) Report on European Governance (2003–2004), Brussels, 22.09.2004 SEC (2004) 1153.
Converse, P.E. (1972) 'Change in the American electorate', in A. Campbell (ed.), *The Human Meaning of Social Change*, New York, NY: Russell Sage Foundation, pp. 263–337.
Cotellessa, S. (2005) 'Lobbying, pluralismo e società civile nella UE', in G. Baldini (ed.), *Quale Europa? L'Unione Europea oltre la crisi*, Salerno: Rubettino, pp. 197–222.
Cotta, M. (2005) 'Elite, politiche nazionali e costruzione della polity europea. Il caso italiano in prospettiva comparata', in M. Cotta, P. Isernia and L. Verzichelli (eds), *L'Europa in Italia*, Bologna: Il Mulino, pp. 17–60.
Cotta, M., Isernia, P. and Verzichelli, L. (eds) (2005) *L'Europa in Italia*, Bologna: Il Mulino.

Craig, S.C., Niemi, R.G. and Silver, G.E. (1990) 'Political efficacy and trust: A report on the NES Pilot Study items', *Political Behavior*, 12: 289–314.
Cram, L. (2006) 'Inventing the people', in S. Smismans (ed.), *Civil Society and Legitimate European Governance*, Aldershot: Edward Elgar, pp. 241–259.
Crepaz, M. and Steiner, J. (2007) *Democracies in Europe*. New York, NY: Pearson-Longman.
Dahl, R.A. (1961) 'Who participates in local politics and why', *Science*, 134(3487): 1340–1348.
Dahl, R.A. (ed.) (1997) *Toward Democracy: A Journey; Reflections 1940–1997*, Vol. 1, Berkeley, CA: Institute of Government Studies Press, University of California.
Dahl, R.A. and Tufte, E.R. (1973) *Size and Democracy*, Stanford, CA: Stanford University Press.
Dalton, R.J. (2004) *Democratic Challenges, Democratic Choices: The Erosion of Political Support in Advanced Industrial Democracies*, Oxford: Oxford University Press.
—— (2006) *Citizen Politics: Public Opinion and Political Parties in Advanced Industrial Democracies*, 4th edn, Washington, DC: Congressional Quarterly Press.
—— (2008) 'Citizenship norms and the expansion of political participation', *Political Studies*, 56: 76–98.
Day, K.M. and Devlin, R.A. (1996) 'Volunteerism and crowding out: Canadian econometric evidence', *Canadian Journal of Economics*, 29(1): 37–53.
della Porta, D. (2006) 'Social movements and the European Union: Eurosceptics or critical Europeanists?', *Notre Europe*, Policy Paper No. 22.
della Porta, D. and Caiani, M. (2006) *Quale Europa? Europeizzazione, identità e conflitti*. Bologna, Il Mulino.
—— (2009) *Social Movements and Europeanisation: an Analysis of Seven European Countries*. Oxford: Oxford University Press.
della Porta, D. and Kriesi, H. (1999) 'Social movements in a globalizing world: an introduction', in D. della Porta, H. Kriesi and D. Rucht (eds), *Social Movements in a Globalizing World*. New York, NY: Macmillan, pp. 3–22.
Denters, B., Gabriel, O.W. and Torcal, M. (2007) 'Political confidence in representative democracies: socio-cultural vs political explanations', in J.W. van Deth, J.R. Montero and A. Westholm (eds), *Citizenship and Involvement in European Democracies. A Comparative Analysis*, London: Routledge, pp. 87–107.
Denters, S.A.H. and Geurts, P.A.T.M. (1993) 'Aspects of political alienation: an exploration of their differential origins and effects', *Acta Politica*, 28: 445–469.
de Tocqueville, A. (1945 [1835]), *Democracy in America*, Vol. 1 (ed. P. Bradley, trans. H. Reeve), New York, NY: Vintage.
de Tocqueville, A. (1945) *Democracy in America*, Vol. 2. New York, NY: Vintage.
de Tocqueville, A. (1969 [1835]) *Democracy in America* (ed. J.P. Mayer), New York, NY: Harper Perennial.
de Vries, C.E. and van Kersbergen, K. (2007) 'Interests, identity and political allegiance in the European Union', *Acta Politica*, 42 (2): 307–328.
Deutsch, K. (1966) *Nationalism and Social Communication*, New York, NY: John Wiley.
Diamond, L. (1999) *Developing Democracy: Towards Consolidation*, Baltimore, MD: Johns Hopkins University Press.
Díez Medrano, J. (2003) *Framing Europe*. Princeton, NJ: Princeton University Press.
—— (2007) 'Democracy, legitimacy and the European Union', in C. de Vreese and H. Schmitt (eds), *A European Public Sphere: How Much of it Do We Have and How Much Do We Need?* Connex Report Series No. 02, Mannheim, pp. 143–169.

Díez Medrano, J. and Gutiérrez, P. (2001) 'Nested identities: national and European identity in Spain', *Ethnic and Racial Studies*, 24(5): 753–778.

Di Palma, G. (1990) *To Craft Democracies: An Essay on Democratic Transitions*, Berkeley, CA: University of California Press.

Dollery, B.E. (2003) *The Political Economy of the Voluntary Sector: A Reappraisal of the Comparative Institutional Advantage of Voluntary Organisations*, Cheltenham: Edward Elgar.

Duchesne, S. and Frognier, A.P. (1995) 'Is there a European identity?', in O. Niedermayer and R. Sinnot (eds), *Public Opinion and Internationalized Governance*, Oxford: Oxford University Press, pp. 193–226.

—— (2007) 'Why is it so difficult to know if national pride leads the way to European identity or prevents it?' *Cahiers Europeens*, 3: 1–18.

Eastis, C.M. (2001) 'Organisational diversity and the production of social capital: one of these groups is not like the other', in B. Edwards, M. Foley and M. Diani (eds), *Beyond Tocqueville: Civil Society and the Social Capital Debate in Comparative Perspective*, Hanover: Tufts University, pp. 157–168.

Eder, K., Hellmann K.-U. and Trenz H.-J. (1998) 'Regieren in Europa. Europa jenseits öffentlicher Legitimation? Eine Untersuchung zur Rolle von politischer Öffentlichkeit in Europa', *Politische Vierteljahresschrift*, Special Issue 29: 321–344.

Edwards, M. (2003) *Civil Society*, Cambridge: Polity Press.

Eichenberg, R.C. and Dalton, R.J. (2007) 'Post-Maastricht blues: the transformation of citizen support for European integration', *Acta Politica*, 42 (2–3): 128–152.

Eliasoph, N. (1998) *Avoiding Politics. How Americans Produce Apathy in Everyday Life*, Cambridge: Cambridge University Press.

Evans, G. and Letki, N. (2006) 'Social capital and political disaffection in the New post-Communist democracies', in J.R. Montero and M. Torcal (eds), *Political Disaffection in Contemporary Democracies: Social Capital, Institutions and Politics*, London: Routledge, pp. 130–154.

Fiorina, M. (1999) 'Extreme voices: a dark side of civic engagement', in T. Skocpol and M.P. Fiorina (eds), *Civic Engagement in American Democracy*, Washington, DC: Brookings/Russell Sage Foundation, pp. 395–425.

Freitag, M. (2003) 'Social capital in (dis)similar democracies: the development of generalised trust in Japan and Switzerland', *Comparative Political Studies*, 36(8): 936–966.

Gabel, M.J. (1998) 'Public support for European integration: an empirical test of five theories', *Journal of Politics*, 60(2): 333–54.

Gabel, M.J. and Anderson, C. (2004) 'The structure of citizen attitudes and the European Political space', in G. Marks and M.R. Steenbergen (eds), *European Integration and Political Conflict*, Cambridge: Cambridge University Press, pp. 13–31.

Gabel, M.J. and Palmer, H.D. (1995) 'Understanding variation in public support for European Integration', *European Journal of Political Research*, 27(1): 3–19.

Gabriel, O.W. (2002) 'Politische Unterstützung', in M. Greiffenhagen and S. Greiffenhagen (eds), *Handwörterbuch zur politischen Kultur*, Wiesbaden/Opladen: Westdeutscher Verlag, pp. 477–483.

Gabriel, O.W. and Kunz, V. (2002) 'Die Bedeutung des Sozialkapital-Ansatzes für die Erklärung politischen Vertrauens', in R. Schmalz-Bruns and R. Zintl (eds), *Politisches Vertrauen. Soziale Grundlagen reflexiver Kooperation*. Baden-Baden: Nomos, pp. 255–274.

Gabriel, O.W. and Zmerli, S. (2006) 'Politisches Vertrauen: Deutschland in Europa', *Aus Politik und Zeitgeschichte*, 30–31: pp. 8–15.
Gabriel, O.W., Kunz, V., Roßteutscher, S. and van Deth, J.W. (2002) *Sozialkapital und Demokratie. Zivilgesellschaftliche Ressourcen im Vergleich*, Vienna: WUV Universitätsverlag.
Gelman, A. and Hill, J. (2007) *Data Analysis Using Regression and Multi-level/Hierarchical Models. Analytical Methods for the Social Science*, Cambridge: Cambridge University Press.
Gilley, B. (2006) 'The meaning and measure of state legitimacy: results for 72 countries', *European Journal of Political Research*, 45(3): 499–525.
Gitell, R. and Vidal, A. (1998) *Community Organizing: Building Social Capital as a Developmental Strategy*. Thousand Oaks, CA: Sage.
Glanville, J.L. (2004), 'Voluntary associations and social network structure: why organizational location and type are important', *Sociological Forum*, 19(3): 465–491.
Gould, R.V. (1995) *Insurgent Identities: Class, Community and Protest in Paris from 1848 to the Commune*, Chicago, IL: University of Chicago Press.
Granovetter, M.S. (1973) 'The strength of weak ties', *American Journal of Sociology*, 78 (6): 1360–80.
—— (1983) 'The strength of weak ties: a network theory revisited', in R. Collins (ed.), *Sociological Theory*, San Francisco, CA: Jossey-Bass.
Green, D.M. (2007) *The Europeans. Political Identity in an Emerging Polity*, Boulder, CO: Lynne Rienner.
Green, M.C. and Brock, T.C. (2005) 'Organisational membership versus informal interaction: contributions to skills and perceptions that build social capital', *Political Psychology*, 26: 1–25.
Gurr, T.R. (1970) *Why Men Rebel*, Princeton, NJ: Princeton University Press.
Gutmann, A. (1998) 'Freedom of association: an introductory essay', in A. Gutmann (ed.), *Freedom of Association*, Princeton, NJ: Princeton University Press, pp. 3–32.
Habermas, J. (1996) 'National unification and popular sovereignty', *New Left Review*, 219: 3–13.
—— (2001) *The Postnational Constellation: Political Essays*, Cambridge, MA: MIT Press.
Haddad, M.A. (2004) 'Community determinates of volunteer participation and the promotion of civil health: the case of Japan', *Nonprofit and Voluntary Sector Quarterly*, 33(3): 8–3.
Hardin, R. (1998) 'Trust in governance', in V. Braithwaite and M. Levi (eds), *Trust and Governance*, New York, NY: Russell Sage Foundation, pp. 9–27.
—— (1999) 'Do we want trust in government?' in M.E. Warren (ed.), *Democracy and Trust*, Cambridge, MA: Cambridge University Press, pp. 22–41.
Haug, C. (2008) 'Public Spheres within Movements. Linking Transnational Movements Research and the (Re)search for a European Public Sphere', Recon Online Working Paper 2008/02: www.reconproject.eu/projectweb/portalproject/RECONWorkingPapers.html (accessed 25 February 2009).
Hay, C. (2007) *Why We Hate Politics*, Cambridge: Polity Press.
Hibbing, J.R. and Theiss-Morse, E. (2002) *Stealth Democracy: Americans' Beliefs about How Government Should Work*, Cambridge, MA: Cambridge University Press.
Hirschman, A.O. (1970) *Exit, Voice and Loyalty: Responses to Decline in Firms, Organizations and States*, Cambridge, MA: Harvard University Press.
Hix, S. (1999) *The Political System of the European Union*, New York, NY: St Martin's Press.

Hooghe, L., Marks, G. and Wilson, C.J. (2004) 'Does left/right structure party position on European integration?' in G. Marks and M.R. Steenberger (eds), *European Integration and Political Conflict*. Cambridge: Cambridge University Press, pp. 120–140.

Hooghe, M. (2003) 'Participation in voluntary associations and value indicators: the effect of current and previous participation experiences', *Nonprofit and Voluntary Sector Quarterly*, 32: 47–69.

—— (2008) 'Voluntary associations and socialization', in D. Castiglione, J.W. van Deth and G. Wolleb (eds), *The Handbook of Social Capital*, New York, NY: Oxford University Press, pp. 568–593.

Hooghe, M. and Stolle, D. (2003) 'Introduction: generating social capital', in D. Stolle and M. Hooghe (eds), *Generating Social Capital: Civil Society and Institutions in Comparative Perspective*, Basingstoke: Palgrave Macmillan, pp. 1–18.

Howard, M.M. and Gilbert, L. (2008) 'A cross-national comparison of the internal effects of participation in voluntary associations', *Political Studies*, 56: 12–32.

Huckfeldt, R., Morehouse, J. and Tracy, O. (2001) 'Disagreement, Ambivalence, and Engagement: The Political Consequences of Heterogeneous Networks', Paper prepared for the Annual Meeting of the American Political Science Association, San Francisco, August 29–September 2, 2001.

Hudson, W.E. (2006) *American Democracy in Peril: Eight Challenges to American's Future*, 5th edn, Washington, DC: Congressional Quarterly Press.

Huntington, S. (1981) *American Politics: The Promise of Disharmony*, Cambridge, MA: Harvard University Press.

Hurrelmann, A. (2007) 'Multi-level legitimacy: conceptualizing legitimacy relationships between the EU and national democracies', in J. DeBardeleben and A. Hurrelmann (eds), *Democratic Dilemmas of Multi-level Governance. Legitimacy, Representation and Accountability in the European Union*, New York, NY: Palgrave Macmillan, pp. 17–37.

Iglič, H. and Font Fábregas, J. (2007) 'Social networks', in J.W. van Deth, J.R. Montero and A.Westholm (eds), *Citizenship and Involvement in European Democracies: A Comparative Analysis*, London: Routledge, pp. 188–218.

Inglehart, R. (1970) 'Cognitive mobilization and European identity', *Comparative Politics*, 3(1):45–70.

—— (1977a) 'Long-term trends in mass support for European unification', *Government and Opposition*, 12(3): 150–157.

—— (1977b) *The Silent Revolution. Changing Values and Political Styles Among Western Publics*, Princeton, NJ: Princeton University Press.

—— (1990) *Culture Shift in Advanced Industrial Society*, Princeton, NJ: Princeton University Press.

—— (1997) *Modernization and Postmodernization*, Princeton, NJ: Princeton University Press.

—— (1999), 'Trust, well-being and democracy', in M.E. Warren (ed.), *Democracy and Trust*, Cambridge: Cambridge University Press, pp. 88–120.

Inglehart, R. and Welzel, C. (2005) *Modernization, Cultural Change and Democracy*, Cambridge: Cambridge University Press.

Jagodzinski, W. and Manabe, K. (2004) 'How to measure interpersonal trust? A comparison of two different measures', *ZA-Information*, 55: 85–97.

Janssen, J.I.H. (1991) 'Postmaterialism, cognitive mobilization, and public support for European integration', *British Journal of Political Science*, 21(2): 443–468.

Job, J. (2005) 'How is trust in government created? It begins at home, but ends in the Parliament', *Australian Review of Public Affairs*, 6(1): 1–23.

Jordan, G. and Maloney, W.A. (1997) *The Protest Business? Mobilizing Campaign Groups*, Manchester: Manchester University Press.

—— (2007) *Democracy and Interest Groups: Enhancing Participation?* London: Palgrave.

Joye, D. and Laurent, A. (1997) 'Associative and political participation in Switzerland and France', in J.W. van Deth (ed.), *Private Groups and Public Life: Social Participation, Voluntary Associations and Political Involvement in Representative Democracies*, London: Routledge.

Kaase, M. (1999) 'Interpersonal trust, political trust and non-institutionalised political participation in Western Europe', *West European Politics*, 22 (3): 1–23.

Kielmansegg, P.G. (2003) 'Integration und Demokratie', in M. Jachtenfuchs and B. Kohler-Koch (eds), *Europäische Integration*, 2nd edn, Opladen: Leske & Budrich, pp. 49–83.

Knodt, M. and Finke, B. (2005) 'Einleitung: Zivilgesellschaft und zivilgesellschaftliche Akteure in der Europäischen Union', in M. Knodt and B. Finke (eds), *Europäisierung der Zivilgesellschaft. Konzepte, Akteure, Strategien*, Wiesbaden: VS Verlag für Sozialwissenschaften, pp. 11–28.

Knoke, D. (1981) 'Commitment and detachment in voluntary associations', *American Sociological Review*, 46: 141–158.

—— (1990) *Organizing for Collective Action: The Political Economies of Associations*, New York, NY: Aldine de Gruyter.

Kohler-Koch, B. (2004) 'Legitimes Regieren in der EU. Eine kritische Auseinandersetzung mit dem Weißbuch zum Europäischen Regieren', in A. Kaiser and T. Zittel (eds), *Demokratietheorien und Demokratieentwicklung. Festschrift für Peter Graf Kielmansegg*, Wiesbaden: VS Verlag für Sozialwissenschaften, pp. 423–445.

Kohler-Koch, B., Conzelmann, T. and Knodt, M. (2004) *Europäische Integration. Europäisches Regieren*, Wiesbaden: VS Verlag für Sozialwissenschaften.

Koopmans, R. (2008) 'Who Inhabits the European Public Sphere? Winners and Losers, Supporters and Opponents in Europeanized Political Debates', in K.Y. Nikolov (ed.), *Adapting to Integration in an Enlarged European Union*. Vol. 2. Sofia: BECSA, 177–215.

Koopmans, R. and Statham, P. (2002) 'The transformation of political mobilization and communication in European public spheres: a research outline', *Europub.Com Research Project*: http://europub.wzb.eu/Data/reports/Proposal.pdf. (accessed 4 March 2009).

Kopecky, P. and Mudde, C. (2002) 'The two sides of Euroscepticism', *European Union Politics*, 3(3): 297–326.

Koslowski, R. (1999) 'A constructivist approach to understanding the European Union as a federal polity', *Journal of European Public Policy*, 6(4): 561–578.

Kriesi, H. (2006) 'Organizational resources: Personnell and Finances', in W.A. Maloney and S. Roßteutscher (eds), *Social Capital and Associations in European Democracies. A Comparative Analysis*, London: Routledge, pp. 118–152.

Kriesi, H. and Baglioni, S. (2003) 'Putting local associations into their context', *Schweizerische Zeitschrift für Politikwissenschaft*, 9(3): 1–34.

Kriesi, H., Morales, L. and Walter-Rogg, M. (2006) 'The political and cultural context of associational life', in W.A. Maloney and S. Roßteutscher (eds), *Social Capital and Associations in European Democracies. A Comparative Analysis*, London: Routledge, pp. 244–268.

Kritzinger, S. (2003) 'The influence of the nation-state on individual support for the European Union', *European Union Politics*, 4 (2): 219–241.

Kumlin, S. and Rothstein, B. (2005) 'Making and breaking social capital: the impact of welfare-state institutions', *Comparative Political Studies*, 38: 339–365.

Kunz, V. (2006) 'Vergleichende Sozialkapitalforschung', in: H.-J. Lauth (ed.), *Vergleichende Regierungslehre. Eine Einführung*, Wiesbaden: VS Verlag für Sozialwissenschaften, pp. 332–352.

Kwak, N., Shah, D.V. and Holbert, R.L. (2004) 'Connecting, trusting, and participating: the direct and interactive effects of social associations', *Political Research Quarterly*, 57(4): 634–652.

La Due Lake, R. and Huckfeldt, R. (1998), 'Social capital, social networks, and political participation', *Political Psychology*, 19(3): 567–584.

Laffan, B. (1996) 'The politics of identity and political order in Europe', *Journal of Common Market Studies*, 34(1): 82–102.

Lane, R.E. (1959) *Political Life: Why and How People Get Involved in Politics*, Glencoe: Free Press.

Lelieveldt, H. and Caiani, M. (2006) 'The political role of associations', in W.A. Maloney and S. Roßteutscher (eds), *Social Capital and Associations in European Democracies. A Comparative Analysis*, London: Routledge, pp. 175–191.

Lelieveldt, H., Astudillo, J. and Stevenson, L. (2006) 'The spectrum of associational activities: from self-help to lobbying', in W.A. Maloney and S. Roßteutscher (eds), *Social Capital and Associations in European Democracies. A Comparative Analysis*, London: Routledge, pp. 81–95.

Lipset, S.M. (1960) *Political Man: The Social Basis of Politics*, New York, NY: Doubleday.

Loth, W. (2002) 'Die Mehrschichtigkeit der Identitätsbildung in Europa. Nationale, regionale und europäische Identität im Wandel', in R. Elm (ed.), *Europäische Identität: Paradigmen und Methodenfragen*, Baden-Baden: Schriften des Zentrums für Europäische Integrationsforschung, Vol. 43, pp. 93–109.

Machill, M., Beiler, M. and Fischer, C. (2007) 'Europe topics in Europe's media. the debate about the European public sphere: a meta-analysis of media content analyses', in C. de Vreese and H. Schmitt (eds), *A European Public Sphere: How Much of it Do We Have and How Much Do We Need?*, Connex Report Series No. 2, Mannheim, pp. 171–213.

Mair, P. (2006) 'Polity scepticism, party failings, and the challenge to European democracy', Uhlenbeck Lecture *24*, Wassenaar: NIAS.

Maloney, W. (2008) 'The professionalization of representation: biasing participation', in: B. Kohler-Koch, D. De Bièvre and W. Maloney (eds), *Opening EU Governance to Civil Society: Gains and Challenges*, CONNEX Report Series, No. 5, Mannheim: CONNEX, pp. 69–85.

Maloney, W.A. and Roßteutscher, S. (2007) 'Assessing the significance of associational concerns: leisure, politics and markets', in W.A. Maloney and S. Roßteutscher (eds), *Social Capital and Associations in European Democracies. A Comparative Analysis*, London: Routledge, pp. 52–78.

—— (eds) (2007) *Social Capital and Associations in Europe. A Comparative Analysis*, London: Routledge.

Maloney, W.A. and van Deth, J.W. (2008a) 'The associational impact on attitudes towards Europe: a tale of two cities', in W.A. Maloney and J.W. van Deth (eds), *Civil Society and Governance in Europe. From National to International Linkages*, Cheltenham: Edward Elgar, pp. 45–70.

Maloney, W.A. and van Deth, J.W. (eds) (2008b) *Civil Society and Governance in Europe: From National to International Linkages*, Cheltenham: Edgar Elgar.

Maloney, W.A., van Deth, J.W. and Roßteutscher, S. (2008) 'Civic orientations: does associational type matter?' *Political Studies*, 56(2): 261–287.

Marks, G. (1999) 'Territorial identities in the European Union', in J.J. Anderson (ed.), *Regional Integration and Democracy: Expanding on the European Experience*, Boulder, CO: Rowman & Littlefield, pp. 69–94.

Marks, G. and Hooghe, L. (2004) 'Does identity or economic rationality drive public opinion on European integration?' *Political Science*, 37(3): 415–442.

Marks, G. and Steenbergen, M.R. (eds) (2004) *European Integration and Political Conflict*. Cambridge: Cambridge University Press.

Maurer, A. (2006) 'Die Vermessung des europäischen Tiefgangs. Extrakonstitutionelle Umwege aus der Verfassungskrise', *Politische Vierteljahresschrift*, 47(2): 264–274.

Mayer, N. (2003) 'Democracy in France: do associations matter?' in M. Hooghe and D. Stolle (eds), *Generating Social Capital. Civil Society and Institutions in Comparative Perspective*, New York, NY: Palgrave Macmillan, pp. 43–66.

McLaren, L.M. (2002) 'Public support for the European Union: cost/benefit analysis or perceived cultural threat?' *Journal of Politics*, 64(2): 551–566.

—— (2007) 'Explaining mass-level Euroscepticism: identity, interests, and institutional distrust', *Acta Politica*, 42 (2–3): 233–251.

Menchik, P.L. and Weisbrod, B.A. (1987) 'Volunteer labor supply', *The Journal of Public Economics*, 32: 159–183.

Michalowitz, I. (2004) 'Analysing structured paths of lobbying behaviour: why discussing the involvement of "civil society" does not solve the EU's democratic deficit', *European Integration*, 26(2): 145–170.

Michels, R. (1959 [1911]) *Political Parties: A Sociological Study of the Oligarchical Tendencies of Modern Democracy*, New York, NY: Dover.

Mill, J.S. ([1861] 1977) 'Considerations on representative government', in *Collected Works of John Stuart Mill*, Vol. XIX, Toronto: University of Toronto Press, pp. 371–577.

Miller, M.K. (2009) 'Debating group structure: how local, translocal, and national voluntary organizations promote democracy', *The Social Science Journal* 46: 47–69.

Minogue, K.R. (1999) 'Creed for Democrats', *Times Literary Supplement*, June 18, p. 8: http://tls.timesonline.co.uk/article/0,,25368-1944286,00.html (accessed 25 February 2009).

Mishler, W. and Rose, R. (2001) 'What are the origins of political trust? Testing institutional and cultural theories in post-Communist societies', *Comparative Political Studies* 34 (1): 30–62.

—— (2005) 'What are the consequences of political trust? A test of cultural and institutional theories in Russia', *Comparative Political Studies*, 38 (9): 1050–1078.

Morales, L. (2004) *Institutions, Mobilisation, and Political Participation: Political Membership in Western Democracies*, Madrid: Centro de Estudios Avanzados en Ciencias Sociales.

Morales, L. and Geurts, P. (2007) 'Associational involvement', in J.W. van Deth, J.R. Montero and A. Westholm (eds), *Citizenship and Involvement in European Democracies*. London: Routledge, pp. 135–157.

Moyser, G. and Parry, G. (1997) 'Voluntary associations and democratic participation in Britain', in J.W. van Deth (ed.), *Private Groups and Public Life: Social Participation, Voluntary Associations and Political Involvement in Representative Democracies*, London: Routledge, pp. 25–47.

Newton, K. (1999a) 'Social capital and democracy in modern Europe', in J.W. van Deth,

M. Maraffi, K. Newton and P.F. Whiteley (eds), *Social Capital and European Democracy*, London: Routledge, pp. 3–22.

—— (1999b) 'Social and political trust in established democracies', in P. Norris (ed.), *Critical Citizens. Global Support for Democratic Government*, Oxford: Oxford University Press, pp. 169–187.

—— (2001a) 'Social capital and democracy', in B. Edwards, M. Foley and M. Diani (eds), *Beyond Tocqueville. Civil Society and the Social Capital Debate in Comparative Perspective*, Hanover: Tufts University, pp. 225–234.

—— (2001b) 'Trust, social capital, civil society, and democracy', *International Political Science Review*, 22 (2): 201–214.

—— (2006) 'Institutional trust and social trust: aggregate and individual relation', in M. Torcal and J.R. Montero (eds), *Political Disaffection in Contemporaty Democracies: Social Capital, Institutions and Politics*, London: Routledge, pp. 81–100.

—— (2008) 'Trust and politics', in D. Castiglione, J.W. van Deth and G. Wolleb (eds), *The Handbook of Social Capital*, Oxford: Oxford University Press, pp. 241–372.

Newton, K. and Norris, P. (2000) 'Confidence in public institutions: faith, culture, or performance? in S. Pharr and R.D. Putnam (eds), *Disaffected Democracies: What's Troubling the Trilateral Countries?* Princeton, NJ: Princeton University Press, pp. 52–73.

Ohmer, M.L. (2007) 'Citizen participation in neighborhood organizations and its relationship to volunteers' self- and collective efficacy and sense of community', *Social Work Research*, 31: 109–120.

Oliver, J.E. (2000) 'City size and civic involvement in metropolitan America', *American Political Science Review*, 94: 361–373.

Olsen, M.E. (1972) 'Social participation and voting turnout: a multivariate analysis', *American Sociological Review*, 37: 317–333.

Orr, M. (1999) *Black Social Capital: The Politics of School Reform in Baltimore, 1986–1998*, Lawrence, KS: Kansas University Press.

Ostrom, E. and Ahn, T.K. (eds) (2003) *Foundations of Social Capital*. Vol. 2, Critical Studies in Economic Institutions, Cheltenham: Edward Elgar.

Oxendine, A., Sullivan, J.L., Borgida, E., Riedel, E., Jackson, M. and Dial, J. (2007) 'The importance of political context for understanding civic engagement: a longitudinal analysis', *Political Behavior*, 29(1): 31–68.

Pache, R. (2001) 'L'insatisfaction croissante des opinions publiques europeénnes', in D. Reyniè and B.Cautrès (eds) *L'opinion publique europeénne 2001*. Paris: Presse de Science Po, pp. 241–248.

Parry, G., Moyser, G. and Day, N. (1992) *Political Participation and Democracy in Britain*, Cambridge: Cambridge University Press.

Pateman, C. (1970) *Participation and Democratic Theory*. Cambridge: Cambridge University Press.

Pattie, C., Seyd, P. and Whiteley, P. (2004) *Citizenship in Britain: Values, Participation and Democracy*, Cambridge: Cambridge University Press.

Pfetsch, F.R. (1997) *Die Europäische Union. Eine Einführung*, München: Fink.

Pollack, D., Jacobs, J., Müller, O. and Pickel, G. (eds) (2003) *Political Culture in Post-Communist Europe. Attitudes in New Democracies*, Aldershot: Ashgate.

Putnam, R.D. (1995) 'Bowling alone: America's declining social capital', *Journal of Democracy*, 6(1): 65–78.

—— (2000) *Bowling Alone: The Collapse and Revival of American Community*. New York, NY: Simon & Schuster.

Putnam, R.D., Leonardi, R. and Nanetti, R.Y. (1993) *Making Democracy Work: Civic Traditions in Modern Italy*. Princeton, NJ: Princeton University Press.

Rabe-Hesketh, S. and Skrondal, A. (2005) *Multi-level and Longitudinal Modelling Using Stata*, College Station, TX: Stata Press.

Risse, T. (2003) 'An Emerging European Public Sphere? Theoretical Clarifications and Empirical Indicators', Paper presented to the Annual Meeting of the European Union Studies Association, Nashville TN, 27–30 March: http://aei.pitt.edu/6556/01/001315_1.PDF (accessed 4 March 2009).

Rohrschneider, R. (1999) *Learning Democracy. Democratic and Economic Values in Unified Germany*, Oxford: Oxford University Press.

—— (2002) 'The democracy deficit and mass support for an EU-wide government', *American Journal of Political Science*, 46 (2): 463–475.

Rosenstone, S.J. and Hansen, J.M. (1993) *Mobilization, Participation and Democracy in America*, New York, NY: Macmillan.

Roßteutscher, S. and van Deth, J.W. (2002) 'Associations between Associations. The Structure of the Voluntary Association Sector', Mannheim: MZES Working Paper 56: (www.mzes.uni-mannheim.de/publications/wp/wp-56.pdf).

Rothstein, B. and Stolle, D. (2003) 'Social capital, impartiality, and the welfare state: an institutional approach', in M. Hooghe and D. Stolle (eds), *Generating Social Capital: Civil Society and Institutions in Comparative Perspective*, Basingstoke: Palgrave, pp. 191–207.

—— (2008) 'Political institutions and generalized trust', in D. Castiglione, J.W. van Deth and G. Wolleb (eds), *The Handbook of Social Capital*, Oxford: Oxford University Press, pp. 273–302.

Salamon, L.M. and Sokolowski, W.S. (2001) 'Volunteering in cross-national perspective: evidence from 24 countries', Working Paper, Johns Hopkins Comparative Nonprofit Sector Project, Baltimore, MD: Johns Hopkins University.

Salamon, L.M., Sokolowski, W.S. and Anheier, H.K. (2000) 'Social origins of civil society – an overview', Working Paper, Johns Hopkins Comparative Nonprofit Sector Project, Baltimore, MD: Johns Hopkins University.

Sánchez-Cuenca, I. (2000) 'The political basis of support for European integration', *European Union Politics*, 1 (2): 147–171.

Saurugger, S. (2007) 'Democratic "misfit"? Conceptions of civil society participation in France and the European Union', *Political Studies*, 55: 384–404.

—— (2009) 'Interest groups and democracy in the EU: a critical appraisal', *West European Politics*, 31(6): 1272–1289.

Sbragia, A.M. (2002) 'The Dilemma of Governance with Government', Jean Monnet Working Paper, 3/02.

Schlesinger, A. (1944) 'Biography of a nation of joiners', *American Historical Review*, 50(1): 1–25.

Schmalz-Bruns, R. (1997) 'Bürgergesellschaftliche Politik – ein Modell der Demokratisierung der EU?' in K.-D. Wolf (ed.), *Projekt Europa im Übergang?* Baden-Baden: Nomos, pp. 63–89.

Schmidt, V.A. (2006) *Democracy in Europe: The EU and National Politics*. Oxford: Oxford University Press.

Schneider, M., Teske, P., Marschall, M., Mintrom, M. and Roch, C. (1997) 'Institutional arrangements and the creation of social capital: the effects of public school choice', *The American Political Science Review*, 91(1): 82–93.

Schulz, T. and Häfliger U. (2007) 'Ein Füreinander im doppelten Sinn. Folgen sozialpolitischer Veränderungen für die Freiwilligenarbeit im internationalen und schweizerischen Vergleich', in P. Farago (ed.), *Freiwilliges Engagement in der Schweiz. Reihe Freiwilligkeit*, Seismo, Zürich.

Schumpeter, J.A. ([1943] 1994) *Capitalism, Socialism and Democracy*, Introduction by R. Swedberg, London: Routledge.

Segal, L.M. and Weisbrod, B.A. (2002) 'Volunteer labor sorting across industries', *Journal of Policy Analysis and Management*, 21(3): 427–447.

Seligman, A.B. (1997) *The Problem of Trust*, Princeton, NJ: Princeton University Press.

Sharpf, F. (1999) *Governing Europe*. Oxford: Oxford University Press.

Shaw, J. (1999) 'Postnational constitutionalism in the European Union', *Journal of European Public Policy*, 6(4): 579–597.

Shils, E. (1991) 'Comments', in P. Bourdieu and J.S. Coleman (eds), *Social Theory for a Changing Society*, Boulder, CO: Westview Press, pp. 126–132.

Sinnott, R. (2005) 'An evaluation of the measurement of national, subnational and supranational identity in cross-national surveys', *International Journal of Public Opinion*, 18(2): 211–223.

Skocpol, T., Ganz, M. and Munso, Z. (2000) 'A nation of organizers: the institutional origins of civic voluntarism in the United States', *American Political Science Review*, 94(3): 527–546.

Smith, A.D. (1992) 'National identity and the idea of European unity', *International Affairs*, 68(1): 55–76.

Statham, P. (2007) 'Forging divergent and path dependent ways to Europe, political communication over European integration in the British and French public spheres', in C. de Vreese and H. Schmitt (eds), *A European Public Sphere*, Connex Report Series, Mannheim: No. 02: 79–142.

Statham, P. and Gray, E. (2005) 'The public sphere and debates about Europe in Britain and France, internalized and conflict driven?' *Innovation*, 18(1): 61–81.

Steenbergen, M. and Jones, B. (2002) 'Modeling multi-level data structures', *American Journal of Political Science*, 46(1): 218–237.

Stoker, G. (2006a) *Why Politics Matters*, London: Palgrave Macmillan.

—— (2006b) 'Politics in mass democracies: destined to disappoint?', *Representation*, 42(3): 181–194.

Stolle, D. (1998) 'Bowling together, bowling alone: the development of generalized trust in voluntary associations', *Political Psychology*, 19: 497–525.

—— (2001) 'Clubs and congregations: the benefits of joining associations', in K. Cook (ed.), *Trust in Society*, New York, NY: Russell Sage Foundation, pp. 202–244.

—— (2003) 'The sources of social capital', in M. Hooghe and D. Stolle (eds), *Generating Social Capital. Civil Society and Institutions in Comparative Perspective*, New York, NY: Palgrave Macmillan, pp. 19–42.

Stolle, D. and Howard, M. (2008) 'Introduction to the symposium', *Political Studies*, 56(1): 1–11.

Stolle, D. and Rochon, T.R. (2001) 'Are all associations alike? Member diversity, associational type, and the creation of social capital', in B. Edwards, M. Foley and M. Diani (eds), *Beyond Tocqueville. Civil Society and the Social Capital Debate in Comparative Perspective*, Hanover: Tufts University, pp. 143–156.

Sudbery, I. (2003) 'Bridging the legitimacy gap in the EU: can civil society help to bring the union closer to its citizens?', *Collegium*, 26: 75–95.

Szczerbiak, A. and Taggart, P. (2000) 'Opposing Europe: Party Systems and Opposition to the Union, the Euro and Europeanisation', *Opposing Europe Research Network*,

Working Paper 1, www.sussex.ac.uk/usis/quicksearch/results.php (accessed 12 September 2008).
Szreter, S. (2002) 'The state of social capital: bringing back in power, politics, and history', *Theory and Society* 31(5): 573.
Tarrow, S. (2000) 'Mad cows and social activists: contentious politics in the trilateral democracies', in S.J. Pharr and R.D. Putnam (eds), *Disaffected Democracies. What's Troubling the Trilateral Countries?* Princeton, NJ: Princeton University Press, pp. 270–290.
—— (2005) *The New Transnational Contention.* Cambridge: Cambridge University Press.
Teorell, J. (2003) 'Linking social capital to political participation: voluntary associations and networks of recruitment in Sweden', *Scandinavian Political Studies*, 26: 49–66.
Teorell, J., Torcal, M. and Montero, J.R. (2007) 'Political participation: mapping the terrain', in: J.W. van Deth, J.R. Montero and A. Westholm (eds), *Citizenship and Involvement in European Democracies: A Comparative Analysis*, London: Routledge, pp. 334–57.
Theiss-Morse, E. and Hibbing, J.R. (2005) 'Citizenship and civic engagement', *Annual Review of Political Science*, 8: 227–249.
Tilly, C. (1978) *From Mobilization to Revolution.* Reading, CT: Addison-Wesley.
—— (2005) *Identities, Boundaries and Social Ties.* Boulder, CO: Paradigm Publishers.
Topf, R. (1995) 'Beyond electoral participation', in H.-D. Klingemann and D. Fuchs (eds), *Citizens and the State*, Oxford: Oxford University Press, pp. 52–91.
Torcal, M. and Montero, J.R. (eds) (2006) *Political Disaffection in Contemporary Democracies: Social Capital, Institutions and Politics*, London: Routledge.
Torpe, L. and Ferrer-Fons, M. (2007) 'The internal structure of associations', in W. Maloney and S. Roßteutcher (eds), *Social Capital and Associations in European Democracies*, Oxford: Routledge, pp. 96–117.
Tyler, T.R. (1998) 'Trust and democratic governance', in V. Braithwaite and M. Levi (eds), *Trust in Governance*, New York, NY: Russell Sage Foundation, pp. 269–294.
—— (2001) 'Public trust and trust in legal authorities: what do majority and minority group members want from the law and legal authorities', *Behavioral Science and the Law*, 19: 215–235.
Uslaner, E. (2002) *The Moral Foundations of Trust*, Cambridge: Cambridge University Press.
van Aelst, P. and Walgrave, S. (2001) 'Who is that (wo)man in the street? From the normalization of protest to the normalization of the protester', *European Journal of Political Research*, 39: 461–486.
van Deth, J.W. (1991) 'Politicization and political interest', in K.Reif and R.Inglehart (eds), *Eurobarometer: The Dynamics of European Public Opinion*, London: Macmillan, pp. 201–213.
—— (1996) 'Politisches Interesse und Apathie in Europa', in T. König, E. Rieger and H. Schmitt (eds), *Das europäische Mehrebenensystem*, Frankfurt a.M.: Campus Verlag, pp. 383–402.
—— (1997) 'Introduction: social involvement and democratic politics', in J.W.van Deth (ed.), *Private Groups and Public Life. Social Participation, Voluntary Associations and Political Involvement in Representative Democracies*, London: Routledge, pp. 1–23.
—— (2000) 'Interesting but irrelevant: social capital and the saliency of politics in Western Europe', *European Journal of Political Research*, 37: 115–47.

—— (2008a) 'Political involvement and social capital', in H. Meulemann (ed.), *Social Capital in Europe. Similarity of Countries and Diversity of People*, Leiden: Brill, pp. 191–218.

—— (2008b) 'European civil society: the empirical reality in the multi-level system of the EU', in B. Kohler-Koch, D. de Bièvre and W.A. Maloney (eds), *Opening EU-Governance to Civil Society*, CONNEX Report Series No. 05, Mannheim, pp. 325–348.

van Deth, J.W. and Elff, M. (2004) 'Politicisation, economic development and political interest in Europe', *European Journal of Political Research*, 43: 477–508.

van Deth, J.W. and Maloney, W.A. (2008) 'The associational impact on attitudes towards Europe: a tale of two cities', in W.A. Maloney and J.W. van Deth (eds), *Civil Society and Governance in Europe: From National toward International Linkages?* Cheltenham: Edward Elgar, pp. 45–70.

van Deth, J.W., Montero, J.R. and Westholm, A. (eds) (2007) *Citizenship and Involvement in European Democracies: A Comparative Analysis*, London: Routledge.

Verba, S. and Nie, N.H. (1987) *Participation in America: Political Democracy and Social Equality*. Chicago, IL: University of Chicago Press.

Verba, S., Nie, N.H. and Kim, J.O. (1978) *Participation and Political Equality: A Seven Nation Comparison*. Cambridge: Cambridge University Press.

Verba, S., Schlozman, K.L. and Brady, H.E. (1995) *Voice and Equality: Civic Voluntarism in American Politics*. Cambridge, MA: Harvard University Press.

Vetter, A. (2002) 'Local political competence in Europe: a resource of legitimacy for higher levels of government?' *International Journal of Public Opinion Research*, 14(1): 3–18.

von Bogdandy, O.A. (2002) 'Europäische Identitätsbildung aus sozialpsychologischer Sicht', in R. Elm (ed.), *Europäische Identität: Paradigmen und Methodenfragen*, Vol. 43, Baden-Baden: Schriften des Zentrums für Europäische Integrationsforschung, pp. 111–134.

von Erlach, E. (2005) *Aktivierung oder Apathie? Eine empirische Analyse zu den Zusammenhängen zwischen der Mitgliedschaft in Freiwilligen-organisationen und politischem Engagement in der Schweiz*, Bern: Dissertation, University of Bern.

—— (2006) 'Politicization in associations: an empirical study of the relationship between membership in associations and participation in political discussions', *World Political Science Review*, 2(1): 1–29.

Ware, A. (1971) *The Logic of Party Democracy*, London: Macmillan.

Warleigh, A. (2001), '"Europeanizing" civil society: NGOs as agents of political socialization', *Journal of Common Market Studies*, 39(4): 619–639.

Warren, M.E. (1999) 'Democratic theory and trust', in M.E. Warren (ed.), *Democracy and Trust*, Cambridge: Cambridge University Press, pp. 310–345.

—— (2001) *Democracy and Association*. Princeton, NJ: Princeton University Press.

—— (2008) 'The nature and logic of bad social capital', in D. Castiglione, J.W. van Deth and G. Wolleb (eds), *The Handbook of Social Capital*, Oxford: Oxford University Press, pp. 122–149.

Weisbrod, B.A. (ed.) (1977) *The Voluntary Nonprofit Sector*, Lexington, VA: Lexington Books.

—— (1988) *The Nonprofit Economy*, Cambridge, MA: Harvard University Press.

White, H. (1992) *Identity and Control: A Structural Theory of Social Action*, Princeton, NJ: Princeton University Press.

Wilson, J.Q. (1962), *The Amateur Democrat: Club Politics in Three Cities*, Chicago, IL: University of Chicago Press.

Wollebaek, D. and Selle, P. (2002) 'Does participation in voluntary associations contribute to social capital? The impact of intensity, scope, and type', *Nonprofit and Voluntary Sector Quarterly*, 31: 32–61.

—— (2003) 'Participation and social capital formation: Norway in a comparative perspective', *Scandinavian Political Studies*, 26(1): 67–91.

—— (2007) 'Origins of social capital: socialization and institutionalization approaches compared', *Journal of Civil Society*, 3(1): 1–24.

Wollbæk, D. and Strømsnes, K. (2008) 'Voluntary associations, trust, and civic engagement: a multi-level approach', *Nonprofit and Voluntary Sector Quarterly*, 37(2): 249–263.

Woolcock, M. (1998) 'Social capital and economic development: toward a theoretical synthesis and policy framework', *Theory and Society*, 27(2): 151–208.

Zald, M.N. and Garner, R.A. (1990) 'Social movement organizations: growth, decay, and change.' In M.N. Zald and J.D. McCarthy (eds), *Social Movements in an Organizational Society*, Brunswick: Transaction, pp. 121–142.

Zmerli, S. (2004) 'Politisches Vertrauen und Unterstützung', in J.W. van Deth (ed.), *Deutschland in Europa. Ergebnisse des European Social Survey 2002–2003*, Wiesbaden: Verlag für Sozialwissenschaften, pp. 229–256.

—— (2008) *Inklusives und exklusives Sozialkapital in Deutschland. Grundlagen, Erscheinungsformen und Erklärungspotential eines alternativen theoretischen Konzepts*, Baden-Baden: Nomos.

Zmerli, S. and Newton, K. (2007) 'Networking among voluntary associations: segmented or integrated?' in W.A. Maloney and S. Roßteutscher (eds), *Social Capital and Associations in European Democracies. A Comparative Analysis*, London: Routledge, pp. 153–174.

—— (2008) 'Social trust and attitudes towards democracy', *Public Opinion Quarterly*, 72(4): 706–724.

Zmerli, S., Newton, K. and Montero, J.R. (2007) 'Trust in people, confidence in political institutions, and satisfaction with democracy', in J.W. van Deth, J.R. Montero and A. Westholm (eds), *Citizenship and Involvement in European Democracies. A Comparative Analysis*, London: Routledge, pp. 35–65.

Zürn, M. (2006) 'Zur Politisierung der Europäischen Union', *Politische Vierteljahresschrift*, 47(2): 424–451.

Index

Italic page numbers indicate tables not included in the text page range. **Bold** page numbers indicate figures not included in the text page range.

accountability 100, 101
activists: associational efficacy 47–9; attachment 187–90; characteristics 13, *14*; description 12; and European support 132, 136, *137*, 138–9, 144–52, 152–3; and internal democracy 107, 112; multi-level analysis 30–4; participation 47–9, 54–5; political efficacy 69–72; political interest 79–83, 132; predictors of attachment *200–3*; and socially active population 27–30, 45–7; territorial identity 199; and trust 161–5, 199–204, 215, 216, 225, 228–9
acts of consent 158, 159
age 22, 51, 98, 113, 197
Almond, G.A. 3, 57, 102
Anderson, B. 182
anti-European political parties 129
Armingeon, K. 106
Armony, A.C. 77
assemblies 108
associational activity: geographic scope 161, 199; individual degree of 161, 167, 172
associational context 225–8, 233, 239
associational engagement 103, 151, 153
associational features 91–2, 199
associational impact 238–40
associational involvement 165–72
associational types 25, 64, *66*, 85–9, 194, 199, 205, **225**
associations: and social integration 181–2; types of 59–60, 194; *see also* organizations; voluntary associations
attachment: collective 182–5; to neighbourhood 166, 167, *169–70*, *174–6*, 177

attitudes: democratic political 233–6; to Europe 131–4, 157–8, 237

Baglioni, S. 25
Barber, Benjamin 77
behavioural characteristics 107–8
behaviourally democratic organizations 108–9
Berelson, B.B. 3
Bowler, S. 59–60
Bowling Alone 1, 208
Braithwaite, V. 209, 210
breadth: of engagement 64, *65*, 98
Brewer, M.B. 184

Caiani, M. 24
Calhoun, C. 182, 184
Campbell, A. 42
Cappellari, L. 21
catnets 183
CID Activists Study 7–9, **11**, 47, 78, 91, 187, 197
CID Organization Study 7, *8*, **11**, 197
CID Population Study *8*, 9, **11**, 45, 61, 107
CID (Citizenship, Involvement, Democracy) project 6–12, 19–20, 131, 186, 240
citizen disengagement 1–3, 231
citizen's model: political efficacy 67–9
Citizenship, Involvement, Democracy (CID) project *see* CID
civic disposition 107
civic empowerment: and civic associations 57 *see also* empowerment
civic engagement: and democracy 77, 103
civic organizations: role of 181

Index

civic-spiritedness 105, 106, 109, *110–11*, 115–18, 233–4
cognitive competence 184, 194, 197
cognitive mobilization 184, 185, 194, 205
collective attachment: arguments 182–5; to municipality and Europe 186–90; predictors 193–204; strength and direction 190–3
commitment 42, 53, 151–2, 194
Committed Multipliers 84–5, *86*, 87–91, 92, *93*, 97, 98
communal-based trust 209–10, 211, 217, 228, 236
'Comparative Nonprofit Sector Project' 23
confidence: in EU 165–72, 199
'consumption model': of volunteering 20–1
contacts score 24, 35; *see also* linking social capital
context 60, 61, 239
contextual factors: organizations 225–8, 233
'critical Europeanists' 135–6, 139, *150*, 151, 152–3
'crowding-out' hypothesis 19, 22, 23, 35, 235
culture-based dimension: political trust 210–11

Dahl, Robert 56, 113
Dalton, R.J. 1, 3
Day, K.M. 21, 22, 26
de Tocqueville, Alexis 40, 102
democracy: and engagement 1–3, 40, 103; internal *see* internal democracy; national 166, *168–70*, 172, 178; and voluntary associations 3–5
Democracy in America 40
democratic deficit 100, 129, 156
democratic freshers 105, 106
democratic graduates 106
democratic participation *see* participation
democratic political attitudes 233–6
democratization 194, 199; *see also* internal democracy
demonstrating 108, 109, *110–11*, 112–13, 114, 118–24
detachment 42
determinants: of voluntary work 20–5
Deutsch, K. 184
Devlin, R.A. 21, 22, 26
Di Palma, G. 211
Diamond, L. 2–3
Díez Medrano, J. 185, 195

discussions, political 84–5, 98, 114, 194
disengagement 1–3, 231
Duchesne, S. 184

economic models: of volunteering 20–1
education 21, 30, 51, 53, 72, 98, 113, 115, 144, 194, 197
efficacy: activists 47–9, 69–72; determinants 55; individual-level determinants of 45; intra-organizational 234; and participation 41–3, 44; political *see* political efficacy; predictions *52*, 53–4
electoral participation 107–8
employment 51, 53
empowerment: fostering 56–7; subjective feelings 62–4, *68*, *70–1*, 235
encapsulated interest 209
endogeneity 67, 73
engagement: breadth of 59, 64, *65*, 98; democracy and 1–3, 103; level of 41–2, 59, 62–4; and social capital 114
ethnic identities 204
EU (European Union): and civil societies 129–30; confidence in 165–72; deficiencies 129–30; legitimacy 156–8, 161–78
EU Commission: and citizen disengagement 1, 100; White Paper on European Governance *see European Governance: A White Paper*
EU institutions: trust in 129, 130–1, 132–4, 207–29, 236
EU treaties 181
'Euro-disaffected' 135–6, 138–9, 145–6, *149*, 151, 152
'Euro-enthusiasts' 135–6, 138, 139, **140–3**, *147*, 152
'Euro-pragmatics' 135, 139, 145–6, *148*, 151
Euro-scepticism 132, 134, 144, 146
Eurobarometer data 131, 144, 207
European attitudes: associational impact on 131–4, 157–8, 237
European Governance: A White Paper 4, 130, 157
European identification 204–6, 238
European institutions: confidence in 195, 199; trust 132–4, 135; *see also* EU institutions
European integration: and citizens' support 129, 131, 153; 'Euro-pragmatics' 135; research on 130–1
European Parliament 156

European politics: contextualizing engagement 91–7; discussions of 83–91; interest in 78–83, 132, **133**
European Social Survey 207
European support: and activists 144–52; and critical Europeanists 152–3; types of 134–7; and voluntary associations 138–9, *140–3*
exchange-based trust 209–10, 211, 224, 228, 236

Ferrer-Fons, M. 24–5, 44
formalization 43–4, 51–2
Frietag, M. 240
Frognier, A.P. 184

gender 113
generalized trust 105, 195
geographic scope 161, 172–3, 194
Gilbert, L. 2, 102, 108
Gilley, B. 158–9
Glanville, J.L. 231
government spending: and voluntary work 19–20, 22–5
group-related trust 163, 165, 167, 172–3, *174*, 177–8, 237
Gutiérrez, P. 185, 195

Habermas, J. 129
Hardin, R. 209
Hay, C. 1
heterogeneous networks 159
Hibbing, J.R. 2, 77
Hooghe, L. 74
horizontal dimensions: of organizational governance 104
Howard, M.M. 2, 102, 106, 108
Huckfeldt, R. 77, 240
human capital 58–9
Huntington, S. 3, 104

identification 181, 190, 204–6
ideological orientation 114, 115, 118, 144, 166–7
imagined communities 182–3, 190, 205
income 72, 113, 115
individual associational involvement 161
individual characteristics: indicators for 92
individual-level determinants: of associational participation and efficacy 45; voluntary work 20–2
Inglehart, R. 184, 190, 193, 194
institutional confidence 194–5, 199

institutionalist perspective 211, 212, 213, 215–16, 228
institutionalization 194, 225–8
institutionally democratic organizations 108–9
institutions *see* EU institutions; European institutions
'interdependence-theory' 23
internal democracy: analysis and results 109–24; data measurement 107–9; effect of 233–4; of groups 100–1; importance of 103–4; role of 104–7
intra-organizational aspects: voluntary organizations 5, 234
intra-organizational democracy 101, 104, 109, 233
'investment model': of volunteering 20–1
involvement: and attachment to Europe 193; breadth of 64, *65*, 98; level of 62–4; types of 59; in voluntary associations 2–3

Janssen, J.I.H. 184
Johns Hopkins Comparative Nonprofit Sector Project 19

Kielmansegg, P.G. 178
Knoke, D. 3, 41, 42, 44, 54
Kriesi, H. 23, 25

La Due Lake, R. 240
Lane, R.E. 58
latent organizational influence 34–5
left–right orientation 114, 115, 118, 144, 151, 166–7
legitimacy: concept of 158–9; EU 129–30, 156–8, 161–78; and European support 136; and internal democracy 101; of voluntary activity 100
Lelieveldt, H. 24, 25
length of membership 72, 106, 109, 115, 151–2, 172, 233–4
level of activity 194
life satisfaction 166, 167, *168–70*, 173, *174–6*, 177
linking social capital 60, 72; *see also* contacts score
local government: as training ground 56; and voluntary organizations 23–4, 35
local networks 183–5
locality effects 233, 238

Maastricht Treaty 181
McLaren, L.M. 185

Making Democracy Work 1, 208
Maloney, W.A. 157
Marks, G. 186
mechanisms: joining and empowerment 58–9
membership fees 194
membership length *see* length of membership
men: and volunteering 21
Menchik, P.L. 20, 21, 22, 26
Michalowitz, I. 101
Michels, Roberto 42, 55
Mill, John Stuart 56, 103
mobilization: cognitive *see* cognitive mobilization; of voluntary work 20, 23, 24, 25, 30, 34, 35–8, 183, 236
multiple identities 186, 190

national differences: political involvement 79–83, 97–8
national identification 144–5
national identity 182–3
neo-Tocquevillean approaches 3, 13, 77, 85, 233–4, 239
nested identities 184–5
networks 59, 114, 159, 190, 197
NGOs (non-governmental organizations) 101
non-actives: attachment 187–90; characteristics *14*; description 13; and European support 132, 136, *137*; and internal democracy 107, 108; and political interest 79–83; and trust 161–5, 167, 215, 216, 229
non-electoral political action 108

oligarchization: of organizations 42
Oliver, J.E. 43
Olsen, M.E. 102
opportunity costs of time 20–1
organizational characteristics 239
organizational determinants 22–5, 53–4
organizational efficacy 72
organizational factors 41, 42, 43–4, 51–2, 151, 235–6
organizations: attributes 35–6; importance of 238–40; types of 59–60, 64, *66*; *see also* associations; voluntary associations
Oxendine, A. 23

participation: activists 45–7, 47–9, 54–5; and associational engagement 103; efficacy and 41–3; electoral 107–8; individual-level determinants of 45; predicting 49–53; rate 109; socially actives 45–7; in voluntary associations 208
participatory democracy 3, 41, 77
participatory habits 233–4
partisan identification 100
party membership 100
passive membership 106–7, 239
Pateman, C. 41, 56
personalized trust 160, 161–5, 166, 167, *170*, 172, 173, *176*, 177–8
'policy-oriented' organizations 25
political behaviour 108
political citizenship 204
political communication 194
Political Culture tradition 56
political discussions 84–5, 98, 194
political diversity 77
political efficacy: concept 58; definition 42; descriptive analysis 62–6; determinants 58–61; and EU confidence 166, *168–70*, 172, 178; explanatory analysis 67–72; research strategy 61; and voluntary organizations 57, 234–5
political interest: in EU 236–7; European politics 78–83, 132, **133**
political involvement: national differences 79, 97–8
political socialization 60
political trust 159, 208–11, *218–23*, 229, 236
Politically Unconcerned 84–5, 91, 92, *96*, 97
predicting: participation 49–53
professionalization: of organizations 42, 43, 49–51, 53–4, 55, 161, **226**, *227*
profiles: European citizens 135–6
protest businesses 100
protest participation 109, *110–11*, 118–24
public-mindedness 105, 106, 107, 233–4
Putnam, R.D. 1, 43, 56, 104, 105, 114, 160, 178, 208

Rabe-Hesketh, S. 26
regional solidarities 183
religion 113, 115
religious people: and volunteering 22
renationalization 129
representativeness 100
research data 6–12
research strategy 6–12
Risse, Thomas 152–3
Rohrschneider, R. 211
Roßteutscher, S. 25, 157

Salamon, L.M. 22–3
Saurugger, S. 101
scepticism 231
Schlesinger, Arthur 102
schools of democracy 102–4, 130, 208, 233–4
schoolyards of democracy 234
Schumpeter, J.A. 3, 104
Segal, L.M. 21
self-selection argument 67, 73, 106, 113, 132, 233, 237, 239
Selle, P. 239–40
'service-oriented' organizations 25
Shils, E. 183–4, 190, 193, 205
Silent Committers 85, **85**, 91, 92, *95*
size: of organizations 43, 49, 51, 53–4, 55, 60, 72, 92, 226–8
Skrondal, A. 26
social activity 165–72
social capital 77, 208–9, 239–40; 'dark side' 3, 100
Social Capital theorists 56, 73
social capital theory 104, 157, 159–60, 208, 210, 212, 224, 228
social influence 159–60
social integration 181–2, 193–4, 238
social networks 59, 114, 159, 190, 197, 208
social participation 134
'social pecking order' 61
social trust 159–67, *168–70*, 173, *175*, 177–8, 208–9, 213, 224, 228–9, 236, 237
socialization 60, 73–4
socially active population 27–30, 45–7, 54
socially actives: attachment 187–90; characteristics *14*; and civic spiritedness 109, 112; description 12; and European support 136, *137*, 138–9; and internal democracy 107; and political interest 79–83, 132; and trust 132, 161–5, 215–16, 225
Sokolowski, W.S. 23
state expenditure: and voluntary work 19–20, 22–5
state legitimacy 158–9
Stoker, G. 1–2, 3
Stolle, D. 106
striking 108, 109, *110–11*, 112–13, 114
Strømsnes, K. 3
subsidies 23, 24, 35, 235–6, 237–8
'substitutive' relationship: state and volunteering 22
suburban dwellers: and volunteering 22

Sudbery, I. 101, 157

take-up rate: participatory opportunities 109
terminal community 184
territorial identities 183–5
tertiary associations 100
Theiss-Morse, E. 2, 77
Tilly, C. 183
time-constraint variables 27–30, 51, 53
time supplied: in volunteering 26
Tocqueville, Alexis de 40, 102
Tocquevillean approaches 77, 102, 130, 240; *see also* neo-Tocquevillean approaches
Torpe, L. 24–5, 44
trans-national democracy 56
transparency 129–30, 156
trust: activists and 161–5, 199–204, 215, 216, 225, 228–9; in EU 162–5; in EU institutions 129, 130–1, 132–4, 207–29, 236; mutual 105, 114; and participation 130; in politicians 100; and socially actives 132, 161–5, 215–16, 225; *see also* communal-based trust; exchange-based trust; generalized trust; group-related trust; personalized trust; political trust; social trust
Turati, G. 21
typologies: of voluntary associations 25, **226**

Uncommitted Multipliers 84, **85**, 91, 92, *94*

Verba, S. 3, 57, 102
Vetter, A. 56
views of justification 158–9
views of legality 158
voluntary associations: and attachment to Europe 205; characteristics 161; and democracy 3–5, 40–2; and European orientation 138–9, *140–3*; impact of 231, 232–3; individual degree of 161; internal democracy of 100–1; involvement in 2–3; local government and 23–4; and networks 183–5; as participatory spaces 42–3; and political interest 78–83; as schools for democracy 102; as schoolyards for democracy 77, 97–9; social influence 159–60; and social trust 208; and trust in EU 225–8; types of 64, *66*, 85–91; typologies 25, **226**

voluntary work: individual-level determinants 20–2; and state expenditure 19–20, 22–5
volunteering 235–6
voter turnout 100, 109–12

Warleigh, A. 101
Warren, M.E. 3, 40–1, 160
Weisbrod, B.A. 20, 21, 22, 26
welfare policy: and volunteering 19–20, 22–5

White, H. 183
White Paper on European Governance 4, 130, 157
Why Politics Matters 1
Why We Hate Politics 1
Wollebaek, D. 3, 239–40
women: and civic-spiritedness 115; and participation 51; and social networks 197; and volunteering 21

xenophobic political parties 129

eBooks – at www.eBookstore.tandf.co.uk

A library at your fingertips!

eBooks are electronic versions of printed books. You can store them on your PC/laptop or browse them online.

They have advantages for anyone needing rapid access to a wide variety of published, copyright information.

eBooks can help your research by enabling you to bookmark chapters, annotate text and use instant searches to find specific words or phrases. Several eBook files would fit on even a small laptop or PDA.

NEW: Save money by eSubscribing: cheap, online access to any eBook for as long as you need it.

Annual subscription packages

We now offer special low-cost bulk subscriptions to packages of eBooks in certain subject areas. These are available to libraries or to individuals.

For more information please contact webmaster.ebooks@tandf.co.uk

We're continually developing the eBook concept, so keep up to date by visiting the website.

www.eBookstore.tandf.co.uk